The Politics

of

Cultural Despair

FRITZ STERN

The Politics

of

Cultural Despair

A Study in the Rise of the Germanic Ideology

University of California Press

Berkeley, Los Angeles, London

University of California Press
Berkeley and Los Angeles, California
University of California Press, Ltd.
London, England

3 4 5 6 7 8 9 0

To My Parents

The prophets prophesy
falsely, and the priests bear rule
by their means; and my people
love to have it so; and what will ye do
in the end thereof?

JEREMIAH V, 31

Contents

Preface to the Paperback Edition (1974)

In the thirteen years of affluence since this book first appeared, the attack on modernity has once again become a dominant theme of our culture. The rebellion of the young—and not only of the young—against the emptiness of a materialist age, against the hypocrisy of bourgeois life and the estrangement from nature, against spiritual impoverishment amidst plenty, against the whole "liberal-capitalist system," has echoed many of the laments of the three critics here discussed. More, the present generation longs for a new communal existence, for a new faith, for wholeness. And once again, the deficiencies of liberal, bourgeois culture have been made shockingly clear in a decade of war, political divisiveness, industrial ugliness. Although in many ways identical with the traditional laments of the right, the outcry this time was linked to a vague leftist orientation; accordingly, the political expression of anti-modernity was not a mystical nationalism, but a utopian socialism, a yearning for a humane Marxism, a Marxism beyond all the realities of previously existing socialist regimes. In Germany, the protest has become quickly frozen into new, political orthodoxies. In America, the political expression of the protest has remained much more pragmatic; the full impact of the disenchantment with modernity has been felt in the cultural realm and in the so-called counter culture. But in all realms, the voices denigrating reason and elevating feeling were heard again, as they have been periodically in our civilization. And once again, implicit in the attack on modernity has been the repudiation, the hatred of the West. At times we seemed to witness analogues to that descent from idealism to nihilism that is suggested in the last chapter of this book.

Paradoxically, as the cultural grievance has once again appeared on the political scene, some historians of the past decade or so have championed a new determinism and once again sought the mainsprings of historical action in economic or eco-

nomically-determined motives. Yet at the same time, within
and without the historical profession, there has been a growing presumption against the notion that material factors alone
are capable of explaining the past. Specific studies, for example, have shown that cultural, spiritual, and psychic factors
must be taken into account if we are to understand the triumphs of irrationality that marked fascism. To the further
exploration of politics as psychodrama, of projective politics,
of the irrational ingredients in all politics, I can hope that this
book may prove useful.

It was written solely as an explication of the past—a past
that haunts us still. If it has acquired a new meaning for the
present, if it helps to focus attention on the persistent deficiencies of a certain kind of unreflective, uncritical modernity and
also on the dangers of exuberant reform movements that in the
name of idealism claim to be immune from accountability,
that in their utopianism propose collective solutions for grievances and aspirations that do not allow for collective solutions,
then the author can gratefully ponder such unanticipated timeliness of his work, even if he would prefer to live in a world in
which the politics of cultural despair had nothing but an historic resonance.

F.S.

COLUMBIA UNIVERSITY

Introduction

This is a study in the pathology of cultural criticism. By
analyzing the thought and influence of three leading critics
of modern Germany, this study will demonstrate the dangers
and dilemmas of a particular type of cultural despair. Lagarde,
Langbehn, and Moeller van den Bruck—their active lives spanning
the years from the middle of the past century to the
threshold of Hitler's Third Reich—attacked, often incisively
and justly, the deficiencies of German culture and the German
spirit. But they were more than the critics of Germany's cultural
crisis; they were its symptoms and victims as well. Unable
to endure the ills which they diagnosed and which they had
experienced in their own lives, they sought to become prophets
who would point the way to a national rebirth. Hence, they
propounded all manner of reforms, ruthless and idealistic, nationalistic
and utopian. It was this leap from despair to utopia
across all existing reality that gave their thought its fantastic
quality.

As moralists and as the guardians of what they thought was
an ancient tradition, they attacked the progress of modernity
—the growing power of liberalism and secularism. They enumerated
the discontents of Germany's industrial civilization
and warned against the loss of faith, of unity, of "values." All
three were foes of commerce and cities as well—heroic vitalists
who denigrated reason and routine. Deeply dissatisfied

xi

with the condition of Germany, they predicted that all Germans would soon suffer from the same anguish that they felt.

As early as the 1850's, Lagarde, a biblical scholar and a lonely, embittered man, decried the decline in German intellectual life and the dissolution of its moral ethos. He became one of the sharpest critics of Bismarck's political successes and a brilliant polemicist against modern Protestantism. In 1890, Langbehn, a failure and a psychopath, wrote a sensational best seller, a rhapsody of irrationality, denouncing the whole intellectualistic and scientific bent of German culture, the extinction of art and individuality, the drift toward conformity. During the following two decades, Moeller van den Bruck, a self-styled outsider and a talented *litterateur,* attacked the Philistinism and liberalism of the Wilhelmine age. After the First World War, he became the leading figure of the young conservatives, and his best known work, *Das Dritte Reich,* published in 1922, provided the German right with its dominant political myth.

Although writing at different times, these three men attacked the same cultural forces in much the same manner. Tirelessly they denounced what they considered the shortcomings of German life, and their complaints illuminate the underside of German culture. Their despair over the condition of Germany reflected and heightened the despair of their countrymen, and through these men we can see the current of disaffection rising until it merged with the nihilistic tide of national socialism.

Above all, these men loathed liberalism; Lagarde and Moeller saw in liberalism the cause and the incarnation of all evil. It may seem curious that they should have fastened on liberalism, the one political force in Germany that perpetually lost. To understand why they did this leads us to the core of their thought. They attacked liberalism because it seemed to them the principal premise of modern society; everything they dreaded seemed to spring from it: the bourgeois life, Manchesterism, materialism, parliament and the parties, the lack of political leadership. Even more, they sensed in liberalism the source of all their inner sufferings. Theirs was a resentment of loneliness; their one desire was for a new faith, a new community of believers, a world with fixed standards and no doubts, a new national religion that would bind all Germans together. All this, liberalism denied.

Liberalism & why Lagardes Langhehn Moeller hated it.

Hence, they hated liberalism, blamed it for making outcasts of them, for uprooting them from their imaginary past, and from their faith.

Their proposed reforms, their utopias, were meant to overcome this liberal world, and their reforms as well as their criticisms reflected the strong subjective element of their thought. "I have no use for abstract truth. I want to bind and liberate my people," proclaimed Lagarde, and like the other critics later, he turned to nationalism and to a new folk-rootedness as the only possible means of redemption.[1] Only some outside agent, they felt, some conspiracy, could have dissolved the ancient unity of the folk; hence by stamping out the agents of dissension and by instituting various reforms, the older community could be reëstablished. For all their individualism and their professed horror of the state, these men had great faith in the efficacy of political and cultural planning.

They were literary racists as well, and Lagarde and Langbehn were vigorous anti-Semites, seeing in Jewish "bacilli," the insidious forces of dissolution. They were frightened by national disunity, which Lagarde sensed and Moeller witnessed, and all three critics explicitly demanded a *Führer* who would embody and compel unity and expunge all domestic conflicts. Their final vision was a new German destiny, a Germany which, purged and disciplined at home, would stand forth as the greatest power of the world, ready at last to rally *Germania irredenta*.

These in brief were the elements of their cultural thought. Together they constituted an ideology, at once an indictment, a program, and a mystique. This ideology I call "Germanic" because its principal goals were the revival of a mythical *Deutschtum* and the creation of political institutions that would embody and preserve this peculiar character of the Germans. All their works were suffused by this mixture of cultural despair and mystical nationalism that was radically different from the untroubled nationalism of their contemporaries. The character of their thought and of their appeal to German society corresponded to a recent German definition of ideology: "A political ideology always possesses the fever of passion, the sense of affective belongingness. It is something driving, an impulse, a spiritual force. . . . A true ideology expresses what one lives for."[2] Still more apt, perhaps, would be Alfred

Fouillée's term, *idées-forces,* because these ideas "united the imagination with the will, the anticipated vision of things with their execution." [3]

The ideas of Lagarde, Langbehn, and Moeller were not clasped in a system, but their import strongly affected the sentiments, the *Lebensgefühle,* of respectable Germans for two generations before Hitler. These *idées-forces* remained, to be sure, a subterranean force, an undercurrent of belief, visible only in moments of crisis. But they nurtured the idealistic rejection of modern society and the resentment against the imperfections of Western ideals and institutions, that contributed so greatly to the debility of democracy in Germany.

The appeal of these *idées-forces* was heightened by the style of Lagarde, Langbehn, and Moeller. All three wrote with great fervor and passion. They condemned or prophesied, rather than exposited or argued, and all their writings showed that they despised the discourse of intellectuals, depreciated reason, and exalted intuition. Humorless and murky, their prose was fitfully lit up by mystical, but apodictic epigrams. For decades they were hailed as Germanic critics and prophets.

I chose these three men not because their ideas were particularly original, but because their thought and their impact on German life demonstrate the existence of a cultural crisis in modern Germany. These three men were the sick analysts of a partly sick society—and as such they played an important and hitherto neglected role in German history. The usual methods of intellectual history would not have been appropriate to this subject. *Ideengeschichte,* the critical exposition of ideas, cannot grasp the style and spirit of these men's work nor would it be enough to sketch their ideas against the background of the time. They wrote directly out of their own sufferings and experiences, and hence the psychic dimensions of their biographies were singularly relevant to their work. These I have tried to suggest, tentatively and without straying into fields that properly belong to psychologists. I attempted to show the importance of this new type of cultural malcontent, and to show how he facilitated the intrusion into politics of essentially unpolitical grievances.

This study, then, takes up the origins, content, and impact of an ideology which not only resembles national socialism, but which the National Socialists themselves acknowledged as an essential part of their legacy. But it will also point to another link, admittedly less tangible—to wit, that the Germanic critics in the peculiar tension between their lives and their ideological aspirations anticipate the type of malcontent who, in the 1920's, found a haven in the idealism of the Hitler movement. This may suggest that while in our historical interpretations of Hitler's triumph we have noted everything, from the dangers of Article 48 of the Weimar Constitution to the role of Big Business, we may not have sufficiently reckoned with the politically exploitable discontent which for so long has been embedded in German culture.

ii

The success of national socialism in Germany should not obscure the fact that the nationalist attack on modern culture is a general Western phenomenon that preceded and has outlived national socialism. In 1927, just before the final rise of national socialism, two European writers of very different persuasion called attention to this movement, labeling it the "conservative revolution" and the "treason of the intellectuals."

The Austrian poet, Hugo von Hofmannsthal, himself a latter-day supporter of the movement, spoke of the many Germans who sought

not freedom but communal bonds [*Bindung*]. . . . Never was a German fight for freedom more fervent and yet more tenacious than this fight for true coercion [*Zwang*], this refusal to surrender to a coercion that was not coercive enough. . . . [It began as] an inner opposition to that spiritual upheaval of the sixteenth century which we usually grasp in its two aspects, the Renaissance and the Reformation. I am speaking of a process which is nothing less than a conservative revolution, of a dimension which surpasses anything that European history has seen so far. Its goal is to achieve a form, a new German reality in which all Germans can participate.[4]

In the same year, Julien Benda, the alarmed rationalist, noted and deplored that in

about 1890 the men of letters, especially in France and Italy, realized with astonishing astuteness that the doctrines of arbitrary authority, discipline, tradition, contempt for the spirit of liberty, assertion of the morality of war and slavery, were opportunities for haughty and rigid poses infinitely more likely to strike the imagination of simple souls than the sentimentalities of Liberalism and Humanitarianism.

He denounced this rise of political passions and the European movement against Jewry, democracy, and socialism, and his particular targets were the intellectuals who "began to play the game of political passions. . . . Our age is indeed the age of the *intellectual organization of political hatreds.*" [5] I hope to show that ours is the age of the *political* organization of cultural hatreds and personal resentments.

Until recently this conservative revolution—let alone its pan-European character—has escaped historians.[6] Its intellectual message has been so elusive and its political manifestations have been so sporadic that few men have recognized the power and pervasiveness of this revolutionary mood. Because of its very illogicality, the term conservative revolution is apt. The movement did embody a paradox: its followers sought to destroy the despised present in order to recapture an idealized past in an imaginary future. They were disinherited conservatives, who had nothing to conserve, because the spiritual values of the past had largely been buried and the material remnants of conservative power did not interest them. They sought a breakthrough to the past, and they longed for a new community in which old ideas and institutions would once again command universal allegiance.

The term conservative revolution as used in this book denotes the ideological attack on modernity, on the complex of ideas and institutions that characterize our liberal, secular, and industrial civilization. For nearly two hundred years this attack has proceeded on many levels, gaining political strength and losing intellectual coherence. Its history is the record of a great vulgarization, favored always by the emergence of social weaknesses and by the spread of modernity to ever new areas of the world. Our liberal and industrial society leaves many people dissatisfied—spiritually and materially. The spiritually alienated have often turned to the ideology of the conservative revolution.

This movement against modernity has gone through many stages. It began as a criticism of modernity in the minds of some romantics; it received its most radical intellectual expression in Nietzsche and Dostoevski, who deepened the attack on modernity by a radical reinterpretation of man and who concluded with a pervasive pessimism concerning the future of the West. The next stage—and these stages represent no legitimate succession of ideas—was the transformation of this cultural criticism into a vague political ideology of the right. Combining cultural criticism with extreme nationalism, these ideologists maintained that the character of modern liberal society was alien to the spirit and tradition of their peoples. This ideology, attuned though it was to the distinct national traditions of each country, was essentially similar in every Continental country. The originators of this ideology were themselves already the victims of modernity, writing no longer as critics but as partisans and prophets. These ideologists appealed to a still less intellectual group—a group I would call, after the machine breakers of the 1820's, cultural Luddites, who in their resentment of modernity sought to smash the whole machinery of culture. It was at this point that the conservative revolution could erupt into politics; usually it took the form of some desperate force of the right that was able, with the help of this ideology, to exploit the spiritual and psychological grievances of masses of men. Modern society harbors many such people, and at moments of private or public strain the cultural discontent may turn into violent political disaffection. In times of health, a society produces fewer such men and can contain this form of discontent; in times of trouble and division, this discontent grows stronger, as society grows less capable of dealing with it.

The intellectual roots of the conservative revolution reach back to a formidable tradition. Rousseau had fathered a new type of cultural criticism, and his followers, particularly in Germany, linked his criticism to an attack on what they called the naïve rationalism and the mechanistic thought of the Enlightenment. Having distorted the Enlightenment, they then held it responsible for every kind of cultural ill, and insisted that enlightened thought was powerless even to grasp these ills. In Germany, from 1770 to 1830, cultural criticism and the denigration of rationalism were often fused, and it was this tradition which was to play so important a role in the formation of the later conservative revolution in Europe. In the West, where modern society was already emerging, a succession of moralists from Carlyle to Burckhardt warned about the particular ills of this new culture. The debate about the democratic dangers to freedom and about the leveling tendency of mass society, so familiar to us today, is an old concern in Europe.

Despite the many differences between them, Nietzsche and

Dostoevski may be regarded as the leading figures of this movement. In their attacks on contemporary culture they pierced to the heart of liberalism and denied its philosophical premises. Man is not primarily rational, but volitional; he is not by nature good nor capable of perfectibility; the politics of liberal individualism rest on an illusion; evil exists and is an inherent aspect of human life; positivistic science and rationalism are divorced from reality and at best only partly valid; the idea of historical progress is false and blinds men to the approaching catastrophes of the twentieth century. Nietzsche was the first to understand the psychological force of resentment and to warn against its soul-destroying power. The catastrophes that he and Dostoevski foresaw would be the more terrible because of the overwhelming fact of the nineteenth century—because, in Nietzsche's words, God is dead.

The historic fact of this decline in Christian faith deeply affected the next stage of the conservative revolution, the stage of the ideologists who did not have Nietzsche's courage to condemn the present without senselessly glorifying the past or promising a final collective redemption. For these men, the loss of religion heightened every other uncertainty, and they said—and often themselves felt—that life in the post-Christian, liberal era was unbearable.*

The conservative revolutionaries denounced every aspect of the capitalistic society and its putative materialism. They railed against the spiritual emptiness of life in an urban, commercial civilization, and lamented the decline of intellect and virtue in a mass society. They attacked the press as corrupt, the political parties as the agents of national dissension, and the new rulers as ineffectual mediocrities. The bleaker their picture of the present, the more attractive seemed the past, and they indulged in nostalgic recollections of the un-

---

* "The unchristening of Europe in our time is not quite complete; neither was her christening in the Dark Ages. But roughly speaking we may say that whereas all history was for our ancestors divided into two periods, the pre-Christian and the Christian, and two only, for us it falls into three—the pre-Christian, the Christian, and what may reasonably be called the post-Christian. This surely must make a momentous difference. I am not here considering either the christening or the unchristening from a theological point of view. I am considering them simply as cultural changes. When I do that, it appears to me that the second change is even more radical than the first." C. S. Lewis, *De Descriptione Temporum. An Inaugural Lecture,* Cambridge, Cambridge University Press, 1955, p. 7.

corrupted life of earlier rural communities, when men were peasants and kings true rulers. Most of them thought that this world had been destroyed by evil hands; consequently they firmly believed in a conspiratorial view of history and society. The villain usually was the Jew, who more and more frequently came to be depicted as the very incarnation of modernity. All of these charges, however exaggerated and distorted, had some basis in reality. If there had been no speculative boom and fraudulence in Germany in the early 1870's and no Panama Scandal in France, it would have been harder, and perhaps impossible, to write this particular kind of indictment of Jewry and modernity. The charges were linked to reality, and that was the precondition of their success.

The chief target of the conservative revolutionaries, however, was liberalism. All the vast and undesirable changes in the lives and feelings of Western man they blamed on liberalism. They sensed that liberalism was the spiritual and political basis of modernity and they sought to equate liberalism with Manchesterism, with the disregard of man's spiritual aspirations, with the acceptance of economic selfishness and exploitation, with the *embourgeoisement* of life and morals. They ignored—or maligned—the ideal aspirations of liberalism, its dedication to freedom, the hospitality to science, the rational, humane, tolerant view of man. For what they loosely called liberalism constituted little less than the culmination of the secular, moral tradition of the West.

That liberalism was much more than an economic or political philosophy has been recognized for a long time. In the 1860's already, Cardinal Newman said of liberalism: "It is scarcely now a party; it is the educated lay world . . . it is nothing else than that deep, plausible scepticism, which I spoke about as being the development of human reason, as practically exercised by the natural man." [7] Nearly a century later, Lionel Trilling said of America that liberalism was our "sole intellectual tradition." [8] It was liberalism in this larger sense that the conservative revolution fought, and by doing so, it could most easily make the leap from cultural to political criticism.

The conservative revolutionaries were not the only, or even the dominant, opponents of liberalism. The Catholic Church, particularly under the reign of Pope Pius IX, some Protestant groups, conservatives, and socialists were agreed on the inadequacy of liberalism.* By the end of the nineteenth century, the liberals themselves changed their political philosophy by gradually adopting a paternalistic program. As a consequence, today's political rhetoric is full of confusion concerning the true meaning of liberalism. Amidst this confusion, some critics persist in blaming liberalism for everything they find undesirable in modernity.

The ideologists of the conservative revolution superimposed a vision of national redemption upon their dissatisfaction with liberal culture and with the loss of authoritative faith. They posed as the true champions of nationalism, and berated the socialists for their internationalism, and the liberals for their pacifism and their indifference to national greatness. At the very least they demanded greater national authority and cohesion, and usually they were partisans of imperialism or national aggrandizement as well. Often their longing for national heroism led them to worship violence, which in turn they justified by arguments drawn from social Darwinism or racism.

These nationalist ideologists appeared simultaneously in almost every Continental country. In the last decades of the century, it became apparent that the ideology of cultural despair and national redemption could arouse the support of a still less intellectualized group, and could thus be carried into politics. The similarities between the three writers analyzed in this book and Maurras and Barrès, D'Annunzio and Enrico Corradini, are inescapable and are reflected also in the simultaneous emergence of their kind of ideology into the politics of their countries. The Action Française and the anti-Dreyfusards, the Christian Socialists in Vienna under Karl Lueger, the pan-Germans and the anti-Semitic parties in Ger-

---

* Of relevance in this connection are Max Weber's remarks: "The church belongs to the conservative forces in European countries; first, the Roman Catholic Church . . . but also the Lutheran Church. Both of these churches support the peasant, with his conservative way of life, against the dominion of urban rationalist culture. . . . It happens nowadays in the civilized countries—a peculiar and, in more than one respect, a serious fact—that the representatives of the highest interests of culture turn their eyes back, and, with deep antipathy standing opposed to the inevitable development of capitalism, refuse to co-operate in rearing the structure of the future." Max Weber, "Capitalism and Rural Society in Germany," in *From Max Weber: Essays in Sociology,* ed. by H. H. Gerth and C. Wright Mills, New York, Oxford University Press, 1946, pp. 370–372.

many, and the Italian nationalists that emerged in 1903—
all of these attested the power and importance of the Ideology
of Resentment.* Perhaps certain aspects of American Populism
could be included here as well. The political organization of
this opposition to liberal society coincided with the weakening of liberal rule itself. At the beginning of the twentieth century, Europeans, for the first time, found solace in nationalist
idealism, in the exultation of heroism, and in the vague social
and imperial promises of minor prophets.[9]

Under the auspicious conditions of declining liberalism,
this political organization of resentment erupted time and
again. It first arose in the 1890's, and it became powerful again
in the late 1920's and early 1930's, under the impact of the
depression and the enfeeblement of democracy. Nor were we
purged of this affliction by 1945. Anyone who remembers the
short-lived Poujadist movement, for example, or McCarthy-
ism, or who reads the columns of our *National Review,* will
be unlikely to pronounce the conservative revolution dead.†

---

* Yet modern critics have often failed to recognize this movement and
its Western dimension. Its initial appearance is sometimes entirely
neglected, as in this recent summary: "The ideologies of the nineteenth
century were universalistic, humanistic, and fashioned by intellectuals. . . . The driving forces of the old ideologies were social equality
and, in the largest sense, freedom." Daniel Bell, *The End of Ideology
in the West. On the Exhaustion of Political Ideas in the Fifties,*
Glencoe, Free Press, 1960, p. 373. A standard work on modern ideologies did not get beyond the unsatisfactory formulation: "Ideologically,
the combination of corporatism and manic nationalism equals fascism."
Eugene Golob, *The Isms. A History and Evaluation,* New York,
Harper & Bros., 1954, p. 560. On the contrary, the problem is to
dissociate this phenomenon from the convenient label of fascism and
to explore the psychological and political roots of this form of discontent. The reason why historians have on the whole ignored the
subject or turned to it only after it assumed the form of national
socialism, is that they are trained to deal with ideas and events, not
with a power of discontent as expressed in unreason and fantasy.
But this kind of subterranean and neurotic force is intrinsically important, and sheds light on the more prominent and healthier elements of society as well.

† I am referring here to the rise of what Richard Hofstadter has called
"the pseudo-conservative revolt" and of whose followers he wrote:
"They have little in common with the temperate and compromising
spirit of true conservatism in the classical sense of the word, and they
are far from pleased with the dominant practical conservatism of the
moment as it is represented by the Eisenhower Administration. Their
political reactions express rather a profound if largely unconscious

Rather we must accept the fact that this kind of rebellion against modernity lies latent in Western society and that its confused, fantastic program, its irrational and unpolitical rhetoric, embodies aspirations just as genuine, though not as generous or tangible, as the aspirations embodied in other and more familiar movements of reform.

Cultural pessimism has a strong appeal in America today. As political conditions appear stable at home or irremediable abroad, American intellectuals have become concerned with the cultural problems of our society, and have substituted sociological or cultural analyses for political criticism. No culture has ever been more solicitous about itself than ours, and in this constant pulse-taking of our cultural health many ills are discovered and often wrongly diagnosed. In the past two decades attacks on our materialism, on the decline of our moral stamina, on all the putative ills of our mass society have been heard from every side. A prominent clergyman has told us that "Americanism without God is synonymous with paganism, nazism, fascism, and atheistic communism," and a professional educator that "the very atmosphere of the university tends to corrode the average student's traditional moral and religious beliefs." [10] We hear as well the familiar call for faith and order in the often strident voices of the Angry Young Men.* Behind the slogans and the unreflective critics is the real suffering of men. There is a discontent in the Western world that does not stem from economic want or from the threat of war; rather it springs from dissatisfaction with life in an urban and industrialized culture—a dissatisfaction that the three critics discussed in this book felt and fostered.

---

hatred of our society and its ways—a hatred which one would hesitate to impute to them if one did not have suggestive clinical evidence." Richard Hofstadter, "The Pseudo-Conservative Revolt," in *The New American Right*, ed. by Daniel Bell, New York 1955, p. 35.

* The English outsiders make the search for authority explicit. As Colin Wilson said: "I believe that our civilization is in decline, and that Outsiders are a symptom of that decline. They are men in reaction against scientific materialism; *men who would once have found their orientation in the Church.* . . . The Outsider's sickness is an instinctive craving for discipline. He is too intelligent to serve a cause that his intellect finds contemptible. Consequently, he must find a discipline that his critical intellect can approve—a moral discipline, a spiritual

iii

Although the conservative revolution was a European phenomenon, only in Germany did it become a decisive intellectual and political force. I believe that this particular reaction to modernity was deeply embedded in German thought and society, and that this curiously idealistic, unpolitical discontent constitutes the main link between all that is venerable and great in the German past and the triumph of national socialism.

There are three main reasons for the appeal of this form of discontent, all of them exemplified in the wide influence that Lagarde, Langbehn, and Moeller van den Bruck had on German thought and politics. First, the style and intent of their criticism were in the line of some of the most important cultural traditions of Germany. Second, their criticism touched upon some of the true weaknesses of German culture, and by its verisimilitude gained credence. Third, the political life of Germany from 1870 to 1933 was marked by the very divisiveness that these men decried, and this in turn facilitated the intrusion of their sentiments into politics. The conservative revolution in general, and the thought of these three men in particular, touched the realities of German life more closely than the similar thought of conservative revolutionaries elsewhere.

There is another reason for the success of the conservative revolution. As we saw, the primary target was modernity as

discipline. But society lacks the Outsider's penetrating critical intellect. In its secret craving for a discipline, for something to follow, it runs after every fire-eating politician, every heart-throb evangelist, every dictator with a programme." According to Stuart Holroyd, "The obstacles which prevent the average modern man from ever attaining to the religious attitude are numerous. Three centuries of humanist culture have bequeathed us a burden of ideas and attitudes which few people ever get around even to questioning, and which are quite incompatible with the religious attitude. Liberalism, the dogma of equality, the faith in scientific method, the myth of progress and the idea of the perfectibility of man, may be cited as examples. We all grew up in the climate of these ideas, and it is difficult for us to shake ourselves free of them. But we must, somehow, if we are to survive as anything more than a race of ingenious little animals." Colin Wilson, "Beyond the Outsider," in *Declaration,* ed. by Tom Maschler, London, Macgibbon and Kee, 1957, pp. 37 and 42; and Stuart Holroyd, "A Sense of Crisis," in *ibid.,* p. 188.

embodied in the rational, liberal, and capitalistic society, which in its political form was shaped, at least on the Continent, by the French Revolution. So far as the German critics opposed this society, they could more easily appeal to a powerful strain in German nationalism. The generation of Arndt and Fichte had already denounced liberal ideas and political institutions as alien, "un-German," and Western. The Germanic critics could more readily dismiss the ideas of 1789 as alien frauds than could Barrès, say, or Maurras. Finally, liberalism and the parliamentary tradition had never been as strong in Germany as in the Western countries, and were therefore easier to attack. In Germany, where liberalism had had so accommodating a character and so unsuccessful a political career, it was easy first to make it despicable and then to despise it.[11]

Lagarde, Langbehn, and Moeller van den Bruck were idealists, and as such they appealed to the educated classes of Germany, whose yearning to be idealistic predisposed them to this kind of appeal. The term "idealist" is ambiguous in English; it is still more elusive in German, where it connotes as well the major philosophical tradition of modern Germany. But the idealism I have in mind was no longer a formal philosophical system. Rather it was an attitude toward life, a set of sentiments and values, that the educated classes inherited from common intellectual traditions and that were gradually adapted to their position in society. Intellectually this idealism was derived from the great works of the idealist period, from Goethe, Kant, and Schiller; it was taught at the higher schools and cultivated in the homes. The residue of the earlier philosophy can be found in the rhetoric of the later period, in the continued predilection for abstract and metaphysical terms, in the implicit belief that the spirit or the idea was the ultimate expression of reality. This idealism involved also the recollection of earlier moral imperatives and esthetic ideals; the great classicist Ludwig Curtius wrote of the ideal of German humanism: "This 'pure humanity' was not a pale abstract theory, but a moral command, directed at each individual, for the reconstruction of his personal life." [12] This command, the essence of what the Germans often called individualism, could best be followed by the pursuit of culture, by literary and esthetic education. The idealism of the later nineteenth century embodied an exceptional veneration for learning, for the cultivation of the self. At its best, this veneration inspired the dedicated energy of Germany's scholars; at its worst, it degenerated into a kind of culture Philistinism, adding a powerful rationalization to the already formidable barrier between the educated and the uneducated classes.[13]

This idealism, with its emphasis on culture and the cultivation of *Innerlichkeit,* did not encourage political participation or even political concern. Neither did the semiauthoritarian political order which Bismarck had installed in 1871. Rebuffed in actuality and turned inward by their beliefs, the German elite tended to become estranged from reality and disdainful of it. It lost the power to deal with practical matters in practical terms; as Friedrich Meinecke put it: "Specifically German also . . . was the tendency to elevate something primarily practical into a universal world-view theory." [14]

Bismarck had created a state that had no constitutional theory; its justification, he thought, was that it worked. Power thinly disguised on the one hand, and spirit emptied of all practicality on the other—these surely were two aspects of imperial Germany. The link between the two realms was the idealization of power; the middle classes, in Max Weber's phrase, "ethicized" Bismarck's achievement of power. This also encouraged a certain idolatry of idealism in politics. Practical ideas and programs were discounted in favor of complete disinterestedness and the right kind of *Haltung* or character.* By the same token, Lagarde, Langbehn, and Moeller van den Bruck, outsiders all, appealed as idealists, whether their ideas had a shred of practicality or not.

Finally, these men appealed to large segments of German society because they were idealistic *and* religious. For the Protestant academic classes had fused Christianity and German idealism so as to forge a *Kulturreligion,* which hid beneath pious allusions to Goethe, Schiller, and the Bible a most thoroughgoing secularization. The religious *tone* remained, even after the religious faith and the religious canons had disappeared. Hence these three men, as well as the conservative revo-

---

* As one example, consider Theodor Eschenburg's description of Ernst Bassermann, the leader of the National Liberals during most of the Wilhelmine period: "His political views were not the product of long reflections, but corresponded to his *Lebensgefühl* and his sensibilities, to his reverent character and to the tradition in which he was raised." Theodor Eschenburg, *Das Kaiserreich am Scheideweg. Bassermann, Bülow und der Block,* Berlin, Verlag für Kulturpolitik, 1929, p. 25.

lutionaries generally, appealed to the religious sentimentality of some, to the genuine desire for religion of others.

This *Kulturreligion* embraced nationalism as well, for it insisted on the identity of German idealism and nationalism. The essence of the German nation was expressed in its spirit, revealed by its artists and thinkers, and at times still reflected in the life of the simple, unspoiled folk. In imperial Germany, this type of cultural nationalism grew, until it found its fullest expression in the First World War, when German intellectuals insisted that they were culturally independent of the West and that the German empire as then constituted fully embodied the supreme cultural values of the German people.

Given this type of idealism, it is no wonder that the German intellectual classes were particularly responsive to the pleadings of Lagarde, Langbehn, and Moeller van den Bruck. Their sentiments proved to have been shared by many people. It is often forgotten that after 1871 many thoughtful Germans were gripped by a mood of mingled pride and disenchantment: pride in the power and the unity of the Reich, disenchantment with the culture of the empire, with the fact that beneath the crust of prosperous politics the old Germany was disintegrating, pulled apart by modernity—by liberalism, secularism, and industrialism. Common were the lamentations about the decline of the German spirit, the defeat of idealism by the forces of realism in politics and of materialism in business. Many would have agreed with Nietzsche's epigram of 1888: " 'German spirit': for the past eighteen years a contradiction in terms." The educated German—the academic, the bureaucrat, the professional man—had for generations occupied a place of distinction just below the aristocrat, and he was now puzzled and disturbed by the rise of a society that accorded equal or superior distinction to men of crasser aims and morals. Dismay was often heard; it appeared clearly in Mommsen's academic addresses, in which time and again he dealt with

the spiritual development of our people under the radiance of good fortune. As the soldier can more easily withstand the dangers and deprivations of war than the intoxication of victory, so we are living before and amidst a spontaneous regeneration of old moral afflictions and a spontaneous generation of new afflictions which spread like an epidemic and which threaten the foundations of our society.[15]

Fear of this "moral decay," as Mommsen called it, was deep-seated, and Lagarde, Langbehn, and Moeller van den Bruck not only thundered against this decay, but offered remedies which generations of unpolitical, idealistic Germans regarded as noble and practical.

As we look back on imperial Germany, we can hardly wonder that the immense cultural upheaval caused such concern. What is surprising, and explicable only if we remember the idealistic insulation of the educated citizens, is that often they mistook change for decline, and, consistent with their conception of history, attributed the decline to a moral failing. Certainly German views on culture were no more realistic than their views on politics. Self-knowledge is no more common among nations than among men; still, few societies in the modern world were so remote from reality as the Germans in the years of the empire.

The real conditions were bad enough and justified some of the fears. With a suddenness that has had no parallel, the industrial revolution changed the face and character of German society. The story of that transformation is familiar enough; in the popular mind, the classical horrors of the industrial revolution are properly associated with England, not with Germany. The patent miseries of late eighteenth-century industrialization did not appear in Germany. The real cost, the psychic cost, has been ignored. Yet the history of Germany from 1871 to 1945 records not only the most extreme economic antagonisms of an industrial society, but the violent resentment against the new industrialism, which in different guises erupted time and again in German life.

To a people sentimental about nature and their ancient towns, the sudden rise of monstrously big and ugly cities was distressing. Nor did Germany do things by halves; by 1910, it had almost as many large cities as the entire rest of the Continent. In those cities a different way of life prevailed. The quiet tone and ordered life of preindustrial society were replaced by a strident tone and by continual change. The pressures of commercialism were heavy indeed, and there was some truth to the charges that the arts and education were in decline. The Protestant Church was losing its power and vitality. And in this changing Germany, there arose the newly emancipated Jews, themselves torn between their old identity and the promise of a new assimilation, who by gaining considerable influence over the cultural life of the nation could be held responsible for some of its shortcomings. Many a German honestly felt that this new society was fundamentally un-German, that the true character of German life had been violated.

Beyond the fear of cultural decline lay a still vaguer sense of malaise concerning Germany's political future. Here too the industrial revolution had wrought immense changes. Bismarck had unified the German states, but the industrial revolution wrecked anew the unity of the German people. The emergence of industrialization under the already repressive and anachronistic regime of Bismarck deepened old and created new class antagonisms. In no other state did feudal and proletarian forces confront each other so directly, for in no other industrial country did the bourgeoisie play so insignificant a political role. The symptoms of these new divisions were clearly manifest, as was Bismarck's alarming use of state power to war against Catholics and socialists. But few Germans understood the causes of these new antagonisms, and justifiable concern was often dissipated in the rhetoric of resentment. If there was political conflict, if the Bismarckian system failed to work, then the fault must lie with the new political machinery, with parliaments, with political parties, with the whole system of incipient democracy. These charges—which Lagarde made with great passion and success—had a certain verisimilitude to them because Bismarck had invested parliamentary bodies with little power or responsibility and hence they seemed to be useless appendages to an otherwise efficient government. Parties were held in low esteem, and the absence of a true conservative party, that is, of a party that was more than a narrow interest group, was a great loss to the political education of Germans. The power of delusion was great, evidenced most clearly by the common longing for a Caesar, for an ultimate authority that would somehow reconcile and transcend all divisions and would realize the one common goal of all upper-class Germans, a great national future. In imperial Germany, interest ruled and sentiment disguised, and it required the penetrating mind of Max Weber to see through the sham and to discern the true condition of Germany. As early as 1895, in his inaugural address, he noted that "to have a declining economic class hold political authority in its hands is dangerous and in the long run incompatible with the national interest." But the bourgeoisie, Weber added, was politically too immature to rule, too prone to yearn for a new Caesar, too willing to substitute 'ethical' for political ideals. Nor did the proletariat possess the statesmanlike qualities that would allow it to rule.[16] Others could not see Weber's vision of political truth, but were oppressed by vague and formless premonitions of disaster.

Cultural discontent, Caesarism, and nationalist hope were the dominant sentiments of many Germans before the First World War. These feelings found expression in the great exaltation of August, 1914, when at last the cultural boredom of the nation was lifted, when politics were suspended, when the nation in danger would soon become the nation triumphant. The exaltation waned, but in its first flush, German intellectuals, most notably Thomas Mann, summed up the whole idealistic, unpolitical tradition of German life by juxtaposing two types of freedom—the Germanic freedom of the inner man and the external freedom of "Western" liberal man.

For large segments of the educated classes, the Weimar Republic was discredited in advance, morally bankrupt before it was established. For four years the Germans had battled the West, and many of them elevated that struggle, too, into the metaphysical realm, believing that the Germanic and the Western characters were antithetical. When the republic did come, it was almost a parody of their fears. This was the liberal state, as they had dreaded it—divided, defenseless, and defeated, the victim of selfish interests at home and abroad. As for the culture of Weimar, could a more dissonant triumph of modernity be imagined? Powerful as cultural despair, Caesarism, and nationalist hope had already been in the prewar consciousness, the very weakness of Weimar inflamed these feelings and made them stronger still.

It was in Weimar that the conservative revolution reached the height of its power. Moeller van den Bruck's *Das Dritte Reich*, a final summary of the resentments and aspirations of the would-be conservatives, had a great appeal to many educated Germans. The pleas of Thomas Mann and a few others for the restoration of political reason and their warnings against the "sentimental brutality" that pervaded the German right were of no avail.* Decades of political delusion had done their work, and many a conservative German shudderingly admired the terroristic idealism of Hitler's movement. The National Socialists gathered together the millions of malcontents, of whose existence the conservative revolutionaries had for so long spoken, and for whose relief they had designed such dangerous and elusive ideals.

---

* In the declining years of the Weimar Republic, Thomas Mann ridiculed the pretensions and the political implications of the conservative revolution. He often chose academic audiences to clarify his position and to dissociate himself formally from a position which at one time had been his own. "Obscurantism—in politics we call it reaction—is brutality; it is sentimental brutality insofar as it tries to hide its brutal and irrational character 'under the impressive mask' of Germanic temperament and loyalty." Thomas Mann, "Von Deutscher Republik," *Bemühungen,* Berlin 1925, p. 151.

I: Paul de Lagarde

and a Germanic Religion

1: The Critic as Academician

One thing I know: I belong not in this time nor in this world. My fatherland has to be bigger.

LAGARDE

Paul (Bötticher) de Lagarde* was a brilliantly erratic scholar and moralist who all his life condemned and excoriated the things he most wanted to love. Always a deeply religious man, he lost his faith in organized Christianity as a student in the 1840's, and thereafter taunted and attacked the Protestant churches. A conservative, he broke with Prussian conservatism in the 1850's, and denounced its reactionary course. A patriot, he thundered against his people's moral decline and prophesied their ruin. Lagarde thought himself homeless, and the great passion of his life was to find a new community, a German nation of dedicated believers.

Lagarde came of age in the 1850's, in that grim decade between the collapse of the revolution and the rise of Bismarck. It was in that decade of public failure and personal disappointments that he conceived his unreasoned pessimism about the future of his people. Nor did Bismarck's successes dispel Lagarde's fears. In some fifty tracts published after 1871, Lagarde warned that the German people were more divided than ever and that their loss of faith and stamina would lead to their annihilation.

But Lagarde sought to be more than a prophet of doom. He believed in a rebirth of Germany and he sought to bring to his people the vision of a Germany reborn. He himself would guide his people to the new Germany. Only a national religion, a Germanic-Christian faith, could effect Germany's

---

* In 1854, he adopted the name de Lagarde, and all his important works were published under that name. His reasons for changing his name are discussed below.

spiritual regeneration. Only the extirpation of liberalism in all its guises, only the inclusion of the Austrian empire—a radical *grossdeutsche* solution—would permit Germany's continued life and growth.

Lagarde's scholarly contributions to philology and religious history, important though they were, have been largely superseded. But his cultural criticism and his vision of deliverance survived him, and had a profound influence on several generations of Germans. Thomas Mann acclaimed him as a *praeceptor Germaniae,* and this he was for all those Germans who were dissatisfied with what they called their humdrum existence in a bourgeois society. At a later time, the National Socialists acclaimed Lagarde as one of their main spiritual forebears, and in the Second World War issued to soldiers an anthology of his work. A dissatisfied nation remembered its prophet of doom and regeneration.

Paul Anton Bötticher was born on November 2, 1827, into an old Saxon family which for generations had sent its sons into the Protestant ministry. From the very beginning, Paul's life was dogged by misery and loneliness: twelve days after his birth, his eighteen-year old mother died.[1] His father fell into prolonged, terrible grief, the more intense for his recollection of an infant daughter who had died the year before. During his years of mourning and withdrawal, the elder Bötticher hated his son, blaming him for his mother's death. Fortunately, there were two maternal great-aunts who cared for Paul, and loved and indulged him.

Paul's father, Wilhelm Bötticher, had originally planned to become a pastor, but had abandoned theology in favor of philology. A heavy religiosity clung to him nevertheless, and all his life he remained a bigoted, cheerless Christian, who thought that unmitigated gloom was the proper mood for a religious home. This devoutly pious egoist terrorized his son just as he did his students at the Friedrich-Wilhelms-Gymnasium in Berlin, where he taught Greek and Latin. He also wrote occasional works of criticism and history, selecting strange subjects like *The Christian Element in Tacitus and the Typically Prophetic Character of his Work Considered in the Light of Rome's Relation to Germany.* His shorter essays included one on the domination of the Jews. Paul once mocked his father's "nauseating book manufacturing," but himself acquired the same passion for publishing and the same versatility.[2] Despite his brooding introspection, Lagarde never realized how much he had been influenced by his father's thought, how much his father's temperament, at once irascible and sentimental, crabbed and generous, resembled his own.

In 1831, Bötticher married again, and within two years Paul had two stepbrothers. A much-beloved little stepsister, born in 1835, died three years later. Within the new family, Paul seems to have been treated as an outsider, an interloper, and his stepmother found it difficult to deal with a child that had such strained relations with his father. Nor did the elder Bötticher relent; as Paul grew older, his father became more tyrannical still, and never talked to his son of his mother. Paul's break with his father was never healed. In 1850, he was called to his father's deathbed, and, to his horror, could conjure up no feeling of grief. This moment of numbness worried him all his life, and the memory of his father oppressed him until his own death.

Lagarde often talked about the sorrows of his youth: "My childhood and adolescence passed along joylessly and far from people; no wonder that books and dreams gained a stronger influence on my life than I could wish for anyone I loved." [3] When his wife asked about his early years, he replied: "It was all so immeasurably sad that you could not fathom it." [4] It is hard to tell how much his reminiscences of woe were truth, how much self-pitying poetry. He seems to have had a fixation on the wretchedness of his childhood, and he blamed his later ills on earlier deprivations. We know that in his dreams and fantasies he mourned and idolized his mother all his life. His feelings about his childhood certainly had a powerful influence on his intellectual life. His dread of loneliness, for example, we find transposed in his plea for a binding German community, in his insistence that true individual strength can be developed only in a fully unified society. His conflict with his father préfigured his resentful and suspicious feelings toward his colleagues and toward all existing authority.

During Lagarde's youth, the great romantic period of Berlin came to an end. He caught a final glimpse of it, and in his autobiographical accounts paints an attractive picture of the Berlin of the 1830's and early 1840's. He also records, proudly, that as a boy he had several times sat on Schleiermacher's lap. But he also witnessed the end of that culture. He noted, for example, that the religious life of the city declined after Schleiermacher's death. Paul's family and their friends ceased altogether to go to church. "A life in and with God existed in Berlin only in the quiet chambers of a few lonely individuals; the city as such did not know it." [5]

Lagarde was a voracious reader, and the romantic writers were his favorites. He read and reread Karl Lachmann's famous edition of Wolfram von Eschenbach, as well as Achim von Arnim, Barthold Georg Niebuhr, and Savigny. He was deeply impressed by Jakob Grimm's German mythology, which was published in 1835. Lagarde's romantic strain was strong and never died. He loved music too, and during his father's absence from the house played the piano.

Paul graduated from the *Gymnasium* in 1844, and entered the University of Berlin at Easter of that year, "still more a boy than a youth." [6] At his father's command, he enrolled in the theological faculty. The university generally, and the theological faculty in particular, had lost much of its distinction since the death of Hegel and Schleiermacher. Lagarde studied under his father's friend, Ernst Wilhelm Hengstenberg, a rigidly orthodox pietist and the leader of the aggressively conservative wing of the Protestant church. According to Hengstenberg, the sole source of truth was the Word of God as revealed in the Bible; any deviation from this dogma marked a step toward atheism, and Hengstenberg, as editor of the *Evangelische Kirchenzeitung,* waged a vicious campaign against all rationalists and liberal theologians. He assumed that his opponents, David Friedrich Strauss, for example, were possessed of Satan, and his polemical tone set a new mark for moral bigotry.* But Hengstenberg was a scholar as well, and Lagarde had the good fortune to hear his lectures on the Old Testament, in which he argued the then unpopular proposition that the Old Testament was as important to Christianity as the New Testament. [7] Lagarde

---

*In the very year that Lagarde began his studies under Hengstenberg, Heine, in his *Deutschland. Ein Wintermärchen,* wrote of the French:

> Sie werden Philister ganz wie wir,
> Und treiben es endlich noch ärger;
> Sie sind keine Voltairianer mehr,
> Sie werden Hengstenberger.

owed much to Hengstenberg, not least this emphasis on the
Old Testament, which remained at the center of Lagarde's
own scholarly concerns. He alternately admired and maligned
Hengstenberg. His other teachers of theology were August
Neander, a converted Jew whom Lagarde detested, and August
Twesten, Schleiermacher's successor, who had no intellectual
pretensions but whose character Lagarde revered. Later, in
Halle, he studied under Friedrich August Tholuck, whose
passionate concern with the purely emotional experience of
religion proved a great inspiration to Lagarde.[8] All in all,
the theologians and their bitter wrangling disappointed
Lagarde and contributed to his repudiation of all forms of
orthodoxy.

The decisive influence on Lagarde was that of the great
poet-philologist, Friedrich Rückert, who taught him Arabic
and Persian. Rückert befriended him as well, and encouraged
his philological interests. Lagarde decided to concentrate on
these, and to put philology at the service of theology, thus
contributing to the work of higher criticism, one of the chief
intellectual enterprises of his time.

In 1845, Lagarde first spoke of his ambition to prepare a
critical edition of the Old and New Testament, to do for the
Bible what the master philologist, Karl Lachmann, had done
for Eschenbach, for the Nibelungen, and for parts of the
New Testament.* Shortly afterward, he specified that the
critical reconstruction of the Septuagint was his goal. By the
time he was twenty, he had already published his first study,
Horae aramaicae, a study of 110 Persian, Armenian, and
Indian words that had been taken over into Aramaic. He was
not satisfied, however, with having mastered these difficult
languages; it was characteristic of Lagarde that in his first

---

* The lives of Lagarde and of Lachmann, who was a generation older
than Lagarde, show curious similarities. Lachmann's ancestors had
been Protestant ministers in Brandenburg, his mother had died when
he was two, he had studied theology and philology, and he had
taught at the same Berlin *Gymnasium* where Lagarde's father had
taught. Like Lagarde, Lachmann identified faulty scholarship with immorality and denounced it accordingly. Like Lagarde, Lachmann found
that his philological work on the Bible pleased his pious heart without
involving him in the dogmatic questions of theology that would have
tortured his scientific conscience. On Lachmann, cf. *Allgemeine
Deutsche Biographie,* Leipzig 1883, XVII, 471–481.

study, as in all subsequent ones, he introduced utterly extraneous subjects that happened to be on his mind.*

The *annus mirabilis* of German liberalism, 1848, passed Lagarde by; his sole political act had been to don the black-and-white cockade of Prussian conservatism. "Consonant with my education and my family ties, I was entirely on the side of the king, whose distaste for a constitution seemed to us fully justified by the consequences which had attended the French constitutional regime." [9] A year later, after the triumph of reaction, his political loyalties were destroyed by the so-called Waldeck case. Benedikt Waldeck, a left-liberal deputy and leading critic of the counterrevolution, was arrested in May, 1849, on charges of treason for having plotted the establishment of a German social-democratic republic. During the trial it became apparent that the spurious charge was being bolstered by evidence fraudulently manufactured by the conservatives themselves. At this, "one of the darkest stains in the heavily stained history of the Prussian reaction," [10] Lagarde's loyalties snapped. He was immeasurably angered by the conservatives and pietists who, like Hengstenberg, condoned the action even after its exposure. Lagarde was now thoroughly disenchanted with the ruling classes of Prussia and wrote scathingly of the timid, reactionary monarchy and its sporadic witch hunts. He was adrift, belonging to neither political camp; he called himself a conservative radical, and opposed all existing parties and powers.

At the same time Lagarde broke with orthodox Christianity, turning with particular vehemence against his father's and Hengstenberg's pietistic views.† "The turning point of my political (and religious) views was the injustice perpetrated against Waldeck. It was not my rational faculty that effected the change; it only showed me the sinful intention of my former friends, and in a few days, and with all my heart, I became a different man." [11]

In 1849, Lagarde received his doctorate *multa cum laude*

---

* Of an enlarged version of *Horae aramaicae,* Rückert complained that it was "mightily blown up with pedantry and unnecessary citations, hence unreadable." Lagarde, *Mittheilungen,* Göttingen 1887, II, 97.

† But intimations of heterodoxy antedated the Waldeck case. Already in 1846, the theologian Tholuck called Lagarde an *anima naturaliter pantheistica,* which he was not, but the remark suggests that Lagarde found it difficult to define his theism in proper theological terms. Lagarde, *Mittheilungen,* Göttingen 1891, IV, 87.

from the University of Berlin for a dissertation on an Arabic theory of colors. He hoped to enter an academic career, but he was too poor to finance his further studies. Thanks to his scholarly achievements and Hengstenberg's help, Lagarde obtained a two-year Protestant fellowship from the city of Berlin, which enabled him to study at Halle. Hengstenberg's help was noteworthy because Lagarde had already attacked him in a highly "inappropriate manner," as he later admitted.[12] In Halle, he wrote his *Habilitationsschrift* on the appearance of Near Eastern words in Greek writings, and began lecturing on Near Eastern languages. But Lagarde disregarded the provision of the stipend that required him to obtain a degree in theology within two years; he arranged instead to have the degree awarded to him, *honoris causa,* by the University of Erlangen. This substitute proved unsatisfactory to Berlin, and his funds were immediately cut off.[13]

The *Privatdozentur,* to which he had been appointed at Halle, offered neither present sustenance nor hope of future promotion. Other attempts at academic preferment failed as well, and, utterly dejected, Lagarde turned to Baron Bunsen, the well-known scholar and Prussian ambassador in London. Because of the latter's intervention, Frederick William IV granted Lagarde a two-year stipend to study in London and begin his projected work of reconstructing the New Testament on the basis of Oriental translations.

In London, Lagarde pursued his philological studies, and acquired some new languages, Assyrian and Coptic among them. His hope of using some important Syrian texts was frustrated by the obstinacy of an English orientalist, William Cureton, who thought to reserve to himself these manuscripts, which he had been the first to edit. Lagarde was consoled when he discovered, in Paris, an important Syrian manuscript, *Didascalia,* which proved indispensable to an understanding of apostolic canon law. He now fell in with Baron Bunsen's work on the *Analecta Ante-Nicaeana,* to which Lagarde appended a critical edition of the *Didascalia.* The Baron praised Lagarde's "very helpful" collaboration.

Lagarde was happy in London. After a few months of living alone, he moved to the embassy, where he was in close contact with Baron Bunsen and, through him, with Britain's political and literary elite.[14] Like so many Germans before him, he was both envious of and enthralled by the English, and, as his later writings were to show, contracted a mild case of *Anglomanie,* a sentimental affliction common in nineteenth-century Germany.* But the cultural discontent he was later to diagnose in Germany had already taken root in England:

Even here in England, among a people that is thought the most religious on earth, discontent spreads ever more widely. The clearest proof of this are the young English poets, especially Alfred Tennyson. Everywhere one gets the sense that their hope is but a phrase, and that only their despair and resignation are truth.[15]

Happy and productive though he was in London, he returned to Halle in October, 1853, six months before his stipend expired. In part this was due to his anxiety about a job and the hope that an earlier return would enhance his chances for an academic appointment. More important, he wanted to rejoin his fiancée, Anna Berger, the daughter of a retired army officer, to whom he had been engaged since 1850, and whom he married in 1854. He had written her long letters from London in which he told of his hopes for marriage: "At the beginning, help me to mold myself into a whole man: bind up those deep and painful wounds of my heart which I could not and should not conceal from you. I acquired them honorably on a dishonorable field of battle." [16] Although otherwise abundantly autobiographical, Lagarde wrote little about his wife. Her recollections suggest that she idolized her husband and comforted him in his loneliness.† Their one deep regret was that they had no children.

---

* Less than a decade earlier, Theodor Fontane had gone to England and formed similar impressions. He praised its freedom and ancient institutions and thought it "a blessed country." Helga Ritscher, *Fontane. Seine politische Gedankenwelt,* Göttingen, Musterschmidt, 1953, p. 49.

† In a revealing letter to her husband, written in September, 1879, on the occasion of her sister's death, Anna de Lagarde expressed her fear that she might die before him. If she should die, he must remember that all she felt was "Thanks to God that He entrusted me into your hands and your love, and thanks to you that you kept me there. . . . Do not withdraw from other people; you can be so much to them. You must only have patience, as you have had with me. Do not be distrustful of yourself nor be unjust to yourself. I want to stay with you to the last, to serve you in your work, and to keep on growing in your light. If not, then you must take care of yourself." Lagarde Archive, Göttingen.

A few months after his marriage, Paul Bötticher—as he had been known until then—took steps to be legally adopted by his maternal great-aunt, Ernestine de Lagarde, whose name he henceforth carried. He had long toyed with this idea, at once difficult and attractive for him. His great-aunt had been his guardian angel, the soul of generosity; she had brought him up, she had financed his first travels, and now, in 1854, she made it possible for him to get married. She, in turn, was delighted to adopt him, for she was the last of her line and without her nephew's action, the family name would die out —as it did, despite his adoption of it. But what of his own family name? He had a strong sense of solidarity with the Bötticher family: he wrote reverently of his immediate ancestors, excepting only his father, whom he mentioned with frigid detachment.[17] But he was sufficiently self-conscious, sufficiently conscious of symbols, and especially of the symbolism of names, to realize that this change was intended as the final rejection of his father, as the final burying of the embittered memories of childhood. To his fiancée he wrote: "It is an absolute necessity for me, it is an end to the past." [18] He would be reborn, as he later urged others to be. Possibly, the aristocratic sound of the name attracted him as well, even though later he denied that the Lagardes were aristocratic or French: they were from Lorraine, he said—hence German—and had fled from Metz in 1684 in order to preserve their Protestant faith. A few years later, his great-aunt left him a large part of her fortune—a prospect that the impecunious Bötticher may or may not have anticipated in 1854.

His professional fortunes, however, were still at a low ebb. Despite Bunsen's and Rückert's support, and despite the numerous texts which he had already edited and published, the University of Halle denied him a professorship, and other universities did likewise. His reputation suffered because of the scathing notices which some of his publications had received. Some of these reviews were harsh and hypercritical, others mischievous and *ad personam*. The organization of his material was criticized, his scholarly arrogance attacked, his originality impugned, his contributions belittled. The reviewers scoured his editions for the inevitable irrelevance and attacked it, often forgetting to acknowledge the painstaking philological work of their indefatigable colleague. A generation later, Lagarde still felt sufficiently angered to republish these notices at his own expense, together with his own vitriolic replies.* Some of the great scholars were gentle, even generous, to him, but this did not mollify Lagarde.† He became thoroughly discouraged and for nearly a decade withdrew from all his friends in the profession. He even cut himself off from Rückert, with whom he had been on exceptionally cordial terms. But this self-imposed isolation grieved him greatly; and in 1863 he wrote to a colleague, "I am glad to have made closer human contact with you; I suppose I shall remain an anchorite all my life and will have to be treated as such." [19]

From the very beginning of his career, Lagarde loathed the guild, as he called it, and in time his contempt hardened into a somewhat paranoiac fear of a professional conspiracy directed against himself.‡ Most of his colleagues, he thought, either plagiarized or traduced him, and all sought to block his advancement.[20] From the early 1850's, Lagarde was on the warpath against the alleged plagiarists of his works. Undoubtedly Lagarde saw more of the poisonous atmosphere of German academic life, and suffered more from it, than did many others, but his belief in a conspiracy against himself has no foundation. What he was really doing was attributing to others his own penchant for calumny and intrigue.

---

* Cf. Paul de Lagarde, *Aus dem deutschen Gelehrtenleben. Aktenstücke und Glossen*, Göttingen 1880. From one of his critics he still demanded "a public apology, which of course could not heal my shattered life." *Ibid.*, p. 109.

† Ernest Renan, for example, facilitated and encouraged his work. On April 23, 1854, he wrote to Lagarde: "My dear friend: I have received your letter with infinite pleasure and I have learned with great joy of the changes which have taken place in your position—changes, it seems to me, on which one can only congratulate you. Notwithstanding your fit of misanthropy, your career, it seems to me, is thriving and secure. It is only a matter of knowing how to wait." Lagarde Archive, Göttingen.

‡ In October 1851, he attended his first and only convention of German philologists and orientalists, and wrote to his fiancée: "What was most repulsive at the meetings was the stench of the guild [*Zunft*], which assailed me everywhere: intellectual proletariat, that labors on its humdrum articles in the sweat of its brow, that does not know that science is to make one free and happy." Anna de Lagarde, *Paul de Lagarde. Erinnerungen aus seinem Leben für die Freunde zusammengestellt*, Göttingen 1894, p. 21. It is unlikely that he struggled to conceal these feelings.

In some ways he himself generated the conditions for his academic failures. On the one hand, he was so eager to be published that he would print texts without any editorial correction or explanation. On the other hand, he thought that because his colleagues were timid and pedestrian, he would have to aim at extravagant heights and speculations. "For me a language is the expression of a psyche, and every psyche is the object of an education by God, that is, of a becoming and a history." [21] That the language and soul of a people were closely related had of course been Herder's contention and Jakob Grimm's inspiration; but Lagarde's colleagues were scientifically minded and repudiated these *a priori* judgments. Lagarde's analysis of a national psyche was usually arbitrary, derived not from evidence but from prejudices. He said, for example, that the Hebrews had no soul and the Persians the greatest soul of all. Such judgments, Lagarde boasted, were intuitive: "Such a matter I do not learn piece by piece, but I see it all at once or not at all." [22] Or again: "Anyone who does not want to see the totality in the individual instance, the whole in one, should at least not pester me with his opinion." [23] This may be engaging evidence of a lively imagination, of what one American scholar has praised as "[Lagarde's] philosophical turn of mind," [24] but it outraged Lagarde's more rigorous colleagues, and unfortunately the truths Lagarde uttered were often unverified, sometimes absurd, or demonstrably erroneous.

Lagarde, in short, stood squarely in his own way. His failure to obtain a university appointment was not due to a conspiracy of frightened colleagues, as he assumed and many of his biographers alleged. He had his share of professional breaks—stipends, patrons, and archival finds—and he had his successes, but he fostered in the guild a sense of himself as a rash, querulous man of principled unreliability. Even Ludwig Schemann, his greatest admirer, conceded that Lagarde's early works were "bold, arrogant, and challenging," as was the man himself.[25]

When no hope was left for a university post, Lagarde reluctantly decided to go into secondary-school teaching. This was not an unusual choice: many of Germany's great scholars —Ranke, Droysen, Lachmann, among others—had done the

PAUL DE LAGARDE AND GERMANIC RELIGION

same, to the inestimable benefit of the *Gymnasia* and without real harm to themselves. In 1854, with the financial help of his great-aunt, he moved to Berlin, and there he stayed until 1866, teaching a wide variety of subjects at a succession of *Gymnasia* and *Realschulen.** Although he enjoyed his teaching and liked his students, he continually cursed his fate as an exile from university life, as an academic jack-of-all-trades. He thought himself competent only in Greek and Latin, and perhaps theology, and he protested often, but vainly, against having to teach almost everything else, including calisthenics. Despite his heavy load, he composed some sixteen monographs, mostly editions of Oriental texts relating to church history, which he had collected while abroad. These, he hoped, would bring him back into academic life, but publishers refused them, and Lagarde had to print them at his own expense. The printing costs had to be met by private tutoring which, in turn, shortened his hours of research. In his last request to Hengstenberg in 1856, Lagarde complained that he was teaching forty-five hours a week and that his evenings were taken up by supervising calisthenics or by tutoring.[26]

In 1861 the Clarendon Press of the University of Oxford presented Lagarde with their five-volume Septuagint edition (prepared by Holmes and Parsons, 1798–1827), and this flattering munificence brought him back once more to the Septuagint itself. Two years later he published a study, "Reflections on the Greek Translation of the Proverbs," which enunciated the principles of textual criticism that ought to be applied to the Septuagint and which "began a new epoch in Septuagint-studies." [27] But the greater his scholarly ambition, the more intolerable a burden his teaching became. Several times he almost obtained a university appointment, but each time he failed; after each failure, especially after protracted and promising negotiations with Giessen, Lagarde's temper flared up and his charges of intrigue and conspiracy became more acrimonious. After a decade of such frustration, he lost all hope for a return to university life.

---

* Only the Gymnasium specialized in classical studies, and until the end of the century the *Abitur* from a *Gymnasium* was the prerequisite for university matriculation. The *Realschulen* excluded Greek and added a second modern language; they prepared students for careers outside the professions.

14

Even in the Berlin school system, despite his success as a teacher, he encountered repeated obstacles to his promotion. His habit of protesting to the Ministry of Education or the city school board, bypassing his direct superiors, about long working hours in unsanitary conditions amidst incompetent colleagues, did not improve his chances. On one occasion he secretly mobilized the fathers of his pupils against the school authorities, an extreme means, even if the end was to secure a more adequate classroom.[28] The final indignity came about in 1865: Lagarde was offered a promotion, but to a newly established vocational school, not even a proper *Realschule,* where he would not have been able to teach Greek and Latin. Exasperated, Lagarde petitioned William I, through the intervention of a friend, General von Brandt, and asked for a royal grant that would allow him a prolonged leave of absence. He assured the king that while he was easily replaceable as a high-school teacher, "another man will not so easily duplicate the studies I have undertaken in order to prepare myself for the writing of works on Biblical criticism and on the earliest history of the Church." He pointed to his heavy burden as a teacher, his meager income, his sacrifice of all the pleasures of life, his knowledge of "languages not easily acquired," and his research, completed but not yet published. He further argued that his health would not permit him to continue his independent work while teaching. Unless help was forthcoming, he would have to abandon his projected "critical edition of the Greek translation of the Old Testament and his commentaries on the Patristic text." [29] The letter was a clumsy compound of insincere modesty and self-conscious arrogance. The subject begged for a favor but warned the monarch of the loss to crown and realm if it were not granted. Nevertheless, William assented and allowed Lagarde a three-year leave with full pay.

At Easter, 1866, Lagarde left Berlin, that "big and loathsome city," which he had long since grown to hate.[30] He settled in the small Thuringian town of Schleusingen, where he witnessed the outbreak of the Austro-Prussian war. The town was besieged by Bavarian troops, but they soon withdrew, and Lagarde exulted at Prussia's victory: "World history is on Prussia's side." [31] Shortly after his arrival at Schleusingen, he published, in revised form, all of his previous essays, omitting only two, which he formally repudiated.* He edited a number of texts as well, and published a critical text of one of the Septuagint books, the *genesis graece,* as a preparatory exercise for the complete Septuagint edition which he thought would require several decades. Meanwhile he hoped to move directly from Schleusingen to a university post.

When, in 1868, the University of Halle awarded Lagarde an honorary Doctor of Divinity, his academic rehabilitation had finally begun. It was clinched the following year, when he was appointed to a full professorship at the University of Göttingen. There he succeeded to the chair of Heinrich Ewald, who has been called "the greatest Old Testament scholar whom Germany so far produced." [32] Ewald, one of the "Göttingen seven" and a loyal Hanoverian subject, was outraged by Prussia's annexation of Hanover and had refused to take the prescribed oath to the Prussian monarch.

With his Göttingen appointment, his election in 1876 to the Göttingen Academy of Sciences (successor to Georg Waitz's seat), and his elevation to *Geheimer Regierungsrat* in 1887, Lagarde had garnered all likely honors. He took pleasure in teaching, and continued to receive generous traveling stipends for his research. Yet, his unhappiness deepened. He had few friends in Göttingen, and vigorous enemies everywhere, and an undiminished capacity for making new enemies. Ewald, his predecessor and former patron, resented his presence, as did many other loyal Hanoverians; the theologian, Alois Ritschl, with whom Lagarde had had pleasant exchanges before, saw him only infrequently. In 1883, on the occasion of the four-hundredth anniversary of Luther's birth, the University of Göttingen planned an appropriate ceremony; Lagarde objected to honoring a sectarian, and Ritschl, though aware of his position, volunteered

---

* Lagarde, *Gesammelte Abhandlungen,* Leipzig 1866. The preface to this work was the occasion of his sole apologetic gesture to the guild. Enumerating the many blessings he had enjoyed during his career, not least the leisure of his leave, he wrote: "All this appears before my soul, and makes me, so blessed, regret every harsh word that I have ever uttered and that I utter even in this volume, prepared under the most trying, agitated conditions. As far as I know I was unfair to no one, but the cause which I wanted to serve by not remaining silent about particularly culpable things I have perhaps more injured than advanced by the just censure of its other servants" (p. xi).

to deliver the principal address, in which he indirectly attacked Lagarde.* A few years later, immediately after Ritschl's death, Lagarde accused Ritschl of all sorts of wrongdoing. Ritschl's son was indignant, a public debate ensued, and Lagarde was forced to retract a few of his accusations of immorality.[33]

Lagarde, on the other hand, would tolerate no criticism of himself and would answer even disinterested comments about his scholarship with invectives and contempt. Not that he practiced the detachment he preached. When he struck at an opponent it was with offensive innuendos and indiscriminate broadsides.† As a polemicist he transcended all limits—and in the Germany of his day these were generously drawn—and cast slurs upon the lives and motives of the most blameless scholars.‡ His polemics, often printed and distributed at his own expense, were frequently wrong in points of scholarship, and alienated not only his victims but the entire guild. His unrestrained anti-Semitism offended a great many people as well. Besides his written attacks, Lagarde denounced his

---

* Ritschl explained the circumstances of his speech to a friend, and added that he had been told that Lagarde "considers Luther a thoroughly unimportant man. But then Luther did not sift any variants of the Septuagint." Otto Ritschl, *Albrecht Ritschls Leben, 1864–1889,* Freiburg 1896, II, 420.

† All German critics mention Lagarde's belligerence, usually with great satisfaction: "He resorted to battle-and-duel expressions even when engaged in his scientific disputes. Lagarde cherished not only the struggle but also the hatred. He wanted to hate." Arno Koselleck, "Die Entfaltung des völkischen Bewusstseins bei Paul de Lagarde," *Historische Vierteljahrschrift,* XXX:2 (November, 1935), 356.

‡ Or even upon their religion: he engaged in a particularly vicious campaign against the scholar Abraham Berliner and capitalized on the opponent's Jewish "character." Dr. A. Berliner, *Professor Paul de Lagarde, nach seiner Natur gezeichnet,* Berlin 1887, is the equally unedifying rebuttal of the accused. Or again, his bitter exchange with Professor David Kaufmann, on the occasion of Lagarde's essay on the Jewish philologist "Lipman Zunz und seine Verehrer," Lagarde, *Mittheilungen,* Göttingen 1887, II, 108–162. Among other irrelevant innuendos, Lagarde played on Zunz's first name, changing it from the German Leopold to the Jewish-sounding Lipman, and Kaufmann, in his rebuttal, obligingly reminded Lagarde: "The name is the person's most private property, as Professor Lagarde should know best of all." David Kaufmann, *Paul de Lagarde's jüdische Gelehrsamkeit,* Leipzig 1887, p. 12. Nothing makes the contemporary blandness of American academic controversy more attractive than these reminders of nineteenth-century polemics.

colleagues and their doings in the public meetings of the faculty. In private, he intrigued and conspired against colleagues, and his unpublished correspondence attests his meddlesome concern for petty academic politics.

Lagarde became increasingly engaged in real politics as well. A few months after his arrival in Göttingen, the Franco-Prussian war broke out, and Lagarde rejoiced at the Prussian victories, the more so as his wife's brothers held important posts in Prussia's high command. His Hanoverian colleagues, still unreconciled to Prussian rule, were more reticent. But Lagarde was fiercely Prussian; on January 2, 1871, he wrote to a friend: "It was criminal not to shell Paris before this. Now let it become a heap of rubble—all except the library, which of course must be spared." * Four months earlier he wrote William I that Alsace and Lorraine as well as Luxembourg "must belong fully and forever to Germany." The king must not be misled by parliamentarians; the president of the Reichstag, Eduard Simson, for example, was too cowardly to ask for Alsace-Lorraine, "but then he is a Jew." [34]

The war stirred Lagarde's patriotism, and for a short time he felt at one with his Prussian compatriots. But this rare sense of community came to a quick and unexpected end. In April, 1872, several German newspapers attacked Lagarde for his alleged servility to Napoleon III, because his name had appeared in a French publication of Napoleon's correspondence with Germans, *L'Allemagne aux Tuileries*.[35] The book had been published in France, to discredit the defeated emperor by documenting his close ties to the Germans. But the French paid little attention to the book, and it was only the German press that exploited the catalogue of distinguished names and pilloried all the German correspondents of Napoleon.†

---

* And put at Lagarde's disposal. As early as September 10, 1870, he asked Bismarck to see to it that about five hundred manuscripts be removed from the great Paris Library and deposited for fifteen years for Lagarde's exclusive use in Göttingen. Helmut M. Pölcher, "Symphilologein," in *Lebendiger Geist*, ed. by Hellmut Diwald, pp. 43–44, and Lagarde Archive.

† Theodor Mommsen was another victim of this inflamed patriotic indignation. He had corresponded with Napoleon, and although Mommsen had refused to collaborate with the emperor on his Caesar study, he was granted imperial authorization to borrow any manuscript in the Paris collections. The French alleged, however,

Lagarde's relations with the Tuileries were not in fact incriminating: as a young man, in 1851, he had sent Prince Louis Napoleon one of his many petitions. He had requested permission to wear the medal which his putative great-uncle, Theodor von Neuhof, had coined for the family in 1736. Lagarde's little absurdity was now widely criticized in Germany, though his sulky offer to resign from the university was declined and his intention to emigrate to England not tested.[36]

Instead of emigrating, Lagarde began his career as a critic and prophet of his nation. His first tract was an attack on the *Kulturkampf* which the Prussian government was then preparing: "When at Christmas 1872 I decided to give the public my essay about the relation of the German state to theology, religion, and the Church, I did so in the hope that it would influence the laws which the state was then expected to adopt as its answer to the attack of the clerics." [37] But there was a more important reason for his growing concern with the condition of Germany. He could not endure the smugness of his countrymen, the patriotic self-adulation that had followed the war and national unification. All this was nauseating to a man who was certain that everything of real value was in decline. His first essay was praised by a few men, Treitschke and Franz Overbeck among them, and Lagarde, heartened by this response, wrote a series of articles about the cultural decay and political divisiveness of Germany. In 1878, he published his *Deutsche Schriften,* a collection of all published and unpublished essays on general subjects that he had written during the preceding twenty-five years. In 1881, he added a second volume of essays, and in 1886 he collected all his essays under the title, *Deutsche Schriften, Gesamtausgabe letzter Hand.* He sent copies of these works to the several members of the court, including the young Prince William,

and the German press echoed the charge, that the imperial government had rewarded Mommsen for his critical reading of Napoleon's edition of Borghesi's works by making a substantial payment to a personal friend designated by Mommsen. The entire correspondence led Mommsen's critics to conclude that he "was one of those German academicians who had flattered the emperor in a disgraceful manner." Theodor Mommsen, "In eigener Sache," *Reden und Aufsätze,* Berlin 1905, pp. 427–431. See also *L'Allemagne aux Tuileries de 1850 à 1870,* ed. by Henri Bordier, Paris 1872, pp. 267–269.

to Bismarck, and to the heads of friendly powers. Gradually, his fame spread.

His writings, as we shall see, were intuitive, unsystematic, and intensely personal. His laments were often informed by his own experiences. His work on theology and German education, for example, contained much that was extraordinarily perceptive in its analysis of what was diseased, and much that was absurdly impractical in its proposed remedies. For Lagarde was never content to be a critic alone: he had a passion for prescribing reforms in the most minute and unrealistic details.

He became the gadfly of his own academic community as well. Pleased to have a measure of power and recognition at last, he intrigued and conspired in order to have his views and friends accepted. Some years after his election to the Royal Academy of Sciences at Göttingen, he submitted to the Prussian government a plan for its total reorganization. His scheme was not without merit, but was killed by premature publicity.[38] Lagarde had created a conspiratorial atmosphere about his proposals, and their failure did little to raise his standing among colleagues. Truculently, he offered his resignation from the academy. These were the things that Schemann had in mind when he reluctantly contradicted Lagarde's widow, who said her husband's loneliness stemmed from the machinations of evil conspirators.[39]

His role as critic took more and more time from his scholarship, but still he blamed the shortcomings of others for his own failures. Consider the cherished Septuagint edition. In 1870, Lagarde sent the Prussian minister of education one of his preparatory studies and announced that "it would be the last study that could be undertaken for the sake of the Septuagint edition."[40] Faced with this ultimatum, the minister solicitously inquired under what conditions Lagarde would be prepared to continue his studies. Lagarde's conditions, which included a substantial salary raise, were accepted; the Franco-Prussian war, however, interfered with the procurement of the necessary manuscripts from foreign libraries, and in May, 1871, Lagarde returned his grants. Earlier he had indignantly rebuffed the minister's suggestion that he be assigned a research assistant. It was hard to be kind to Lagarde.

In the 1870's Lagarde blew alternately hot and cold about

the Septuagint edition. In 1880 he announced once more the resumption of his work, and was immensely cheered when a group of British scholars, headed by the orientalist William Wright, offered to promote his work by awarding him a supplementary salary. This he declined, but requested, and received, a subsidy of one hundred pounds. In 1883 he published a critical fragment of Lucian's fourth-century edition of the Septuagint, wrongly thought by Lagarde to have been the official text for the patriarchates of Constantinople and Antioch. Originally he had added to the text innumerable variants, so that the first chapter of Genesis had to be printed, in small type, on ten specially large octavo pages. Realizing the impossibility of this, he swung to the other extreme of printing only one text, often uncorrected by any variants. Not once in this period did the printer receive a complete manuscript; installments would dribble in and Lagarde would enter variant readings from other manuscripts only in proof. Rahlfs, the Septuagint scholar and a student of Lagarde, called the Lucian text "Lagarde's greatest failure." [41]

In 1883, Lagarde submitted his Lucian fragment to William I; the rest, he said, would not be forthcoming: "Hindrances solicitously placed in my path" by colleagues made completion of the work impossible. He thanked the emperor for his several grants and begged him to order enough copies of this fragment (publication costs borne by Lagarde) to distribute to every *Gymnasium* in the Reich.[42] This was refused. Lagarde continued his monographic work, but his German peers still withheld their recognition, and he again concluded that a conspiracy was afoot. His burden was too heavy, and on New Year's Eve, 1884, he announced the suspension of all his systematic work in theology and philology: "All these years I have worked as much as twenty men and am now as exhausted as fifty men." [43] A year later, Professor Althoff asked him about the Septuagint work; Lagarde promised to resume it if "public recognition of an unequivocal nature" were accorded him, and if his salary were increased so that he could spend a third of each year at foreign libraries.[44] He did prepare some more fragments, but as he wrote to his friend and colleague, Alfred Schöne, in 1891: "My Septuagint studies are devouring the Septuagint." [45]

After he suspended his work on the Septuagint, he announced the preparation of a complete, critical edition of the

Psalter, based on the Greek text. This too, he abandoned. Indeed, none of his more ambitious plans was ever fulfilled.* At the time of his death there was general agreement that no man could have been equal to the execution of such gigantic feats of scholarship. In the 1880's, again at his own expense, he published four volumes of *Mittheilungen* and one volume of *Abhandlungen* which contained a miscellany of his monographs. Over the years he invested a large sum this way, several times his annual university salary—and his returns, through sales, were small indeed.

These last studies consisted of critical editions of texts in Greek, Latin, Syrian, Chaldean, Arabic, Coptic, and Persian, with an occasional foray into Armenian literature.[46] By an unhappy fate, this, like his earlier work, won most of its support and praise from foreigners, especially Englishmen.† In a long review essay on Lagarde's works, S. R. Driver, an important English Biblical scholar, offered the most generous praise:

Such, in Germany, are the works which a single man can produce in five years, more and better than most Englishmen could produce in a lifetime. Certainly such productivity is phenomenal even in Germany: if we mistake not, Theodor Mommsen . . . is Lagarde's only superior, perhaps even his only equal. But in the comprehensiveness of his learning Lagarde stands absolutely alone. . . . Whatever be the subject under discussion—the meaning of some recondite word, the sense of a passage from the fathers, the reading of a manuscript, the explanation of a passage of the LXX. or other version—he illustrates it from every source and every side with a brilliancy, an acuteness, and an originality which may truly be said to be unsurpassed.[47]

Such praise of Lagarde was rare, especially in the Germany of his day. After his death, the world of scholarship treated

* With one exception—he completed, in 1888, a new edition of Bruno's Italian writings: Paul de Lagarde, *Le opere italiane di Giordano Bruno*, 2 vols., Göttingen 1888. Not affection, but hatred for Bruno prompted Lagarde to undertake this work. "I wanted to get to know the sea from which the mills of our free-thought draw their water." Lagarde, *Ausgewählte Schriften*, 2d ed., ed. by Paul Fischer, München 1934, p. 201. Henceforth cited as *A.S.*

† Among the latter, S. R. Driver, William Wright and John Keith-Falconer were the most distinguished and effective supporters. On several occasions one or the other of them approached Lagarde with offers of financial assistance.

him more kindly. Whatever the flaws of his own efforts, Lagarde had persistently described the kind of ›critical scholarship that still had to be done, and this, by common consent, was in itself a contribution of high merit.*

In 1891, Lagarde went to Rome on his last research trip. After his return, in October, his health began to fail; toward the end of that year, unknown to anyone save his wife, he entered the hospital and was operated on for cancer of the stomach. A few days after the operation, on December 22, he died. Although he had formally left the Protestant Church, and no minister could appear at the graveside, Lagarde had requested a church service. After considerable difficulty, the university obtained a municipal chapel, where the university's prorector, the great classical scholar Ulrich von Wilamowitz-Moellendorff, at his own request, delivered the funeral oration.†

It is a lonely man [*stiller Mann*] who now enters the realm of eternal silence; to many of his colleagues he was a total stranger, to few only did he become and remain close. . . . He scattered the seeds of great ideas and emotions and those developed in a thousand hearts. A wind, too, he sowed, and reaped a storm; not even at his grave will the passions, hatred and love, calumny and adoration, subside.

But Marc Antony was wrong: "The good that men do lives after them, and so it shall be with Paul de Lagarde." Wilamowitz recalled Lagarde's unique achievements in scholarship —("There is probably no one among us who can correctly spell the languages in which he published texts")—and said of his greatest ambition: "There exists no task more difficult and therefore more beautiful" than his projected edition of the Old Testament.

---

* "Paul de Lagarde is the man to whom, probably, living students of the Septuagint must look up to as the leader of modern progress. . . . Lagarde laid down certain rules for the study of the text of the Greek Old Testament, which still, on the whole, represent the prevailing views and practice." Richard R. Ottley, *A Handbook to the Septuagint*, London, Methuen, 1920, pp. 71, 93.

† Of course, Wilamowitz could not have known that Lagarde had opposed his call to Göttingen; in a letter to Friedrich Althoff, powerful councilor of the Prussian Education Ministry, Lagarde wrote: "Wilamowitz is not the right man for us—and that for a very definite reason," which remained unspecified. Letter of April 4, 1883, Lagarde Archive.

But the deceased was not only a savant, indeed the core of his being is not thus touched. . . . As a prophet he spoke about state and church, education and worship, about society and morality. Nor did he lose heart when his voice remained a voice in the wilderness. He felt himself a prophet. And he had a right to do this: for his was a prophetic nature.

Wilamowitz concluded by invoking other prophets of the spirit, Augustine and Giordano Bruno, Rousseau and Carlyle, who, like Lagarde, were essentially religious men, who succeeded through "the full engagement of their subjective faith," and who, again like Lagarde, endured much suffering.[48]

In a letter to his father-in-law, Theodor Mommsen, Wilamowitz explained his part in the funeral: "It seems likely that he [Lagarde] bequeathed his entire fortune to the Academy of Sciences here.* Also, of course, it fascinated me to try to grasp the problematic nature of this man who seemed to me both curious and significant. Since he had been *persona ingratissima* to the Ministry, [my participation] might be held against me, but I do not care." Mommsen, who had been deeply offended by Lagarde's anti-Semitism, merely rejoined: "In Lagarde there was much that could have become a great man, but . . . ," and he left the inexplicable unexplained.[49]

Lagarde missed more than greatness. He was a troubled man, whose fleeting moments of contentment did not prevail against his heavy, self-imposed burden, against his melancholy, his lack of inner self-sufficiency. This man, who made the most exorbitant demands on himself and others, who labored most prodigiously, whose ambitions knew no bounds, dissipated his efforts and failed time and again in his self-appointed tasks. In part, no doubt, this was due to the sheer magnitude

---

* Lagarde had in fact willed his possessions, including his library, to the Academy of Sciences, subject to a great many conditions. As Wilamowitz put it: "Not without self-denial, the academy accepted the legacy and the royal government approved this acceptance, and in this way both bowed before the will of a man who had sought the highest, but on his own terms." Ulrich von Wilamowitz-Moellendorff, *Reden und Vorträge*, Berlin 1901, p. 91. In 1893, Lagarde's library was sold for 30,000 marks to New York University, where it was maintained as a separate unit—the Lagarde Library—until recently. It constituted one of the best Oriental libraries in America. I am grateful to Dr. Theodor F. Jones, former director of the University Heights Library, New York University, for permission to borrow some of Lagarde's books. Dr. Jones told me that Lagarde's old desk chair, shaped in the form of a saddle, had long been at the library, but had recently disappeared.

of his intellectual appetite; perhaps it was also a persistent failure of concentration. For Lagarde, this kind of failure must have been particularly agonizing; he so freely arraigned his colleagues for lesser deficiencies, and he so often said, with gratuitous acerbity, that scholarship was a moral act, and flaws in it a moral failing.

William James once defined self-esteem as a fraction: $\text{Self-esteem} = \frac{\text{Success}}{\text{Pretensions}}$.[50] Lagarde's fractions would have revealed the intensely unhappy, frustrated man that he was, an impression confirmed by his wife's remark: "In actual fact Lagarde possessed too little, not too much self-esteem [*Selbstbewusstsein*]." [51] He suffered from soaring pretensions, fragmentary performance. As a scholar he had not come close to his goal; as a patriot, he shuttled back and forth, as we shall see, between impossible expectations and bootless despondency. A lover of children, he died childless. Always in search of friends, he possessed few. And he could never shake off the terrible regret over his mother's death, nor the terrorizing memory of his father.

The most unrestrained expression of his loneliness appeared in his occasional poems, some of which he published and all of which were published posthumously by his widow.[52] Their style was wooden and heavy, and the lines were often in the form of abbreviated declarative sentences, without rhyme or beauty. But, like his prose, they were suffused with the passion of his suffering and longing. An admiring critic characterized Lagarde *"as the poet of the most Germanic and the most pious nostalgia."* [53] As late as 1887, he wrote with unabated grief:

> Oh mother, yourself a child, when giving birth,
> As my playmate, why did you not stay,
> How could I grow up, with whom?
> And hence a child I remained to my old age.

And again:

> The worst in life
> Is silent loneliness,
> In which the soul forgets all speech,
> And neither speaks nor hears,
> But as a petrifaction of days bygone,
> Is left like rubble on the road.

But the rage of the lonely man was also expressed:

> We have loved long enough
> Today we start to hate.

In many ways Lagarde with his tempestuous moods had remained a child, wounded, frightened, craving the affectionate recognition of others, yet so fearful of losing his independence that he rebuffed and insulted the very friends he sought. Certain of a conspiracy against him, he privately intrigued and publicly berated, until even his friends pulled back, bewildered and exasperated.

But his readers and followers knew nothing of this sadness. They only heard the insistent speech of a prophet, calling them to greatness. And they thought Lagarde a true prophet.

2: The Idealism of Antimodernity

The Germany that we love and that we yearn to see has never existed and perhaps never will exist. LAGARDE

Lagarde was one of the great critics of imperial Germany. His *Deutsche Schriften* became a classic in cultural criticism; few other works dealt so comprehensively and ruthlessly with the hidden weaknesses of Bismarck's empire: the loss of faith, the disunity of the people, the corruption of education and the decline of morality. None combined this criticism with such passionate nationalism, and it was this combination that gave Lagarde his immense appeal.

Lagarde first turned to *Zeitkritik* when he was forty-five years old. Until then, except for two political speeches delivered in 1853 but not published, he had devoted himself to his scholarly work, and his only contact with the official world had been his intermittent conflict with it. Throughout the 1850's and 1860's, he felt estranged from German politics, and by 1872 his mood and the mood of his countrymen were radically different. While they were exulting over their military victory and national unification, Lagarde was looking ahead to the disasters he thought would overwhelm the new Reich. In his *Deutsche Schriften* he sought to warn his people against the new and terrible dangers that would annihilate their true character and ultimately destroy Germany itself.

He wrote as a prophet; he neither reasoned nor exposited, but poured out his excoriations and laments, his intuitive truths and promises. There was nothing limpid or systematic in his work; within each essay he skipped from subject to subject, alternating abstract generalities and concrete proposals. The pervasive mood of the book was despair and the dominant tone a kind of whiny heroism.

As a lonely figure, uncommitted to any cause or party, Lagarde saw the weaknesses of every group in the new Germany. Much of what he wrote was exasperatingly remote from reality, yet some of his prognostications were remarkably perspicacious. He had the quickened sensibility of a wounded man and was therefore more closely attuned to the sufferings of other men and the shortcomings of his culture than those healthy people who were caught up in the bounding advance of their society.

Lagarde's plans for the restoration of religion, politics, and education—which are discussed in the following chapters—were held together not by any inner logic or philosophy, but by his vision of the nature of men and the destiny of Germany. Essentially he was a moralist who saw the world and men in simple moral terms. Although the Germans of his day had succumbed to all sorts of evils and temptations, the German people still had a unique calling for the heroic, moral life. As a prophet, he sought to teach his people to conquer its foes and recover its past greatness. It was *hubris* of Lagarde to avow and even believe that he was the prophet who would prepare Germany's rebirth. Nor did he want to be a prophet of God alone; he thought of himself, and was hailed, as the prophet of Germanism, of the *Volkstum* that was still unspoiled.

Lagarde believed man to be a creature of will and energy and sentiment, for whom reason was of secondary importance: "The core of man is not his reason, but his will. . . . For like everything that is good, knowledge also enters through the will, whose wings are sensibility and imagination, and whose driving force is love." [1] Man was a spiritual being, and the needs of his soul were far more important and irrepressible than the needs of his body. When Lagarde insisted that he was the last defender of German individualism, he was not thinking of political rights at all; he thought of himself as the last champion of the German character. He wanted to remake society so that the great individuals could realize themselves and that no one would be deprived of his right to fulfill the plan that God had fashioned for him.

Like so many believers in human greatness, Lagarde was oppressed by the frailty of men, afraid always that he would succumb to a new temptation. Lagarde thought that the German character would perish in material comfort, for men can thrive only on adversity and can grow only in perpetual struggle. Work and suffering ennoble, and the worst vice was self-indulgence. The idea of human equality was a fraudulent myth, and the recognition of inequality a psychological necessity, because "man's greatest joy is to revere other men, or to put it less extravagantly, to recognize other men above themselves, and to love and be loved by these men." [2]

Lagarde's moral thought was not original. We recognize the traditional fusion of Protestantism, especially Lutheranism, and the Prussian ethos. We recognize as well some themes from the German romantic writers and from the literature of the wars of liberation. But for Lagarde this moral insight also possessed an existential truth: he was idealizing and justifying his own life of suffering and disappointment.* In his heroic view of man's moral life, Lagarde's personal experience and resentment and the general propositions of cultural criticism most clearly coincided.

Lagarde's passionate nationalism was molded by the same moral view: "I am incapable of understanding the life of a state in any other way except as an analogue of the individual life of a person. . . . The nation, like the individual, has a soul, and in the last analysis, for nations as well as individuals, the soul alone possesses value." [3] Therefore all the material triumphs of imperial Germany counted for nothing, indeed were an evil, because they endangered the German soul. Lagarde's criticism was quickened by his nostalgic recollection of an earlier, uncorrupted Germany, where the heroic essence of Germanism, of *Deutschtum*, had prevailed, and had been embodied in a unique race of German heroes. His quarrel with modern Germany arose not because it tolerated injustice or bred poverty, but because it enfeebled that older type of man and destroyed the traditional virtues.

The German soul could be saved only by a rededication to common purposes and tasks. Each nation had a task assigned

---

* There are countless passages in which Lagarde paid tribute to his experience of adversity. Reflecting on all the obstacles of his career, he once wrote: "Without this hard school I would not have become the free man that I am, and freedom—inner independence from the world and turning towards God—means more to me than any scientific achievement." Lagarde, *Symmicta*, Göttingen 1880, II, 138.

to it by God, and Lagarde thought to identify the national tasks for his people. They were to culminate, as we shall see, in Germany's imperialist destiny, in her colonization of *Mitteleuropa*. Beyond imperialism was Lagarde's vision of a Germany reborn, when the soul of the nation and of all its citizens would be fused by a new religion and protected in a new community of Germanic believers. Toward that utopia Lagarde directed his political efforts and his plans for reform.

Clearly Lagarde's perspective was different from the dominant outlook of the nineteenth century. He sneered at the real, the practical world; he distrusted positivism, loathed materialism, and mocked progress. He asked questions and set up goals that were different from those of his liberal, enlightened contemporaries. He had contempt for the business world. The cheerful commonplaces of the patriotic *literati* enraged him and intensified his own commitment to the problematical and tragic.* If life had no more to offer than safety, profit, and a little pedantry, if all risks and sacrifices had been taken out—it was a miserable, empty life. Lagarde always thought that he was a solitary fighter; actually he belonged to those nineteenth-century dissenters whom Eric Bentley has described as heroic vitalists. Lagarde's faith in heroic vitalism, mixed as it was with a strong nationalist bias, became the foremost prejudice of his temperament, the springboard of his judgment.

It was a rankling, exacting prejudice for Lagarde to burden himself with. Such exalted images are rarely realized; few men regard the world as a perpetual battleground and few states emulate Sparta. The nineteenth century, with its universal Podsnappery, hid and denied its heroism, and it appears heroic only to us, in retrospect. It is only recently that we have discovered and begun to envy the admirable energy of our inner-directed ancestors.

---

* He thought in fact that the literati were the characteristic expression of every soul-destroying force in modern Germany: "On the surface of the new Reich swims the *Literat*. . . . This poisonous weed must be extirpated from our streams and seas, as must the political system without which this weed could not survive. [Then] the clean mirror will reflect the flowers of the shore and the stars of heaven, the ancient gods will reemerge from the depths, and no one will harbor us any ill will." Lagarde, "Die Religion der Zukunft" (1878), *Deutsche Schriften,* 3d ed., München 1937, p. 276. Henceforth cited as *D.S.* The first time a particular essay is cited, its date of composition will be given.

Lagarde saw nothing but decline.* The old Germany was rapidly disappearing, and in its place arose a secular society, a new Babylon, that worshipped Mammon and devoured men. Scattered throughout the *Deutsche Schriften* were the distorted criticisms of modernity that were characteristic of men with utopian inclinations, and that could have been composed by Carlyle or Tennyson as easily as by Lagarde. The evils of the industrial society, particularly in its infancy, were great; they were made more unbearable still by those writers who tortured the minds of men by nostalgic dreams of a past that never was and prophesied a future that could never be, all the while vilifying, but not explaining, the present.

Lagarde had no difficulty in enumerating the manifestations of cultural decay. Time and again he complained about the general retreat from morality, the creeping decline of excellence, the collective descent into passive slothfulness. Nothing was immune from the leveling threat of the rising masses. A frivolous cheapening of standards was evident everywhere, and if it persisted "we shall all sink into nothingness: for the capital resources of our intellectual life, which we possessed in 1870, have been nearly exhausted in this last period of our history, and we are face to face with bankruptcy." [4] The language, for example, was steadily being corrupted: "Our speech has ceased to speak, it shouts; it says cute, not beautiful, colossal, not great; it cannot find the right word any more, because the word is no longer the designation of an object, but the echo of some kind of gossip about the object." [5] The penalty of continuous passivity will be collective death: "All spiritual forces should be set free, all sham stamped out, every organization of idealistic intent allowed and encouraged: if this were done, it would be a joy to be alive. Instead, it is a punishment today to have to witness the withering away of our nation." [6]

Lagarde assumed that most Germans were unhappy and

* And saw it everywhere. How easily he converted a random episode into further proof of a general decline can be seen from this brief account which he sent to his wife in August 1871: "In Cassel, at the railroad station, there were three Hessian peasant women, old, weatherbeaten, worn out by work and grief. They could only have talked of misery and sorrows, and they looked to me as if they were emigrating from this new Germany that is so liberal, so powerful, and so utterly un-German. We worship foreign gods—that is our undoing." Anna de Lagarde, *Erinnerungen,* p. 93.

that the new commercial society bred nothing but this discontent and resentment. He assumed, in short, that everybody would sooner or later be afflicted by the same despair that oppressed him. Already in 1853, in his first essay, he wrote: "We are all thoroughly discontented." [7] Thirty-five years later, after Germany had been successfully unified, he complained: "Our life is more joyless than anyone can imagine." [8] This was the insistent theme of his cultural criticism. No work was done that pleased, no art produced which was creative, no faith existed which ennobled and inspired. The typical *Bürger* chased after comfort and success, with no sense for the world beyond. Nothing but dissatisfied and disgruntled hedonism. Nothing but mediocrity, dull, drab middle-class life, materialism and cultural sterility. "The nation is bored: therefore individuals through smoking, reading, theater-going, bar-loitering, home-gardening, and the addiction to humor magazines try to dispel their awareness that ciphers like themselves cannot stand being alone for any length of time at all." [9] His charges against the emptiness of urban existence and against the corruptive impact of commercial life rounded out the usual picture of the conservative-esthetic protest.[10] "Better to split wood than to continue this contemptible life of civilization and education; we must return to the sources [of our existence], on lonely mountain peaks, where we are ancestors, not heirs." [11] Lagarde feared the consequences of this cultural anguish, yet by his work spread it ever more widely.

Before 1871, Lagarde could hope that the political unification of Germany would effect a spiritual regeneration as well; but Bismarck's Reich quickly dashed his hopes. *This* form of unification, he charged, would not inspire the nation to a new burst of creativity, but immeasurably hasten its spiritual collapse. "There has never been a creation as joyless as this one." * The young had not been swept up by any sudden

---

* Lagarde, "Vorrede" (1885), *D.S.*, p. 99. Lagarde of course was not alone in that judgment. In 1873 Nietzsche published the first of his *Unzeitgemässe Betrachtungen* in which he warned against the common mistake of believing Germany's military victory also proved the superiority of its culture. Nothing could be more dangerous; actually he foresaw "*the defeat—yes, the extirpation of the German spirit in favor of the 'German Reich.'*" See *David Strauss, der Bekenner und der Schriftsteller,* in *Nietzsche's Werke,* Leipzig, Naumann, 1906, II, 4. While Nietzsche and Lagarde may have been the most outspoken critics of Bismarck's creation, others soon chimed in. See D. Wilhelm Lütgert, *Das Ende des*

patriotic enthusiasm, and they were bored by the political or military ambitions of the Reich: "They want to fight a war for a concrete ideal, they want danger, risk, sacrifice, and death, and do not want to regurgitate the platitudes that their grandfathers had already chewed on." [12] In every possible way the new Reich stunted the growth of the free individual and thus annihilated the only source of cultural vitality. "Everything depends on the human being, and Germany lacks nothing so much as men; there is nothing toward which Germany, with its adoration of the State, of public opinion, of *Kultur,* and of success, directs so much hostility as toward the individual, who alone can bring it life and honor." [13]

This mounting disgust with modernity was the underlying passion of Lagarde's cultural criticism and of the ambitious reforms he proposed. For twenty years he explored the causes, the symptoms, and the cure of Germany's spiritual collapse, discovering in turn that the Jews, the liberals, the academicians, were the cause, and a new religion, a new body politic, a new nobility, and a new educational system the cure. That many of his strictures were just and incisive cannot be gainsaid. Every critical thinker in Germany had similar misgivings, and like-minded criticism, often just as intense, has been heard in Western countries of late, reaching an alarming crescendo in our own country. Lagarde's inadequacy lies rather in his analysis, in his intemperate and unhistorical personification of social deficiencies, in his paradoxically liberal belief that social tinkering could effect vast spiritual reforms. One is struck as well by the pathological prominence of Lagarde's conspiratorial view of society. His picture of Germany was no different from his picture of Göttingen, where the pure Lagarde was beset by worthless colleagues. In his cultural criticism, this conspiratorial view accounts for the brutality of some of his plans, but it has as its complement Lagarde's heroic conception of men and nations. It was the heroic image that allowed him to appear to himself and others as an idealist, as a disinterested fighter for old values and transcendental ideals.

Lagarde was an idealist in the several senses in which Ger-

Idealismus im Zeitalter Bismarcks, Gütersloh 1930, pp. 224–255, for a discussion of the "German pessimism" which sprang up immediately after unification. A suggestive interpretation can be found in Otto Westphal, *Feinde Bismarcks. Geistige Grundlagen der deutschen Opposition von 1848–1918,* München and Berlin 1930, pp. 94–147.

mans have used this term during the past century.* In his esthetic-heroic view of men and nations, in his pseudo-religious faith in the irrational, the supernatural, and the divine, in his glorification of the *Genie,* he was close to the historical movement of the late eighteenth century, known as Idealism. In his depreciation of the political and economic man, of the common man of everyday life, and of the political culture that adapts itself to him, he appeared as an idealist because he had turned his back on modernity, on practicality, because he preferred to legislate for an implausible future rather than to reform an intractable present. The ultimate goals of Lagarde's cultural criticism appeared idealistic, the immediate reforms often involved physical violence and brutality. Again we are reminded of certain characteristics of Lagarde's biography: since childhood, he had been accustomed to hate concretely, but to attach his love to an ideal object that was dead and beyond recovery.

To many Germans, then, Lagarde was an idealist, in the same way that Hitler was to be an idealist for another generation, and in a way that Marx and Bismarck never were. He helped to establish the idealism of antimodernity, and, as we shall presently see, he incorporated into his program of reform radical provisions for violence and tyranny. But these, as Lagarde's reputation was to prove, could be sanctioned without depriving the resentment against modernity of its idealistic respectability.

---

* And he was invariably hailed as an idealist. In an important catalogue of right-wing heroes, published during the Weimar Republic, we find Lagarde characterized as "an idealist in politics. . . . He knew perfectly well that politics had to be concrete and practical, but just because the concrete is so unidealistic, the *Realpolitiker* in Germany must be an idealist." Franz Hahne, "Lagarde als Politiker," in *Deutscher Aufstieg. Bilder aus der Vergangenheit und Gegenwart der rechtsstehenden Parteien,* ed. by Hans von Arnim and Georg von Below, Berlin, Schneider, 1925, p. 287.

3: The Germanic Religion

Thou shalt not kill; but needs't not strive
Officiously to keep alive.   ARTHUR HUGH CLOUGH

Shame on the man who, while his neighbor's
house is ablaze, pursues learned studies about the
nature of fire, instead of extinguishing the fire.
Pure theology is worth nothing; today's world is
basically evil and immoral; to improve it must be
the chief goal of our lives and labors.   LAGARDE

Lagarde used to say "I am nothing but a theologian, and my interest in all other things has its center in my theology." [1] It was true that ever after his loss of faith in organized Christianity, theology and the renovation of religious life in Germany engaged his mind most persistently and profoundly. His religious thought was the creative synthesis of his scholarship and his will to reform, and it was as a religious thinker, as a free-lance theologian and critic on the fringes of orthodoxy, that Lagarde had the most lasting influence on German thought.* His criticism of Christian dogma, his satire of tepid Protestantism and his attack on political Catholicism were deservedly famous, and his prophecy of a new national religion

---

* A most impressive testimony to this influence was Ernst Troeltsch's dedication of the second volume of his collected works to "the memory of Paul de Lagarde." In his article "The Present State of Theology and Religion," first published in 1903, Troeltsch wrote of Lagarde: "One of the most stimulating and important theologians, if at the same time one of the strangest. . . . His *Deutsche Schriften,* cast in such powerful prose, have finally made the impact that his great and important ideas deserve. . . . [And this not only among theologians] but especially among laymen; he placed the gravity and the greatness of all these questions before their heart and conscience." *Gesammelte Schriften,* Vol. II: *Zur religiösen Lage. Religionsphilosophie und Ethik,* Tübingen 1913, pp. 19–20.

that would somehow spring from the still uncorrupted German *Volk,* from the untutored classes, struck a responsive chord in a society that was uneasily secular.

In Lagarde's religious criticism and prophecy all the strands of his experience were fused. Here we find the romanticism of his youth as well as the mature scholarship of his later life, here we find traces of the disappointed critic of his time as well as of the son in rebellion against his father and against his father's faith. The hope of Lagarde's life was to find a new faith, a new Jerusalem: a haven after a lifetime of unintended solitude.

Nowhere did Lagarde's activism show up more forcefully than in his essays on religion. He wanted to be a national reformer, a spiritual educator of the Germans: "I have no use for abstract truth. I want to bind and liberate my people." *
His readers he called "the members of my congregation," his message expounded his free-thinking amalgam of pietism, rationalism, and romantic imagination. Tirelessly he inveighed against the futility and error of the existing faith and proclaimed the desperate need for a new one.

Lagarde's break with orthodoxy came in the late 1840's and early 1850's.† But the first stirrings of doubt and disillusionment came earlier, in his father's house where he noticed the discrepancy between pretension and reality.‡ As a child he observed the decline of religious life after Schleiermacher's death, and in later years he made light of Schleiermacher's attempted synthesis of philosophy and religion: "In the mornings

---

* *"Ich will mein Volk binden und befreien."* Lagarde, *Symmicta,* Göttingen 1880, II, 106. Lagarde's uncommon usage of *binden* is certainly an echo of the Gospel's *"Wahrlich, ich sage euch: Was ihr immer auf Erden binden werdet, soll auch im Himmel gebunden sein, und was ihr auf Erden lösen werdet, soll auch im Himmel los sein."* Matthew, 18,18.

† Franz Xaver Kraus, the Alsatian Catholic reformer, wrote of Lagarde: "He often said to me that he was an arch-heretic, and still this heretic was one of the most god-fearing beings whom I have encountered on this earth. The reflection of eternal light shone in the face of this stranger to this world." Quoted in Rudolf Grabs, *Paul de Lagarde und H. St. Chamberlain,* Weimar 1940, p. 12.

‡ Nietzsche, the son of a Protestant minister, and an even more radical critic of Christianity than Lagarde, once pointed out the importance of these early impressions: "As children of preachers, a great many German philosophers and academicians had their first view of ministers in childhood, and hence ceased to believe in God." Quoted in Ernst Benz, *Nietzsches Ideen zur Geschichte des Christentums und der Kirche,* Leiden, Brill, 1956, p. 174.

Schleiermacher played religion on the G string and in the afternoons philosophy on the D string; on request the other way around"; and in a pun on his name, Lagarde continued: "Schleiermacher's death did not so much create a gap as it showed that the abyss which even then was yawning had not been bridged by him for the educated classes but had merely been veiled [*verschleiert*] by him." [2] At the university, Lagarde encountered the fierce conflicts within Protestantism, the battle between rigid orthodoxy on the one hand and liberal theology on the other. Between these extremes were the ineffectual mediators who failed to understand that between Hengstenberg, for example, and David Friedrich Strauss there could be no reconciliation. Nor was it possible to define a common ground between the Pietists and the rationalists. In his years of study Lagarde discovered at first hand the power of the higher criticism, and he came to realize that no valid theology could be constructed until the groundwork of philological work had been laid. His projected edition of the Septuagint was intended to provide this groundwork.

Lagarde's revulsion from organized Christianity came at a time of deep crisis for the churches of Germany. The theological uncertainties and divisions proved the more dangerous as Christianity itself was subjected to radical attacks from the outside, most notably from the left Hegelians. The important works of Ludwig Feuerbach and Bruno Bauer appeared early in the 1840's and further encouraged the turning away from religion on the part of the educated classes. Lagarde was a sensitive observer of this growing indifference to and discomfort about religion that characterized especially the bourgeois Protestant world. The revolution of 1848 proved a still greater shock to the churches. Protestantism responded by drawing still closer to the throne and thus becoming still more estranged from the people. For the Catholics, the revolution had been the signal to enter political life, to rally believers to common political action.

Lagarde warned against political Catholicism and against the Protestant drift toward a renewed tightening of the bonds between a frightened monarchy and church.* He condemned

---

* Modern scholars have judged the postrevolutionary developments within Protestantism in much the same manner. In his semiofficial history of the Protestant Church, Karl Kupisch indicts the Protestant Church of the 1850's and concludes: "Long before socialist propaganda could

the whole tendency of official Protestantism which he identified with the religious policy of Frederick William III and which was epitomized by the king's establishment of the Union of Lutheran and Reformed Churches. According to Lagarde, this union worked to the detriment of both confessions and was a worthy monument to the reign of Frederick William III, "one of the most disastrous kings which Prussia ever had." [3] Nor did the policy of Frederick William IV, of his camarilla, or of his religious advisers promise any improvement.

By 1853, Lagarde began publicly to denounce the *Lumpentheologie* of his day.[*] A quarter of a century before Nietzsche's avowal that God is dead, Lagarde reported the spiritual bankruptcy of Christianity, proclaimed the death of religion in Germany and fulminated against the surface religiosity that had supplanted true faith. In the succeeding decades, Lagarde elaborated his criticism of the existing churches and of the religious life in Germany, and he sharpened his attack on all contemporary theology. He insisted ever more urgently that only his own national religion of the future could save Germany. His program of reform, as we shall see, proved the usual composite of soaring fantasy and minute details. Throughout this later phase, Lagarde remained impervious to developments in theology and politics, and merely built further on his own ideological foundations. The one exception was his im-

---

carry its work to the masses, this [Protestant] church was made up of 'visitors' to divine services and ever more lost its character as a congregation." *Zwischen Idealismus und Massendemokratie. Eine Geschichte der evangelischen Kirche in Deutschland von 1815–1945*, Berlin 1955, p. 69. Of the same period, William O. Shanahan writes: "At a decisive moment, German Protestantism had cast its lot with the authoritarian and the agrarian traditions of European life, openly scorning the urban and industrial and liberal world that was coming into being. German Protestantism thereby veiled the loss of the common man's allegiance, for by committing itself to monarchical authority, Protestantism could not take the side of the people." *German Protestants Face the Social Question*, Vol. I: *The Conservative Phase 1815–1871*, Notre Dame (Ind.) 1954, p. 301.

[*] In 1853, he wrote to his fiancée from London: "You write that I am far more orthodox than before. Not that I know of. It only seems this way to you because here I do not have to confront a victorious reaction, complete with [Johann Wichern's] *Innerer Mission* and with an unscientific, deceitful theology. The opposition disappears, and with it the bitterness and sharpness which an opposition to our *Lumpentheologie* necessarily evokes." Anna de Lagarde, *op. cit.*, p. 31.

mediate denunciation of the *Kulturkampf* which he thought a stupid, liberal attack on Catholicism that was bound to fail.*

Lagarde's theological thought was a highly idiosyncratic and unsystematic combination of his own religious feelings and of the several, often contradictory, strands of prevailing theological and historical opinion. Lagarde himself was a sentimental theist, a religious being, capable of feeling awe, reverence, and a sense of the mysterious. God he regarded as the creator and the redeemer of man, who for each man and each nation had conceived a unique destiny. History was the human approximation of that destiny, "but in the historical world, next to the spirits of light there marches a dark spirit, which is called sin, and whose traces are to be found everywhere, and whose acts can be recognized at every step." [4]

His theism had drawn inspiration from the pietistic and romantic movements, and the latter especially had quickened his own religious sense and his understanding of the religious experience of others. On the other hand, it was compatible with his commitment to theological rationalism, and with the philosophical skepticism and philological criticism introduced by Lessing and the German Enlightenment. His passionate belief that religion and the capacity for a religious life were the necessary elements of survival for men and nations, without which they would gradually dry up, expressed his inner experience as well as his historical judgment. Religion was not merely a kind of social cement for him, as it was for so many thinkers of the nineteenth century; it was rooted in man's ineradicable desire for a link with God and the supernatural. It was a reaching out for the sublime and the inexplicable, a human striving for excellence beyond itself, and hence the condition of all human improvement.

But the existing Christian religions had lost their power, and Lagarde repudiated them, thus finding himself again as a reluctant outsider.† His indictment of Christianity consisted

---

* Lagarde was one of the very few non-Catholics who at once opposed the *Kulturkampf*. Another prominent non-Catholic was Konstantin Frantz who in 1872 published his *Religion des Nationalliberalismus,* which denounced the liberal ideology behind the *Kulturkampf* in much the same manner and temper as Lagarde did.

† Walter Nigg classified Lagarde as an "outsider" among Christian liberals, arguing that so heretical a believer could only be ranged

of two parts, an historical attack on the authenticity of its dogmas and a critique of its contemporary institutions. His aim was primarily negative: to clear away the rubble of the past and so prepare the ground for the building of a new national temple.*

Lagarde was a ruthless critic of the content and authenticity of Christian dogma. He threw the whole battery of higher criticism against the Church, and added some idiosyncratic shafts of his own. Like so many critics before him, he sought to strike down the walls of false dogma beneath which the true faith lay buried. "Fourteen centuries have molded the Christian religion. It is not the work of a single person, not the sole work of Jesus, but the result of many efforts by many men and many peoples. . . . [Now] it is doomed to extinction because of the Jewish elements which it absorbed." [5] It was not only that some of the fundamental dogmas of the Church— the trinity and infant baptism, for example—lacked even a shred of justification in the Bible. The root evil was simply this: the Gospel, "which is an exposition by a religious genius of the laws of the life of the spirit," had been turned into Christianity, "a new substance made up of the Jewish, Greek, and Roman elements fused with the Gospel." [6] By the mid-nineteenth century, the *Evangelium* and Christianity were entirely different things, and the Gospel, so long imprisoned and perverted by the Church would have to be liberated from it.†

---

among the liberal opponents of orthodoxy. *Geschichte des religiösen Liberalismus. Entstehung, Blütezeit, Ausklang*, Zürich and Leipzig, Niehans, 1937, pp. 286–288.

* Or, as he put it at the end of his major essay on religion: "Only truth will make us free, and my political essays have no other end than to destroy the sham in education, in the treatment of religious and political questions, to destroy that sham ruthlessly and thus to pave the way for that liberating truth. . . . We want freedom, but not liberalism; we want Germany, but not Jewish-Celtic theorems about Germany; piety, not a dogmatics that has lost its bite because of a muzzle to which the government carries the key. . . . We want the recognition, education, and transfiguration of our own nature, but we do not want to be driven by a Russian coachman, on a French leash, whipped by a Jewish scourge." Lagarde, "Die Religion der Zukunft," *D.S.*, p. 285.

† In an effusive letter, Franz Overbeck, the Basel theologian and friend of Nietzsche, thanked Lagarde for his essay on religion, and commented: "I must think back many a year before I can recall a theological work that gave me as much of an intellectual feast as did yours. . . . As far as such a new idea as your distinction between the

The Christian image of Jesus was itself an intolerable distortion. To glorify His death, and not His life, His agony, not His life-giving joy, His sacrifice and not His teachings, was the unforgivable, the monumental Jewish perversion.* It had been enshrined at the center of Catholicism: for what did the Mass—the Lord's Supper or the *Abendmahl,* terms that Lagarde mocked and despised—seek to commemorate, indeed to repeat, but His death. This was the result of the typical Jewish penchant for celebrating the unique historical event and not the eternal spirit that informed it. As always with Lagarde, the culprit was close at hand. Paul, the Jew, "the utterly unauthorized . . . who even after his conversion remained a Pharisee from head to toe," who had never known Jesus and who had deliberately avoided the surviving disciples, debased and corrupted the Gospel of Jesus by admixing Jewish beliefs and customs with it.[7] Lagarde hated this Saul—and tiresomely derided his adoption of another name.† "Nothing

Gospel and Christianity is concerned, you will not expect ready understanding, least of all from someone who in this matter is not altogether uninhibited." Letter of February 1, 1873, Lagarde Archive. Overbeck had called Nietzsche's attention to Lagarde's essay, and Nietzsche in turn urged his friend Rohde "not to neglect this short and most astonishing work which says fifty things wrongly, but fifty things rightly and truthfully, thus a very good work." *Friedrich Nietzsches Gesammelte Briefe,* 2d ed., Leipzig 1903, letter of January 31, 1873, II, 394.

* Shaw, of course, also derided "Crosstianity" and "the central superstition of the salvation of the world by the gibbet." Preface, *Major Barbara,* New York 1907, pp. 30–31.

† St. Paul and the Old Testament had already been attacked by German philosophers of the eighteenth century. Lagarde's polemics harked back to Fichte's denunciation of St. Paul, but other European thinkers had been equally hostile to St. Paul. At the end of his book on St. Paul, Renan wrote: "After having been for three centuries, thanks to orthodox Protestantism, the Christian teacher *par excellence,* Paul sees in our own day his reign drawing to a close." *Saint Paul,* transl. by Ingersoll Lockwood, New York, Carleton, 1869, p. 330. Lagarde's attack, in turn, had a profound influence on Nietzsche whose "first stirrings of distrust of St. Paul came from Lagarde." Charles Andler, *Nietzsche. Sa vie et sa pensée,* 2d ed., Paris, Gallimard, 1958, I, 485. These first stirrings were echoed in his later outbursts: "That it [the Bible] also tells the story of one of the most ambitious and obtrusive of souls, of a head as superstitious as it was crafty, the story of the apostle Paul—who knows this, except a few scholars? Without this strange story, however, without the confusions and storms of such a head, such a soul, there would be no Christianity; we should scarcely have heard of a small Jewish sect whose master died on the cross. . . .

that Paul said of Jesus and the Gospel carried the stamp of reliability. . . . How can we have any dealings with a church that is built on such foundations?" If people prefer Paul's version, they should acknowledge that "Paul, not Jesus, is our Saviour." * If they do not, then Christianity must rid itself altogether of its Jewish legacy.

To divorce Christianity and Judaism even at this late stage would be a recognition of an unambiguous historical truth and of Jesus' own intent. He was not the Messiah of the Old Testament. This inspired mortal, this transcending religious *Genie* of all human history, had in fact been a conscious rebel against Pharisaic Judaism. When Jesus said, "I am the Son of Man," he really meant, according to Lagarde's casuistry, "I am not a Jew." The original act of rebellion should now be consummated, the Jewish past disavowed.†

The Christian churches, guardians of these false and corrupt dogmas, had degenerated in their workaday practices, in their whole temporal being, as well. The ancient temples were

---

That the ship of Christianity threw overboard a good deal of its Jewish ballast, that it went, and was able to go, among the pagans—that was due to this one man, a very tortured, very pitiful, very unpleasant man, unpleasant even to himself." *The Dawn. The Portable Nietzsche,* ed. and transl. by Walter Kaufmann, New York, Viking, 1954, pp. 76–77. A characteristic difference between Lagarde and Nietzsche was that the former used his attack on St. Paul in order to vent his anti-Semitism, whereas Nietzsche, praising the Jewish tradition from which St. Paul came, provided an important psychological interpretation of his conversion.

* But note Shaw's remarks as well: "The conversion of Paul was no conversion at all: it was Paul who converted the religion that had raised one man above sin and death into a religion that delivered millions of men so completely into their dominion that their own common nature became a horror to them, and the religious life became a denial of life. . . . He would have been quite in his place in any modern Protestant State; and he, not Jesus, is the true head and founder of our Reformed Church, as Peter is of the Roman Church. The followers of Peter and Paul made Christendom, whilst the Nazarenes were wiped out." Preface, *Androcles and the Lion,* New York, 1919, pp. xcvii, ciii.

† In this, Lagarde anticipated the radical wing of the late nineteenth-century liberal theologians, Adolf Harnack among them, who demanded the separation of the Old and the New Testament. For some of the later nationalistic heresies, the German Christians, for example, Lagarde became a patron saint. They regularly invoked him to justify their anti-Semitism, their blatant assertion that Jesus was an Aryan, their pagan brew of a Germanic faith.

crumbling on their false foundations, the ecclesiastics were impotent, the congregations dwindling, and faith was disappearing from the life of man. Lagarde was as ruthless with Christian institutions as he was with Christian dogma.

Protestantism, the faith of his pietistic father, he loathed. "Any religion, even fetishism, is superior to the hodgepodge of insipid, cowardly sentimentality and stale, decaying remainders of Christianity which today we call Protestantism." [8] His vitriolic attacks were meant to alert his contemporaries to the decline and fall of Protestantism, to the fact that the Protestant religion had in fact ceased to be alive. For all its distortions and extravagances, his indictment contained many insights and some truths, and his astringent voice, loud and unabashed in its denunciation of conventional pieties, disturbed many a dogmatic slumber. He was one of the few men—of his time or ours—who sensed, correctly, that the decline of Protestant faith in nineteenth-century Germany was an historical development of incomparable importance.

Lagarde's attack on Protestantism, in which scholarship was peppered by polemics, was bent on proving that the faith of the Reformation had been a misbegotten child of Catholicism, that its development had been the gradual unfolding of ineffectuality, interrupted by brief moments of pernicious power. In matters of dogma the Reformation had retained most of the Catholic tradition, itself fraudulently evolved, but had repudiated the apostolic authority which hitherto had protected the unity of faith and dogma. Lagarde ridiculed the Protestant claim to have ensconced the Bible and the individual conscience as the new sources of authority. The major dogmas of Christianity, after all, could not be justified by any interpretation of the Gospel, however liberal. As for the only distinctly Protestant belief—justification by faith—Lagarde argued that faith had so completely disappeared from contemporary life as to make it a mockery.

The creative impulse of the Reformation had withered almost at once: "If Luther was ever valid, his validity ceased in 1546," when he died.[9] If Protestantism was ever a live force, it ceased to be one in 1648 "for when it received the solemn permission to live, it had lost its last excuse for existence." [10] Its political consequences had been lamentable: "By sanctioning the princes' rebellion and by thus introducing caesaropapism," it had surrendered Germany to barbarism.[11] The existence of petty principalities, that too was Protestant handiwork; Bismarck's unification, the *kleindeutsche,* anti-Austrian solution, could be laid at the door of the Protestants, indeed was their greatest crime of the century. The continuing divisiveness within the new Reich was of Protestant design as well—witness the *Kulturkampf:* "Protestantism is the cause of the fatherland's disunity." [12]

Nor were the cultural achievements of German Protestantism more impressive. The most cherished possession of the Protestants, the Luther Bible, Lagarde sought to scrap as obsolete.* After 1648, Protestant theology had dried up and by the nineteenth century "pietism and rationalism [had] devoured Luther's Protestantism." † Its one beneficent consequence had been achieved by its very ineffectuality: it had been so weak that it was unable to thwart the intellectual and artistic life of the peoples under its control and thus, indirectly, it promoted the resurgence of German culture. On the other hand, its utter insignificance was attested by its failure to mold or affect this resurgence: "I simply deny that the Protestant system or Church had any essential influence on Lessing, Goethe, Herder, Kant and Winckelmann." [13] In fact, the influence was all the other way; every strain of German thought penetrated the ever soft and malleable life of Protestantism, until it had become a kind of *Kulturreligion.* Protestantism, in short, "will eat out of any hand." [14]

Protestantism had been turned into a respectable shell for secularism. People belonged to churches "for the same reason that they buy insurance before boarding an excursion train: through orthodoxy they try to buy themselves protection against the consequences of possible, but highly improbable,

---

* Lagarde nurtured as personal and intense an animus against Luther and his liberal admirers as against St. Paul, whose teachings had of course been an inspiration to Luther. Lagarde complained of Luther's boorishness, of his uncouth demagogy, and he depicted him as a major malefactor of Germany.

† Lagarde, *A.S.,* p. 296. Here again Lagarde anticipated later theological criticism. Ernst Troeltsch, for example, was to contend that after the eighteenth century a different type of Protestantism arose, a neo-Protestantism, an amalgamation of Reformation and Renaissance, that was ready to assimilate the modern world. Cf. Ernst Troeltsch, *Gesammelte Schriften,* Vol. IV: *Aufsätze zur Geistesgeschichte und Religionssoziologie,* Tübingen 1925, pp. 292–296.

accidents." * The truly religious had long since been cast out of the temple in favor of the money-changers.

The temple itself was poorly appointed. With its historic impulse spent, its theology decaying, its identity ambiguous, Protestantism could neither recruit eminent ministers nor retain powerful congregations. The abolition of clerical celibacy had so proletarized the priesthood that only the mediocre entered the ministry. "The Protestant ministers of whatever sect are but the theologically tainted projections of political velleities; worms which take on the hue of the fruit which they feed on." [15] A fashionable exception, Schleiermacher, for example, could confer distinction and even glamor to the ministry, but could not perpetuate a reforming tradition. His parents and their friends, Lagarde recalled, had attended Schleiermacher's every sermon; but after his death ceased almost altogether to go to church.† "The people are no longer Protestant . . . the Bible is no longer read in its entirety; a few verses satisfy the congregation . . . faith has disappeared from life." [16]

For Protestantism Lagarde had the contempt reserved for the pretentious weak: it was "an episode in history, not an epoch." [17] For Catholicism he harbored a characteristically ambivalent feeling, a mixture of awe and hatred, envy and resentment. If the one was too spineless for him, the other was too powerful and pervasive. The institutional strength of Catholicism, its doctrinal certainty, its magnificent ritual, above all its persistently successful appeal to the flock—all these he admired. But the Church was un-German, indeed anti-German, and the greater its strength, the weaker the true German community.

As for Catholic dogma, Lagarde's central objection was to the Eucharist, to the historically invalid and religiously in-

---

* Lagarde, Über die gegenwärtige Lage des deutschen Reichs" (1875), *D.S.*, pp. 158–159. The "soft side" of Protestantism, the growing secularization of the Church itself, the approximation of sermon, ritual, and clerical dress to secular bourgeois life, is sensitively depicted in Franz Schnabel's *Deutsche Geschichte im neunzehnten Jahrhundert*, 2d ed., Vol. IV: *Die religiösen Kräfte*, Freiburg im Breisgau 1951, Book 2, esp. chapters 8 and 10.

† Somewhat maliciously Lagarde recorded how the grown-ups would come home from a Schleiermacher sermon and exult: "Today he was again divine! [*Heut' war er wieder göttlich!*]." Lagarde, *A.S.*, pp. 60, 14.

tolerable doctrine of transubstantiation. But his attack was concentrated on neo-Catholicism, on the new Church Militant, for "the Catholicism with which the Reformers battled has been dead for three hundred and fifty years, or, if one prefers, has been a-dying ever since that time." [18] Modern Catholicism is an altogether new construction, which preserves the old name and the traditional forms only in order to persuade the world of its ancient identity and to preserve its ancient privileges. In fact, however, the Jesuits had built a new Church, organized to combat the forces of modernity. The dogma of papal infallibility, recently promulgated, was "the closing act of the founding years of this neo-Catholic church; it bears the same relation to the new Catholicism as Nicaea bore to the old." [19]

This new Catholicism Lagarde called Jesuitism—another instance of that specious labeling by which specific institutions or movements could be blamed for all manner of amorphous evil. The Jesuits, he claimed, had mobilized the Church against the menacing forces of the national state and of science. In the contemporary world, Jesuitism embodied the Church's uncompromising negation of modernity; it rejected the findings of science and hence forced a divorce between spirit and materialism to the mounting benefit of the latter. It defied the principle of nationalism as well, and hence in its appearance in national states the new Catholicism is "the born enemy of every state and nation." [20]

Lagarde denounced the *Kulturkampf* on simple pragmatic grounds: it would end in failure, as indeed it did. The state could not conquer the Church, Catholicism could be routed only through the emergence of a rival national religion. The *Kulturkampf*, moreover, might align Catholic countries with the Vatican against Germany and make the next war not only racial but also religious.* After Bismarck had called off the *Kulturkampf*, Lagarde noted with pleased surprise that it had brought about neither a spontaneous upsurge among the faithful nor even isolated conversions. The years of the Catholic Church were numbered, too.

Having demonstrated the inadequacies of all existing faiths,

---

* Lagarde, "Diagnose" (1874), *D.S.*, pp. 105–108. A year later, this was much bruited about in Germany and the notorious war-in-sight crisis of 1875 was predicated on the danger of a clerical alliance— Italy, France, Austria—against Protestant Germany.

Lagarde intoned the old dream of a Germanic-Christian faith. The reign of a universal faith was ended, and Protestantism had failed utterly to present a national alternative. The new heroic faith would have to be a cleansed version of Christianity, appropriate at last for the German character. Even some of the old pagan rites would have to be revived.

The key to the new religion was to be theology, defined by Lagarde as a comparative, historical study of all religions. "The Queen of the Sciences," as he called theology, is the knowledge "of the history of the city of God [*Das Wissen um die Geschichte des Reiches Gottes*]." [21] Theology would thus recover the essence of the divine in its historic unfolding, in its many transitory manifestations. It would reveal the Gospel as the latest and fullest revelation of the divine, and it would point the way to a new, post-Christian faith.

Just as theology should clear away the rubble of antiquated Christian doctrine, so the government of the new Reich should do everything in its power to hasten the demise of all existing confessions. The state should divorce itself completely from all religious groups; according to German custom, this would have ended the public collection of church taxes as well as the granting of state subsidies.[22] At the same time, the responsibilities of the several confessions should be enlarged so that their burden would become heavier. Every confession should have its own schools, maintained at its own expense. The state should restrict itself to a few regulatory controls; it should supervise the finances of the churches and prevent the four Protestant sects from attempting a merger.* A little intramural rivalry might further weaken the Protestant churches. All laws relating to the training of ministers should be reduced to the one ordinance that only men born and educated in Germany could enter the ministry. Protestant seminaries should be forcibly removed to the remote borderlands of Germany, where, without injuring the Reich, they could assist in the colonizing efforts abroad. Shorn of public recognition and assistance, the churches would have to fend for themselves, and Lagarde cheerfully assumed that some of the weaker Protestant congregations would soon give up the

---

* The Lutherans, the Calvinists, the Evangelical Church, and the *Protestantenverein*, originally a South German nonecclesiastical and decidedly liberal association, striving to bring modern culture and religion in closer harmony.

ghost and rally to the new national religion. "If the so-called Protestant Church in Germany would have to be supported by voluntary contributions—the synagogues thrive on these contributions, at least externally—the Protestant Church would disappear within ten years." [23] Withal, the state needst not strive to keep the Church alive.

The state should effect one other institutional change. It should abolish the Protestant and Catholic faculties at German universities. Theology should cease to be an exegesis of Christian dogma; it should become a comparative study of all religions. This science should not be entrusted to men who had taken oaths to uphold a specific theological position and whose primary task was the education of clerics for a particular confession. The new theology would reveal the essence of all religion and thus help fashion the religion of the future." *

In his essay on the religion of the future, Lagarde tried to sketch the outlines of the new Christian-German faith.[24] The Jewish elements would have to be purged, the distinctive Protestant dogmas had already withered away. The sacraments of baptism, confirmation, penance, and marriage would be retained, and the Eucharist would have to be given a new symbolic meaning. The new sacrament should impress on the believers that they were men, born with the need to eat and drink, and destined to die. For the rest, Lagarde asserted that religious practices must spring from the new soul of the religion and hence could not be prescribed in advance.

The essence of the religion of the future would be a fusion of the old doctrines of the Gospel with the "national characteristics of the Germans." [25] Different people required different faiths; the universality of Catholicism had become insufferable. The new religion would have to express the special ethos and the destiny of the German people. "The basic principle of the new community must be that religion is the consciousness of the plan and purpose of the education

---

* Franz Overbeck devoted a respectful, if not wholly sympathetic, section of his *Über die Christlichkeit unserer heutigen Theologie*, Leipzig, Fritzsch, 1873, to Lagarde's radical redefinition of theology. Concerning Lagarde's notion that the new theology should be the pathfinder of the Germanic religion, Overbeck wrote: "Theologies have always followed their religions, in fact the more energetic and harmonious the original drive of these religions, the later their theologies appeared" (p. 85).

of the individual, of peoples, and of humanity." [26] But what was this national character of the Germans and what the divine plan for its future? Lagarde invoked Madame de Stael's definition of the superiority of the Germans: "The independence of intellect, the love of loneliness, and the peculiar selfhood of the individual. After reading this, those who know the character of the new German Reich will, with tears in their eyes, realize how German our Reich is." [27] In Bismarck's Germany moral austerity and independence had been annihilated and the conditions for a religious resurgence were thoroughly unfavorable. "We have never had a German history, unless the regular, progressive decline of the German character constitutes that history." [28] The new religion would have to arrest that decline and recover and preserve the old Germanic virtues. It would have to propagate Germany's cultural uniqueness and her imperial destiny.

The new religion would have to come for "if we do not find men for this endeavor and find them soon, we may as well renounce the future of the fatherland. Germany would then exist for a while longer, but would cease to live almost at once. . . . Germany in the future will be a secular state in a heavenly dress, a despotism that calls itself freedom." [29] But whence was the new religion to arise? The state could do no more than publicly abjure all links with the existing churches. Religious consciousness springs instinctively and spontaneously from a people's common aspiration, and the educated classes were incapable of such an inspiration. They had become un-Germanic, and only the lower, uneducated classes still retained some of the original Germanic genius, some *Naturwüchsigkeit*. But would they be able to break through the crust of civilization and of erudite indifference? Lagarde feared not, and as his hope for a spontaneous rise of the new religion waned, he banked more and more on a heroic leader who could embody the people's inchoate religion: "Only the pure, strong will of a Single Man can help us, a regal will, but not parliament nor statutes nor the ambition of powerless individuals." [30]

Lagarde also invoked the old Christian doctrine of rebirth (*Wiedergeburt*), which had latterly reappeared as the central doctrine of the Pietists. Rebirth signified the gift of a new spiritual life through Jesus, the transformation of a sinful man into a creature of grace. To Luther this was tantamount

49

to God's gift of faith to man; to the Pietists and Schleiermacher it involved the inner experience of the religious
person, the consciousness of being in communion with God,
which was antecedent to dogma. In claiming the doctrine of
rebirth for his national religion, Lagarde further loosened
it from its Christian matrix.* He regarded rebirth as an
incontrovertible fact of all human experience, hence as a
valid basis of his hope for a religious revival. He pushed the
idea of rebirth from a Christian to a secular mystical meaning, down the treacherous slope toward the theology of
politics. For his heroic program he invoked God's sanction,
avowing that God's will and the Germanic religion coincided.
By the 1920's, the idea of a national or racial rebirth had
become a poisonous weapon for nationalistic critics, the more
powerful for its religious ring.

Lagarde's oft-repeated proposals for the national religion
of the future mirrored the ambiguity and erratic idealism
of his position. At once rationalist and mystic, historian and
believer, Lagarde experienced to the full the religious quan-
dary shared by so many other nineteenth-century intellectuals
who labored to demolish what they wished to worship.
Lagarde with half his being was a scientist, and his intellect
suspected the heart of the genuine believer. He did not seek
to strip Christianity of its mysteries in the manner, say, of
David Friedrich Strauss; rather he sought to mix with it a
secular mystique, to unite a Christian heaven and a German
earth in one impenetrable mystery.†

---

* Nor was Lagarde the only one to do so. As Fischer recently noted
for the period before 1848: "It was characteristic of the tracts of
many politicians as well as of the sermons of ministers that the
meaning of words like salvation, rebirth, resurrection, and revelation,
were changed from their genuinely religious sense to a political and
national sense." Fritz Fischer, "Der Deutsche Protestantismus und die
Politik im 19. Jahrhundert," *Historische Zeitschrift,* CLXXI:3 (May,
1951) 477.

† Lagarde refused to discuss the philosophical premises of his religion
of the future. In a long, admiring letter, the philosopher Paul
Natorp, congratulating Lagarde on his essays, expressed his own reluctant doubt: "My doubts concern the major controversial point,
the belief in the personal God and in personal immortality." He
also inquired: "What is to be done? Instead of the many immodest
words, we need a modest deed. Show us the way." Lagarde's characteristic reply was: "It is self-evident that I do not regard your doubts

Lagarde was not alone in his calling for a new religion. The great minds of the nineteenth century all grappled with God, faith, and religion. Some sought to bury Christianity, others to revive it, many were brooding over the fate of a faithless world. The thought of a purely secular world was as intolerable as the thought of a controlled clerical society. Rousseau had pointed to the necessity of a civil religion, and the nineteenth-century Germanic critics—although most of them loathed Rousseau—echoed his belief that without a compelling religious sanction the secular state would perish.* Fichte had already proposed a national religion, and by the second half of the century, many cultural critics sought some kind of religion. Jakob Burckhardt, for example, wrote in 1874: "If the German spirit out of its innermost and its most peculiar strength should react once more against this sombre tyranny, if it should succeed in setting up against this tyranny a new art, poetry, and religion, then we are saved; if not, not. I say: religion, for it will fail without a superworldly will which would counterbalance this entire hubbub [*Rummel*] of power and money." [31] Burckhardt had no clear image of this religious revival nor did he mean to be a prophet. There were a thousand reasons why men felt as Shaw did: "Government is impossible without a religion: that is, without a body of common assumptions." [32] They all felt an outraged sense that the man of nineteenth-century science and liberalism, all reason and self-interest, was a monstrous abstraction.

Certainly Lagarde's demand for a national religion was part of his abiding hatred of liberalism and of modern culture. The new religion would become the spiritual basis for a new state, for a new hierarchical community that would

---

as anything that separates us. But I neither can nor want to enter into any philosophical discussion. Religion has the same relation to human life that metaphysics has to intellectual life. They are both immanent, even if people have no sense of it." As to what can be done: "The people should be warned. Every deed that strives after the ultimate would be useless now. Jesus today would end in prison or in an insane asylum; Zarathustra, Buddha, and Confucius as well."

* Letters of January 24, 1879, and February 2, 1879, Lagarde Archive. Following common German usage, the Germanic critics considered and vilified Rousseau as the democratic theorist *par excellence*. Their animus blinded them to the simple fact that their best ideas on men, nature, and education, on antiurbanism and antiparliamentarianism, were but distorted and intemperate adaptations of Rousseau's thought.

accept the teleological belief that God had placed men at different stations in life for different purposes.[33] Lagarde sensed as well that the conflicting loyalties of Catholics and Protestants, North and South Germans, liberals and conservatives, and the continuing tensions among the social classes, had not been, and could not be, reconciled by the mere promulgation of political unity. The political act lacked the compelling power which could subordinate the conflicts among particular interests and ancient loyalties to the common purpose of a radically new society. The new religion alone could overcome the diversities of belief and the divisiveness of modern society; it alone could ensure the permanence of Germany's unification and the imperial future of the Reich. In some ways, then, Lagarde's religion was little more than a mystical nationalism with a Christian veneer.

The dilemma for him was the impossibility of "creating" a religion by fiat, and the unlikeliness of its creation by the spontaneous will of the people. In the last years before his death, Lagarde's despondency deepened as he grew more and more convinced that his cherished hope was impossible of fulfillment. "What other nations achieved in the deepest solitude of undisturbed youth, Germany has to do in the bright light of the nineteenth century amidst the newspaper reporters and telegraph wires: to perform heroic deeds in an age of paper money, stock jobbery, party newspapers, and general education. We are stricken by the necessity of having to do in 1878 what should have been done in 878." [34]

4: The Germanic Nation

The Germans are idealists even in their hatred. We do not hate external matters as do [the French], but in our enemies we hate the profoundest, the most essential that is in them, their thoughts. HEINRICH HEINE

When people talk of the unity of Germany, they almost always think of the unity of political leadership; I contend that unity has to be understood as the unity of the governed. The former without the latter would be mere force; to demand the former when the latter prevails would be unnecessary, for it would come about by itself.

LAGARDE

In all his works, Lagarde thought to serve but one goal—the spiritual resurgence of a united German people. That was the aim of his religious thought, and it also dominated his political thought, of which he was intensely proud.* In fact, no sharp distinction between his religious and political thought can be drawn: he sought to recapture in the political realm what had been lost in the religious. The disastrous secularization of the German soul could be overcome only if her political life could be charged with a religious purpose and sanction. Lagarde's vision was of a new Reich, a new political community of believers, that would worship the new Germanic religion.

This was a very different goal from that of the conventional conservatives who wanted to protect throne and altar. Lagarde

---

* "My political essays have been of greater utility than my theological studies; I rejoice that on several important issues I have mightily contributed to a shift in public opinion." Lagarde, *Symmicta*, II, p. 143.

thought neither deserved protection; his conservatism embraced a traditional view of human nature, but had nothing to do with the defense of existing institutions or interests. Lagarde, as we saw, turned against the Prussian monarchy at the same time that he lost his faith in orthodox Christianity. From that time on, he constructed his own political theology. He drew up plans and programs for a new Reich that would expunge all domestic conflict and would foster and prescribe the heroic moral life of the past. Because his interest in politics was spiritual and ethical, his ideas remained impervious to fact or political change, and he himself remained the lonely, ever dissatisfied critic that he sought to be.*

Lagarde first turned to politics during the time of the Waldeck trial, at the beginning of the "reactionary 1850's," when the liberals had been discredited by their failure and the conservatives by the nature of their victory. He recoiled from the conservatism of the Prussian monarchy, dominated as it was by selfish Junkers, and he despised the liberals, who, he hoped, would never recover from their ignominious defeat. His disillusionment with Germany was heightened by his visit to England, where he thought he saw a united people, a popular monarchy, and a responsible gentry—all things that Germany lacked. On his return in 1853, he proclaimed himself a radical-conservative, opposed to every party and position that existed in the fatherland.

The 1850's were a decade of general discontent.† Lagarde's "inner emigration," his disappointed rejection of German politics, coincided with the great flow of outward emigration. The revolution had settled nothing and unsettled everything. The postrevolutionary settlement in Germany had few supporters and fewer still thought that a divided and illiberal Germany could long endure. In Prussia, Frederick William IV regretted the concessions he had made to the liberals in 1849, and his reactionary camarilla and some of his ministers sought to balance formal concessions by actual repression. Just as

---

* Even an admirer of Lagarde's conceded that "however valuable Lagarde's fundamental views particularly on politics are, many of his suggestions belong more readily in the realm of fantasy than in the realm of practical political thought." Käte Schiffmann, *Lagardes Kulturanschauung,* Münster 1938, p. 41.

†"This is an evil time!" was the opening sentence of Wilhelm Raabe's popular *Die Chronik der Sperlingsgasse,* which appeared in 1854.

the wars of liberation were followed by the harshness of the Carlsbad decrees, so the 1848 revolution was followed by the semilegal persecutions of political dissenters. But the Prussian monarchy only lost further ground by these half-hearted measures of reaction; even the Prussian minister of the interior, Otto von Manteuffel, noted in a private memorandum in 1856 that the political conditions in Prussia allowed "people at home and abroad to identify the government with one newspaper [*Kreuzzeitung*], whose unabashed tendency to replace the Prussian monarchy of the Grace of God by a government of Junkers and Pietists has gathered on itself all the scorn and hatred of the nation." [1]

For Lagarde this period of general dissatisfaction provided an auspicious beginning. The failure of a political system is always an invitation to dreamers and cranks, as well as for serious reformers, and it was easier to devise programs of radical change amidst universal feelings of discontent than in a period of stability. Although Lagarde's work was intuitive and idiosyncratic, and although he acknowledged no intellectual influences, he was in his formative years closely attuned to the thought of some of the dominant conservative thinkers. In the 1850's, philosophers and publicists tried to define a conservative creed, and all of them, most notably Friedrich Julius Stahl and Wilhelm Heinrich Riehl, condemned the nascent capitalistic and commercial order and hoped to restore in some form the idyllic life of the small town, of the self-sufficient farmer and artisan. Lagarde's persistent concern with the social question and his plans for a restored patriarchal system corresponded to the main themes of the romantic conservatism of Frederick William IV's camarilla and of most conservative publicists and Protestant ministers of the period.[2] Lagarde also followed the new direction in anti-Semitism which fastened on the economic role of the Jews. In all these matters Lagarde was less specific and systematic than his contemporaries, but he breathed the same nostalgia as they did for a Germany that was free of all the social evils of a liberal, commercial society. The nostalgia of the right had as its counterpart the utopias of the left; the 1850's were critical years in the history of socialist theory, especially Marxism, and Lagarde's passionate concern for the unity of the German people reflected his fear that the working classes would become alienated from the existing order.

The two lectures that Lagarde gave in 1853, and that were published some twenty-five years later, contained not only his indictments of the German princes in general and of the Prussian monarchy in particular, but also all the themes and prejudices of his later political writings. Central to his political thought was a dualism which he posited between "state" and "nation," a dualism meant to correspond to that between body and soul.* The state, like the body, was simply a machine that performed certain tasks; it required the guidance of a spiritual entity that could give it purpose and direction. By itself, the state was tyrannical, and its bureaucrats were irresponsible martinets, upon whom Lagarde heaped endless abuse. Like other conservatives of the time, Lagarde vilified Hegel, the idolator of the state, whose philosophy was the "poison" of German youth and the comfort of the unscrupulous *Machtpolitiker*. Far from being the divine idea on earth, the state, regardless of its form, regardless of its representative institutions, annihilated individuality.

Lagarde's conception of the nation was a mystical corollary to his Germanic religion. A people can become a nation only through the collective acceptance of its divinely ordained mission. Once a nation, it has but one will, and all conflict is banished from it. Lagarde's nation was much more absolutistic than Hegel's conception of the state, which provided for the autonomy of civil society. Lagarde's nation had no bounds; it embodied the immanent unity of like people, and its will was beyond challenge. By prescribing to the Germans what their divine task was, Lagarde hoped to fuse them into a nation. The more exacting the mission, he thought, the more fervent would be the response of the people.

Germany's mission, Lagarde announced, was the colonization of all non-German lands in the Austrian empire. "Magyars, Czechs, and other similar nationalities that live under the sceptre of Austria are an historical burden." [3] They must give way to the superior culture of the Germans. Germany's

---

* Lagarde's dualism of state and nation anticipated the distinction between *Gemeinschaft* and *Gesellschaft* which, in 1887, Ferdinand Tönnies introduced in his work of the same title. Tönnies' *Gemeinschaft* and Lagarde's *Nation* are nearly identical, though their respective counterparts are different. Both sought to overcome the liberal, atomistic society. Tönnies readily acknowledged the impact that Lagarde's political writings had on him.

imperialist task would also strengthen another scheme of Lagarde's, the establishment by fiat of a new German gentry. Finally, the unity of the German nation could be achieved only by the extirpation of the twin agents of dissension—the liberals and the Jews.

Considering his goals and prejudices, it is little wonder that Lagarde felt immeasurably forlorn in the new empire. His own ideal of a unified nation was of course not realizable, and he came to look upon Bismarck's creation as the very antithesis of his ideal. He sensed that the new empire was drifting toward liberalism, however much Bismarck's autocratic rule or the constitutional safeguards disguised this drift. Above all, the tone of the new Reich was crude and commercial, not cultured and heroic, and Lagarde assumed that the spiritual life of the nation had been emasculated. Lagarde's nationalism was of a different order from that of his compatriots; he yearned for something spiritual, and they rejoiced at Germany's magnificent material power. Lagarde, therefore, belonged to those Germans who did not leap after success and did not embrace Bismarck's *Realpolitik*. He clung to his own mystical vision and condemned all those who were willing to accept anything less than the unattainable.

He gloried in his self-assigned role as Bismarck's principal theoretical opponent. Time and again he predicted the end of the second Reich, and warned against the deepening divisions within the society. Germany, embattled at home, was endangered by a ring of foreign enemies as well. He thundered against Bismarck's self-denying policy regarding Austria, against the very idea of *Kleindeutschland*. Germany's destiny, he insisted, demanded her dominion over all of *Mitteleuropa*. He approved neither of Bismarck nor of any of his political opponents, and throughout his life remained a conservative adrift. To a friend he once described his political predicament: "I have no home anywhere, not even in the fatherland. For while you are facing with eye and heart the new world, I live with every breath in a past that never was and which is the only future I crave. I am an alien in all places." [4]

The focus of Lagarde's attack on Bismarck's Germany was the continuing divisiveness of the new Reich. The political act of unification had not created unity, indeed, the institutions of the empire were breeding new conflicts. He fulminated in particular against the *Parlamentarismus* and the multiple-party system, because these embodied and exacerbated conflict, rather than resolving it. The Reichstag should be replaced by an advisory Council of State, composed of legislative experts. The people should be represented only in local assemblies; on a national scale, a Prussian and a German diet should be created, drawn in part from the provincial estates (half-elective, half-hereditary bodies) and in part from members of the local chambers of commerce.[5] Universal suffrage was but a farce which left the real powers —the political parties—in command. The elected representatives turned themselves into a political priesthood which acted without concern for the people.[6] Lagarde shared the common German suspicion of political parties and of the compromise and log-rolling that went with them.* Parties were a means of misrepresentation. Toward the end of his life, more and more insistently he called for a *Führer* who would so completely represent the people that in him they would be united and his command would be their will. Such a *Führer* was all the more important in his analysis because Germany with its many kings and princes had ceased to be a monarchy: "The emperor is a president of the republic, whom we have agreed to call emperor." †

Lagarde's incisive, often shrewd, strictures against Bismarck's Germany emphasized his differences with the Conservative party. Time and again he condemned the conservatives for merely trying to cling to the status quo and their own privileges; true conservatives should conserve only those forces that were alive and creative, that is, only those that served men's souls:

The purpose of the [true] Conservative party can therefore be reduced to one principle. It seeks to give every man the right, and

---

* He had not always felt this way. In England, in 1852, Lord Derby said to him: "Seven-eighths of all business would be done by Whigs exactly in the same way as by Tories." Lagarde hoped that German parties would some day approximate this ideal, but by the 1870's he had given up this hope. Lagarde, "Über die gegenwärtigen Aufgaben der deutschen Politik" (1853), *D.S.,* p. 25.

† Lagarde, "Die nächtsten Pflichten deutscher Politik (1886), *D.S.,* p. 450. In 1886, Lagarde sent young Prince William, the later William II, a copy of his *Deutsche Schriften;* he flattered him as "the *Führer* of German youth," hoping, as William himself was to hope in time, that he would prove to be the long-anticipated democratic Caesar.

so far as it is within its power, the opportunity, to become actually what God had wanted him to become from the beginning. Contrary to the fashionable philosophy of the day, we are convinced that the world is a totality, ordered toward a goal, and that its disorder is only a means to our education. We are also convinced that every man, truly everyone, has a definite place in the world, that is assigned to him and only to him.[7]

Lagarde sought to rally the conservatives to become the guardians of the individual and of the nation against the tyranny of the state and the arbitrariness of its bureaucrats. In his program for the Conservative party he dwelt on some traditional liberal sentiments: "The state is not sovereign. The monarchy, religion, science, and art are *sui generis* and are therefore superior to, and outside of, the state. And if the state dares to bend them to its will, they shall confront the state as enemies." [8] The inadequacy of official conservatism was similar to the inadequacy of its main ally, official Protestantism: both believed, out of principle and out of self-interest, in the uncritical acceptance of authority, and it was this unthinking subservience, this mere time-serving, that enraged Lagarde.

Dissatisfied with existing conditions and the existing opposition to them, Lagarde found himself in the characteristic predicament of conservative revolutionaries; he had to propound radical innovations in order to attain a conservative society. Often his proposals violated his own dictum that laws are useless without the spontaneous sanction of national approval. One of his most cherished schemes—the introduction of a new German nobility, which he elaborated in the most painstaking detail—depended clearly on the prior presence of social traditions and habitual deference. In this instance, as in many others, Lagarde legislated with the abandon of any doctrinaire rationalist reformer, hoping that laws and institutions would in the end arouse the binding sentiments of loyalty and affection.

In his proposals for a new German gentry, first advanced in 1853, and clearly inspired by the English society which he had so recently observed and admired, he looked toward a new tier of social power between the leveling masses at the bottom and the arbitrary and nearly omnipotent power of the state at the top.[9] Throughout the 1850's and 1860's, there were strong protests by enlightened aristocrats and by moderates everywhere against what they called the arrogant irre-sponsibility of the Junkers.[10] Lagarde lashed out against the incompetent and impoverished Junkers who performed none of the functions of a gentry. He proposed that all families who had for several generations rendered certain kinds of public service should be granted patents of lower nobility. These families—provided they professed a Christian faith for six generations—would organize themselves into self-governing units. They would elect a head of the family, they would maintain an ancestral home on a rural estate where the aged and indigent members could be cared for, they would try their own members before their own courts for any violation of the austere code of honor they were pledged to obey. Any member sentenced by a criminal court to a loss of civil rights would be forced to renounce his name and emigrate to another country with an arbitrary number as his sole identification. The new gentry was really the old Germanic clan in modern dress; in Lagarde's rhapsodic recital one could hear the forest murmurs of a primitive German past.

The new nobility would serve as a model for every other group in German society. It would be a bulwark of individual-ity against every form of repression; it would be the prototype of other islands of freedom and self-government within the state. At the same time these noble families on their ancestral manors would become the centers of monarchical loyalty and national dedication within the Reich. They would strengthen the enfeebled institutions of the family as well, and would reknit the familial ties that had snapped in a commercial society. And the revival of the family—"that tactical unit which the ethos [of a people] leads into battle against sin and nature"—would usher in a new epoch in German life.[11]

The negative expression of Lagarde's dedication to a Ger-manic or folk community was his violent hatred of all divisive agents in German society and of modern open society in general. He loathed the new industrialized life, with its impersonal, purely commercial ties, and longed for some rural idyl where a harmonious hierarchy had prevailed. Capitalism was evil, and all parasitic carriers of it should be extirpated. It was characteristic of this kind of conservative protest against capitalism that the main grievance was directed against those institutions—stock jobbing and banking, for example—that seemed to violate the sacred principle that a man should earn his daily bread. At bottom was a revulsion against the worship of money, against the elevation of traders over heroes. The injustices of capitalism, the exploitation and alienation of the workers, were rarely mentioned.* His hatred of the modern economic society fastened on two villains, the Jews and the liberals. They were the agents of a gigantic conspiracy aimed at the heart of Germany.

Lagarde wrapped his incredibly ferocious anti-Semitism—the product of all his twisted being and of all his diverse intellectual concerns—in a respectable cloak of nationalist idealism. With both horror and envy, he identified the Jews as a proud, invincible nation whose religion had nothing to do with the Old Testament but consisted of an unshakable faith in its own nationality. In other words, the Jews possessed the very unity that the Germans lacked, and it enabled them to be "at least in Europe the masters of the non-Jews. . . . The Jews as Jews are a terrible misfortune for every European people." [12] They were "the carriers of decay and pollute every national culture, they exploit the human and material resources of their hosts, they destroy all faith and spread materialism and liberalism." The Germans, Lagarde charged, have only themselves to blame for this alien domination: "They are much too soft to resist these Jews who have become hard-bitten through Talmudic discipline. . . . Because I know the Germans I do not want the Jews to be allowed to live together with them. . . . Every Jew is proof of the enfeeblement of our national life and of the worthlessness of what we call the Christian religion." [13]

In his first anti-Semitic outburst, in 1853, Lagarde repudiated racialism: "Germanism is not a matter of the blood, but of the spirit." † Even after racial anti-Semitism had become popular in Germany, he dubbed it a crude form of materialism, scientifically meaningless. "Of course the Jewish

---

* This anticapitalistic sentiment was of course endemic in the Western world; its history has yet to be written, and when it is, it most likely will reveal that this anticapitalistic mood sprang not only from nostalgia for the simple life of some lost Arcadia, but also from nostalgia for a religious faith that seemed doomed to extinction at the same time.

† Lagarde's untranslatable jingle runs: *"Das Deutschtum liegt nicht im Geblüte, sondern im Gemüte,"* "Über die gegenwärtigen Aufgaben deutscher Politik," *D.S.,* p. 30.

question is a racial question too, but no idealistically inclined person can ever deny that spirit could and should conquer race." [14] He himself befriended several Jewish students who had succeeded in "purifying" themselves. At times he argued that German culture could assimilate Jews through education, intermarriage, or conversion. But conversion to what he considered threadbare Christianity seemed an improbable solution; why should Jews trade "their coarse but warm clothing for our trashy rags?" [15] In the last analysis they only had the choice between abandoning their Jewishness, or being expelled from Germany and from the eastern territories that Germany was to colonize. If neither happened and the Jews were simply allowed to linger on, then Germany would become *"verjudet,"* a word that Lagarde may not have coined but that he certainly popularized and that later had a central place in National Socialist rhetoric. However much Lagarde may have leaned toward the ruthless solution of expulsion, he never quite surrendered the hope that the Jews could be shorn of their religious and national identity. Hence the National Socialists, otherwise so appreciative of Lagarde, were justified in their frequent lament that he had not understood the inexorable laws of race.

His scruples about racism notwithstanding, Lagarde's anti-Semitism grew steadily more violent. He warned against a sinister and successful conspiracy of world-wide Jewry against Gentiles, especially against Germans: "The *Alliance Israélite* is nothing but an international conspiracy—similar to Freemasonry—to establish Jewish world domination; in the Semitic field, it is the same as the Jesuit order is in the Catholic." [16] The Jews had gained control of the press, and through "the Palestinization of the universities, of the law, of medicine and of the stage," they controlled all thought.[17] Jews and capitalists were synonymous, and Lagarde demanded their simultaneous destruction. The state should at once seize all credit and banking facilities, thus depriving the Jews of their means of existence.* With "this usurious vermin" no com-

---

* The identification of Jewry with the evils of capitalism became popular in Germany in the early 1870's, at the time of the great stock-market crash. Bismarck was frequently attacked because of his close ties to his Jewish banker, Gerson von Bleichröder, and several pamphlets denounced the "Bismarck-Bleichröder era," which they said dominated Germany. The Stöcker movement of the late 1870's

promise was possible: "With trichinae and bacilli one does not negotiate, nor are trichinae and bacilli subjected to education; they are exterminated as quickly and as thoroughly as possible." [18] Few men prophesied Hitler's work with such accuracy—and approval.*

The brutality of Lagarde's utterances far exceeded the moderate anti-Semitism that was then common among German conservative critics. To those who deplored modernity and the open society the Jew was an obvious target. After the middle of the past century, the Jews, exploiting civil rights only recently gained, rapidly captured an important place in the cultural life and the urban economy of Germany. There began as well a steady influx into Germany of Jews from eastern Europe, and hence the argument that the Jews were non-Germans and therefore nonassimilable acquired a specious plausibility.[19] Certainly the Jews, German and non-German, were overwhelmingly attracted to the larger cities, where they engaged and excelled in such traditionally denigrated enterprises as journalism, finance, and commerce.[20] Hence it became customary to identify Jews with all the hateful innovations of the new age.† Paradoxically, this antimodern element in anti-Semitism modernized the ancient prejudice and gave it renewed impetus in industrial Germany. The old charges about ritual murders and other crimes of religion were not particularly persuasive in a secular society, but the

---

also embraced this mixture of anticapitalism and anti-Semitism. In their struggle for power the National Socialists played on the same theme and several times introduced legislation for the expropriation of all Jewish-owned credit institutions.

* Nor did the National Socialists forget this prophecy. In 1944, when they were carrying out their policy of extermination, an anthology of Lagarde's work was distributed by the army and contained Lagarde's demand for murder. See Paul de Lagarde, *Ich mahne und künde*, Breslau 1944, pp. 57–63 for "The Jewish Question. The Jews, A National Misfortune."

† In 1894, Hermann Bahr published a study of anti-Semitism based on his interviews with German and European writers and public figures, and concluded that "German anti-Semitism is reactionary, it is a revolt of the petty bourgeoisie against industrialization, of Germanic [teutschen] youth against the freedom of modernity." Hermann Bahr, *Der Antisemitismus. Ein internationales Interview*, Berlin, Fischer, 1894, p. 214. It is symptomatic of Lagarde's great appeal that Bahr, the avowed foe of anti-Semitism, wrote admiringly of Lagarde; cf. his *Tagebuch*, Berlin, Cassirer, 1909, pp. 16, 24, 109, 114, and 133.

identification of Jew and modernity became an immensely powerful component of anti-Semitism, though one that has often been overlooked.*

The Jews had "natural allies, the liberals," and Lagarde's attack on them was more pervasive, if less vitriolic, than on the Jews.[21] Like most of the Germanic critics after him, Lagarde thought that both Jews and liberals were the agents of subversion, conspiring against the true Germanic society of faith and hierarchy. For Lagarde, liberalism was not primarily a political creed nor a particular set of political institutions; it was the dominant, diabolical, and thoroughly alien force in German culture, the force impelling toward sham and modernity. Its characteristic protagonist was the academician, its primary sin the German educational system with its barren accumulation of disparate bits of miscellaneous knowledge.†

Lagarde's main polemic against liberalism was appropriately entitled: The Gray International.‡ Liberal ideals, borrowed from abroad, were drab and un-German. Like the Red In-

---

* Even Jakob Burckhardt warned in 1880: "To the Semites I would recommend a great deal of sagacity and moderation, and even then I do not believe that the present agitation will die down again. . . . The Semites will particularly have to atone for their totally unjustifiable interference in all sorts of affairs, and newspapers will have to rid themselves of their Semitic editors and journalists if they want to survive. Such a thing [anti-Semitism] can break loose suddenly and contagiously from one day to the next." *Jakob Burckhardts Briefe an seinen Freund Friedrich von Preen, 1864–1893,* January 2, 1880; Stuttgart and Berlin 1922, p. 137. Burckhardt's advice may be boggled at, but it reflects his deep concern lest the wave of social animus swallow up the Jewish population of Europe. Five years earlier, Meyer Carl Rothschild wrote to Bleichröder: "As for the anti-Semitic feelings, the Jews themselves are to blame, and the present agitation must be ascribed to their arrogance, vanity, and unspeakable insolence." Letter of September 16, 1875, in the S. Bleichröder Archive, New York.

† As a twenty-six-year-old, he already wrote in a letter to his fiancée: "I hate the mere word liberal because I have never met a single liberal who would not become the most inconsistent man of the world and who would not be willing to defend any tyranny whatsoever, provided he could be the tyrant. Altogether the world is becoming ever bleaker, and hardly anything remains except to cultivate one's personality as clearly, purely, and powerfully as possible." Anna de Lagarde, *Erinnerungen,* pp. 38–39.

‡ Lagarde's title was probably suggested by a fiercely anti-Semitic work of C. Wilmanns, *Die "Goldene" Internationale und die Notwendigkeit einer sozialen Reformpartei,* Berlin 1876.

ternational and the Black International, "Liberalism was homeless and hence of the greatest danger to every nation." [22] But unlike the other internationals, it had no hard, clear set of doctrines. Implicitly it rejected the uniqueness of the Germans and hence denied the need for any unique German forms of life; any ideal or institution would do, so long as it promoted comfort and a certain kind of progress. As early as 1853, Lagarde had written: "Our liberalism is always an object of pity for me," and twenty-five years later he ranted against "the principles of 1789 which have been transplanted to Germany and whose representatives we call liberals." [23] Like all Germanic critics after him, Lagarde was repelled by the liberals' tolerance: "This is the enemy we have to fight, because it—this brand of tolerance—is fatal to everything serious." [24]

Liberalism was also blamed for promoting materialism and Philistinism, for destroying metaphysics, converting scientists and educated men into mere fact finders, for encouraging dilettantism. The liberals eschewed the total view, the whole picture, and hence had no thorough-going *Weltanschauung* and no understanding of the religious life. They were pagans, he charged, and pedants as well, and he railed against this unpalatable combination. Tying Hegel and liberalism together—as did many conservatives of the 1850's—Lagarde alleged that both were responsible for feeding Germans every scrap of knowledge from the past instead of encouraging the development of a new and authentically German spiritual life. Liberalism, in its utter sterility, was responsible for all the cultural ills of the age. In Lagarde's hands it became a term of abuse which stood for cosmopolitanism, for materialism, for false individualism and tyranny, for oligarchy and democracy; the term comprehended everything—and nothing. It was the secular equivalent of Evil. In the end, even Lagarde's uncritical biographer had to conclude: "The liberals had more or less to accept the responsibility for all that did not suit [Lagarde] in the modern world." [25]

Certainly the political machinery and the economic institutions of liberal Germany did not suit him. His denunciation of Manchesterism, of the unfettered capitalistic society, was entirely in keeping with the dominant mood of German conservative critics. It is an important fact that at the very moment when German capitalism entered its exuberant maturity,

German intellectuals and industrialists turned strongly against *laissez-faire* and condemned it as a foreign importation.* Ever since, Germans have been loath to admit that domestic conflict and competition were inevitable concomitants of modern society. Like so many other Germans, Lagarde believed that the denial of the existence of conflict was in itself tantamount to its abolition.

Lagarde had no such compunctions about conflict abroad. From the 1850's on, he was an ardent imperialist, insisting that the colonization of the East was Germany's divinely assigned mission. The same blend of the practical and the mystical, the same concern with the spiritual resurgence of the Germans that characterized Lagarde's reforms for German society at home, marked his militant proposals for German expansion abroad. At a time when most Germans were exulting over the unification of Germany, Lagarde prophesied that *Kleindeutschland* would go down in disaster, as indeed it did.† He never relented in his attacks on the chancellor.‡

---

* The great crash of 1873 provoked a storm of protest against unbridled capitalism and Jewry. Lagarde himself often cited the Jewish *Börsenschwindler* of that time, and here he was close to such scurrilous and popular writers as Otto Glagau, who wrote *Der Börsen- und Gründungsschwindel in Berlin*, 4th ed., Leipzig 1876. See also Paul W. Massing, *Rehearsal for Destruction. A Study of Political Anti-Semitism in Imperial Germany*, New York 1949, chap. 1.

† There were a handful of other *grossdeutsche* diehards, of whom Constantin Frantz was the most influential; after the debacle of 1945, their views were widely and sympathetically reëxamined. See Robert Saitschick, *Bismarck und das Schicksal des deutschen Volkes. Zur Psychologie und Geschichte der deutschen Frage*, Basel 1949, chap. 8, for a sympathetic account of Lagarde's attack on Bismarck. In his essay "Das Problem Bismarck," *Hochland*, XLII (October, 1949), 1–27, Franz Schnabel weighs carefully the various alternatives to Bismarck's *Kleindeutschland* which Lagarde and Frantz had urged. Hans Lohmeyer, *Die Politik des zweiten Reiches, 1870–1918*, Berlin, Neff, 1939, II, 49, calls these two "the only truly important publicists who opposed Bismarck and the new Reich."

‡ He nevertheless sent Bismarck a copy of his *Deutsche Schriften*, emphasizing that he was his "political opponent": "Although I serve with different arms from your Highness, I serve the same secular and divine monarch as you and I will fight and, if necessary, even die, for what is your cause too: the true, that is the eternal, honor of the German fatherland." Anna de Lagarde, *op. cit.*, pp. 106–107. The book was also sent, with covering letters, to Prince William of Prussia and Prince Alexander of Bulgaria, as well as to some fifty public figures.

He never wavered in his belief that German destiny demanded a *Grossdeutschland,* and even more, German hegemony over *Mitteleuropa.*[26] The reasons adduced for this expansion were manifold—Lagarde frequently invoked the claims of nationalism or of defense—but ultimately they all sprang from his discontent with the existing Germany, from his belief that a great national mission would at last bring forth a truly united and dedicated nation.

Throughout his life Lagarde preached that Germany's destiny lay in the east, that Germany must rule and colonize the vast lands of eastern and southeastern Europe, then uneasily ruled by a decrepit Austria and a contemptible Russia. In his first essay, written in 1853 after the failure of 1848 and the temporary triumph of Austria, he demanded that Germans colonize all non-German territory within the German *Bund.* "This is a task that is capable of unifying the Germans." [27] Any German receiving state charity or parish relief ought to be settled in Bohemia or Moravia, Hungary or Istria. Others should be allowed to forego military service if they chose to settle in those areas.[28] Once there, these German colonists, formerly impoverished, would be assigned large homesteads and adequate supplies of cattle. Such a prosperous class would constitute a kind of landed gentry among the natives, and would assume the political and cultural leadership of their new land. By having a creative purpose, this gentry would distinguish itself from the incapable Junkers of Prussia. This scheme, moreover, would remove a large number of Germans from the artificial life of the cities.

To impart an air of plausibility to this plan of national expansion, Lagarde pleaded its likely benefits to peace and progress. Germany, he argued, was vulnerable to military attack and its defense could be secured only if eastern Poland, "from the Vistula to the Pinsk marshes, and Alsace and the entire Lorraine area east of the Ardennes can be annexed to Germany." [29]

Even after 1871, Lagarde feared that Germany was not viable, that it "would go to ruin because of its location between enemies and unreliable allies, because of the ensuing necessity always to be armed to the teeth, because of the financial burden imposed by this necessity of living in a state of armed peace." [30] The only alternative to mounting danger and ultimate disaster was vast expansion; Belfort and the other border fortresses must be wrested from France and the entire Austrian empire must be colonized and annexed. "Austria has no other purpose than to become Germany's colonial state." [31] The greatest menace was Russia, which in the short run would seek to block Germany's eastward push, and in the long run would hurl its inexhaustible manpower against its western neighbors. If Russia were to refuse to surrender Poland, the Balkans, and a sizable strip of the Black Sea coast to Germany, then "it forces us to war. . . . The Germans are a peaceful people but they are convinced of their right to live for themselves, as Germans, and convinced that they have a mission to perform for all the nations of the earth. . . . Obstruct the Germans . . . in their fulfillment of their mission and they acquire the privilege to use force." [32] There is a subdued joy in Lagarde's contemplation of a war with Russia. In some ways he was preaching the preventive war that Bismarck always indignantly refused to wage. Lagarde was haunted by Russia's potential greatness: "What we may expect once Russia has satisfactorily trained its army and built all its railroads is just as easily predictable as what in fifty years America, nurtured on Europe's marrow, will challenge us with. Both countries will enter their years of political indiscretion [*Flegeljahre*], those years in which the consciousness of strength and the absence of serious purpose combine to produce insolence." [33]

While there was still time, Germany should make itself invincible in *Mitteleuropa*. Here Lagarde's plans were the usual blend of fantastic aims and minute practical details. He prescribed the German colonization of Poland and deemed the first step the immediate expulsion of all Polish Jews. Further "population transfers"—Lagarde's own words —would consist of moving the Slovenes, Czechs, Magyars, and other non-German peoples within the Austrian empire to definitely assigned areas where they could live and die in regulated oblivion. The Germans would then completely dominate central Europe, indeed would be able to plunge beyond it, until they had conquered colonial lands as far east as Asia Minor. Much of this was inspired by what later came to be popularly known as the *Lebensraum* argument; Lagarde felt certain that these colonizing schemes would at once relieve Germany's overpopulation. All immigration to America would end, and the melting pot would no longer transmute noble Germans into base Americans. In eastern Europe, colonists would become more Germanic than the Germans.

In his last essay he drew up the most explicit proposals for an Austrian-German union.[34] The two emperors should conclude an indissoluble alliance; if either throne should fall vacant because of the death of a monarch without an heir, the other dynasty would succeed to the throne. The Austrian emperor would send his non-German nationals—except for Jews, who should be forced to leave altogether, and Italians, who could stay—to specific areas within the empire; all other areas would be immediately opened to large-scale German immigration. The two empires would form one customs area and would adopt common nonliberal institutions. Gradually the two empires would merge, and the German nation, together at last, would live a safe and purposeful life. Europe, too, would attain peace—the peace of German hegemony.

Not that peace was in itself a positive good. Like so many other critics of the time, Lagarde idealized war, and over and over again asserted that by war a nation gained strength, vitality, and dedication. This endless call for blood was of course a protest against the liberal hope of perpetual peace. Strife and bloodshed, he held, were the essential elements of progress, and this brutal doctrine could flourish more easily because the three wars for German unification had been relatively sparing of human lives.* War appeared as a moral necessity that a large country could easily afford.

Lagarde's views on war underscore the speciousness of his other "realistic" justifications for his imperial plans: to reduce taxes, to decrease immigration overseas, to insure peace, and to save the Germans in Austria. His political ideas were all too often unpolitical fantasies; through politics he sought to gain spiritual ends, to reach and transform the moral life of man. In the last analysis, none of his *ad hoc* arguments in favor of imperial expansion revealed the inner spring of his intention: he thought of conquering other peoples and of imposing German rule on them as a means of saving Germany from itself, from its incipient cultural decay.

---

* In the three wars between 1864 and 1871, the total number of Germans killed was 33,351. Gaston Bodart, *Losses of Life in Modern Wars,* Carnegie Endowment for International Peace, Oxford, Clarendon Press, 1916, pp. 56, 61, 148.

"Only the Germanizing of the countries along our eastern border is a deed of the nation, which now vegetates passively, and which by reading and smoking comforts itself about its nullity." [35] This massive challenge would revive German energy and would make Germans conscious of their common world-historical task. He did not consider his program as part of a scramble for power, but as the execution of a spiritual duty. No wonder he cared little for the possible repercussions of his plans, for the political realities of Germany's military situation. How unimportant they were, compared with the immense effect that the policy of national aggrandizement would have on the German spirit.

Here is the dynamic which gave Lagarde's nationalistic ambitions their force. His ambitions were not born of the conviction of Germany's greatness; they arose instead from the misgivings about Germany's fate which so oppressed his mind. This is the significant jump which placed the Germanic critics in the vanguard of tribal imperialism. Feeling alone and discontented in their culture, these zealots wanted war and conquest to bring peace and purification at home.

5: The Corruption of

German Education

One of the most frequent complaints that runs through Germany like an epidemic is the complaint that idealism, at least for our youth, is dead, and that hence nothing of substance can be expected from Germany. . . . [But] if a child is naughty, it is the parents' fault.   LAGARDE

Lagarde spent his life close to the schools and universities of Germany. If there was one world that he knew well, it was the academic world, and his essays on education demonstrated this familiarity. He was a harsh critic of all that he had seen— and suffered—and his sombre view of the weaknesses of German education was tinged by his deep resentment. By averring that German academic life had been so corrupted by the liberal spirit of the new Reich that it was incapable of producing cultivated and idealistic youths, Lagarde wrote off the last hope for the spontaneous regeneration of Germany. His thoughts on education strengthened the impact of his cultural despair.

Lagarde began his attacks on German academic life in 1874, at a time when most Germans and all foreigners believed that German academic training was second to none, that German universities were models of intellectual discipline and erudition.* Just as it was once said that Waterloo had been won on

---

* As but one example, consider a remark made by Lord Bryce about the Germans: "There is no people which has given so much thought and pains to the development of its university system as the Germans have done—none which has profited so much by the services universities render—none where they play so large a part in the national life." Quoted in John Theodore Merz, *A History of European Thought in the Nineteenth Century*, London 1897, I, 159.

the playing fields of Eton, so now, on both sides of the Rhine, it was said that the superiority of German schools had helped Germany conquer France. For decades Americans had been admiring and adapting German institutions, and the influence of German education on America has been powerful and persistent.

Lagarde dissented from this general acclaim. According to him, German education was rapidly declining because of the corrupt spirit of the new Reich. How could the schools escape the general collapse of morality, the emergence everywhere of the commercial spirit, of materialism, and of spiritual *sans-culottism?* Worst of all, there was no religious faith and "without God, there can be no education because without ideals, without eternal life, without responsibility before the final judge, there can be no education." [1]

Germany, moreover, was locked in a spiritual "civil war," fought for the time being only by calumny and vileness, but nevertheless rendering impossible the formulation of a uniform educational system.[2] Nor could any society hope to give a real education to a large number of its citizens: "Democracy and culture [*Bildung*] are mutually exclusive." [3] A catalogue of Lagarde's complaints about modern education would include nearly every criticism that we ourselves have heard about progressive, democratic education.*

Lagarde was not entirely alone in his pessimistic views on German education.[4] Schopenhauer and Nietzsche, for example, derided the German professor and denounced the pedantry and Philistinism that he carried into German life. In 1872, in his lectures at Basel, "On the Future of Our Educational Institutions," Nietzsche had also warned against the pressures of Germany's commercial mores against her humanistic education.† Both Lagarde and Nietzsche denounced the steadily

---

* A survey of American higher education discusses similar criticisms of modern American education, but makes the distinction between the deficiencies of education in a democratic society and the as yet insufficiently realized advantages of *democratic* education. Richard Hofstadter and C. DeWitt Hardy, *The Development and Scope of Higher Education in the United States*, New York, Columbia University Press, 1952, pp. 65–71, 107–113.

† "Two apparently hostile forces, in their actions equally pernicious and in their results finally converging, dominate at present our educational institutions which were originally, however, based on totally different principles. One is the drive toward the greatest possible *extension of*

declining standards of teachers and students, and warned that the product of Germany's educational mill would be nothing more than a pretentious and dissatisfied mediocrity.[5]

But Lagarde's attacks differed from those of Schopenhauer and Nietzsche because he was nationalistic, Germanic, and to some extent antihumanistic. They would have abhorred his insistence on a German religion, and his belief that a program of communal remedies could save Germany's educational system.

The form of Lagarde's attack, as always, consisted of three parts: the statement of extravagant expectations and ideals, a distorted and hypercritical view of actual conditions, and a prescription of concrete reforms. His ideals were a mixture of nationalistic and religious sentiments, as illustrated by his belief that the Germans had a unique calling to be men of learning. In his formal speech at the opening of the University of Czernowitz, Lagarde proclaimed: "Providence—who could deny it—has endowed each German in his cradle with the drive toward truth and science."[6]

But Providence, he feared, was being thwarted by the schools and universities; the native drive of Germans toward truth was being stifled, and Germanic individuality annihilated. Youth was being corrupted by the sins and comforts of the old, and the future of the nation was being mortgaged to the education of the present. The reformer who dreamed of heroes, of a new faith, and a united nation, railed against schools that produced soulless robots, tutored by poor teachers, corrupted by false knowledge, and prepared for the wrong

education and the other the drive toward *minimizing and weakening it.* . . . In the face of these fatal tendencies of extension and weakening, one would despair utterly, were it not possible to rally two other forces, truly German and truly rich in promise for the future; I refer to the drive toward the *contraction* and *concentration* of education as the antithesis of the greatest possible extension, and the drive toward the *strengthening* and the *self-sufficiency* of education as the antithesis of minimizing it. A warrant for our belief in the victory of the last-named principles can be found in the fact that both the forces we consider pernicious are so opposed to the timeless purpose of nature, as the concentration of education for the few is in harmony with it, whereas the first two forces could only create a culture that was false to the very roots." "Über die Zukunft unserer Bildungsanstalten," in *Aus dem Nachlass, 1869–1873,* in *Nietzsche's Werke,* Leipzig, Naumann, 1906, I, 277–278.

kind of life. There would have to be new schools to mold the new German nation.

The existing educational system, Lagarde charged, perpetuated the sham and superficiality of German life. The schools were enveloping the nation "with a tough slime of cultured barbarism [*Bildungsbarbarei*], this most revolting of all barbarisms which makes life in Germany unbearable now." [7] Lagarde wrote this in 1874, unaware that Nietzsche had condemned the *Bildungsphilister* two years earlier.* Both were revolted by the sterile, intellectually passive consumers of culture, by the parasites feeding on the past. Lagarde proposed that the only way to escape this slime and reëstablish the conditions for cultural creativity was by educating a few individuals thoroughly and letting the great majority of people subsist on nothing more than the elementary skills.

Consequently Lagarde rejected the very premise of German education, the ideal of "general education" [*allgemeine Bildung*], the education of the many in all the traditional humanistic disciplines. The very intention of acquainting students with the accumulated wisdom of the Western tradition infuriated him. To adopt this goal for the *Gymnasium* promoted stupidity and pretentiousness, and education thus conceived became nothing more than the requirement that all educated people should "have heard of everything at some time." [8] The mere study of past thought was no achievement; it smothered spontaneity and sentiment, and would never lead a student to the proper end of education—the knowledge of the divine plan. Anticipating the frequent complaints of later generations of students, Lagarde attacked and ridiculed the *Gymnasium's* emphasis on the classical world, and contended that it ill-prepared the student for life in modern Germany.†

---

* As early as 1843, Joseph Görres had warned against the *zivilisierte Barbarei* which was threatening the West. As quoted in Franz Schnabel, *Deutsche Geschichte im neunzehnten Jahrhundert*, Vol. IV: *Die religiösen Kräfte*, 2d ed., Freiburg im Breisgau 1951, p. 170.

† In 1907, Ludwig Gurlitt, well-known reformer and critic, attacked general education and wrote: "But I need not pursue this struggle against so-called general education; this diseased ideal, which German schools unfortunately served for a century and for whose sake countless German children were sacrificed as to a moloch, is at last, thank God, in its final agony." Gurlitt repeated other strictures of Lagarde's as well. Ludwig Gurlitt, *Die Gesellschaft. Sammlung sozialpsycho-*

"Is there no soul in Germany that protests against the pleasure of being an heir to some 5,000-odd years, none that feels that this inherited wealth impoverishes because it oppresses us, because it forces us not to be ourselves?" [9]

Lagarde insisted that Hegel, his favorite villain, had been responsible for this emphasis on encyclopedic knowledge, that he had in fact encapsuled all previous knowledge in his system and had then succeeded in saddling the Prussian schools with this regurgitated thought. The accomplice had been Hegel's disciple Johannes Schulze, who in the 1820's and 1830's had worked under Baron von Altenstein in the Prussian Ministry of Education. By foisting Hegel's system on the *Gymnasien,* Altenstein and Schulze had adulterated the older ideals of general education. Lagarde of course exaggerated Hegel's influence—the original inspirers of *allgemeine Bildung* were Fichte and Wilhelm von Humboldt—but it was nevertheless true that Altenstein and Schulze did cram a good deal of Hegelianism into the Prussian schools.[10]

Lagarde's attacks on Altenstein and Schulze overlooked the many issues on which he and they agreed. They accepted, for example, the general view of conservatives, particularly prevalent in the 1850's, that most teachers were dangerously subversive and should be held culpable for the revolution of 1848.* Altenstein believed moreover that the curriculum in the primary schools and for the lower social classes should be restricted to the three R's, and to singing, religion, and a bit of patriotic folklore. Nor could Lagarde have quarreled with

---

logischer Monographen, ed. by Martin Buber, Vol. XVI: *Die Schule,* Frankfurt am Main 1907, p. 37 and *passim.*

* Certainly Frederick William IV felt this way. Addressing Prussian teachers in 1850, he said: "All the misery which has come to Prussia during the past years is to be credited to you and only to you. You deserve the blame for the godless pseudoeducation of the common people which you have been propagating as the only true wisdom and by means of which you have destroyed faith and loyalty in the minds of my subjects and turned their hearts away from me. . . . These [teachers'] seminaries, every one, must be removed from the large cities to the small villages, in order that they may be kept away from the unholy influence which is poisoning our times. . . . I am not afraid of the populace, but my bureaucratic government . . ,. is being undermined and poisoned by these unholy doctrines of a modern, frivolous, secular wisdom. But as long as I hold the sword hilt in my hands, I shall know how to deal with such a nuisance." Quoted in J. Tews, *Ein Jahrhundert preussischer Schulgeschichte,* Leipzig 1914, p. 126.

Altenstein's credo: "I do not think the principles enunciated will raise the common people out of the sphere designated for them by God and human society." [11]

Lagarde maintained that the worst threat to higher education was the new system of providing material advantages for its recipients. Characteristic of this commercialization of learning, he thought, was the Prussian law, first adopted at the beginning of the nineteenth century and after 1871 extended to the entire Reich, which allowed students who had attended the *Gymnasium* for a minimum of six years to volunteer for a one-year term of military enlistment instead of being conscripted for the compulsory three-year term. According to Lagarde, three-fifths of all students in secondary schools attended only to gain this, or some other kind of privilege, and left school as soon as they had attained their nonscholarly ends. The regular course of study at the *Gymnasium* encompassed a nine-year curriculum, and the large number of students who left after six years depressed the level of the entire school. The minority, who were intent on receiving a full nine years of education in the humanities, were held back for six years of their careers by the certificate-hunting majority.

Lagarde pointed to the great increase in the number of students in the *Gymnasium* and warned that because of this great and sudden expansion the supply of good teachers was insufficient. Therefore "the meanest mediocrity is nowadays hired at once and poisons still further the already poisoned conditions." [12] Inferior students were being taught by barely competent teachers. To put a premium on the holders of a doctorate was a senseless procedure; the dissertation was a mechanical exercise of a highly specialized and unoriginal nature, and had nothing to do with the candidate's potential talent for teaching. Mediocre dissertations should no longer provide an automatic entry into the classroom. Poor teachers, with or without doctorates, should be dismissed by the state and assigned to research jobs instead. In the future, mechanical exercises, note-taking, and feats of memory should no longer dominate the life of the students; instead, better teachers should encourage and develop spontaneous, sustained thought. At the present time, "three things are the harvest of our education: poor eyesight, a yawning disgust with everything that once existed, and an incapacity to face the future." [13] The root of the evil was that "too much is demanded in our schools"—a complaint that by 1890 had become generally accepted and in that year resulted in the reduction of the students' load.[14]

Nor should education be a profitable road to riches; it should once again become practical and hierarchical. It should be a function of social status and intellectual promise: the lower classes should have a severely limited vocational training; the future rulers of Germany, the chosen few of high intellect and character, should be given a new and far more intensive training. Women should be confined to the rudimentary learning of grammar schools, with a smattering of civics added; if they aspired to more, their husbands could instruct them at a later time. The *Gymnasium* should be maintained for especially gifted boys, but no privileges should be accorded its graduates. The ideal of general education should be abandoned as an unattainable and undesirable goal, and the curriculum altered accordingly. History was struck from the curriculum altogether: too few teachers were capable of studying history while teaching it, and without such study the historian could not achieve the one indispensable requirement of his discipline, objectivity. The few who achieved it barely filled the necessary university posts. To allow a nonqualified historian to teach would lead to the propagation of dangerous political prejudices.[15]

Lagarde's most cherished reform called for the creation of a few state schools in which the intellectual and political elite of the nation would be educated. "I demand that by seriously giving a real education to a few, regardless of birth, and chosen solely for moral and intellectual capacity, a class shall be created which will be trusted by the people and govern for the people." [16] In rural areas, far from the indulgence of parents and the sinful diversions of urban life, these schools would raise the leaders of the future—about 50,000 men, or .4 per cent of the entire male population. The state would impose the most rigorous intellectual and moral standards. These schools were not to be polluted by the greatest evils of student life, smoking and drinking. This appeal to abstinence and hardiness underlines the similarity of conception and purpose between Lagarde's dedicated school for potential rulers and the later *Ordensburgen* which combined National

Socialist ideology and Spartan discipline to train National Socialist leaders.

Lagarde looked to the day when all schools would give instruction in his new religion. But until this religion had taken hold, he believed that the state should encourage every Christian faith to have its own elementary schools. If Jews wanted their own schools—with special provisions for anachronistic dietary laws, and the like—they should emigrate to Palestine. To raise young children without religion was a moral crime, while to allow them to choose their own faith in a state school was to exceed their capacity.

Lagarde also attacked the German universities, and added his poisonous shafts against the figure of the German professor, who throughout the nineteenth century was alternately maligned and revered. Considering the humiliating rebuffs which Lagarde had suffered, or imagined he had suffered, at the hands of academics, it is little wonder that he berated his colleagues so furiously, and only occasionally made a gesture toward guild loyalty. The university professors, he charged, wielded unmatched power in German society and, given their incompetence and immorality, caused untold damage. They "are now the class which dictates fashion." [17] Despite the exaggeration of this remark, one is reminded that in imperial Germany the university professor did enjoy great power and prestige and had, in fact, become the showpiece of the liberal middle class, just as the officer represented the ideal of the nobility.

Lagarde had battled the guild all his life, and the scars remained. He had contempt for his colleagues and tried to show their moral frailty and academic incompetence. Most academics, he maintained, were liberals; the academic life was an extension of the liberal mind, and Lagarde often insisted that academics were responsible for all sorts of cultural evils, even for the dishonesty of the daily press and for the infidel tone of everyday life. These were not uncommon feelings among some of the uneducated people and among the clerical and feudal elite; nor was Lagarde the only academic to denigrate his profession. Still, the vigor with which critics like Lagarde fulminated against the academics attested anew their hostility to liberal, bourgeois society and their suspicion of the merely intellectual life.

The scholarly achievements of academics were dismal as well, Lagarde complained. Themselves the product of academic degeneration, they perpetuated the evils of the system. Their preparation was inadequate, their devotion to learning deficient, their teaching ability inferior. Just as he had ridiculed the concept of general education in the *Gymnasium,* so he contemptuously dismissed the universities' pretensions to prepare students adequately in several disciplines in three years. The anticlerical laws of 1873, requiring a final examination in philosophy, history, literature, and theology for all divinity students, would make "certain that at least the Protestant theologians would become still paler, more superficial, and more untruthful than they already are." [18] He himself refused to examine students in any but his own immediate fields of specialization, and he exuded a sense of self-righteousness toward colleagues who felt free to examine in fields that lay beyond their own narrow specialties.

Teachers were as shallow and irresponsible as the students they taught; they were too indolent to broaden their knowledge while teaching, or even to keep abreast of their own disciplines. More stipends should be made available to students and teachers, but only to those who neither smoked nor drank—nor kept a dog. Scholarly publications could not find a market in Germany, as witness Lagarde's own works. Once more banking on mechanical measures to induce qualitative changes, Lagarde proposed that no public or university library in Prussia should circulate books published after 1520. These the scholars should be forced to buy.[19]

After the beginning of the *Kulturkampf,* Lagarde demanded the confiscation of all ecclesiastical benefices and the subsequent establishment by the Reich of several academies for scholars—to be financed from the confiscated endowments. There the serious scholar, freed from the demands of teaching, could pursue his scholarly interests at the expense of the state. That such a permanent divorce between the scholar and the teacher violated Lagarde's principle concerning the inseparability of good teaching and active research did not trouble him. The state would appoint the members of these academies and indicate the general direction of the work to be pursued. The only prerequisite for an appointment was membership in a "Christian or post-Christian religion"—a frivolously obvious exclusion of Jews.[20]

The universities meanwhile should rid themselves of all outside pressures. Lagarde proposed that the governmental supervision of the universities, which included the power of appointment, should devolve from the government in Berlin to the provincial authorities. This decentralization would cut the ground from under the "Berlin hustlers." [21] He also demanded that all nonacademic societies at the universities, especially the fraternities, should be dissolved: the unrelieved pursuit of knowledge was the student's sole purpose. Nor was studying to be rewarded beyond its own intrinsic value. University graduates were to receive no special privileges and no automatic preferences in employment. Students who violated the rigid discipline were to be expelled by the state—a provision which Lagarde extended to secondary-school students and teachers as well.

In 1890, William II called together the leading educators of Germany and charged them with the task of revising the curriculum of the secondary-school system. In his address, he demanded tougher physical training and a more vigorous cultivation of the Germanic consciousness. Lagarde, to his chagrin, was not invited to this conference, despite the fact that his strictures on education were widely known. Thus Lagarde's only major attempt to put his ideas into practice was his effort to revamp the Göttingen Academy of Sciences —and that effort, too, ended in failure. In 1876, he was elected to the academy and shortly thereafter proposed its total reconstruction. It should be greatly enlarged and precise duties entrusted to it: "We all live by having duties. Institutions, too, live by duties." [22] The two urgent tasks of the historical-philological branch of the academy should be the writing of the history of the ancient Saxon Duchy and the exegesis of the Talmud. Lagarde demanded that theologians, physicians, and jurists be excluded and stipulated that in addition to historians and philologists only the mathematical-physical disciplines should be represented. On the other hand, membership should be opened to qualified professors from Kiel and Rostock. Once enlarged, the Göttingen academy could successfully challenge the supremacy of the Berlin Academy of Sciences. In time, he thought, other regional centers would spring up and would loosen the stranglehold which the Berlin academy exercised over German scholarship. The evils of centralization, he thought, were demonstrated by the dictatorship of the Paris academy.

All of these plans were still-born. Lagarde prepared them in secret and asked the Prussian ministry to enact them without revealing the author's name. As it turned out, his sponsorship became known, the plans were dropped, and Lagarde sulkily announced that in the event of any changes in the academy he would resign. This, he added, would be done lest any vilifier should charge him with having advocated these reforms in the hope of self-advancement. With this equivocal gesture, Lagarde ended his efforts to reform the German educational system. Much that was useful and even noble in his plans was defeated by his crabbed manner and his extravagant presumption. But generations of students and reformers found in his strictures the justification for their own discontent with Germany's educational institutions.

6: The Prophet Remembered

> *If much that appears in this volume [of collected essays] seems to be commonplace, it became commonplace only through me. It is the fate of prophets that they are forgotten when what they preached is actualized. I shall thank God if as a political figure I shall soon be forgotten: then the great future which I prophesy and demand shall have arrived.*　　　LAGARDE
>
> *You, mein Führer, have rescued from oblivion, the works of Nietzsche, Wagner, Lagarde, and Dühring—works which foretold the doom of the old culture.*　ALFRED ROSENBERG TO ADOLF HITLER, PARTEITAG 1934.

After his death, Lagarde's fame as a national prophet, far from sinking into oblivion, steadily grew. He had not been a born leader, a charismatic man; throughout his life, his intemperate presumption, his annoying withdrawals and demands, had offended friends and enraged foes. It was only after his death, when his thoughts were unencumbered by his obstinate being and when his laments about German culture acquired greater plausibility, that his name came to be invoked by many people and various causes, always as a respectable, irreproachable representative of moral righteousness and nationalistic idealism.

Lagarde deserved to be remembered. For all his eccentricities and absurdities, he had been one of the first to sense the existence of a cultural crisis in imperial Germany. Amidst the stability and success of Bismarck's Reich, he had felt something of the inner hollowness of the Reich; in the Wilhelmine period, after Lagarde's death, many Germans came to see those same flaws and perplexities, epitomized, as they then were, by the emperor himself. Lagarde had warned against the threat of dissension at home and of conflict abroad, and all his fears found belated justification in the growing political antagonisms before 1914, in the defeat and revolution of 1918, in the peace of 1919. He had been one of the first German nationalists to voice his despair about the future of German culture. The fatalities that he predicted, occurred; events caught up with the mood of despair that he had helped to foster. No wonder then that he was remembered as a prophet, and as a teacher too. His appeal to austerity and duty, his call for sacrifice and purity, inspired those Germans who before and after the First World War were dissatisfied with the emptiness of their private and public lives.

It is a commonplace that intellectual influence cannot be measured in quantitative terms; hence the steady increase in the circulation of the *Deutsche Schriften* is in itself insufficient evidence of influence.* We know also that there was a growing public for Lagarde which in addition to the *Deutsche Schriften* absorbed several anthologies of his work and bought a large number of picture postcards that carried pithy patriotic messages culled from his writings. In the late 1920's, at the time of the centenary of his birth, there appeared many commemorative pamphlets and articles, extolling Lagarde, and many scholarly studies of his political and religious thought which were also wholly sympathetic to him.

But Lagarde's importance to the cultural life of Germany was much greater than these data suggest. By the versatility and passion of his thought he evoked enthusiastic responses among very diverse men and groups. He appealed simultane-

---

* A few months before Lagarde's death, the *Deutsche Schriften* went through a second printing at the Dieterichsche Verlagsbuchhandlung in Göttingen. A third printing followed in 1903. The book made a profound impression on the nationalistic publisher, J. F. Lehmann, who, in 1908, decided to add it to his publications. His plan was delayed, however, and it was not until 1924 that Lagarde's *Deutsche Schriften* and the supplementary volume, *Ausgewählte Schriften*, appeared under ·J. F. Lehmann's imprint. Thereafter, the first volume was reprinted three· times, and the *Ausgewählte Schriften* twice. J. F. Lehmann always carried *Deutsche Schriften* with him, and when the Bavarian revolutionaries in 1919 placed him in jail, he found the book "a genuine treat." *Verleger J. F. Lehmann. Ein Leben im Kampf für Deutschland*, ed. by M. Lehmann, München, Lehmanns, 1935, pp. 34, 110, and 159.

ously to some of the leaders of Germany's cultural elite and to some of the disreputable groups in the political and cultural underworld of imperial and Weimar Germany. By his double appeal, he helped to create an affinity of outlook between these extremes, these seemingly incompatible groups in German society—an affinity that neither group was aware of, that was never made explicit, but that contributed nevertheless to the great emotional outbursts of national unity, in August, 1914, and again in the years of the decline of Weimar and the rise of National Socialism.

The diversity of his appeal corresponded to what might be called the two sides of Lagarde. Already in his lifetime there were two images of Lagarde: there was the "soft" and the "hard" Lagarde, the former appealing to reasonable critics of modern culture, to men brooding over the prospects of religion and morality in a suddenly transformed, secular world, and the latter appealing to men and groups that had cast their discontent into definite, often ruthless, programs, be it organized anti-Semitism, imperialism, or aggressive nationalism. In between were those men who grasped but a particular slice of Lagarde's thought—his reflection on education, for example, or his critique of theology.*

The soft Lagarde was admired by men who saw in him the great idealist and reformer, the prophet who sought faith, truth, spiritual values, and who condemned secularism, materialism, and the workaday world. After the publication of his first essay, he received glowing tributes not only from Germans, but from distinguished foreigners as well. In 1875, Thomas Carlyle, a man with whom Lagarde had a marked affinity in thought and temperament, wrote: "It is many years since I have met with so much faithful independence of thinking and real originality in any book, German or other, that has come before me." He commended Lagarde's views on Protestants and Papists, and added:

Your notion of the Jews, which has a fine spice of satire in it, amused me considerably. But above all things, I was interested by

---

* Among those who had been most powerfully influenced by Lagarde's critique of education was Ludwig Gurlitt, who carried the banner of Lagarde into his frequent battles against officialdom. See, for example, Ludwig Gurlitt, *Der Deutsche und sein Vaterland. Politisch-pädagogische Betrachtungen eines Modernen,* 8th printing, Berlin 1903, esp. pp. 82–83.

what you say towards the end of the book, that there is no real gain to any nation, except by the restoration of some real religion to it. This is to me the truth of truths; and I am anxious in a high degree to hear what farther you may please to utter upon this highest matter.[1]

Even T. G. Masaryk, the eminently humane father of the later Czechoslovak republic, congratulated Lagarde: "Please accept my monograph on suicide as a feeble contribution to the noble endeavors to which you have dedicated head and heart." *

After his death, the soft Lagarde began to appeal to a growing number of educated Germans. To invoke Lagarde in those years was to attest one's patriotic idealism, to prove one's hatred of everything un-Germanic, to take a stand for the "yea-saying," the irrational, the creative forces of culture against the negativism and materialism of mere intellectualism. In many circles, Lagarde was turned into a comfortable substitute for Nietzsche, who to so many Germans seemed abstruse and dangerous. Lagarde, moreover, had the inestimable advantage of being a nationalist, whereas Nietzsche, his bourgeois readers thought, was at best ambivalent on that score. Some sensitive men like Ernst Troeltsch, Friedrich Naumann, Hermann Bahr, Richard Dehmel, Christian Morgenstern, and Ludwig Curtius were deeply moved by Lagarde's earnest faith, his national ethos, his individualism, his scorn for German education.[2] We have already seen how warmly Franz Overbeck and Paul Natorp responded to Lagarde's religious thought. When Thomas Mann referred to Lagarde as the *praeceptor Germaniae*, he was not only paying his personal tribute to the man, but was also aptly describing Lagarde's position in Wilhelmine Germany.[3] Georg Quabbe, a brilliant and spirited German conservative of the post-1918 period, wrote of Lagarde's "sublime conservatism," and noted that such was his intellectual appeal and such the rapacious

---

* Masaryk to Lagarde, March 14, 1881, Lagarde Archive, Göttingen. Five years later, Masaryk wrote: "If I take the liberty of sending you my study on concrete logic, I do so out of a deep-felt need in some way to express my gratitude for your *Deutsche Schriften*. At a later time I shall deal with them more specifically, that is, correct some of your political accusations, for example, of the Czechs, because I do not believe you wrote with detachment on this point. Of course this in no way impairs my sincere esteem for you." October 30, 1886, Lagarde Archive, Göttingen.

penchant of liberals for raiding conservative thinkers, that Lagarde would someday become a liberal hero: "I hope to be around still when they [the liberals] pull off the neat trick of proving the liberal character of Lagarde's thought; if he had not delivered so many inextinguishable kindnesses to the Jews, this would have been tried long ago." *

In fact, neither Jews nor liberals proved to be impervious to the idealism of this *praeceptor Germaniae*. In 1901, for example, a Jewish intellectual, Efraim Frisch, introduced Christian Morgenstern, the poet and translator of Ibsen, to Lagarde's *Deutsche Schriften*. Lagarde's unrelenting pessimism, his yearning for a new faith attracted and inspired Morgenstern, and led him to revere Lagarde as he had earlier revered Nietzsche, and as he was later to admire Rudolf Steiner, himself an avid reader of Lagarde. Morgenstern hailed Lagarde, "this greatest legislator of the German present—for Nietzsche is no legislator in that sense— . . . this proudest and most precipitous mountain range," as the man who led him away from society and back to the Bible. "For any man who does not time and again perish because of Nietzsche and Lagarde, only to be resurrected by them, for him these two were never born." Morgenstern's highest praise and his most characteristic estimate were expressed in his remark about Ibsen's *Brand*: "There I see [Ibsen] stand next to Lagarde and Nietzsche as the third great defender of the spirit of discipline [*Zuchtidee*] against the modern principle of *laisser-faire, laisser-aller.*"†

---

* Georg Quabbe, *Tar a Ri. Variationen über ein konservatives Thema*, Berlin 1927, pp. 109–110. It was characteristic of Lagarde's double reputation that Quabbe, his great admirer, had nothing but magnificent scorn for racism and the *völkische Idee*, which, after all, Lagarde had helped to father: "Indeed a ridiculously simple cure: we throw out the Jews and the Poles, marry among ourselves, and if things get hot, we will go in for a little eugenics, and then bliss will reign." *Ibid.*, p. 16.

† As late as 1906 Christian Morgenstern wrote in his diary:

> Zu Niblum will ich mich rasten aus
> Von aller Gegenwart.
> Und schreibt mir dort auf mein steinern Haus
> Nur den Namen und 'Lest Lagarde!'
> Ja, nur die zwei Dinge klein und gross:
> Diese Bitte und dann meinen Namen bloss.
> Nur den Namen und 'Lest Lagarde!'

Friedrich Hiebel, *Christian Morgenstern. Wende und Aufbruch unseres Jahrhunderts*, Bern, Francke, 1957, pp. 63–75.

The image of Lagarde as the German legislator *par ex-cellence* was particularly important to all the cultural critics, all the educators, who denounced modern culture—in its totality or in some specific aspects—as un-Germanic.* During the First World War, when German intellectuals sought to refute Allied claims that the democratic progressive West was fighting a militaristic, reactionary Germany, they frequently argued that the German imperial regime was more representa-tive and democratic than the mechanical vote-counting systems of the Western democracies. Thomas Mann's *Betrachtungen eines Unpolitischen,* the epitome of this avowal of cultural independence, sought to prove that the unpolitical, spiritual nature of the Germans set them fundamentally apart from men in other societies. Mann readily fell back on Lagarde's sharp differentiation between the genuine *Volk* that was always right and the democratic collection of individuals, of egoists, that was almost always inimical to the *Volk.* Lagarde's commitment to the *Volk* as the ultimate source of power, Mann contended, was still conservative, despite its apparent democratic implications. Conservatism did not mean "to keep everything that existed, but to keep Germany German and that is all. And it is German above all not to confound the *Volk* with the individual atoms that compose the mass." The artist who reflects on Germany's fate "can only repeat, out of his own deepest conviction, what the giants of our people, Nietzsche, Lagarde, and Wagner, have said, that democracy in the Western sense and flavor is alien to us, something trans-lated, something 'present only in the press,' and something that can never become German life and truth." [4]

To the growing number of intellectuals who, before and after the First World War, brooded over the inadequacy of a purely secular society, Lagarde appealed with particular force. As the yearning for a new faith deepened, Lagarde's belief that religion was indispensable and that contemporary Christianity was dead, received widespread, troubled assent. Whether the envisioned goal was an esthetic-aristocratic surrogate for re-

---

* To list all critics who at one time or another acknowledged or exhibited Lagarde's influence would be a massive, futile enterprise. I am not asserting that Lagarde was a formative influence on them, but that in the more or less serious literature of lament before 1933 he appeared regularly as the guarantor of truth and the prophet of national resurgence.

ligion, as the Stefan George circle hoped, or a refurbished, socially conscious Christianity as Friedrich Naumann planned, the impact of Lagarde was unmistakable. Already in 1903, Ernst Troeltsch wrote: "The great religious movement of modern times, the reawakened need for religions, develops outside the churches, and by and large outside theology as well." And in this connection Troeltsch took note of Lagarde's growing influence: "His powerfully written *Deutsche Schriften* have . . . won him an influence worthy of his great and important ideas." Even if he himself never reached an ultimate position on religion, his theological thought reawakened "the desire for it in the hearts of others, and had an influence not only on theologians, but especially on laymen, and placed the gravity and greatness of these [religious] questions before their heart and conscience." [5]

Lagarde appealed to those artists and intellectuals of the pre-1914 generation who were proud of Germany's magnificent successes, but appalled by the price it had paid and troubled by premonition of great national disasters.* They were troubled, too, by the old question: *"Was ist deutsch?"* What was the essence of their people, the character that they must strive to preserve, the purpose they should further? They found answers to these questions in their reading of Lagarde, and they acknowledged him as a central figure in their intellectual lives.

That he should have been so unqualifiedly accepted by this group attests anew the essentially unpolitical nature of so many German intellectuals who concerned themselves intermittently with politics. In praising Lagarde, they remained unperturbed by his brutal side, by his immense capacity to hate, by his desire to destroy Jews, liberals, *literati,* and, if need be, the non-German peoples of Central Europe. They remained unperturbed as well by his ungenerous utopianism, by his dream of a Germanic community with its intimation of perpetual order and spiritual regimentation.

While contemplative Germans saw only the "soft" Lagarde,

---

*As one critic put it in 1913: Lagarde's "ideas are more alive among us today than at any time before; what he preached, prescribed, and prophesied appears to the Germans of today far more clearly, far more urgently, and far more possible, than it appeared to those who still saw him among them." Max Christlieb, "Paul de Lagarde," *Die Tat,* V:1 (April, 1913), 2.

the right-wing activists and devout anti-Semites saw only the "hard" features of his thought, careful to justify themselves and their program by pointing to the idealism of Lagarde.* A few groups embraced both sides of Lagarde; the high priests of German culture, the Wagner court at Bayreuth, for example, celebrated Lagarde as a great anti-Semitic prophet of pure *Deutschtum*. While both Wagner and Lagarde were alive, it proved hard to forge a link between them, despite Wagner's public appeal for ideological comradeship with Lagarde and despite warm letters from Cosima, assuring Lagarde that she and her husband "certainly shall do everything in our power to give [the *Deutsche Schriften*] wide circulation." †

For one thing, Lagarde could not endure the music of the future, and this, of course, was the sin of sins for the master.‡ In the last months of his life, Lagarde did pull closer to the Bayreuth court, now presided over by the formidable Cosima, who was supremely patriotic and high-minded even in her crassest commercial dealings. Lagarde's sudden death frustrated

---

* Franz Mehring, the socialist writer, reviewed Anna de Lagarde's memoirs and stressed the alleged influence that Lagarde had on Prince William, later William II. Lagarde "was one of those sparkling, muddleheaded men who are too clever to howl with the capitalistic wolves and too cowardly to leave the capitalistic fleshpots. Next to Nietzsche he has become the apostle of those funny fellows who as Bismarck's hired writers enjoy a thriving business and at the same time pretend that they are the saviors of the betrayed nation. They usually add citations from Lagarde in order to make their empoverished stew a little tastier." "Man nennt das Volk," *Die Neue Zeit,* XIII:8, part 1 (November 15, 1894), 225.

† In 1878, in the *Bayreuther Blätter,* Wagner published for the first time his essay "Was ist Deutsch?" which he had originally written in 1865. In a postscript bewailing the un-Germanic culture of the new Reich he admitted that he could no longer define what was German, but "could not Konstantin Frantz be of admirable help to us? And certainly Paul de Lagarde as well? Let these two consider themselves to have been sincerely solicited to answer this fateful question for the instruction of our poor Bayreuth *Patronatverein.*" *Gesammelte Schriften und Dichtungen von Richard Wagner,* 3d ed., Leipzig, Fritzsch, 1898, X, 53. Also a letter of Cosima Wagner to Lagarde, February 6, 1876, Lagarde Archive.

‡ In February, 1881, Lagarde saw a performance of Siegfried in Munich: "I was bored to extinction. Four hours of recitative is intolerable. . . . I am completely cured of Wagner; of my own accord I shall not again expose myself to such suffering." Nor did he hesitate to make his distaste known to some of the professional Wagnerites. Quoted in Rahlfs, *Paul de Lagarde,* p. 75.

these plans for active collaboration, but posthumously Bayreuth sought to make him into a Germanic immortal. The *Bayreuther Blätter* devoted its June, 1892, issue to a memorial of Lagarde and emphatically recommended his work to its readers. Ludwig Schemann, one of the most prolific of Bayreuth Germanics and racists, and later the author of a full-length biography of Lagarde, summarized his life and work and concluded that "for the comprehension of Lagarde's whole being one must above all remember that he always considered himself the prophet and guide of his people—which, of course, he actually was." For Schemann this legacy consisted largely of his struggle against the Jews: "Not since the days of Schopenhauer and Wagner has a German thinker so mightily opposed this alien people, which desecrates our holy possessions, poisons our people, and seeks to wrest our property from us so as to completely trample on us, as Lagarde has." [6] It was this image of Lagarde, the anti-Semitic prophet of a purified and heroic Germany, which the political Wagnerites and the *Bayreuther Blätter* kept alive. Houston Stewart Chamberlain, Wagner's son-in-law and intellectual disciple, wrote: "For us, the *Deutsche Schriften* have for a long time belonged to our most precious books, and we consider Lagarde's unabashed exposure of the inferiority of the Semitic religious instincts and of their pernicious effects on Christianity as an achievement that deserves our admiration and gratitude." [7] Although critical of Lagarde's lack of consistent racism and his pessimism about the future of Protestantism, Chamberlain always paid tribute to his Germanic character and mission. Actually Chamberlain's influence was more restricted than Lagarde's: Chamberlain was something of a public philosopher under William II, and appealed to the vanity of his compatriots, but by the same token he failed to touch the many groups, including the literary elite, that found itself in opposition to Wilhelmine Germany. Only an outsider like Lagarde could appeal to other outsiders.

The ferocious Lagarde was the patron saint of the emergent anti-Semitic or *völkische* movement.* During the last decade of his life, he was in touch with some of the leading anti-Semitic

---

*"The great spiritual movement of Germanic-racist character that stands behind the anti-Semitic movement is above all based on Paul de Lagarde." Adolf Bartels, *Der völkische Gedanke. Ein Wegweiser,* Weimar 1923, p. 24.

organizers and publicists, among them Theodor Fritsch, Friedrich Lange, and Nietzsche's brother-in-law Bernhard Förster, who never tired of proclaiming their indebtedness to his teachings.* Their crusade was primarily aimed at eliminating all Jewish participation in German cultural life.[8] Lagarde's relations with these men were not always smooth.[9] He declined Fritsch's request for a portrait, saying his personality ought to be kept out of the public eye: "It should not become known because the harsh seriousness of my nature is displeasing and would only harm the good cause." † Even these fellow-warriors he rebuffed, often accusing them of plagiarism, lack of respect, and other acts of ill will. Most enduring was his influence on the *Verein deutscher Studenten,* founded in 1881, which "for the Germanic-racialist position was even more important than the anti-Semitic parties." [10] The *Verein* early discovered in Lagarde's anti-Semitism the moral justification of its prejudices and honored him as one of its patrons.‡ Lagarde also belonged to the handful of heroes that the later *Wandervogel* acclaimed.[11] To them he appeared as the sworn enemy of their fathers, hence their friend. Other student associations cherished his memory as well, and the *Burschenschaftliche Bücherei* devoted one of its official publications to a detailed, sympathetic exposition of Lagarde's thought.[12]

Many of the anti-Semites were also concerned, as Lagarde had been, with the birth of a nationalistic faith, and his religious ideas encouraged the later Germanic Christians in their

---

* Another member of this group wrote in retrospect: "For a long time Lagarde has been my spiritual leader." Max Robert Gerstenhauer, *Der völkische Gedanke in Vergangenheit und Zukunft. Aus der Geschichte der völkischen Bewegung,* Leipzig 1933, p. 11.

† Letter to Fritsch, July 8, 1888, Lagarde Archive. Lagarde and some of his anti-Semitic correspondents signed their letters with the patriotic salutation, *"mit deutschem Gruss,"* later used extensively by the National Socialists.

‡ Lagarde's "idealism" comforted many an anti-Semite; the one-time president of the Pan-German League, for example, records that "in our efforts to maintain the proper spiritual and moral level in these matters [the Jewish question] we received powerful support from the works of Lagarde, Count Gobineau, and Houston Stewart Chamberlain. At the end of the century, I plunged into them, and I do not know from which of these three great men I derived the most profit." Heinrich Class, *Wider den Strom. Vom Werden und Wachsen der nationalen Opposition im alten Reich,* Leipzig 1932, pp. 87 ff.

search for a faith that would Germanize Christianity, that would tear away from Christianity its Jewish and universal elements, reconcile the competing confessions and preach a gospel of German heroism. Lagarde had a particularly powerful influence on the various sects of the *Deutsche Christen,* that sizable, and for a while extremely important group of German Protestants who in the early 1930's threw their support to the National Socialists. As early as 1921, the *Bund für deutsche Kirche* was organized, and the imprint of Lagarde's teachings was clear and acknowledged from the start.[13] The movement spread, and amalgamated with similar groups in other parts of Germany. What they had in common was Lagarde's heritage: the desire to convert Christianity into a polemical, anti-Semitic, nationalistic faith and organization that would supplant the old and decadent tenets of a perverted and universal Christianity. In this distortion of Christianity and in the mass desertion from the Christian faith—one of the most obscure and most important aspects of the rise of national socialism— Lagarde's thought played a central role.*

Lagarde's imperialist schemes were cherished by most of the nationalistic groups. The Pan-German League, which I shall discuss later, took over his Continental imperialism and became the strictest guardian of an aggressive Eastern policy [*Ostmarkpolitik*].[14] Defenders of the *grossdeutsche* program hailed Lagarde as one of the first men to have seen the shortcomings of Bismarck's Reich.[15] During the First World War Lagarde was frequently acclaimed by the annexationists, and some of his ideas were echoed without specific acknowledgment, in the most celebrated work on Germany's wartime mission, Friedrich Naumann's *Mitteleuropa.*

After the war and the November revolution, Lagarde's became one of the most frequently invoked names by all those

---

* Even a cursory examination of the abundant—and appalling—literature of the Deutsche Christen reveals how often Lagarde was invoked by them. In the early and decisive years of the Nationalist Socialist struggle against the Protestant Church, for example, the inside jackets of all publications of the Deutsche Christen in the Rhineland cited Lagarde—and only Lagarde—as "the pioneer of a Christian faith consonant with our [Germanic] character." Or again, "Paul de Lagarde was one of the fiercest proponents of a *Nationalkirche* in the Protestant camp." Kurt Thieme, *Aus dem Wieratal ins Reich! Ursprung und Aufbruch deutschen Christentums,* Weimar, Verlag deutscher Christen, 1939, p. 77.

Germans on the right who hated the republic but had no desire to go back to what they remembered as the bad old days before 1914. All the little patriotic leagues, all the amateur writers for the countless little journals and broadsides, found Lagarde a source of inspiration and respectability. Even the militant men of the Free Corps found the old German scholar inspiriting. One of them remembered that when in 1921 the students at Göttingen organized themselves into the Free Corps *Oberland* "to defend German soil in Upper Silesia, Lagarde was in our hearts, because in him patriotism and piety were most deeply intertwined." [16] A philosopher celebrated Lagarde as the central defender in the late nineteenth century of the Germanic spirit against Cartesianism, against the arch-foe of German philosophy, and interpreted his attack on contemporary Christianity as in effect constituting an attack on the enfeebling, rationalistic tradition of Western Christianity, embodied originally in monotheism.* Whenever any of these groups sought to express their intellectual commitments, to rationalize their great passionate longing, they fell back on Lagarde as one of the earliest fighters for militant *Deutschtum*.†

The evidence of Lagarde's postwar fame is great indeed and justifies the conclusion of several observers who have spoken of a "Lagarde Renaissance" in the 1920's. The National Socialists, of course, furthered a revival of Lagarde's anti-Semitic and imperialist thought, and Alfred Rosenberg, in his *Mythus,* repeated many of Lagarde's strictures against Christianity and insisted that the National-Socialist movement marked the fulfillment of his Germanic dream: "Amidst the ecstasy over the second Empire a prophet [Lagarde] posited the Germanic-Nordic-Western dream, and almost alone, set up the proper goals for it." [17] For a short time, the National Socialists realized Lagarde's hopes for a *Grossdeutschland* and for vast population transfers that would strengthen the Ger-

---

* Franz Böhm, *Anti-Cartesianismus. Deutsche Philosophie im Widerstand,* Leipzig 1938, pp. v, 274 ff., considers the history of German philosophy as one massive protest against Cartesian rationalism and optimism and attributes this insight to his critical study of late nineteenth-century thought, "and in particular to my concern with Lagarde."

† Again as a mere example we should note that the *Jungdeutsche Orden* acclaimed Lagarde's memory, as did most of the lesser organizations of the conservative revolution. See Klaus Hornung, *Der Jungdeutsche Orden,* Düsseldorf 1958, pp. 69–76.

man element everywhere in Central Europe. This, of course, does not imply that the National Socialists were dependent on Lagarde for inspiration; it would be closer to the mark to say that they used him, as others had used him before, as a spiritual legitimization, as a cloak of respectability.*

Lagarde's influence, then, grew with the passage of time and with the accumulation of Germany's disasters. As the country raced through war, defeat, and totalitarianism, it proved ever more hospitable to Lagarde's peculiar blend of hope and gloom. Of course, his had not been the only voice that cried out against modernity. Just before his death, he found a devoted, if erratic, disciple in Julius Langbehn, who privately and publicly protested his intellectual kinship to Lagarde. Langbehn's avowed intent to promote Lagarde's gospel bore fruit when, shortly before Lagarde's death, he successfully persuaded Lagarde's publisher to risk a second edition of the *Deutsche Schriften*. More important, Langbehn's own immensely successful book, *Rembrandt als Erzieher*, which appeared anonymously in 1890, summed up in a new form and with different emphases, the several themes and purposes of Lagarde's work. In this way, Langbehn's *Rembrandt als Erzieher* was destined to announce the next stage in the evolution of the Germanic ideology.

---

* Under the National Socialists, Lagarde's work was continually reprinted and new anthologies were prepared. In addition to the several new printings of the *Deutsche Schriften* and to the anthologies already cited, there appeared a brochure, *Nationale Religion*, ed. by Georg Dost, Jena, Eugen Diederichs, 1934, and a book entitled, *Deutsche Schriften*, ed. and selected by Wilhelm Rössle, Jena, Eugen Diederichs, 1944.

II: Julius Langbehn

and Germanic Irrationalism

7: The Critic as Failure

Among pillars
Fallen,
Among temples
Desecrated,
Among people
Cultivated,
Among girls
Corrupted,
I walk and find no rest.
LANGBEHN

A new age, still unfamiliar to itself, with its intellectual concerns still undefined, will often gain self-knowledge for the
first time from a programmatic book, even a bad book. For the
decade of the 1890's, everywhere in the Western world a
creative, groping, innovating period, such a book, at least for
Germany, was Langbehn's *Rembrandt als Erzieher,* published
in 1890.

The decade was one of strife and unrest, when the cultural
discontent which previously had been the complaint of a few
artists and intellectuals became the faddish lament of the
many. The revolt against modernity, the attack on civilization, gathered force, hundreds of voices inveighed against all
sorts of evils and repressions, and multitudes of people everywhere were repeating these imprecations. Nietzsche, ignored
during his creative period, was suddenly read and admired,
Ibsen was played and praised, Nordau's *Degeneration* vehe-
mently debated. Everywhere, and not only in Germany, sprang
up the cry for greater freedom, for self-expression, for more
experience and less theorizing, for a fuller life, for the recognition of the tortured, self-torturing individual. The intensity of
this awakening in Germany can be gauged by the instantaneous

success of Langbehn's book. The decade that ended with the exuberant fling of the German Youth Movement began with this wild book, this breathless tirade, this rhapsody of irrationalism.

However wild and chaotic the book was, its intent was unmistakable: to condemn intellectualism and science, to denounce modern culture, to praise the "free" individual and the true Germanic aristocrat, to revive the German past. Rembrandt, celebrated as a German, was to be the teacher of a new and final German reformation. Art, not science or religion, was the highest good, the true source of knowledge and virtue. And the old German virtues, now lost, were: childlike simplicity, subjectivity, individuality. *Rembrandt als Erzieher* was a shrill cry against the hothouse intellectualism of modern Germany which threatened to stifle the creative life, a cry for the irrational energies of the folk, buried for so long under layers of civilization. The tone of Langbehn's book, at once prophetic and personal, projected the intense sufferings of the author, himself an extreme representative of a particular type of discontented critic.

Julius Langbehn was born on March 26, 1851, in the small town of Hadersleben in Schleswig, a countryman of Friedrich Hebbel, and of a people known for its narrow-minded stubbornness.* His mother was descended from a talented family of pastors in Schleswig, one of whom had studied under Luther.[1] His father's ancestors, rooted for untold generations in the stark Holstein country along the shores of the Baltic Sea, had seldom been anything more than day workers or weaver's apprentices, except for a few small-time farmers. Langbehn's father, however, had moved up in the world; he was a philologist, trained at the university, and in the 1840's he became the assistant principal of the local *Gymnasium*. If the larger world about the Langbehns had remained at peace, they could in all probability have assured their son a comfortable, happy childhood.

Actually, three months after his birth, his father's career was wrecked by the political repression which everywhere had

* "[There is] a certain Holstein temper, full of fanaticism and hatred. Hebbel was the most powerful exemplar, Langbehn belonged to it too." Alfred Lichtwark, *Briefe an Max Liebermann,* ed. by Carl Schellenberg, Hamburg, Trautmann, 1947, p. 262.

followed the 1848 revolutions. In Schleswig-Holstein, the Danes, who during the revolution had defeated German efforts to conquer these provinces, sought to suppress the nationalist adherents of the German cause. Langbehn's father was one of these, and in the summer of 1851 he was dismissed by the Danish authorities for refusing to adopt Danish as the primary language in his school.

Harried and jobless, the elder Langbehn left Schleswig and sought a livelihood in Holstein, a country ruled by the Danish crown but belonging to the German Confederation.[2] His patriotism was not rewarded, and the family had to go from town to town looking for help and employment and finding neither. At last they settled in Kiel, where the father became a tutor in some patrician families. His work yielded a meager income, and the parents found it difficult to care for their three sons, of whom Julius was then the youngest. A fourth boy was born in 1856.*

Julius grew up in Kiel, oppressed by his family's struggle with penury. Little is known about their family life beyond the rather conventional picture of a harsh, disciplinarian father and a gentle, loving mother who acted as the comforter —the picture which Langbehn himself composed as an adult. His father early introduced him to heady reading: "As a boy I was always occupied with Homer and the *Nibelungenlied,* with Ossian and Scott. And beech-tree forests and the Baltic Sea. That is real hero's fare." [3] In 1863, he entered the Kiel *Gymnasium;* during his second year his father died, and his mother became the sole support of the family. She worked at various jobs, sapping her strength until life at home became more and more difficult. After his graduation, Langbehn entered the University of Kiel as a student in the natural sciences. His small municipal stipend did not suffice, and he had to support himself by doing odd bits of work and by soliciting subsidies from friends and strangers.[4] Heedless of his mother's entreaties, he left home and moved to a student's quarter.

At the outbreak of the Franco-Prussian war, the nineteen-year-old Langbehn volunteered at once for military service.

---

* Julius's oldest brother, a postal clerk, afflicted with a chronic lung ailment, died, a bachelor, in 1884. Despite his limited resources, this brother repeatedly contributed to Julius's support. The second son, a sailor, was drowned in 1864. The youngest Langbehn emigrated to Colorado in 1881, where shortly afterward he died of tuberculosis.

Quickly trained in the infantry, he fought in the battles around Le Mans and Orleans, was made a lieutenant, but soon thereafter was discharged because of a rheumatic ailment. The Franco-Prussian war left Langbehn—as it left Nietzsche—with a loathing for war; "the rawness and the brutality of life" appalled him.[5] The memory of this wretched experience prevented Langbehn from ever espousing battle and martial vigor as a cultural blessing in the manner of Lagarde and Moeller.

Langbehn returned to Kiel to study chemistry, but with the financial help of a wealthy merchant he was able, in 1872, to move to the University of Munich. There, though still poor and largely self-supporting, he cast about for a more attractive career. Bored by the natural sciences and the rigors of the laboratory, he became enthralled by the world of art, by the talk of artists and art students, who seemed to him more alive and sensitive than the natural scientists. Munich, with its gay Bohemian life at Schwabing, delighted him; his new friends encouraged him to begin the study of art and archaeology. A year later, shaken by the news that his mother had suffered a mental breakdown and had been committed to an institution, and still uncertain about his career, he decided to run away from Munich and his responsibilities.* He traveled to Venice on foot. Effusive letters to friends at home tell the familiar tale of the incredulous German entranced by the beauties of the South. He took a variety of jobs which sustained him and provided him with the means of further travel.

Langbehn returned to Munich in 1875, where for the next five years he studied art and archaeology and prepared his doctoral dissertation on early Greek statues of the winged victory.[6] His principal teacher was the well-known archaeologist Heinrich Brunn, and between teacher and pupil an excep-

---

* His mother remained in the asylum, her condition unimproved, until her death ten years later. The nature of her illness has been much disputed. Langbehn's disciple, Nissen, was delicately vague about her illness; see Benedikt Momme Nissen, *Der Rembrandtdeutsche Julius Langbehn*, Freiburg im Breisgau 1927, pp. 25, 60–61. The art critic, Cornelius Gurlitt, who had once been a friend of Langbehn's, explicitly spoke of her insanity; see his "Der Rembrandtdeutsche," *Die Zukunft*, LXIX (December 18, 1909), 376. The well-known German psychiatrist, Hans Bürger-Prinz, reviewed the medical history of Langbehn's family and diagnosed his mother to have been psychotic and schizophrenic, with a persecution mania that was fixed on her children. Hans Bürger-Prinz and Annemarie Segelke, *Julius Langbehn der Rembrandtdeutsche. Eine pathopsychologische Studie*, Leipzig 1940, pp. 10–11.

tionally close relationship sprang up, reflecting their mutual admiration. In 1880, Langbehn's dissertation was at last completed; he had already passed his examinations, in his major fields with an "excellent," in philosophy with a "bare pass."

Brunn befriended Langbehn, and Brunn's son, some fifty years later, remembered the delight with which the entire family greeted the frequent visits of "this handsome man, this great blond German. . . . Strangely, as often as Langbehn's figure appears to my mind's eye, in dream or thought, it always possesses something transfigured, and the more time passes, the more transfigured it becomes." [7] But Brunn was not spared Langbehn's stubborn side; his help was often spurned, as was his hope that Langbehn would follow an academic career. Instead, Langbehn went out of his way to defy academic conventions; his dissertation, for example, was defiantly printed in Gothic type.

In 1880, Brunn recommended Langbehn for a stipend from the Imperial Archaeological Institute at Rome. The request was refused, partly because the guild regarded Brunn as not being enough of a philologist, and partly because of Langbehn's insufferable arrogance at his decisive interview.* A year later, when the grant was offered, Langbehn nearly refused it. In the end he relented and went to Rome, and immediately became embroiled with the secretary of the institute, who had dared to criticize him in some minor financial matter. His work bogged down because of the very grandiosity of his plans, and the practical suggestions of Brunn he rebuffed with so much insolent anger that Brunn began to speak of his megalomania. In spite of all, Brunn sought to find him a university post, but Langbehn balked at being chained to an academic discipline. On Langbehn's return to Munich, master and pupil broke—with all the requisite formality— and Langbehn, on leaving Brunn's house for the last time, threatened "to go to Hamburg and become a bootblack." [8]

---

* Langbehn blamed Mommsen, "the well-known archpriest of Berlin intriguers," as he called him, for his failure to obtain the stipend. Langbehn retaliated for this supposed rebuff by public and petulant attacks on Mommsen. Mommsen had in fact—and characteristically— sought to help the young Langbehn. But years later, when *Rembrandt als Erzieher* appeared and a friend praised it to Mommsen, he replied: "Your standards seem to have greatly declined with age." Lothar Wickert, *Theodor Mommsen. Eine Biographie*, Vol. I: *Lehrjahre 1817– 1844,* Frankfurt, Klostermann, 1959, p. 280.

A decade later, from anger and the passionate desire to be an outsider, Langbehn asked the University of Munich to strike his name from the list of its graduates: "It is my intention . . . to divest myself of the title of doctor." When the dean notified him of the faculty's decision not to act on his request, Langbehn chose his own means: he tore up his diploma and mailed the pieces to the university, to signify his contemptuous resignation. Over the protest of three members of the faculty senate, it was resolved not to press charges against this unprecedented insult.*

Langbehn had been relatively content during his protracted student life.† Many of his earlier ties he severed; shortly after his Italian trip, he withdrew from the Lutheran Church, with which his ancestors had been so closely identified. His new faith was art, his new friends were artists or art students. He was happiest in the company of three young painters, Karl Haider, Wilhelm Leibl, and Hans Thoma, all of whom painted his portrait. His life inclined toward Bohemianism, touched occasionally by his later obsession for secrecy and isolation. "I care nothing for the so-called bourgeois traditions; I would never barter away my happiness for them." [9] Occasionally his unconventionality went too far: "In 1880 he was fined thirty marks by the police for damaging property—

---

* In his recent account of this episode, the historian Karl Alexander von Müller concluded that: "[Langbehn], odd duck that he was, was nevertheless a harbinger of the coming disaster. His life, like his book, constitutes the early signs of the deep inner upheaval toward which the age was drifting with ever greater rapidity. For him to break the tie to the official institution of science and for the institution not even to suspect that here something more than a scrap of paper had been torn to shreds, but to believe that it would suffice to make a note in the files—both were symptomatic of the age about to begin." Müller knew from first-hand experience, from his own ready collaboration with the National Socialists, the depths to which the enterprise of science could sink. Karl Alexander von Müller, "Zwei Münchener Doktordiplome," in *Festgabe für seine königliche Hoheit Kronprinz Rupprecht von Bayern*, ed. by Walter Goetz, München-Pasing 1953, p. 193.

† The most informative picture of Langbehn as a student was left by Charles Waldstein, a Jewish archaeologist at Cambridge, who had been a pupil of Brunn's and a friend of Langbehn's. Waldstein's description suggests a talented, eccentric, moody, and undisciplined man. Langbehn later broke with Waldstein, partly because the latter was unable to find him a job in England, partly because of his growing anti-Semitism. Cornelius Gurlitt, "Langbehn, der Rembrandtdeutsche," *Protestantische Studien*, No. 9 (Berlin 1927), pp. 28–31.

sufficient proof indeed that he lived the fast student life." [10]

Even Langbehn could not remain a student forever, and in 1880–81, after more than a decade of intermittent attendance at the university, he chose a career, or rather, he reached a negative decision: he disdained all employment. To a friend he wrote: "I shall now cease to study the past, instead I shall *construct the future*." [11] One more trip to Rome and Athens, and then his education would be complete, and he would tackle in earnest his plan for the reform of German culture and the rebirth of the German people. For the sake of that future, he made presumptuous demands on the present he condemned, on acquaintances whom he insulted. He pretended to turn his back on society, protesting his contemptuous indifference to it, but still hoping that it would seek him out, celebrate, support, and crown him.

For the next decade Langbehn traveled, studied, wrote, always intent on his reform, of which the first installment was to be the Rembrandt book. He trotted from museum to museum, from library to library, indefatigably collecting material for "the book"; he settled briefly in Berlin, Hamburg, Frankfurt-on-Main, Frankfurt-on-the-Oder, and a score of other places. He used to boast that "what I know I have acquired by traveling," and that his journeys gave him the insights into men and cultures that inspired his thought.[12] Dresden became his favorite city—"the only place in Germany where I could remain forever"—and he stayed there from 1885 to 1892. His *Wanderjahre* were impoverished; and in Dresden he shared a room with two laborers serving them as cook and bootblack in return for the undisturbed daytime use of the room.[13] He found it easy to associate with and to humble himself before simple folk—a characteristic he later erected into a principle of his reformist code.

During that decade Langbehn went to absurd lengths to conceal his obscure identity, to disguise what no one was particularly anxious to discover. He alternately cherished and resented his self-constructed isolation. At times his poverty forced him to hunt up friends or generous supporters. On those rare occasions when he chose to break out of his isolation, his highly engaging traits created a favorable first impression. Tall, ascetic, and slightly melancholy, his appearance seems to have been as striking and impressive as his versatile conversation. Cornelius Gurlitt, a respected German art critic, recalled his first meeting with Langbehn: "Our disputations continued . . . [about] politics and cultural questions, poetry and science, problems of race and faith. He was my superior in all knowledge and everywhere seemed to possess opinions which to me at least were new. . . . I have never been a good dialectician, but here I encountered a razor-sharp, cold blade, swung by a fiery hand, and I was unusually powerless." Their meeting ended with Langbehn accepting a monthly subsidy of fifty marks from Gurlitt, and still the latter concurred with Langbehn's parting remark: "The time will come when you will be proud of today's conversation." [14]

Other men, no less accustomed to good conversation than Gurlitt, were also impressed by Langbehn, and even Bismarck had no regrets at having received him.* Women, in particular, were dazzled by his intellectual virtuosity; Frau Sophie Sömmering, a novelist who wrote under the pen name of Arthur Helding, remembered her first meeting with him, at which he refused to divulge his identity. She was certain, however, that he was "an important personality. . . . In his conversation he was irresistibly clever, scintillating as if filled with a thousand electric sparks." [15]

It was in the 1880's, when Langbehn lived alone and without recognition, that he developed an intense *culte du moi,* an obsession with the self, a glorification of it, an elaborate pretense of self-sufficiency. It was then that he turned his habitual narcissism—he could sit for hours before his own portrait, caressing it—into a conscious principle of life. His behavior became more and more unbalanced, and the gap between his ideal self-image and his actual conduct all the more agonizing. He craved friends and affection, only to rebuff both when he found them; he sought renown and recognition, yet devised the most elaborate disguises and feats of disappearance. He exalted as supreme such virtues as strength, health, and self-sufficiency, only to beg—insolently to be sure—for favors that would sustain him, only to be

---

* Bismarck, in 1891, is said to have invited the author of *Rembrandt als Erzieher* to his estate at Varzin. Langbehn stayed for two days, and his host later described him as "a man of child-like modesty whom one has to push into talking, which is all the stranger since he seems to write with sledgehammers." Bismarck had skimmed the *Rembrandt* and was "delighted" that it had achieved such a popular success. Max Bewer, *Bei Bismarck,* Dresden 1891, pp. 27–30.

plagued by recurrent paranoiac fears that unless he bought and prepared his own special diet, his enemies would succeed in poisoning him. He had an unbounded sense of his own importance, yet he suffered immensely from even the most innocuous, often imaginary slights. In his dealings with men and ideas, he was rigid and uncompromising; his portraits and judgments bear no nuances, no subtle shadings. Men either submitted to him totally or were cut off. His affective life, in short, was dogged by deprivation and disappointment, and his contacts with other persons, of either sex, were painful and immature. His refusal to work deepened his isolation, rendered him more dependent on the bounty of others, and made him still less capable of mastering life. Gradually he faded into a phantom world of his own, remote from reality, surrounded by books, pictures, fears, and daydreams, obsessed with thoughts about himself.*

How difficult it was for Langbehn to have any kind of

---

* Langbehn's sanity has been called into question by friends, critics, and psychiatrists. Hans Thoma, for example, believed he was "a highly intelligent man, but crazy." Herman E. Busse, ed., *Hans Thoma. Sein Leben in Selbstzeugnissen Briefen und Berichten*, Berlin, Propyläen, 1942, p. 135. Nissen, of course, insisted that his master was thoroughly sane and that his habit of breaking with people sprang from his excessively rigorous morality. The most detailed and authoritative study was made by Hans Bürger-Prinz, who thought Langbehn's works "were a good example of the complex nature of the schizophrenic form of experience and expression." He concluded that "the mixture and simultaneous presence of an inability to face life with a desire to improve the world, of infantilism, frailness and defenselessness with falseness, frigidity, and extreme aggressiveness, of autistic rejection of wealth, of bizarreness of thought, of superficiality, shallowness and rudeness—these are the major characteristics which define the case. "Über die künstlerischen Arbeiten Schizophrener," in Oswald Bumke, ed., *Handbuch der Geisteskrankheiten*, Vol. IX, part v: *Die Schizophrenie*, ed. by K. Wilmanns, Berlin, Springer, 1932, p. 692. In 1940, Bürger-Prinz returned once again to "the Langbehn case," and in his thorough study seems less certain that Langbehn was schizophrenic; he may have suffered from paranoia, but in the main, Langbehn's psychic disturbance was not attributable to the emergence of a specific disease, but to the heightening of long-present character traits. Bürger-Prinz and Segelke, *Julius Langbehn . . .* , p. 180 and chapter viii. A recent student of genius maintains that "Langbehn undoubtedly possessed many personal traits which suggest that he deviated considerably from the norm," but that this does not justify the diagnosis of schizophrenia. Rudolf K. Goldschmit-Jentner, *Vollender und Verwandler. Versuche über das Genie und seine Schicksale*, Hamburg, Wegner, 1952, pp. 196, 185–197, and *passim*.

stable relationship is exemplified by his fitful contacts with Lagarde, whom he regarded highly. He wrote to him in 1887, praising the morality and patriotism of the *Symmicta*. His first request, still modest, if somewhat unusual, was for the loan of the *Deutsche Schriften,* which he alleged he could neither buy nor borrow. He did not divulge his name: "Who I am is of no consequence, but I am a German—that I can aver." [16] A desultory correspondence (through Lagarde's publisher) sprang up, the two men met once or twice, and after two years Langbehn began to demand Lagarde's exclusive affection. To Lagarde's wife he confided: "For the present I lead an incomparably lonely existence. On top of Mont Blanc it could not be lonelier. I see much, but no one sees me." [17] In 1890, when he sought to make himself, or rather his book, visible, he tried to commandeer Lagarde's help. Lagarde should draft, or at least sign and circulate, an endorsement of it. When Lagarde hesitated, Langbehn grew testy, his deference evaporated, and thinly concealed resentment took its place. The relationship limped along; Langbehn had antagonized another benevolent supporter, and had convinced himself afresh that the world was against him.

To the outside world, and to his ever-changing, ever-shrinking group of friends, Langbehn justified his self-importance by pointing to the Rembrandt book, which he had begun immediately after his break from academic life, and which he intended as the Bible of a new, reformed Germany. For the sake of this unwritten work he made extravagant demands on friends and acquaintances. He solicited subsidies from a number of people, always assuring the donors that they were the true beneficiaries of these transactions. Generosity was to be its own reward, and he would fall into a rage if a friend dared to criticize him, or an acquaintance inquired too closely into this mysterious book for whose benefit such great sacrifices had been made.

Friends had to be exclusive lovers and dumb disciples, and any gesture of independence sufficed to arouse such jealous anger that a break became inevitable. He broke with Karl Haider, who had pleaded that he was a husband and a father as well as a friend: "Whoever avows to be my true friend must place that friendship above all else." [18] With Hans Thoma he broke because the painter refused to bar his house to old friends who displeased Langbehn. A friend of

Thoma's, who had also been a friend of Langbehn's, asked the latter why he was avoiding him: "Have I hurt your feelings? Do I offend you?" To which Langbehn replied: "Yes, if I had been God, I would have created you differently." [19]

Many friends recoiled from summonses similar in nature to this, addressed to an old comrade from the battlefield:

> I have found a vocation for you . . . namely to support me annually with a thousand marks for my living expenses and this not as a sacrifice for me, but for the fatherland. I hereby give you my word that it is a worth-while inconvenience. I conceive of this relation as a kind of life-long marriage—like the brothers Grimm, Luther and Melanchthon, etc. . . . I am certain that with this division of labor we will get along together. Of the above-mentioned pairs, one, after all, was always the less important. . . . [My duties] essentially consist of planning, not executing a reform of the entire cultural life of Germany.[20]

For a time people would respond to these pleas, then cease to do so, and funds would again become scarce. During these lean periods Langbehn had to fall back on such humiliating makeshifts as tutoring or writing occasional, anonymous articles for newspaper *feuilletons*. Any suggestion that he should seek permanent employment aroused Langbehn's suspicion that the Maecaenas was getting weary—a suspicion that sufficed to choke off any further contact. Only willing donors found admittance to the circle of Langbehn's patrons.

In the winter of 1889–90, Langbehn interrupted the composition of his book and embarked on one of the oddest adventures of his life. Having heard of Nietzsche's collapse, he resolved "to save" him, and, though a stranger to Nietzsche and to his family, he implored Nietzsche's mother to leave her son in his charge. Frau Nietzsche welcomed Langbehn warmly, authorized his visits to the Jena asylum, and exclaimed to her daughter that "God has sent me an angel." [21] For two weeks Langbehn talked and walked with Nietzsche every day, and with great satisfaction reported that he had succeeded in rekindling Nietzsche's intellectual interest and in winning his intense gratitude.* Simultaneously he launched

---

* Langbehn's comments about Nietzsche were couched in condescending sentimentality; to Nietzsche's mother he wrote that her son's "memory and knowledge are astonishing. . . . He is a child and a king, and he must be treated as the royal child that he is—that is the only proper method." Quoted in Carl Albrecht Bernoulli, *Franz Overbeck und*

a campaign of vilification against the asylum physicians and sought to poison Frau Nietzsche's mind against two of Nietzsche's friends, Peter Gast and Franz Overbeck. Langbehn insisted that he alone could rescue her son from his afflictions, if only she would entrust the patient to his exclusive care. Nothing less than formal guardianship would do, and he proposed to remove Nietzsche to Dresden and place him there under his sole supervision. Frau Nietzsche would have to sign the following pledge: "The undersigned binds herself under oath . . . to avoid all written and oral communication with her son Friedrich Nietzsche," except by permission of Langbehn, the guardian.[22] At this, even Frau Nietzsche balked, whereupon Langbehn angrily rescinded the offer. Franz Overbeck naturally objected to this interloper and finally persuaded the mother and Peter Gast that Nietzsche should be shielded from him. Langbehn left Jena when Nietzsche, while being lectured by his visitor, flew into a rage, overthrew the table in the room, and stormed out of Langbehn's presence. Nietzsche, it will be recalled, still had sustained periods of lucidity at that time.

Although Langbehn's intellectual relation to Nietzsche is obscure, there is no doubt that he felt a particular affinity for the lonely prophet. Langbehn expected to play a role analogous to Nietzsche's, only greater, purer, and more constructive. I think it probable that Langbehn thought his *culte du moi* and his idiosyncrasies of style were Nietzschean, just as later on young would-be geniuses mastered the gestures, but not the qualities, of Nietzschean greatness. Nietzsche, after all, had boasted of his loneliness, had retired to the magnificent isolation of the Engadine—though he had preserved, unknown to the public, a circle of trusted friends. Langbehn's rescue operation presaged, in melodramatic fashion, how the sickliest elements of German life were later

---

Friedrich Nietzsche. Eine Freundschaft, Jena 1908, II, 317. A decade later, after Nietzsche's death, Langbehn wrote to Bishop Keppler about Nietzsche's character, which he admired, and his work, which he detested: " 'Atheists' like Shelley and 'Anti-Christs' like Nietzsche are simply truant school boys whom one has to bring to the correct path. In regard to Nietzsche I had this very intention, but circumstances were stronger than I was. . . . I cannot read a page without, quite literally, becoming physically ill. I consider him, in short, a pure soul, into which the devil entered." Quoted in Nissen, *Der Rembrandtdeutsche*, pp. 132–133.

to swoop down on a defenseless Nietzsche, and appropriate him for their own purposes.

Once more in Dresden, Langbehn made the final arrangements for the launching of his book. He expected that his *Rembrandt als Erzieher* would not only take its place alongside Nietzsche's *Thoughts Out of Season* and Lagarde's *Deutsche Schriften,* but would surpass both in popularity and lasting influence. Despite its wretched style, its disjointedness and intermittent triviality, his book, written according to the title page "by a German" and published by the Leipzig firm of C. L. Hirschfeld in January, 1890, had an instantaneous success. Langbehn himself directed the publicity, and the phenomenal sale of the book was in part due to his remarkable business acumen. His preparatory circular announced the book as a "bugle call to the young and aspiring German generation of today which represents the future. To secure the greatest possible audience for this book its price was fixed at only two marks." *

The author's anonymity heightened its appeal. Langbehn's name would have meant nothing to the public, but the mystery invited literary guesswork, and the book was variously attributed to Lagarde, Nietzsche, Hinzpeter, who had been William II's tutor, numerous divines, and a host of other notable contemporaries. Lagarde was most often mentioned as the likely author.† In the first two years, the book went through thirty-nine editions.[23] Even after publication, Langbehn continually revised the book; in 1891, for the thirty-

---

* I found a copy of the circular in the Lagarde Archive. The publisher had been most hesitant to plunge into this venture, and consented only when Langbehn's friend, Woldemar von Seidlitz, guaranteed the printing costs. The publisher, moreover, was outraged by Langbehn's unalterable insistence that the book must sell for no more than two marks, and he was reconciled to such unorthodoxy only when Langbehn accepted his condition that he should receive no royalties. "Money is dirt," Langbehn told the incredulous publisher. Bürger-Prinz and Segelke, *Julius Langbehn,* p. 82.

† Even before Langbehn "revealed" himself to Lagarde, the latter had guessed that Langbehn was the author. Lagarde certainly did not want to be held responsible for the book; the Lagarde Collection of the University Heights Library of New York University includes Lagarde's copy of the Rembrandt book, in which are inscribed in his own handwriting scathing comments about Langbehn's many stylistic infelicities. See also Lagarde, *Ausgewählte Schriften,* p. 281, for his repudiation of the authorship.

seventh edition, he added two new chapters, one in praise of anti-Semitism, the other in restrained appreciation of the Catholic Church.

The book turned out to be a critical as well as a commercial success. Many leading critics wrote searching, and on the whole favorable reviews; this astounding reception I shall discuss in chapter 10. In two years' time, however, interest waned, and the book gradually disappeared from the book stores. Its influence persisted, though in a more subterranean fashion.

Encouraged by this acclaim, Langbehn hoped to score another hit, this time with a slim collection of his poems. But this second venture, *Forty Poems,* by an author again identified as "a German," proved to be an unmitigated fiasco.* The poems were not only bad stylistically, but bordered on the pornographic. The state prosecutor of Schleswig-Holstein threatened to launch a suit, and Langbehn quickly disappeared from sight in order to escape legal proceedings. The book was withdrawn, despite Langbehn's insistence that in the light of his personal purity the charge of indecency was ludicrous. To be sure, only a few of the poems were erotic, but these were coldly explicit about the pleasures of sexual gratification.[24] Almost all express a desperate craving for friends, for love, erotic or Platonic. What prompted him to publish these poems is not clear, especially as he always boasted—probably with justification, and repressed regret—of his chastity and purity. Gurlitt suggested that his purpose in publishing the questionable poems—and Langbehn had alluded to a purpose—may have been to forestall any condescending criticism of his asexual life.[25] Many of his friends recoiled from these poems, and their repugnance deepened his sense of isolation. It confirmed his suspicion that, his initial success notwithstanding, he remained misunderstood. The few friends who remonstrated with him directly were dropped with deliberate brusqueness.

Shortly after this episode, Langbehn made one last effort to revive the popularity of his first book; he published, again

* Glöss, the publisher, nevertheless had a marble plaque erected on his house, on which in gold letters was written: "In this house were printed the *Forty Poems. By a German.*" See F. W. Glöss, "Der Rembrandt-deutsche," *Die Zukunft,* LXX (January 15, 1910), 95, who added that Langbehn never paid his share of the printing costs.

at Glöss, *Der Rembrandtdeutsche, von einem Wahrheits-freund* (by a friend of truth). The book reprinted two favorable reviews of the Rembrandt book by P. W. von Keppler, Catholic professor of theology at Tübingen and later bishop of Rottenburg, and added 666 epigrams by and about Langbehn, although a few were contributed by Max Bewer and Heinrich Pudor.* The imperious demands for help which he had previously served on his friends were now brought before the public, mixed again with a strong dose of self-adulation. Even his devoted disciple, Nissen, found the book full of "intellectual arrogance and unbounded pride." [26]

After these two failures, Langbehn completely vanished from the public eye; neither his remaining friends nor his publishers could find him. In 1891, he returned to Kiel for a short time, but his "free manner with the [male] students was often misconstrued." [27] In anger, Langbehn resigned from Teutonia, his old student fraternity, and went back to Dresden. He left Dresden shortly afterward in order to escape another subpoena served in connection with the *Forty Poems,* and settled in Vienna. There he compounded his isolation by living as a recluse, eating simple vegetarian fare which no one but he himself could prepare. Even here he had a brush with the law, this time because his landlord objected to his having had twenty-five trees cut down in the garden, without permission, because "they impaired his view." Three trials ensued, Langbehn was found guilty in each, but he fled the country before the judgments could be enforced.

It was about this time, during his hermit-like existence, that his great desire for a disciple was at last fulfilled. In 1891, he met the Frisian painter Nissen, nineteen years younger than himself, who became his follower and remained loyal until his master's death. Nissen pledged his complete subordination to Langbehn who accepted him as "helpmate, secretary, servant, and sworn friend." [28] The close companionship never led to equality or intimacy; the familiar *du* was banned forever. Langbehn at once began the education of his disciple by making him conscious of his deficiencies, and Nissen gratefully recorded the stages of his intellectual improvement. He was particularly struck by Langbehn's despair

---

* With Max Bewer he broke a short time later, when he discovered that this vigorous anti-Semite had a Jewish mother. Bürger-Prinz and Segelke, *Julius Langbehn,* p. 98.

over Germany's political future; Langbehn believed that only men like Vienna's demagogic mayor Karl Lueger offered any hope at all.*

Threatened by numerous law suits, Langbehn reluctantly left Vienna and, in 1894, visited Italy, southern France, the Basque coast and the Canary Islands. A year later, he was forced to return to Germany, and the search for funds started again. Rather than interrupt his own unfettered life, he persuaded Nissen to settle down as a portrait painter in Hamburg in order to support them both. In the meantime, he continued his travels, settling briefly in Lübeck, then moving on to Rotterdam and Würzburg. During those last years as a solitary wanderer, he so deliberately flaunted his incognito that landlords frequently suspected him of being a fugitive from justice or an escaped lunatic.

Harried, homeless, intermittently insolvent, his life by then knew neither joy nor recognition, nor even companionship. Old friends he had rebuffed, new ones he found more and more difficult to make, and his one disciple was usually far away. Nothing was left but the belief in his own mission, and for its sake he refused all work that might delay his projected reforms. He allowed an ever wider gulf to separate him from society, and in the end he turned his back on the world of art as well. Walls of his own making were to shield him from enemies of his own fancy. His energy flagged, his creative powers were dissipated, and during the last fifteen years of his life he produced virtually nothing.

In this decade of isolation, after the publication of the Rembrandt book, Langbehn gradually drew closer to Catholicism. Despite his earlier criticisms of the Roman Church, his cultural aspirations had never been fundamentally antithetical to the Church. He had sought a national rebirth through art, but art he regarded as synonymous with mysticism, and hence a form of religion. Rembrandt was the symbol of that reform, the resurrected prophet who could destroy the false art of naturalism and, by his example, prove that the goal of art was not the creation of beauty alone, but the attainment of the most sublime and fullest truth. In the search for that truth, Langbehn believed art and religion

---

* Nissen, *Der Rembrandtdeutsche*, pp. 220, 342. Only a few years later, Adolf Hitler concluded that Lueger "was the greatest German mayor of all times." Hitler, *Mein Kampf*, New York 1940, p. 72.

coincided, both alike mediating between man and the divine.
At the very time of his retreat from art, Catholics alone seemed to reach out to him; amidst growing indifference to his work and program, encouragement came only from them. On his travels he felt that the people in Catholic lands exuded a joy of life, a natural virtue, and a child-like goodness that had long since disappeared from Protestant areas. In the mid-1890's, he first began attending Catholic services, and rejoiced in the esthetic pleasure which they afforded him. In 1898, he begged Bishop Keppler to help him find the road to faith. Their active and intimate correspondence demonstrated that Langbehn's conversion was not the result of an intellectual quest: "I have ever been a child and precisely as such do I feel myself drawn to the motherly character of the Catholic Church . . . it means spiritually to return to the womb." *

Langbehn, who had always demanded total subordination from his friends and disciples, did not withhold his own from the Church. He rejoiced in the authority of the Church, adored the legends of the saints and of their miracles and insisted that these supernatural works vouchsafed the truth of the traditions of the Church. At the beginning of his formal instruction, he avowed his belief in all the dogmas of the Church; the very haste of this acceptance disconcerted his Dominican instructor, who feared that emotional fervor was usurping the place of the proper study of theology.[29] The dogma which Langbehn most readily accepted was original sin: "We are born with a heavy sin, and most men acquire heavy sin." [30]

As a last loving gesture for lower Germany (*Niederdeutschland*), Langbehn resolved to enter the Church in Rotterdam. During January, 1900, he was instructed in the faith by a Dominican priest, in February he was baptized, and a month later he received his first communion. Ecstatically he reported to Nissen that his happiness was now complete.

---

* *Langbehn-Briefe an Bischof Keppler*, ed. by Benedikt Momme Nissen, Freiburg im Breisgau 1937, p. 1, letter of March 3, 1899. Keppler had long been an outspoken critic of German society and especially of the Jewish influence on it: "[The Jews] are a thorn in the flesh of Christian peoples, suck their blood, enslave them with chains of gold and with the tin sceptre of poisoned pens, and contaminate the public fountains of culture and morality." Quoted in Ludwig Schemann, *Die Rasse in den Geisteswissenschaften*, München 1928, I, 385.

Soon after his conversion, Langbehn resumed his tasks as a reformer, this time of the Church itself. He denounced the "liberal" wing of the Roman Catholic Church which sought to compromise with modern culture. He exhorted Keppler to fight secular education and to reaffirm the sanctity and the unbroken tradition of the Church. In 1902, for the last time, Langbehn's call for reform reached a wide audience; in a sermon largely written by Langbehn, Bishop Keppler condemned liberal Catholicism and counseled steadfast adherence to the fundamental dogmas of the Church. He warned against all attempts to conquer the evils of modern culture by compromising with their defenders, and the entire sermon breathed Langbehn's undiminished hatred of the modern intellectual. Keppler's defiant words were widely discussed and even Pope Leo XIII expressed "the greatest joy" at reading this rebuff to the movement of modernism.[31] Langbehn, however, wanted to push the struggle even further, and shortly after this speech quarreled with the bishop. Keppler wrote him that from now on "each has to go his own way and serve God according to his own conscience." [32] Langbehn plunged into the struggle for Catholicism with the same self-assurance with which he had fought for the Rembrandt reform; at times he was afraid of his own certainty: "I feel so strong intellectually—in gifts and knowledge—that I fear it will keep me not so much from humility as from true simplicity [*Einfalt*]." [33]

Nissen followed Langbehn into the Catholic Church; in 1903, the two men settled in Munich where Nissen continued to earn their joint livelihood by painting. Just before his break with Bishop Keppler, Langbehn begged him to secure Nissen the permission to paint Pope Leo XIII. This was granted, and both Nissen and Langbehn went to Rome where the portrait was executed and the pope received the two converts in an audience for pilgrims.

In the last years before his death, Langbehn wrote almost nothing, but continued to ponder the reform of Catholicism. The old hope of the Counter Reformation, the reconciliation of the Protestants, ran strong in him, and he thought seriously of taking up lay preaching. In 1906, he and Nissen traveled to Switzerland and then spent the winter in Salzburg. Their return to Munich in the early spring of the following year coincided with the rapid decline of Langbehn's health; on

April 30, 1907, on his way south to a warmer climate, he died of cancer of the stomach.

Nissen, his companion on this trip, now had to fulfill his last orders. Langbehn, still alternately seeking and rebuffing the world around him, had insisted that his death must remain a secret and had asked to be buried in the small Bavarian hamlet of Puch, under a linden tree, which had served as shelter for Saint Edigna, a French princess, who in the twelfth century had forsaken royal pomp to save her soul as a hermit. There Nissen buried him and placed a stone marked J. A. L. over his grave. Only years later, and amidst an acrimonious controversy, did the public penetrate Langbehn's last secret.[34]

8: Art and the

Revolt against Modernity

> *To lead men back to natural spontaneity and simplicity, away from the artificial and the artful, that is my true vocation.* LANGBEHN

Langbehn's book was like his life: obscure, confused, and contradictory. The very title, *Rembrandt als Erzieher*, set the tone of vague allusiveness, at once suggestive and mysterious.* Despite a brave show of order and organization—the book was divided into five main parts, each part painstakingly divided under some thirty titled subsections—it was a thoroughly undisciplined, undigested work. There was little coherence and less logic as Langbehn playfully skipped from topic to topic, from idea to idea, alternating triviality with prophecy, personal impressions and prejudices with penetrating insights and bold ideas for reforms. The aphoristic style, contrived, cumbersome, and clumsily imitative of Nietzsche's later prose, heightened the sense of chaos which the book exuded.† Add to this the incessant and banal play on words,

---

* Langbehn's title, it is assumed, was suggested by Nietzsche's *Schopenhauer als Erzieher;* Goethe had entitled a short note, *Rembrandt als Denker.* After Langbehn's success, this form proliferated and a number of brochures appeared, offering, satirically or seriously, Bismarck, Moses, Moltke, and Höllenbreughel as educators. In 1894, Friedrich Naumann wrote his pamphlet on Jesus' social gospel, *Jesus als Volksmann.* After the war Martin Havenstein's *Nietzsche als Erzieher,* Berlin 1922, was published.

† This lack of order and organization attested Langbehn's unsystematic mind and his haphazard way of preparing the Rembrandt book. In the early 1880's, a university friend discovered that Langbehn was collecting a vast miscellany of information under a great many unconnected headings. This must have been the beginning of the Rembrandt book —disjointed notes, bits of unrelated knowledge, which in the end were placed, seemingly at random, in his great mosaic. Langbehn also corresponded with various acquaintances, hoping to elicit some expert substantiation for his wild deductions in all sorts of highly technical

the tiresomely pretentious derivation of meanings from words and names, the whole display of a kind of mystical philology, and one wonders how this wearisome diatribe could have attained such popularity.

But what would be deficiencies in a work of scholarship may be assets in a work of prophecy. Chaos and absurdity may suggest great, impenetrable depths, and repetition may weary the reader into belief. Idiosyncratic forms of construction and punctuation suggest an irrepressible individuality, and the absence of such pedestrian qualities as the acknowledgments of intellectual debts, is surely proof of genius. Secular prophets can dispense with gods or footnotes. It sufficed that Langbehn scattered the names of all great culture-heroes throughout the book, and thus displayed his erudition. He leapt from laments to prophecies, from wild charges against the present to sublime visions of the future. But no argument, no bridge of reason that could be challenged or discussed—nothing, except an occasional foe or scapegoat that accounts for the presence of evil. Such a book is nearly impervious to criticism; it is either ignored or celebrated. Langbehn's Rembrandt was celebrated because it expressed that curious mood of despair and hope that had suddenly gripped so many Germans.

Rembrandt als Erzieher defies classification; one fact alone is clear, that it has precious little to do with the real, the historic Rembrandt. This is neither a biography nor a study in esthetics; Langbehn's Rembrandt was the personification of a cultural ideal, just as Nietzsche's attack on David Friedrich Strauss was a polemic not against a man, but against a state of mind and a cultural condition. Langbehn's work ranged far and wide over countless topics, but its mood and purpose are inescapably clear. Rembrandt, perfect German and incomparable artist, was pictured as the antithesis of modern culture and as the only possible model for Germany's "third reformation." * He was the ideal type, the measure

---

fields. Cf. Hermann Brunn, "Julius Langbehn, Karl Haider, Heinrich von Brunn," *Deutsche Rundschau*, CCXVIII (January, 1929), 32.

* Luther's first reformation, rooted in the German people, was partly undone by the second, or Lessing's, reformation which, emanating from the mind, failed to reach the masses. Rembrandt's reformation would be a synthesis of the previous two. *Rembrandt als Erzieher. Von einem Deutschen*, 33d ed., Leipzig 1891, pp. 165–170. Hereafter cited as *Rembrandt*.

of all things: "An attempt is made . . . not to measure a man by his age—but an age, today's present—by a man." [1] The age, needless to say, was made to suffer from this preposterous effort to compare incommensurables. Langbehn's Rembrandt embodied the highest form of life, art, and individuality. Present-day Germans, on the other hand, were depicted as pygmies, torn from their native soil and tribe, enslaved by a corrupt kind of learning. They were not masters of the right kind of mystical art. Rembrandt should point the way to the restoration for man and society of all the life-affirming qualities: simplicity, spontaneity, intuition. Science, commerce, and technology must vanish; art, individuality, and the primitive life should be enthroned as the deities of the new age.

Langbehn lacked the critical faculty which alone could have cast his intuitive impressions and vague aspirations into some kind of an analytical scheme or order. What emerged instead was a crude, even absurd, *Weltanschauung,* a pseudo-religious, philosophical, mystical way of looking at the world, a characteristic mixture of thought and dream that has enjoyed great popularity in modern, secular Germany.[2] The core of Langbehn's *Weltanschauung* was negative and nostalgic. He rejected contemporary culture, sneered at reason and feared science, and the temper of his criticism evinced a desire not so much for the reform as for the annihilation of modern society. This rejection of modernity, and of the rational-scientific tradition which he identified with it, was the pervasive element of the book. However incoherent its expression, the book was dominated by a consistent aspiration toward a form of primitivism which, after the destruction of the existing society, aimed at the release of man's elemental passions and the creation of a new Germanic society based on Art, Genius, and Power.

Langbehn had several reasons for seizing upon Rembrandt as the prophet of this new society, not the least of which was his own devotion to the painter, an esthetic judgment in advance of the popular revival of Rembrandt in our own century.* Rembrandt's chiaroscuro suggested the mysterious

---

* Langbehn's choice of Rembrandt was undoubtedly influenced by the fact that among his patrons in the 1880's were some of the leading Rembrandt scholars of Germany, notably Woldemar von Seidlitz and Wilhelm Bode. The well-known Hamburg museum director, Alfred

depths and contradictions of human life, and for Langbehn this was clear proof that the knowledge intuited by art was far superior to the knowledge deduced or researched by science. The "dark" side of Rembrandt, the anticlassical bent which made the age of Enlightenment neglect him, derived from a kind of simple religion of awe and faith, not of dogma. Except for Shakespeare, who appears as the lesser hero of the book, Langbehn could not have selected an artist more easily converted into his kind of ideal. Fact and fantasy mingled of course, and fantasy predominated, but Rembrandt at least allowed for a considerable measure of verisimilitude.*

Lichtwark, with whom Langbehn had been in close touch, was particularly insistent that the exclusive hold which classical and Renaissance painting had on German sensibility should be broken, and that the study and appreciation of Dutch art, especially of Rembrandt, should be cultivated. In 1886, he complained that "with us, there has not yet grown up a generation that had implanted in it the same yearning for Rembrandt's art that is drilled into us for Raphael's art." Rembrandt "reached the highest intensity of life's truth." Alfred Lichtwark, "Rembrandt und die holländische Kunst," in *Eine Auswahl seiner Schriften*, ed. by Wolf Mannhardt, Berlin 1917, II, 261–262. Nor was it entirely novel to dwell on Rembrandt the thinker; the leading French critic, Eugène Fromentin, in his epoch-making *Les Maîtres d'Autrefois*, published in 1875, spoke of Rembrandt as performing "the labor of an analyzer, a distiller, or to speak more nobly, of a metaphysician, rather than a poet. . . . By this faculty of second sight, thanks to his somnambulistic intuition, he sees farther in the supernatural than any one." (Quoted from the translation, *The Old Masters of Belgium and Holland*, Boston 1882, p. 311.) Langbehn of course popularized this view of Rembrandt, and his work quickened the Rembrandt cult which permeated the prewar generation in Germany. Two years after his book appeared, modern girls began sporting Rembrandt hats (see the stage instructions to Gerhart Hauptmann's *Kollege Crampton*, 1892). For Germans, Rembrandt came to be a unique culture hero, a master artist and philosopher. The sociologist Georg Simmel, who had given Langbehn's book a sympathetic review, wrote the most serious appreciation in this genre, *Rembrandt. Ein kunstphilosophischer Versuch*, 2d ed., Leipzig 1919, in which he elaborated some of Langbehn's themes and emphasized Rembrandt's Germanic individualism and anticlassicism. Other writers, notably Spengler and Alfred Weber, continued this tradition.

* Langbehn's book received favorable, if occasionally puzzled, notices from Rembrandt scholars. The first such review was by Wilhelm Bode, and appeared in the eminently respectable *Preussische Jahrbücher*, LXV:3 (March, 1890), 301–314: "Although Rembrandt is only the thread by which the author unfolds his tapestry, his appraisal of the great master is based on the knowledge of his works and a fine understanding of his nature. What he says about him is often new and

There was as well the proper relationship between man and artist, between wretchedness and genius, to fit the idealized image of the artist in distress. Rembrandt's paintings captured the inexplicable elements of his being and of mankind, and his art—as his life—was defiantly individualistic. It was this unconquerable individuality of Rembrandt which should inspire the Germans to throw off the pettiness and passivity of their present lives. Finally the book extolled Rembrandt for his spontaneity, willfulness, and above all for his untranslatable quality of *Volksthümlichkeit*—belonging to, expressing, yet transcending his people and its traditions.* Rembrandt was "the most German of German artists," or more precisely, the most *Niederdeutsche,* the greatest representative of the most creative tribe of Germans.† By his *Volksthümlichkeit,* Rembrandt should inspire the Germans to return to the sources of their unity and individuality, to their oldest popular traditions. Only by being themselves, by belonging to their people and accepting their past, could present-day Germans become free individuals again.

---

surprising, always brilliant and presented with the warmth of glowing admiration for the artist. . . . [The book] is certain of a distinguished place in the Rembrandt literature" (p. 303). The French scholar Emile Michel reviewed it in his article "Les biographes et les critiques de Rembrandt," *Revue des Deux Mondes,* CVIII:3 (December 1, 1891), 652–660. Carl Neumann's authoritative study, *Rembrandt,* devotes eight pages to Langbehn and concluded: "*Rembrandt als Erzieher* is not a work of art history. But the world of art would do well to ponder what has been rightly felt in this book and to grasp the phenomenon of Rembrandt in such a way that its full force be made fruitful for our art as well as our life." 3d rev. ed., München, Bruckmann, 1922, I, 30.

* *Volksthümlichkeit* has no exact English equivalent. Father Jahn first used it in his book, *Deutsches Volksthum,* 1810, and meant the unique character of one nation as against other nations. Soon after Jahn and long before Langbehn, the term lost its original meaning and came to signify qualities of the lower classes, of the uneducated, the uninhibited. This is Langbehn's sense. "A man of the people" suggests a similar meaning, but lacks the mystical implications of the German phrase. See Jakob and Wilhelm Grimm, *Deutsches Wörterbuch,* Vol. XII, part 2, Leipzig, Hirzel, 1951, p. 499.

† In the next chapter we shall see how important this concept of *Niederdeutschland* was for Langbehn. He meant by it his native region of northwestern Germany as well as the spirit of this allegedly self-contained tribe of unspoiled, sturdy peasants who alone had remained truly Germanic. Linguistically *hochdeutsch* had replaced *niederdeutsch,* but Langbehn championed its surviving form, *plattdeutsch.*

Rembrandt was a man of infinite contradictions, and Langbehn fastened on this rather human quality as proof that all contradictions in thought and society could be reconciled, if only the will to harmony would find the right formula. If Rembrandt could transcend his own contradictions and achieve greatness, then, Langbehn argued—in a characteristic flight of illogic—every man and every people could. In this and other ways, Langbehn used the Rembrandt symbol as the means of verbally reconciling antitheses, of creating a specious harmony out of conflict and diversity, and of conquering complexity by fashioning verbal formulas. In Langbehn's hands, the symbol, by being confused with reality and endowed with a life and a force of its own, lost all its meaning.

Rembrandt of course *can* instruct, but not if this education is taken literally, not if real conflicts in politics or philosophy are resolved by a sort of Rembrandt mediation.* Langbehn had a passion for "thirds," for syntheses, for a higher form which would reconcile and combine in a new form previous antitheses. He expected that these abstruse "reconciliations" or syntheses—vague adaptations of Hegel's dialectics—would be actualized by society; his faith in the power of abstractions was great—and attractive to his readers.

Langbehn's opening sentences, often cited by later writers, informed the reader of the range of his cultural criticism:

It has gradually become an open secret that the contemporary spiritual life of the German people is in a state of slow decay; according to some, even of rapid decay. Science everywhere is dissipated into specialization; in the field of thought and literature, the epoch-making individuals are missing. The visual arts, though represented by significant masters, lack monumentality; . . . musicians are rare, performers abound. Without question the de-

---

* Nietzsche wrote of Schopenhauer: "The most difficult task remains: to say how a new circle of duties may spring from this ideal, and how one can connect oneself through ordinary activity with such a transcendental goal, in short, to prove that this ideal *educates.*" And Nietzsche answered concretely: "These new duties are not those of a lonely individual, but one belongs with them to a mighty society, held together not by external rites and laws, but by a fundamental idea. It is the fundamental idea of culture itself, in so far as culture places before each of us only one task. *To promote the creation of the philosopher, of the artist, and of the saint within and without us and thus to contribute to the perfection of nature.*" See *Schopenhauer als Erzieher*, in *Nietzsche's Werke*, Leipzig, Naumann, 1906, II, 256, 263–264.

mocratizing leveling atomistic tendency of this country expresses
itself in all this. Moreover, the entire culture of the present is . . .
turned backward; it is less concerned with the creation of new
values than with the cataloguing of old ones. . . . The more
scientific it [culture] becomes, the less creative it will be.[3]

One theme dominated the entire book: German culture was
being destroyed by science and intellectualism and could be
regenerated only through the resurgence of art and the rise
to power of great, artistic individuals in a new society.

Hatred of science dominated all of Langbehn's thought
just as hatred of liberalism had dominated Lagarde's thought.
Neither critic defined the object of his hatred, and in reality
for both of them the two terms had become synonyms for
evil. To Langbehn science signified positivism, rationalism,
empiricism, mechanistic materialism, technology, skepticism,
dogmatism, and specialization, in fact everything but the disinterested and devoted quest for knowledge. He loathed
science both for what it was and for what it did. He hated
men who, in Wordsworth's phrase, "murder to dissect," who
disembowel the living for the sake of an abstraction or a
formula. Undoubtedly he hated science as well because it
presumed to penetrate the mystery of life and nature, to make
comprehensible a universe that Langbehn wanted left
shrouded in poetic obscurity. "Has the scientific, specialized,
microscopic culture of today advanced the human soul in
any important way?"[4] The impatience which had driven him
from the laboratory and the exuberance which had led him
to art inspired his book; and his impulsive choice of a profession, now given some intellectual justification, was meant
to encourage others to accept and relish their antiscientific
inclinations.*

Langbehn had good reason to single out natural science
as the dominant element in German intellectual life, and his
confused misunderstanding of it paralleled, in an exaggerated
form, the uncertainties of the scientists themselves. By the
mid-nineteenth century, the natural scientists in Germany had

---

* Nor was there anything exclusively German about this revulsion from
science. Johan Huizinga, in his splendid *Mein Weg zur Geschichte,*
Basel 1947, recalled a movement of the eighties in Holland, "which
taught us to put science way below art, to seek our true life in our own
innermost depth—which was a great blessing—and not to care about
politics and such things, which was a great error" (p. 22).

won their battle against the *Naturphilosophen* and were gradually tightening their hold upon the universities. For so long under the tutelage of philosophers and metaphysicians, the scientists in their triumph disavowed philosophy entirely and proposed to build their systems merely on "facts," gathered in minute research, arranged by inductive reasoning and tested by rigorous experiments. The ideal of science, endowed with the prestige of success and the moral justification of devoted, often self-effacing service to truth, won acceptance in ever new fields. The ethos of the scientist represented the most marvelously disciplined faith in human intellect. Scientific specialization followed and was rewarded by startling discoveries in new and autonomous subjects, but some of these discoveries, such as those in physiology and psychology, were particularly objectionable to a mystic and a vitalist like Langbehn. Helmholtz demonstrated that optical and physiological phenomena could be reduced to quantitative relations measurable in terms of classical mechanics, and Wundt made a number of analogous discoveries in psychology. While their diligent students painstakingly toiled in these newly established fields, bolder spirits, led by the enormously successful popularizers Büchner, Moleschott, and Haeckel, threw all scientific caution to the winds, and, generalizing from these beginnings, preached a scientific materialism that was more comprehensive but no less crude than that of some of the late eighteenth-century philosophers.* In this view of the universe, only matter—that is, the atom in its infinite combinations—had reality; the human mind and will as independent forces were condemned as the figments of the "idealistic" imagination. A few scientists protested against this new metaphysics, but neither their colleagues nor the larger public paid them any heed, and their ineffectual words do not invalidate the conclusion of a foremost student of this period: "The history of nineteenth-century Germany dis-

---

* They *did* preach: The association of German Monists, founded in 1904, sponsored Monistic Sunday sermons, many of them delivered by Haeckel's disciple, Wilhelm Ostwald. Frederic Lilge, *The Abuse of Learning. The Failure of the German University*, New York 1948, pp. 81–82, as well as the chapter "The Idolatry of Science." For a description of these sermons, which were a mixture of popular science and ethics, and for their role in German cultural life, see Hedda Eulenberg, *Im Doppelglück von Kunst und Leben*, Düsseldorf n.d. (*ca.* 1950), pp. 148–163.

closes the detachment [of the sciences] from speculative thought and the magnificent expansion of specialized scientific fields, but it discloses as well that simultaneously and because of this, the tradition of universal and humanistic thought vanished." [5]

Langbehn's onslaught on science and scientism coincided in time but not in spirit or method with the beginning of a world-wide critique of the philosophical foundations and the cultural effects of mechanistic science and of positivism particularly. This wider movement necessarily lies outside the purview of this study, but even a mere listing of the outstanding figures—Nietzsche, Butler, James, Dilthey, Bergson, and Freud—reminds one of the seriousness, the power, and the ultimate success of this group. Despite important individual differences, together they achieved the overthrow of dogmatic scientism.[6] In the face of their critical thought, many of the mechanistic and simplicistic concepts of scientism had to be abandoned. It was they who created the bases for modern psychology and physics, and for much of the recent thought in philosophy and history. Langbehn had nothing in common with these men save that all attacked late nineteenth-century science; Langbehn's intent, temperament, training, and above all, the quality of his mind, set him apart.

There were some superficial similarities between Langbehn's charges and those of Nietzsche, but it would be wrong to infer from this an influence or an identity of views. Both quarreled with the dominant tendencies of the time; but Nietzsche attacked science because of the increasing narrowness of this particular generation of scientists. He was anti-Darwin because the Darwinists violated his view of human freedom, and he was critical of mechanistic, soulless science. But his roots were deep in the Western humanistic and scientific tradition, and he sought to preserve the freedom and intellectual vitality of that tradition from the dogmatism of an ephemeral aberration. Langbehn's attack, on the other hand, was the irritated gesture of a man unwilling to admit the validity of science, unwilling to recognize the supremacy of intellect, unwilling even to study the findings of science. His was the prototype of the modern antiscientific temperament, yearning for mystery and religion, and disdainful of intellectual effort.

He allowed the possibility of science, provided it would turn into an intuitive, mystical endeavor: "Only a science of laws, a science of the spirit [*Geist*] can really be called a science and that kind of science stands close to art." The inductive method, Langbehn averred, could never lead to an understanding of what he alternately dubbed *Geist des Ganzen* or *Tektonik der Natur;* only after the structure had been intuitively grasped could the facts acquire meaning. As a positive example of this "science" he cited Goethe's theory of colors and asserted that its total wrongness was preferable to, say, Darwin's "partial" truths. The latter, whom he considered the most representative scientist of the age, "delivered bricks, not buildings" and should have enunciated a cosmological theory which would have lent meaning to the facts of evolution. Germany's "greatest scientist" had been Kepler, whose scientific work proceeded from an artistic impulse, from the search for harmony.* Following Kepler's example, "real" science should spring from intuition and thus the mystical element of science would be reinstated. In any case, "the vocation of science is to submerge [*untergehen*] itself in art, for such a submission [*Untergang*] only marks its exaltation." [7]

Contemporary scientists, as well as most humanists and historians, were far from capitulating to art or intuition. They were concerned with facts, and they knew that the search for truth depended on painstaking toil and unswerving impartiality. But in Langbehn's view, scientific work required unbounded subjectivity; scientists should rely primarily on their judgment and sentiment.

The final end of false science is to register facts, the final end of true science is to pronounce value judgments. Of course the latter must precede the former, and the false science is false precisely because it is only half a science. . . . [The academics'] 'objectivity,' which treats all things as equal is just as untruthful as that modern 'humanitarianism' which treats all men as equal.

---

* By an odd coincidence, a group of neo-vitalists, believers in the life force and opponents of the Monistic Association, organized the *Keplerbund* in 1907. Theobald Ziegler, *Die geistigen und sozialen Strömungen Deutschlands im neunzehnten Jahrhundert*, Berlin 1911, pp. 315 and 329. See also Hans Driesch, *Geschichte des Vitalismus*, Leipzig, Barth, 1922, chapters 2–4, for a discussion of vitalism since 1850.

Quoting Swedenborg, he charged that this false kind of science was dull, that it did not "speak with the light cheerful voice of the heart,"—science as child's play.[8]

Nowhere was subjectivity more essential than in historical work, where, Langbehn charged, Ranke's prescription of objectivity had produced sterility. Here of course Langbehn was presaging a more general and critical appeal for subjectivity, as demonstrated, for example, in the writings of Dilthey and Croce. In his attacks on contemporary historians Langbehn singled out Mommsen and likened him in his exclusively intellectual outlook to Erasmus; both, he said, had sacrificed their souls to their intellects and Mommsen would share Erasmus's fate of being forgotten by the German people. It is ironic that Mommsen should have been his principal target: Mommsen, more than many of his colleagues, allowed his political passions to inform his great narrative work.

Historians should not only be subjective but also patriotic and "racial." They should take full cognizance of the psychic factors in the history of peoples. The next great task should be a collective history of "German folk customs, costumes, and physical characteristics" which would quicken national consciousness. Historians must above all remember that "the water of objectivity is good; but the wine of enthusiasm must not be left out; only the two together yield the right mixture." [9]

Langbehn was merely stating a cultural fact when he linked science and increased academic specialization, but by a characteristic simplification he distorted the significance of specialization: "The men of intellect, today no rarer nor of lower quality than ever, are being practically ground to pieces by the great mill of specialization." [10] He attacked German universities and German professors, adding nothing but spleen to the criticism earlier pronounced by Schopenhauer and carried on by Burckhardt, Nietzsche, and Lagarde. The major sins of the academicians were intellectual narrowness, personal cowardice, atrophied emotions, and professional dishonesty.* Those Germans who bow to the judgment of the

---

* After brilliantly dissecting the character of modern scholars, Nietzsche concluded: ". . . he is in his essence and by his origin *unproductive,* and has a certain natural hatred of the productive; and that is why there is an endless feud between the genius and the savant. The latter wish to kill, dissect, and comprehend nature, the former to increase it

specialist "are no better than those earlier Germans who bought indulgences from Tetzel." [11] As the archetype of the modern professor, Langbehn singled out Emil Du Bois-Reymond and vilified his philosophical and literary addresses. Yet Du Bois-Reymond had done precisely what Langbehn had counseled; he had transcended the limits of his specialty and pronounced on general questions.* But the academics were all bad, and exaggerating a common German prejudice, particularly among the young, he concluded: "The professor is the German national disease; the present German education of youth is a kind of Massacre of the Innocents." [12]

Scientists and academicians were held responsible for sham education (*Halbbildung*), and Langbehn merely paraphrased Nietzsche when he condemned these "barbarians of culture." [13] Unlike Nietzsche, however, Langbehn did not enter the controversy over German education as a defender of the humanistic traditions, but instead sought a more robust, primitive climate for German culture. Too much respect had been lavished on books and bookish learning: "The letter kills, the picture is alive." [14] All the celebrated pedantry of German schools he loathed:

Many a stolen tear which a blond child secretly wipes from his eyes may yet prove a far heavier burden on an education-mad pedant of today than he thinks. . . . In our children we defend the future of our people; we cannot tolerate that these children are sacrificed to the Moloch of a false culture. We cannot let them be crippled, tortured, and miseducated. And perhaps some day there will come a big child, that "hidden emperor," who will revenge all these little children.[15]

In later editions he sharpened his attack on the pedantic peddlers of education and on the whole system of educating

---

by a new living nature. . . . Happy periods did not need or know the savant; the sick and sullen time ranks him as its highest and worthiest." *Schopenhauer als Erzieher,* in *Nietzsche's Werke,* Leipzig, Naumann, 1906, II, 285.

* For Emil Du Bois-Reymond's leading role in the struggle of scientists against vitalists and *Naturphilosophen,* cf. the illuminating comments in Ernest Jones, *Sigmund Freud. Life and Work,* Vol. I: *The Young Freud 1856–1900,* London, Hogarth, 1953, pp. 45–48. Du Bois-Reymond's philosophical assay, *Über die Grenzen des Naturerkennens,* 1872, in which he answered *ignorabimus* to the questions of the ultimate nature of matter and energy and of the origin and structure of human thought, had started a widespread controversy. Langbehn also attacked a rather fatuous lecture of Du Bois-Reymond's on Faust.

everyone; he pleaded for the training of "an aristocratic minority of the nation," for the unfettering of the child's energy and imagination.[16] He commiserated students who were taught to dissect history and the classics, rather than led to grasp the total meaning of an age or of a literary work.*

The real threat to Germany was overeducation and the continued neglect of health and physical training. Not book-learning, but the character and stamina acquired in struggling with nature would properly prepare the young. The English had far better mastered the necessity of balancing the training of mind and body, and he urged their example upon the Germans. If Berlin's fifty thousand bars would be closed and an equal number of public baths constructed, the member-ship of the Social Democratic party would dwindle rapidly.[17] This emphasis on physical prowess and political conservatism recalls the mood of Heroic Vitalism from which Langbehn was never far removed.[18]

Langbehn's vitalism prompted his attack on the prevailing *science* of medicine. In some passages of uncanny prognostica-tion, he championed hypnotism, emphasized the interrelation in most diseases of mind and body, and called "for a partially psychic healing therapy" to take the place of chemical and physical therapy. The human body, he charged, was neglected by contemporary medicine and imprisoned by contemporary fashion: "Modern culture, like modern dress, is only a mum-mification. [*Vermummung*] [19] He battled against these forms of repression, but he said nothing about the repression of sexuality, nothing in the whole book about love. Here, it would seem, his own uncertainties and deprivations were sustained by the prevailing tabu about the subject.†

---

* Langbehn's thought found a distant echo in the principles of National Socialist education, as witness a widely hailed speech by Hitler's *Reichskommissar* for education, Bernhard Rust: "The decisive thing is not whether the youngster knows the battle plans of Salamis and Cannae, or whether he is able to recite all the lovely sentences of Homer, but it is decisive whether he grasps the heroic spirit and whether the significance of Salamis comes alive again." Quoted in Cuno Horkenbach, *Das Deutsche Reich von 1918 bis Heute* (volume for 1933), Berlin, Verlag für Presse, Wirtschaft und Politik, 1933, p. 111.

† The Germanic critics generally avoided any discussion of love, mar-riage, or sexuality. Here they dared not follow Nietzsche, who before Freud had been the most radical German thinker on the subject;

Langbehn's diatribes against modern education always included his avowal that he was the defender of the child; the purity and certainty of its instincts were recurrent themes in his thought and, in some ways, foreshadowed the religious phase of his life. Even in an urban culture the child had retained its closeness to nature and possessed an immediacy of perception which the overeducated adult lacked. "Simplicity is the panacea for the evils of the present." [20] In the new Germany the talents and joys of the child would be preserved in the adult; even now the "genuine and pure" Germans had retained more of the childlike in their nature than had other peoples and none more so than his own unspoiled folk from *Niederdeutschland.* There is unquestionably something attractive in this plea for childhood, especially in an age when ignorance and prejudice about childhood ran strong;* but the reverse of this idyllic glorification was Langbehn's unrelenting warfare against intellect. Certainly his cult of the child conveyed in yet another form his commitment to a new mystical primitivism.

In fact Langbehn had made every effort to woo the young. He was one of the first nationalist critics to propagate "the cult of youth." † His book ended with repeated incantations

---

rather they adhered to the conventional morality of German writers —that of German upper-class culture generally. Even if the Victorians were not really Victorians—and this is what scholars seem to think now —the Germans were, and an essay on Sex and Repression in Imperial Germany would be most illuminating. As one example, consider Theodor Fontane's complaints about German biographies: "Dove's essays about the Forsters and the Humboldts are instructive, but leave me dissatisfied insofar as they are modeled after the conventional rules of biography writing in Germany and put themselves under the to me intolerable obligation of 'beautifying for ever.' If one could only decide to write the history of the Humboldts truthfully and authentically, to dwell, for example, on the sexual irregularities [*Uncorrektheiten*] of, I think, both Humboldts (certainly of one), then the portrait of their lives would be ten times more interesting, not from the point of view of common gossip, but from the physiological-psychological point of view." Theodor Fontane, *Briefe an Georg Friedlaender,* ed. by Kurt Schreinert, Heidelberg 1954, letter of December 5, 1884, pp. 2–3.

* Mrs. Frances Hodgson Burnett's *Little Lord Fauntleroy* appeared in 1886, and in the following year two German editions evidenced the popularity of the book. Langbehn was warring against this type of sentimentality.

† Few of the reformers or political movements of the nineteenth century

to German youth: "The new intellectual life of the Germans is not a matter for professors, but for the German youth, especially for the uncorrupted, un-miseducated [*unverbildeten*] and uninhibited youth. Right is on its side." [21]

Langbehn's vilification of the dullness and mediocrity of adult, Philistine society perpetuated the nineteenth-century tradition of contempt for the bourgeoisie. After 1871, Germany had lost her artistic style, her "monumentality," her great individuals. But in his thundering against bourgeois life, one can hear the peculiar note which the National Socialists later tirelessly blared forth. The bourgeoisie had become "rootless," alienated from folk and nature, had lost its *Volksthümlichkeit* and childlike nature (*Kindlichkeit*) and thus had forfeited the prerequisites of manhood and greatness. And again, like so many of his conservative contemporaries, Langbehn roundly condemned all urban and especially all metropolitan communities.

Berlin epitomized the evil in German culture: "Spiritually and politically, the provinces should be maneuvered and marshaled against the capital." * The poison of commerce and materialism, or, as he sometimes called it, the *Amerikanisierung* of Germany, was corroding the ancient spirit of

---

had singled out the young as the agents of reform and progress. After the First World War, the fascist movements everywhere directed their appeal to youth, and their opponents—often in self-defense—had to do likewise.

* *Rembrandt,* p. 133. Far from being the accepted and respected capital, as Paris and London were, Berlin was widely considered as an ugly upstart among German cities. In a country where antiurbanism ran strong, every mammoth city was suspect, but Berlin doubly. A history of antiurbanism, both as an idea and as a movement of practical importance, would constitute a timely and important study. Theodor Fontane may serve as a witness once again: "Bismarck who is so often right is right also in his distaste for huge cities. You write yourself that 'with a little less "Getting-on" [*Carrière machen*] we would have more truth in the world. Certainly. And not only more truth, but also more simplicity, and unaffectedness, more honor, charity, even more knowledge, industry, and thoroughness generally. And what does Getting-on mean other than to live in Berlin, and what does Berlin mean but to get-on? To be sure a few people need the large city because of their jobs, but they are lost, particularly lost for their jobs, if they cannot practice the difficult art of living in the big city and at the same time of *not* living there." *Briefe an Georg Friedlaender,* letter of December 21, 1884, p. 3.

the Prussian garrison town;* even the natural defenders of the old order, the aristocracy and officer corps, capitulated before the new power, Mammon, and allowed the *nouveau riche* into society. Forty years later, millions of Germans were to echo the charge that "the crude cult of money, a North-American and at the same time a Jewish characteristic, predominates in Berlin more and more."[22]

Science, pedantry, and the hubbub of modern life had nearly killed the German spirit. As was characteristic of the Germanic critics, Langbehn drew up a list of remedies for Germany's regeneration. These will be discussed in the next chapter. The heart of all these reforms was contained in the prophecy that an Age of Art should replace the currently prevailing Age of Science.

In Langbehn's scheme, art and science were the two great antagonists, wrestling for the soul of the modern German. For Langbehn, the triumph of life-giving art over cold, deadening science was every bit as inevitable as the triumph of the proletariat over the bourgeoisie was for Marx, and, like Marx, he sought to guide and speed up historical inevitability.

Before turning to the often absurd means that Langbehn proposed for the enthronement of art, we must try to answer

---

* From the 1870's on, conservative writers in imperial Germany expressed the fear that the German soul would be destroyed by "Americanization," that is by mammonism, materialism, mechanization and the mass society. It is ironic that the first person to use the phrase in that sense was Langbehn's arch villain, Du Bois-Reymond, who in 1877 warned that European culture was in danger of being overwhelmed by *Amerikanisierung,* that is, by excessive realism and technology. See Otto Basler, "Amerikanismus. Geschichte des Schlagwortes," *Deutsche Rundschau,* CCXXIV (August, 1930), 144. Americanism meant modernity, and to critics like Langbehn it must have seemed appropriate that the opposition movement within Catholicism known as modernism had originated in America, and that in the 1890's its program—a form of liberal deviationism—came to be called Americanism. The dispute over Americanism became sufficiently important, in France and Germany as well, that on January 22, 1899, Pope Leo XIII dispatched an encyclical, *Testem benevolentiae,* to Cardinal Gibbons of Baltimore, condemning Americanism, especially the view that "the Church ought to adapt herself somewhat to our advanced civilization and, relaxing her ancient rigor, show some indulgence to modern popular theories and methods." *Documents of American Catholic History,* ed. by John Tracy Ellis, Milwaukee, Bruce, 1956, pp. 553–562, and Albert Houtin, *L'Américanisme,* Paris, Emile Nourry, 1904, a study later put on the Index.

—as Langbehn did not—why *art*, why this worship of art as the sole redeemer, why Rembrandt as educator? Langbehn's silence is itself significant; to him it was an obvious matter, a new version of an old and powerful German myth.

That art was the highest good of a society, that it had a sublimity and timelessness which no other human pursuit possessed, that it could soar to the highest form of truth, and that it should be a teacher of man and a guide to morality— these had been beliefs that had originated in the *Sturm-und-Drang* period, in that first marvelous outburst of liberated genius that later generations still sought to emulate. Accompanying this apotheosis of art was a solicitous concern with the artist, with his life, his struggles, his genius. Quite apart from his creations, from his ability, in Carlyle's phrase, "to read the open secret of the universe," the artist was thought to personify the human condition, to embody the quintessence of man, at its most violent and intense, and no theme is more characteristic of modern German literature than the struggle between the artist and the Philistine. These beliefs, modified and elaborated by their adherents, persisted throughout the nineteenth century, despite the growing challenge by the devotees of science. With the veneration of art often went the belief that great art was peculiarly German, that the Germans had a special calling for the creation and cultivation of the arts. As early as 1773 appeared a little volume, *Von deutscher Art und Kunst,* and this linkage of character and art, this attempt to define an artistic style that was uniquely German and a uniquely German character that could be grasped by its art, proved one of the most powerful and persistent myths of German culture.* It could of course easily be bent into a xenophobic weapon, and from the time of the French Revolution this began to happen. There was German art and un-German, that is, foreign, Western, art.

---

* Of course the romantic movement throughout Europe wrought a similar change in the conception of art. A recent work by Raymond Williams, *Culture and Society, 1780–1950,* New York 1958, examines this change in English culture and notes that the very terms art and artists acquired new meaning in the romantic period: "*Art* came to stand for a special kind of truth, 'imaginative truth,' and *artist* for a special kind of person, as the words *artistic* and *artistical,* to describe human beings, new in the 1840's, show" (pp. xv–xvi and *passim*). The identification of art and national genius was of course a European phenomenon, but it played a particularly powerful role in Germany.

In the beginning—during the romantic movement in Europe —there was a necessary and universal rebellion against the tyranny of French conventions and classical forms; and in the end, in the recent past, there was the exhibition of "decadent art" in Hitler's Munich.

In the interval, at different times and with different men, the purely esthetic view of art as against the functional, often national, view predominated. In Schopenhauer's philosophy, art, especially music, offered salvation from the tragedy of senseless, ceaseless strife. Schopenhauer's influence was great, in Germany as well as abroad, but the greatest figure in the German apotheosis of art—barring a brief, later repudiated, moment in the young Nietzsche's life—was Schopenhauer's one-time disciple, Richard Wagner. Felicitously combining profit and doctrine, Wagner constructed a Germanic ideology of art, of which his *Gesamtkunstwerk,* fusing not only all the arts, but philosophy and religion as well, was the noblest example. Bayreuth was to become the national Mecca, the temple of German character and art.

Although critical of Wagner, Langbehn shared his view of the power of German art. The age of faith had been replaced by the hated Age of Science, and the new Age of Art would mark a synthesis of the two. The right kind of "populistic" (*völkisch*) art loomed as the only possible surrogate of religion, as the only remaining means of spiritually ennobling life. It could fuse religion and philosophy, truth and beauty, and become the incarnation of the national genius. Langbehn banked on art as the only possible means of redemption, as earlier reformers had banked on a religious revival or created utopian visions of social justice. It would heal the divisiveness of the people, for a people committed to a common esthetic experience could overcome its material antagonisms and evolve a new secular version of the idealized medieval community, a latter-day Nürnberg of the Meistersinger. A people's art would teach all Germans the essence of their being, it would teach them to know themselves. Bismarck had provided the externals of unification, but a secret emperor, a great artist-hero, would have to furnish the deeper, internal unity.*

---

* This too was an old romantic idea: "The fragmentary nature of modern civilization was regarded as not beautiful; art was looked upon as a means of cohesion, and to it was assigned the highest purpose." Franz Schnabel, *Deutsche Geschichte im neunzehnten Jahrhundert,* Vol. I: *Die Grundlagen,* 4th ed., Freiburg im Breisgau 1948, p. 262.

Art—at least in Langbehn's day—was also undemocratic and nonscientific, and hence an age of artistic preëminence would also have to be an age of the revived elite, the artist as hero—this would restore the proper, nonmaterial view of life. Individuality would flourish, and the gifted few, once again dominant, would inspire a revival of folk art. It would work yet another revolution in the view of man—the scientific or mechanistic view of man had superseded the spiritual outlook, and only art could probe and portray the mysteries of man and nature. Not foreseeing the deepening of the rational comprehension of man through modern psychology and psychoanalysis, Langbehn saw in artistic and intuitive understanding the only alternative to the intolerable materialistic view of man. In his vision of the future, art would not be one element in a harmoniously developed and broadly humanistic culture—as in Germany's classical age or indeed in Rembrandt's Holland—but the great antagonist of science, the conqueror of modern culture. To worship art in Langbehn's manner was to go primitive, to return to some form of tribal fetishism.*

Not every form of art could achieve these grandiose goals—whenever art is so elevated it is in danger of being censored. With alarm, Langbehn noted and condemned some of the new directions in German art. Of Wagner, for example, he was highly critical, objecting especially to the composer's arrogance which was so contrary to the humility of the true artist and of Rembrandt and Shakespeare in particular. " 'Simplicity and quiet greatness' Wagner does not offer. . . . he is nervous and makes nervous." [23] Or, still more prejudicial to Wagner, he is too modern in his hankering after mere theatrical effect: "He out-meyerbeered Meyerbeer. [*Er hat Meyerbeer übermeyert*]." In an aside nowhere fully amplified, Wagner was labeled "a romantic, not a classicist; for that reason alone he is second-rate." [24]

Langbehn also lashed out against the exponents of *l'art*

---

* The belief that art is "truer" than reason or science was still widely held in the 1920's, when Thomas Mann parodied it: "Poetry and art, at least romantic poetry and *German* art—these surely embody dreams, simplicity, feeling, or still better *Gemüt;* they have nothing in common with 'intellect,' which is, very much like the Weimar Republic, to be considered a matter for Jew boys [*Judenjungen*], to be held in contempt by patriots." "Von deutscher Republik," *Bemühungen*, Berlin 1925, p. 174.

pour l'art as triflers, and he denounced the then emerging
school of German naturalists as coldly scientific—and how
could Langbehn approve of the crude realism of Gerhart
Hauptmann and the other naturalists who were then for the
first time being produced on the stage? Art should ennoble,
and literature that exposed social iniquities or unconventional
passion was anathema to Langbehn.* Emile Zola, the father
of European naturalism, he attacked "as the archenemy of the
people." All Germans should learn to hate him, but beyond
angry name-calling about his "brutality of feeling and pride
of knowledge" Langbehn's indictment was vague, though
vehement. The animus is not hard to explain: Zola was the
prime literary foe of all conservatives because they sensed in
his work an immense force that even then was pushing German art ever closer to the modern democratic age.[25] For
Langbehn, art was much too serious, too sacred in purpose, to
be free; a scientific bent in art seemed sacrilegious. Art therefore would have to be regulated; it must have its roots in the
elemental passions of men, and it must be spontaneous, primitive, populistic, moral but not intellectual. The works of the
two painters, Aloys Fellman and Wilhelm Leibl, already
"point to the artistic tendency of the future." [26] Both painted
in a popular manner; and "the new German art will have to
base itself on the peasantry, the best and simplest expression
of the *Volksthum*." [27]

But how to institute this right kind of art? Leadership and
direction were needed, and Langbehn insisted that only if
Germany were governed by *Kunstpolitik* could the new age be
ushered in.† Politics should become the handmaiden of art,
transcending military concerns and party politics.‡ *Kunst-*

---

* Langbehn's censorious comments on modern art were echoed a few
  years later when parliamentarians of the center and the right sought to
  amend the so-called Lex Heinze on the suppression of procurers in
  such a way as to repress virtually all modern art, including the
  naturalistic dramas of Sudermann. Ziegler, *Die geistigen und sozialen
  Strömungen Deutschlands im neunzehnten Jahrhundert*, p. 652.
† Literally: the politics of art, but "esthetic politics" might be a better
  translation for this neologism. In a fuzzy and confused way, Langbehn's
  Kunstpolitik recalls Ruskin's *The Political Economy of Art*, London
  1857.
‡ Or fuse them, for " 'Art and war' is a Greek, a German and an Aryan
  watchword. . . . In the very name of the Anglo-Saxon poet this union
  of art and war celebrated its greatest triumph: Shakespeare means a
  spear shaker [*Speerschüttler*] and names always have a reason." *Rembrandt*, p. 211. This is a fair sample of Langbehn's pretentious trifling.

politik, Langbehn implied, would have to proceed on two levels: in the direct encouragement and regulation of artistic genius and in the promotion of a milieu favorable for artists, which would have to include the destruction of all cultural obstacles to artistic greatness. This in turn depended on the growth of *Volksthümlichkeit,* that is, of a culture in which the traditional or folk habits of a people are protected so that the artist can commune with his unspoiled people. In the end a vigorous folk art would match the achievements of the new artistic Titans, and the genius and the masses—complementary forces, according to Langbehn—would destroy the cultural dominance of the Philistines. "The military and artistic development of the future Germany involves an anti-Philistine development." [28]

Kunstpolitik called for a much more extended education in the arts, and Langbehn's proposals in this field fell on particularly receptive ears among German educators.[29] "To regard art as something alien from real life is always a sign of artistic decadence; art should deepen everyday life, not turn away from it; the former is a classical aspiration, the latter romantic." [30] First, he urged the cultivation of artistic talent among the young, the training of their senses, not only of their minds. Second, art was to become a practical force in culture through the reform and purification of architecture and interior decoration. The atrocities of contemporary urban housing should be replaced by esthetically attractive constructions which in turn would restore a measure of joy to the people.

Above all, this new Age of Art would have to be preceded by a new moral order; Rembrandt was the symbol of *Kunstpolitik* and "the influence of [his] character on German art is unthinkable without its simultaneous influence on the moral and intellectual life of the whole nation." [31] Here Langbehn was left in a dilemma characteristic of the Germanic critics: salvation would come through art, and art would come after salvation. Out of such an imaginary predicament only an imaginary, a hidden leader, could deliver the people, and it is to this leader that we now turn.

9: Art, Politics, and the Heroic Folk

Neither soil, nor speech, nor state, but the Volk
in its oneness is the Fatherland.   LANGBEHN

*The concepts of state and people, people and men
of culture should not be blown up into artificial
contradictions, but should be reconciled to become
a natural harmony. The ultimate aim of the
education of the individual and of the people is
to reconcile, not to divide, to fuse to unity the
upper and the lower, the external and the internal
elements of human life.*   LANGBEHN

Like so many Germans of his time, Langbehn was unpolitical.
He cared neither for the theoretical questions of political society nor for the practical issues of power, diplomacy, and conflicting interests within the state. To ignore such practical
questions was highmindedness. Langbehn disdained political
life and scoffed at the suggestion of friends that he should
found and lead a party of his own, a reform movement of
"social aristocrats." * To be acceptable to Langbehn, politics
had to be ennobled by unpolitical ideals, enveloped by a mystique at once deprecating the present and glorifying the future.
Such "estheticizing" of politics and power was quite common
in imperial Germany. [1]

---

* By an odd coincidence, Arno Holz, the German naturalist, wrote a
play, *Sozialaristokraten,* in 1896, which depicts the decline of a foot-
loose *litterateur,* a Nietzsche disciple and former academic, who began
his life as an idealist, as a man who believed only in individualism and
"in unpolitical politics," not in superman but in supermanhood. After
being jailed because of an article on free love, he wound up as the
Reichstag candidate for the Antisemitic party, preaching that "what
the bedbug is in private life, the Jew is in the body politic." Between
the type whom Holz portrayed in his play and Langbehn, whom he
certainly did not have in mind, there was a strange resemblance.

Langbehn's own ideas on politics, his reforms, precise and brutal though they often were, are linked to his *Kunstpolitik,* to his irreproachable desire for a revival of art and a restoration of morality. Art was to excuse politics, and politics to produce art, and both were to inspire and perpetuate a moral reform of Germany.

The link between art and politics was the *Volk,* that mythical repository of character and strength, of which every conservative German dreamed. "Whoever wants to raise German art, must first raise the German *Volksthum.*" [2] Following Herder, though without mentioning him, Langbehn insisted that great art could spring only from the *Volk,* from an organic community, from a specially cultivated nativist soil. Without this earthy sustenance, the artist would perish.* In his analysis of the prerequisites of art, Langbehn came close to the views of the materialists and the naturalists, whose program, enunciated in the late 1880's, he detested:

A work of art is only the product of different forces working together: of the individual, of the populistic tradition [*Volksthum*], of the conditions of the age; if these three factors are simultaneously and jointly active, then something great is born. All the political and social relations are important for a work of art, if indeed not more important than the artistic work itself. . . . Under all circumstances the spiritual development is totally dependent on the political development.[3]

How unromantic, how unheroic this notion of a society, producing an artist! How Philistine the implicit denial of the artist as a free spirit, as a man above society! Langbehn, like all the Germanic critics, praised individuality as the highest good, as the most characteristically German attribute, while, less explicitly believing in a rigid determinism. The individualism of the Germanic critics was a slippery notion, as it had to be in order to avoid the political conclusions of liberalism and democracy. The real source of individuality was the *Volk* or the community, and only by restoring it, if necessary through compulsion, could freedom and greatness be achieved.

Langbehn lamented the disappearance of this dumb, life-

---

* As he once put it, not without justification: "After squeezing the *old* Goethe like a lemon, our culture should remember the *young* Goethe, who in his early work fulfilled the demands for maturity of spirit and true *Volksthümlichkeit.*" Langbehn, *Der Geist des Ganzen,* ed. by Benedikt Momme Nissen, Freiburg im Breisgau 1930, p. 43.

giving *Volk*. To revive it became his task, and for the sake of that goal he turned political. Part III of his book was therefore entitled *Deutsche Politik*, and over fifty pages he scattered his comments on the ills and likely remedies of German society. His political excursions were vague and even more abstract than his thoughts on other subjects, and certainly more abstract than the common German practice of elevating concrete issues to a metaphysical realm.* His intent, not clear to himself, was to end all politics, to subdue this hateful innovation of modernity, to extirpate the ideas and institutions of 1789 which had made such headway even in Germany. In Rembrandt's Holland or in young Goethe's Germany, there had been no political struggle, and hence, so the critics believed, no divisions. Today, on the contrary, a superficially unified Germany, still divided by antagonistic classes, competing confessions, rival regions, could not recover the *Volksthümlichkeit*, the one *Volk*, that Langbehn so ardently desired. Hence his mystical invocation of the people's rebirth, of a *Führer*, of a "hidden emperor" who would once more rally and unite the people, and abolish politics as well. Only Rembrandt or Christ—and in the later editions of the book, Christ, the "probable Aryan," was pronounced indispensable—could inspire a Germanic rebirth, a reintegration of Germans into one cohesive people, governed, for its own sake, by its aristocratic leaders.

But how had this heroic folk perished? Langbehn gave no answer—none of the Germanic critics ever explained how this noble people, this race of heroes, could have lost its unity and strength. More or less openly, they all pointed to one sinister figure—the Jew—who even then was gnawing at German culture, corroding and corrupting the character of the true German. Here was the outsider worming his way in, climbing ever more ostentatiously into positions of power. The link between Langbehn's desire for populistic primitivism and his anti-Semitism is clear, even if it was not stated in his writings. The ultimate cause of German decay was modernity itself,

---

* The abstractness of German political theorizing is not peculiar to Langbehn, or to the group here studied. In his work on the early Ranke, Laue observes: "The German vocabulary is replete with abstractions which are made the grammatical subjects of active verbs. Action, in other words, proceeds from abstractions, not from individuals alone." Theodore H. von Laue, *Leopold Ranke. The Formative Years*, Princeton, Princeton University Press, 1950, p. 92.

that complex of new and violent forces that had destroyed the traditional society and the traditional faith. But the immediate cause was the Jews and their brethren, the academics.

At first Langbehn drew a sharp distinction between ortho- dox and assimilated Jews. He accepted orthodox Jewry as a valuable complement to the German people, and he wrote warmly about a few Jews, particularly Spinoza and Rahel von Varnhagen. But he vilified those Jews of his own day who had abandoned and repudiated their own traditions in order to become modern, secular Germans. During the last quarter of the nineteenth century, the larger part of German Jewry had become secularized, converted, or had joined the reformed wing of Judaism, which, like liberal Protestantism, was a kind of culture-religion. He scorned Mommsen's advocacy of the mass conversion of Jews to Christianity: "Religion is not a coat that one puts on and off at one's pleasure." [4] Here Lang- behn touched on the central issue facing German Jewry: the choice between assimilation, and the ultimate extinction of their identity, or the maintenance of their identity and the acceptance of their apartness. By and large, progressive Jews, encouraged by enlightened, secular Germans, chose the former path, and joined their gentile contemporaries in a common veneration of *Kultur* and German learning. There was opposi- tion to this, of course. From within Jewry came many warn- ings, some merely politic, others deeply principled: the Jews ought not to embrace so fully and so openly an alien culture for some day the Germans would wreak vengeance on the Jew- ish appropriators and dispensers of German culture. The de- bate was carried on sometimes publicly, more often privately, because the very process of assimilation touched on some of the deepest questions of faith and national consciousness con- fronting Jews and Germans alike.* Langbehn preached a

---

* A few weeks before the appearance of *Rembrandt als Erzieher*, the issue was raised publicly when a Jewish writer, Conrad Alberti, pub- lished a widely hailed preposterous denunciation of Jewry, "Judentum und Antisemitismus," *Die Gesellschaft*, No. 12 (December, 1889), pp. 1718–1733. "I can assert boldly that among the young generation of Jews, suffused with modern *Bildung*, there is not a man who in the depth of his soul is not convinced of the superfluousness, harmfulness and rottenness of Jewry." Alberti argued that with the decline of faith in God the Jews had lost their justification for a separate existence, and that they had become a mere clique that "was a preëminent participant in the corruption and stagnation of all conditions." The solution was total assimilation, *provided* the Germans would cease being anti-

war of extermination against all assimilated Jews: "They are a poison for us and must be treated as such. . . . They are democratically inclined; they have an affinity for the mob; everywhere they sympathize with decadence." [5] In later editions he became more vitriolic still and even invoked Lessing, Germany's apostle of toleration, on behalf of the anti-Semitic campaign:

The modern Jew has no religion, no character, no home, no children. He is a piece of humanity that has become sour. . . . The aspiration of present-day Jews for spiritual and material domination evokes a simple phrase: Germany for the Germans. A Jew can no more become a German than a plum can turn into an apple. . . . Now that the Jews are the oppressors and the enemies of all German being [even] Lessing would fight them to the death.*

Semitic, because Jews could not be expected to assimilate under fire. If the Germans facilitated this process, then at some world's fair, 150 years hence, "the last Jew would be exhibited as a rarity." Many a moderate German, alarmed by the rising power of the Jews, also counseled patience. Fontane, for example, wrote: "Morality aside, the enmity against the Jews is nonsense, because it is simply impractical. Everybody I know here, especially the military and the nobility, are eminently dependent on the Jews and are daily becoming more so. . . . There is no other way but to hold one's tongue and to be content with gradual Christianization." *Briefe an Georg Friedlaender,* letter of November 9, 1892, p. 197. Shortly before the outbreak of the First World War, when extreme anti-Semitism had been on the wane for some time, the debate was renewed; cf., for example, Werner Sombart's *Die Zukunft der Juden,* Leipzig 1912, which argued that the policy of assimilation was bankrupt and that Jews should retain their national self-consciousness, and a controversial statement by a Jew, Moritz Goldstein, in *Der Kunstwart,* XXV:11 (March, 1912), 281–294, in which he defined the problem of the Jews in the following manner: "We Jews administer the spiritual property of a people that denies us the right and the ability to do so." His prescription was more self-respect for Jews, and he suggested that those Jews "who all the time deal in German culture, who pretend as if, and who persuade themselves that no one recognizes them—these are our real foes. They must be pushed out of their all-too-visible posts where they represent Jews as a false type of Jew, they must be silenced, and gradually exterminated [*auszurotten*]."

* *Rembrandt,* 49th ed., pp. 348–351. Note the biological analogy. It was in those years that German naturalism, Gerhart Hauptmann in particular, dealt with questions of eugenics, with the hereditary character of alcoholism, insanity, and other diseases. To some people the racist agitation against Jews must have seemed more plausible because of this new, widespread concern in hereditary ills and vices.

Oppressors of what? Langbehn did not say, but most likely he was referring to the ever more conspicuous role of Jews in the arts, particularly in the theater and as critics. By the time he wrote *Der Rembrandtdeutsche* in 1892, he concluded ominously: "For us, the Jews are only a passing pest and cholera." [6]

German youth, he urged, should take the lead in combating the poisonous influence of Jewry. The student fraternities, he noted, had always barred Jews, and the officer corps and the Jesuits also knew that the only good Jew was the excluded Jew. The Jesuits admitted no one who had had any Jewish ancestors in the preceding five generations, and he recommended that a similar *Ahnenprobe* be instituted in Germany as a condition for citizenship.[7]

Despite his frequent use of racist rhetoric, Langbehn was not a full-fledged racist—a fact that the otherwise appreciative National Socialists frequently lamented. Racism was probably too "scientific" for him, and his own brand of partial or intermittent racism was more like a mystical poetry of blood. But in later editions and writings, he emphasized more sharply the role of race and blood as the determinants of the Jewish question. He believed, of course, that the Germans were Aryans and that "only German blood should rule over Germans; that is the first and fundamental right of our people." [8]

If one reviews the wide range of anti-Semitic thought in imperial Germany, one is struck by the odd combination of a vague, even feeble motive and a precise and brutal intention.[9] In Langbehn's book or life, for example, anti-Semitism did not play a large role; his attacks on the Jews appeared on a handful of pages. But what a disproportion between argument and conclusion, between the briefly stated grievance and the call for extirpation! There was no personal experience that could have aroused his hatred; unlike Lagarde, he had no Jewish colleagues and he made no mention of ever encountering obnoxious Jews. To him it had become an article of faith that Jews and modernity were one, and the fury of his anti-Semitism sprang from his resentment of everything modern. He hated the Jews for encouraging the Germans to succumb to science, democracy, and educated mediocrity.* Of course the Jews

---

* Needless to say, there was a great deal of truth to the view that the Jews championed the forces of modernity. L. B. Namier, in discussing the expansion of European society and thought between 1750 and 1914,

favored liberalism, secularism, and capitalism. Where else but in the cities, in the free professions, in an open society, could they escape from the restrictions and prejudices that lingered on from the closed, feudal society of an earlier period? They were, and in a sense, had to be, the promoters and profiteers of modernity, and for this Langbehn, and so many others like him, could not forgive the Jews.

It was easier to champion orthodoxy for Jews than to pre-scribe the traditional Christian faith for Germans. Langbehn's longing for religion was strong, but it was sublimated in his early writings—before his conversion—in his call for an Age of Art. Obviously, the Germanic critics could not preach the simple revival of the old, non-Germanic faith, the less so as Christianity in Germany had played a divisive role, and the great passion was for a religion, a mystique, that would *bind* and unite. The Christian dogma, moreover, had been seri-ously damaged by a century of scholarship and higher criticism, and Christian ethics had been reëvaluated by Nietzsche in a manner particularly cogent and inescapable for the Germanic critics. Hence Langbehn's flight to art, to a realm where mysticism and nationalism, faith and metaphysics, could be fused.

Much to the scorn of his clerical reviewers, Langbehn did not place religion among the major headings of his book. His comments on religious questions were scattered haphazardly, and his attitude was characteristically ambiguous. "To trans-late Christianity into everyday life, as Rembrandt did artis-tically, will always remain one of the principal tasks of the Germans. And the German people will have to stick to Chris-tianity as long as they acquire no better basis for their spiritual existence. Until now this has not happened." [10] This *faute de mieux* faith was a disemboweled kind of Christianity. "Reli-gion is nothing solid but fluid." Modern Germans need a more virile and active Christianity, and in that spirit a new *Imita-tion of Christ* should be written. Christ himself would always

says: "Two races headed the movement, though under vastly different conditions—the British and the Jews; they were the pioneers of capitalism, and its first, and perhaps chief beneficiaries. . . . they are now the two most urban communities . . . have the largest percentage of black-coated workers and professional intelligentsia; and are threatened by the rise of the corresponding classes in countries in which they live dispersed." *In the Margin of History,* London 1939, p. 56.

remain *one* of the great teachers and some form "of living, fluid, individual Christianity is acceptable to modern man as well." [11] The instinct for religion, even for Christianity, is born anew with every child, but the form and ritual of belief had to change with the times.* Langbehn harbored no sympathy for the modernist movement within Christianity, and yet he had unwittingly embraced its view of the evolutionary character of religious dogmas and practices. Although a foe of science and rationalism, he failed to rescue Christianity from the higher critics and from the much-vilified relativists; in fact, their ideas had entered his own thought, for he and the other cultural critics were exposed to all "winds of doctrine."

Although nonsectarian from indifference, Langbehn at first seemed much closer to Protestantism than to Catholicism. The tenor of his religious thought pointed to the primacy of faith over works, and to the more Germanic character of Lutheranism. He celebrated Luther, Rembrandt's historic complement, as the true German hero who in his work and thought had synthesized art and religion. "Art is subjectivity, and subjectivity is faith. The German hero of faith [*Glaubensheld*], Luther, even apart from his religious significance, is the supreme hero altogether. Germany first recognized itself in him." [12] Art moreover could flourish only in Protestant regions, where "inwardness" had replaced the Catholic worship of externals. As proof of this dubious contention he drew an antithesis between Rubens and Rembrandt. And religion *was* subordinate to art: "Goethe, Rembrandt, Luther: a culture that does homage to these three kings is the true Saviour [*Heiland*] of the Germans." [13]

Langbehn's Catholic reviewers pounced on this sacrilegious confusion of art and religion.† Beginning with the 37th edi-

* Langbehn's peculiar form of trifling did not stop at religious matters, as witness these examples: "In money, German attar is more valuable than oriental attar; in the same way, German Christendom is more valuable than oriental Christendom. . . . Aryanism is Childlikeness and is Christianity: these three factors of life are identical. Christ himself is the typical child, the child in its noblest form, the child of God." *Rembrandt*, p. 311.

† There were two major reviews of *Rembrandt als Erzieher* by Catholics. A. Baumgartner, a Jesuit critic of great prominence, subjected the book to a withering attack; no other review ever rivaled the gusto of his demolition. *Stimmen aus Maria-Laach. Katholische Blätter*, XL (1891), 86–104. A strikingly sympathetic review appeared anonymously in the *Historisch-politische Blätter für das katholische Deutschland*,

tion, in 1891, Langbehn whittled away at his favorable remarks about Protestantism and added a new section on Catholicism. There he simultaneously depreciated Luther—"history goes beyond its great personalities"—and gently pushed him closer to the Catholic camp, by stressing his kinship to the Catholic mystics of the fifteenth century. All Protestant writers—from Shakespeare to Lagarde—had "a pro-Catholic vein" and present-day Germans should recognize that the Catholics were in some ways even more Germanic and certainly more artistic than the Protestants.[14] In his last book in 1892, he acknowledged that only the Catholics had given him an intelligent and sympathetic hearing, and concluded: "The Rembrandt book does not rest on a specific confessional basis. If ultimately one wanted to ask: 'for or against Christ,' then the answer of the *Rembrandtdeutsche* would certainly be: Christ today, tomorrow, and forever." [15] But the strange dialogue between the anonymous author of the Rembrandt book and the anonymous contributor to the *Historisch-politische Blätter* continued, and the latter, though welcoming Langbehn's strides toward Catholicism, correctly noted that Langbehn was still far from being a Christian.

For Langbehn's purposes, neither religion nor anti-Semitism was enough. To restore the unity and purity of an earlier Germanic community a revolution in politics and morals would be necessary. Everywhere he diagnosed symptoms of division and decline, and the struggle among antagonistic interests. Far from approximating the general will, politics had become the arena for enfeebling conflicts. The very quality of his political writing attested his strongest wish—and that of the Germanic critics generally—: the abolition of politics and the substitution of command and mystery, of charisma. All this was fuzzy and obscure, as it would have to be, because no one in the 1890's could have foreseen the means whereby charismatic leadership could replace modern representative government. The wish, however, was there, disguised, half-articulated, but the stronger for not being clearly recognized

---

and this review—as well as two subsequent articles in the same journal —were identified as having been written by the theologian and later bishop, P. W. von Keppler. Keppler's reviews, it will be remembered, had a great influence on Langbehn; he republished the first two in his *Der Rembrandtdeutsche. Von einem Wahrheitsfreund.* Dresden 1892, and eventually became a good friend of Keppler's.

nor expressed, and therefore relatively impervious to critical attack.

Langbehn dimly perceived the connection between social inequality and political conflict, and he sought to destroy the latter without impairing the former. He deprecated the cultural consequences of capitalism and *laissez-faire,* and he contrasted modern Mammon worship with the legendary simplicity of an earlier age. The most immediate problem was the dissatisfied and alienated worker, because only men without property and hope are likely to start revolutions. The relation between ruler and ruled, employer and employee, should be neither antagonistic nor equal, but should be rendered harmonious by a revived paternalism, by higher wages, by giving the worker some stake or property in society, and by other incentives which would replace the cash nexus of the industrial society. Langbehn's intent was close to that of the corporatists, and many of them would have agreed with his characteristic slogan: "Equality is death, hierarchy is life." [16]

The political arm of the alienated worker was the German Social Democratic party, and Langbehn proposed that it would have to be "nationalized," that is, transformed into a nationalistic-socialist movement. He too demanded that the proletariat be reintegrated into the *Volk.* The proper intermediaries were the nobility; social democracy could be conquered only by a "social aristocracy based on historical and traditional relations and hence at one with the healthy elements of the lower class." [17] With his usual elaborateness, he played on the derivation of *Adel* [nobility] from *edel* [noble], and he admonished the nobility to live up to its noble obligations. Nobles and princes should attend to the welfare of the disinherited, who would then accept their place in a hierarchical community. "The task is to provide food and drink for the hungry and thirsty people, at first quite literally." [18] None of this could be done by mechanical or democratic means: "After the French Revolution, comes the German reform; after equality, differentiation." [19] Langbehn was invoking the old dream of a social monarchy, of a "liberal aristocracy," of a proletariat that would rediscover the pleasures of habitual deference. Political and social problems were once again reduced to the realm of simple morality; if each German would recover the civic virtues of an imaginary, organic past then all tensions and antagonisms would cease.

The best, the truly authentic German was the peasant. He was the *Volk* incarnate; his virtues, his virility, had once constituted the strength of the people. Rembrandt, not surprisingly, turns out to have been a peasant, a spiritual peasant to be sure. His robust simplicity, his faith, his massive physique —all these marked him as a peasant, and if Germans cannot entirely plow under their urban monstrosities, then at least this spiritual peasantry should be refurbished. It is, of course, in an allegorical sense that this characteristic thought must be understood: "In the end the peasant may yet kill the professor; what is robustly original in the nature of the German may yet predominate and prevail over the artificial element of that nature." [20] But allegory can, and did, turn into action. The peasant stood for all that remained unpolluted in society, for all that remained fixed and rooted, and his greatest political virtue was his cheerful subservience—a quality rarely encountered among "modern" Germans.

Even as the Nordic gods had their abode in Valhalla, so this idealized peasantry had a last place of survival, *Niederdeutschland*. There, in that northwestern plain of Germany, the noblest and toughest of the peasants had lived, and there, Langbehn asserted, the traditions of the peasantry, the customs and costumes, the dialect and faith, still survived. Actually *Niederdeutsch* was an elastic term, as were all symbols of the Germanic critics. Anyone whose ancestors had once lived there, remained a *Niederdeutscher*, and hence Langbehn's hymn to the Boers, as "the only surviving old Germans." * The great culture heroes, Rembrandt of course and Shakespeare too, were *Niederdeutsche*, and in more recent times, Bismarck was, and Langbehn, and even Johnny Appleseed! [21] The idealization of the *Niederdeutsche* as the more than perfect peasant, has a long history in German folk mythology, and with this respectable ancestry, it found a ready place in Langbehn's curious imperialism.

It was characteristic of Langbehn to construct this ideal type of the *Niederdeutsche*, who no longer corresponded to any living reality. But it was dangerous as well, because it introduced still another division into Germany's political life, and Langbehn was already concerned about the existing divisions. The political and cultural antagonism between Prussia

---

* *Rembrandt*, p. 125. He made much of the Boers; a few years later the populace at large celebrated these dour country cousins.

and the Reich—superficially suppressed by Bismarck, but a source of great annoyance even to him—reappeared in Langbehn's pages in a transfigured form. Prussia and Germany represented cultural opposites and only the proper union could effect the desired rebirth of Germany. Prussia was "cold," all outward, and estranged from Germany because of the many alien races that had mixed their blood with Prussian blood—Slavs, Jews, and Frenchmen. Therefore Prussian culture was empty. Germany, on the other hand, was "warm," *volksthümlich,* and its culture bore great promise. The marriage of the two would yield excellent offspring: Prussia, as was to be expected, was the male partner, Germany the female, "and it is certain that the intellectual talents are always derived from the mother, and that therefore in regard to the intellectual fruits of such a marriage, the German character will have to be decisive." *

Germany, however, was governed by parliamentarians and party men, not by peasants. The German tradition of sneering at parliaments and parliamentarians is nearly as old and widespread as the contempt for Jews and journalists. Soon after the French Revolution, German publicists began to denounce the presumption and futility of national assemblies, of men "mechanically elected," each living off and hence perpetuating particularist interests in society. The failure of 1848 heightened this disdain for parliamentary bodies, and the ineffectual wrangling of the Reichstag, so assiduously and contemptuously advertised by Bismarck, perpetuated this sentiment. Langbehn was thus merely playing a new variation on a conservative theme when he attacked *"Fraktionsmenschen"* (members of the same parliamentary group) "as part-men, therefore as nomen, who rejoiced at the departure of the great chancellor [Bismarck] as school children rejoice at the departure of a strict teacher." These men were the agents of Germany's progressive decline. Bismarck was gone, lamented by only a few, especially among the young, who knew that "in Bismarck the character of the German people had once more become personified." [22]

Langbehn hated democracy, because it was based on the

* *Rembrandt,* p. 203. The formulation was of course idiosyncratic, but the distrust, even disdain, of Prussia, these were common feelings among a part of the cultural elite of imperial Germany. The great change came, as will be seen below, at the time of the First World War.

principle of human equality and run by human mediocrity. In the near future Germany would have to be rescued by a "Caesaristic-artistic . . . single individual. . . . Democracy is a body that yearns for a head, and that is why it so often acts headless and why it so easily finds a head, be it a demagogue or a Caesar." * Unity could be effected only through a leader, a *Führer,* who could intuit and express the true nature and will of the people. Etymologically, *Volk* implied following, and the German people had preserved its capacity to obey, its "monarchical calling." A new leader was needed who would "set the dead masses into motion; he deserves to rule. Not in the manner of a tyrant, but in the way in which Bismarck ruled over Germany, that is, by realizing the feelings, aspirations, and demands of his people, at times, it would seem, even against their will." [23] But Bismarck was gone, and all that was left, said Langbehn, was a republic with a crowned head, a Hohenzollern dynasty that lacked the power and the popularity of the Hohenstauffen. We need more pomp, more circuses. Unwittingly he provided a preview of William II's imperial circus, of his uneasy lurches toward popularity.

This active emperor needed a silent counterpart, "the secret emperor," the true unifier of German culture.† This folk hero would be on the scale of another Luther or Shakespeare, and he would rise to be the acknowledged legislator of all Germans. Langbehn shuttled back and forth between describing a cultural hero and a political *Führer.* Culture and

---

* *Rembrandt,* pp. 267–268. Note the slight discrepancy in the two references to Caesar. Actually Langbehn's ideal of a *Führer*—and that of so many of his contemporaries—was a looking backward at the image of an irresistible Caesar, and not a looking forward to a modern political leader of the twentieth-century variety. For a sympathetic review of the Caesar legend from Napoleon to Nietzsche, by a disciple of Stefan George, see Friedrich Gundolf, *Caesar im neunzehnten Jahrhundert,* Berlin 1926.

† Long after the popularity of the Rembrandt book had faded, Langbehn continued to promise the coming of this secret emperor that would rescue Germany. On countless occasions he would intimate that he himself was one of these emperors, or at least their prophet. The theme of a secret emperor is of course an old one in German mythology, and usually focused on Barbarossa in his Kyffhäuser mountain. See also Albrecht Mendelssohn Bartholdy, *The War and German Society. The Testament of a Liberal,* New Haven 1937, p. 99, who notes that in the north and northwest—in *Niederdeutschland*—the prevalent political view was republican, except for the widespread legend of the secret emperor.

politics were mixed, as always, just as abstraction and reality were thoroughly confounded, and the link between culture and politics was the moral effect of the former which would reform the spirit of the latter. Political disunity was essentially a moral failing, and hence moral reform would resolve all political conflict. More than that, it would enable Germany to take its rightful place as *magister mundi*. For the precept that "the best shall rule applies to people too and that is why the Germans have a calling to world domination." [24] Langbehn's progress from an imaginary secret ruler over culture to German supremacy in the world is not quite as odd or unique as it might seem; the popular defense of German imperialism always invoked the superiority of German *Kultur,* the hope

> Und es soll am deutschen Wesen
> Einmal noch die Welt genesen.*

Like so many of his contemporaries, Langbehn adduced a whole string of reasons for Germany's imperialist destiny. He made passing references to the dangers facing Germany. Her military and industrial power necessarily aroused the jealous hostility of her neighbors, her frightfully exposed location in the heart of Europe ordained that "in the European state system she either dominates or is dominated. A third pos-

---

* The couplet is Emanuel Geibel's, the thought is much older. The notion that the superiority of German culture was a legitimate warrant for Germany's supremacy in Europe was first enunciated at the time of Germany's spiritual awakening and political humiliation, that is, at the time of the great revolution. Schiller, for example, regarded German *Bildung,* a blending of classical thought with northern morality, as constituting the *Weltsendung* of the German people. In the nineteenth century, with the rise of German power and, ironically, the decline of German *Bildung,* the concept of a spiritual mission or domination was gradually materialized. In a profound, if hopelessly anachronistic essay, *Untersuchungen über das europäische Gleichgewicht,* Berlin 1859, Konstantin Frantz defined Germany's national calling *not* to be political unification in slavish imitation of the Western powers, but continued disunity and the spiritual leadership of a European community of peoples. Lagarde and Langbehn helped to approximate an old ideal of the spirit to a modern defense of political imperialism. Also see Ludwig Dehio's brilliant essay, "Gedanken über die deutsche Sendung 1900–1918," for a discussion of Germany's inability, unique among modern imperial powers, to define normative values that would justify and popularize German imperialism. *Deutschland und die Weltpolitik im 20. Jahrhundert,* München 1955, pp. 71–106.

sibility does not exist. As long as she is unified, she will dominate." A page later, he spoke of a world domination that would be essentially spiritual, though physically active as well. Yet another page, and he was preaching the "spiritual annexation" of Holland and Denmark—*Niederdeutsche* countries, of course—for their own sake, "so that they will not dullen because of the narrowness of their horizons." Germany must establish an empire from Amsterdam to Riga, and "she must collect all her children around her. That is the best policy of state and spirit. It is a family policy." [25]

Charles Andler, that scholarly detective of the roots of German imperialism, interpreted *Rembrandt als Erzieher* as "the first sign of the new philosophic Pan-Germanism" that emerged after the dismissal of Bismarck and in opposition to his weaker successors.[26] Although one can boggle at Andler's assessment of Langbehn's importance to the Pan-German movement, there can be no question about the centrality of imperialism in his political thought.* All the strands of fantasy came together in his timely plea for expansion, all his hopes for regeneration would be quickened by imperialism. Push the frontiers back, and the peasantry will expand and multiply, the *Niederdeutsche* element will be strengthened, the *Volk* will become healthier, the secret emperor more powerful.

The ultimate justification of imperialism was German culture, the very culture which he had set out to denounce. It seems incongruous for Langbehn to justify German imperialism by appealing to German culture when the rest of the book proclaimed the decline of that culture. To understand this apparent paradox, to understand this leap from despair to aggression, is to probe deeply into the roots of what I have here called the politics of cultural despair.

Discontent with culture and discontent with his own place in it inspired the pervasive pessimism of Langbehn's book. Germany's celebrated achievements in science and politics were vilified, and the failures of the age magnified and maligned. Langbehn could not bear to stop at diagnosis; he lacked the detachment, the "timelessness" that Nietzsche pre-

---

* Langbehn was proud of his appeal to Germans abroad: "*Rembrandt als Erzieher* is a pan-German book. In Austria, Russia, Scandinavia, England, Holland, and North America it received greater acclaim than in Germany." *Der Rembrandtdeutsche. Von einem Wahrheitsfreund*, p. 64.

scribed and possessed. He sought to be the prophet of doom *and* regeneration. He itched to play the activist, to become the "secret emperor," to lead others and thus himself, out of the maze of self-inflicted hatreds and frustrations. Despair had ultimately to yield to the promise of redemption. Hence the insistence on the several steps to regeneration, the healing powers of a Rembrandt, on the still slumbering powers of the *Niederdeutschen*—all these were verbal constructions designed to combat the deeply rooted sense of despair. Likewise the imperialist destiny which promised the regeneration of Germany and, paradoxically, was justified by Germany's cultural superiority which imperialism had yet to achieve. Langbehn, so earnestly thinking himself the heir of German idealism, scorned *Realpolitik* as well as economic self-seeking, but arrived at an identical program of aggressive expansionism from entirely idealistic—that is to say, abstract—premises. These premises had the further advantage of being infinitely flexible; they could be used to justify any deed or ambition. Seen in this light, his imperialism must be understood as a complement, not a negation of his cultural despair. Not Bismarck's quiet acquisition of a colonial empire, but the later, and largely unsuccessful, howling after a *Weltreich* sprang from this barely disguised sense of despair and discontent. The leap from Rembrandt to imperialism may have been particularly far-fetched and fanciful, but in the Germany of the 1890's all roads led to a place in the sun, and everything beginning in mystique ended in politics.

10: Langbehn and the Crisis

of the 1890's

Not since Goethe's Werther *and Schiller's* Räuber *has a truly important literary work had such a decisive impact as the Rembrandt book. People seek to disguise the impact now, but it will break through again.*   LANGBEHN

The signs of internal decay multiply: selfishness and the most reckless careerism have taken the place of a fine sense of honor and noble benevolence. The hearts of people are invaded by brutality and destructive ideas, while on the outside there arises today a dead, for us unprecedented, Byzantinism. With all this, our youth is becoming ever dumber, in a specialized sort of way, sheep follow the ram that happens to leap forward, and drinking to the leader and repeating each other's phrases have taken the place of independent thinking. In the past, things became 'fashionable' if one person, but not everybody followed; now a slogan or a catchword seizes people with the force of an epidemic, which a single person can hardly escape and which persists until a certain section of society is disinfected.

THEODOR FONTANE

Langbehn's confused lament caused an immediate and unprecedented sensation. Bookdealers exhibited the book as "the most important work of the century," critics praised, queried, or condemned it, and, above all, it *sold;* it was read, discussed, ridiculed, and acclaimed by thousands of people.[1] Langbehn had caught the mood of a groping, discontented, and aspiring people, and they in turn welcomed his book as an articulation of their own inchoate feelings of discontent. *Rembrandt als Erzieher* appeared anonymously, as if written by and for Everyman, an Everyman that stood uneasily before a tumultuous decade.

The book, so long in the making, came out at a propitious moment. To be sure, it had been preceded by isolated stirrings of revolt and discontent, by the first signs of yet another Young German rebellion against the old order, but that order had seemed imperturbable, even impervious. In 1890, when Rembrandt, the mythical educator and *Kunstpolitiker,* appeared, Bismarck, the *Realpolitiker,* the embodiment of tradition and authority, was cast aside. After his dismissal, the old order was visibly in retreat, and the decade that followed saw new, and often immensely promising departures in politics and thought, in the arts, in science, and in popular taste.* Most of these new departures Langbehn had in some fashion or other anticipated, above all the intensification of a *Reichsverdrossenheit,* of a dissatisfaction and ennui with the political culture of the new empire. This mood was not exclusively German; it was in fact a stormy analogue to the "psychic crisis" that gripped the United States at the end of the nineties, to the fever that seized France at the time of the Panama Scandal and the Dreyfus Affair, to the endemic eruption of populist nationalism and political anti-Semitism.† In Germany this psychic crisis was reflected in the great anti-Semitic victories of the early 1890's, in the ideology of the economically aggrieved agrarians, in the growing influence of the Pan-Germans, and above all in the youth movement at the end of the decade. And all these movements—as well as the intellectual and artistic innovations of the decade—seemed to echo the

---

* No general history of that brilliantly confused decade has yet been written, but H. Stuart Hughes's *Consciousness and Society. The Reorientation of European Social Thought,* New York 1958, is an excellent analysis of the intellectual movements that began in that decade. He notes that in Germany "an initial sign of the changed times was the appearance in 1890 of . . . *Rembrandt als Erzieher,*" p. 43.

† The psychic crisis in America was first analyzed by Richard Hofstadter in "Manifest Destiny and the Philippines," *America in Crisis. Fourteen Crucial Episodes in American History,* ed. by Daniel Aaron, New York, Knopf, 1952, pp. 173–200. Actually this psychic crisis seems to have afflicted most peoples in the Western world, and one of the common elements of it was a fierce revulsion against modernity.

mood and aspirations of the Rembrandt book. Fulfilling some promise of the book, these varied and contradictory movements insured the survival of its thought, even after the initial excitement had waned. Before the First World War, to proclaim oneself a "Rembrandtdeutscher" was to attest a noble commitment of the heart, a longing for a better and more artistic national future. After the war, the book enjoyed renewed popularity and several new editions appeared. Catholics and conservative critics of the Weimar Republic kept Langbehn's influence alive.*

No other work of the Germanic critics penetrated German culture so deeply, no other mixture of cultural despair and nationalist hope ever proved so popular. Rembrandt and art were the guarantors of respectability, and provided the Germanic ideology at the moment of its widest appeal with a conservative, idealistic, and thoroughly acceptable guise. The nihilistic and brutal undertone went largely undetected, the more so as the German public was accustomed to extraordinary violence in speech and polemic.

The sale of *Rembrandt als Erzieher* far exceeded Langbehn's own grandiose hopes. Week after week the sales increased, and new printings appeared. The critics could not ignore so overwhelming a success, and their attention to the book increased the sales still further. In the early months, the sale of the book was as much the cause of curiosity as the contents themselves. In the first year, sixty thousand copies were printed; in the first two years more than forty printings were sold. By 1893, interest began to wane, but the book remained on the market and continued to sell; in the mid- and late twenties, sales soared once again. By the end of the Second World War, at least 150,000 copies, including several posthumous editions and involving at least four different publishing houses, had been sold.[2]

The book became the great literary fad of 1890, not only among the general public but among the academic and artistic

---

* In 1922, Carl Neumann, in his authoritative *Rembrandt*, 3d ed., München, Bruckmann, 1922, I, 28, wrote: "The book had a great impact, and if we hear less about it now, it is because the best part of Langbehn's thought has been accepted by public opinion and appears self-evident. The author was right in much of what he wrote, and if his explanations often seem strange to us, we should hold to his theses, and remember that lawyers and judges make decisions, but that young law clerks write the opinions."

elite of Germany.* It became "the Spengler book of the nineties, a Spengler book before the catastrophe." [3] Its sales, in fact, approximated that of the later Spengler sensation, which in eight years sold—to a much larger reading public—100,000 copies.[4] It is significant—as well as mystifying—that many reviewers, including some of Germany's leading critics, hailed extravagantly what a recent, able critic has called "the shoddiest of literary wares." [5] There was some dissent, of course, but the book—or the storm it had created—was taken seriously, and the critical reception of the book facilitated its immense influence. After the First World War the philosopher Rudolf Eucken wrote: "Since the [original] appearance of this book, I have consciously lived through its effects and its history. . . . It has more and more proved to be a mighty force in German life." [6]

The public, not the critics, were the first to discover the book; in most instances, the reviewers merely confirmed, elaborated, and occasionally questioned what was by then an established success.[7] In 1890 and 1891, almost every major newspaper and quarterly carried a review. In the same years, an unprecedented spate of books and pamphlets, for or against the Rembrandt book, burst upon the book market, and some of these, especially the more obviously satirical ones, went through several printings as well.† Whether parodies or seri-

---

* As the merest example, consider Ernest Seillière's recollection that in 1890, when he was a student at Heidelberg, there "appeared a book which had tremendous sales and which became the topic of conversation for my teachers and fellow-students. It was called *Rembrandt als Erzieher* . . ." Ernest Seillière, *Morales et Religions Nouvelles en Allemagne. Le Néoromantisme au delà du Rhin,* Paris, Payot, 1927, p. 69; for the essay on Langbehn, see pp. 69–125. Again Cornelius Gurlitt in the standard work, *Die Deutsche Kunst des neunzehnten Jahrhunderts,* 3d ed., Berlin 1907, p. 470, recalled that the book "was ridiculed because of its numerous weaknesses and suffered a flood of mocking answers. But it was the first book in decades that was really read by artists."

† The most adulatory pamphlet was Max Bewer, *Rembrandt und Bismarck,* Dresden 1891, which in a few weeks went through ten printings. Bewer, a journalist and something of a poet, thought it "a mystical coincidence that at the time of Bismarck's dismissal there appears a book that tries with passionate genius to awaken the natural feeling of the German people. . . . It is a book for the ages. . . . It is a brilliant breakthrough against the materialistic West and at the same time a bold leap into the infinite" (pp. 38, 46, 66).

ous tracts, these replies to Rembrandt kept the literary controversy alive for several years.[8]

More important than the tracts were the countless serious reviews which appeared in the daily press and, with enviable rapidity, in every type of periodical. Even *Kladderadatsch,* the humor magazine, carried a large cartoon, showing a classroom in which Rembrandt as a teacher was brandishing a switch at several boys who were carting paintings in and out.[9] The critics were unanimous on one point: this was a strange book, and its public reception was unprecedented, puzzling, and highly significant. They disagreed as to why the book should have been so successful, just as they disagreed on all other aspects of the work. What pleased some outraged others, and what some viewed as the essence of the book, others totally ignored. No reviewer could ignore Langbehn's idiosyncratic style, and most critics echoed at least the positive part of Georg Simmel's summary in his long review in the *Vossische Zeitung:* "Never before have I heard such common and on the whole unimportant ideas elaborated with such sparkling spirit and in such original style." [10] The reviewers usually picked the theme closest to their own interests, and neglected the others. The first reviews tended to be favorable, indeed enthusiastic, but this was before Langbehn's revisions outraged some powerful groups, especially the Jews, the liberals, and some earnest Protestants.* Reviewers were impressed by the idealism of Langbehn's discontent, by his moral earnestness, by his sincerity, and—the timid among them—by his success. While conceding minor blemishes, they would always extol the book's lofty purpose and distinguished merit. Only a few—and those not the best-known reviewers—dissented and attacked the pretentious folly of the work or the ignorance of its author.

The world of art was delighted with the Rembrandt book and rejoiced at the success of a work that prophesied the rebirth of German art. By a meaningful coincidence, Langbehn's book appeared a short time after the founding of several widely

---

* In 1892, Langbehn explained the decline in his popularity: "The mendacity of the German (?) reviewers in the daily press is clearly demonstrated by the fact that they praised the author of the Rembrandt book to the skies until he uttered one word against the Jews; from that day on, he was continually maligned." *Der Rembrandt-deutsche. Von einem Wahrheitsfreund,* p. 42.

hailed periodicals dedicated to the arts.* All of these had a large and distinguished audience, and their several reviews of Langbehn's book marked important milestones in its career.

A front-page review which appeared six weeks after publication in *Der Kunstwart* was generally attributed to its editor, Ferdinand Avenarius:

The book itself and even more the storm which it evoked in the first five weeks—so exceptional for a book of this type—are of symptomatic importance for our time. . . . In the main, *Rembrandt als Erzieher* offers its readers few thoughts of striking originality. Not only Nietzsche and Lagarde, but the works of *many* contemporary critics . . . anticipated several of the thoughts of this work, and *Der Kunstwart* itself may point in good faith to [its own] articles . . . as proof of how close its aspirations are to the direction in which the unknown author travels. The chief significance of this work lies in the fact that the author molded in his heart a coherent *Weltanschauung* out of the diverse elements of his thought, a *Weltanschauung* which, new as it is, becomes at once typical of a *Weltanschauung* of hundreds, even thousands of Germans. In this sense *Rembrandt als Erzieher* is truly a work of deliverance.[11]

By stressing Langbehn's "symptomatic importance," his link to Nietzsche and Lagarde, and his promise of salvation, Avenarius anticipated the most persistent themes of the critics. Very much in the same vein was Friedrich Pecht's review which appeared on the front page of his periodical, *Die Kunst für Alle:*

"This book, so rich in ideas, deals with the future of art in our country and gives the editor of this magazine a particular satisfaction. On the basis of theoretical considerations, the book's thoughtful author came many times to the same conclusions as we had, slowly and laboriously after fifty years of practical experience. . . . Here we have a book so correct in its ideas that it should be read in its

---

* In 1885, Friedrich Pecht began publishing *Die Kunst für Alle;* in October, 1887, Ferdinand Avenarius founded *Der Kunstwart;* and on January 29, 1890, appeared Otto Brahm's *Freie Bühne für modernes Leben,* published by Fischer, Berlin. In March, 1890, Stefan George decided on the publication of another and self-consciously esoteric periodical, *Blätter für die Kunst.* The first issue appeared in October 1892 and proclaimed its faith "that art will have a magnificent rebirth." Friedrich Wolters, *Stefan George und die Blätter für die Kunst. Deutsche Geistesgeschichte seit 1890,* Berlin, Bondi, 1930, pp. 29, 42–43.

entirety, the more so as this book, now already in its third printing, offers useful suggestions on every page." [12]

Die Gesellschaft, the mouthpiece of German naturalism and realism and the defender of Zola, wrote of the book that sought to demolish Zola: "Praised by all the giddy-headed romantics as the new gospel of the Germans, the book is undoubtedly the work of a very good head and a brave heart. . . . [But] it estheticizes without end, as if we lived in a world which had not even heard at second-hand about the social question or social anguish and social need." [13]

More flattering was the thirteen-page review by Wilhelm Bode, Germany's most eminent Rembrandt scholar, which appeared in the March, 1890, issue of the widely read *Preussische Jahrbücher.* We have already noted that Bode praised Langbehn's empathy with Rembrandt; the book as a whole he called "a polemic, derived from the innermost life of the German spirit, which intends to find through a diagnosis of today's frequently corrupt conditions the basis for the necessary rebirth of German art and culture." [14]

Bode's review dealt primarily with questions of art, but his comment on the necessary rebirth of German art and culture struck a common note. Other critics also singled out this promise of redemption, yet it remains puzzling that even the most judicious critics of the day were so struck by the forcefulness of Langbehn's views or were themselves so attuned to them, that they failed to see, or having seen forgave, the feebleness of the argument and the atrociously bad style. Georg Brandes, who was a kind of secretary-general of European culture, and who had just delivered his pioneering lectures on Nietzsche, announced:

In the most disciplined of all European peoples, there has appeared once again a writer who preaches individualism. . . . The unknown author of *Rembrandt als Erzieher* is a very knowledgeable and clever man, original enough to be always interesting even when he becomes a bit tiresome, and sufficiently of his own age to express much that one is familiar with from reading the best German books and from conversation with the better Germans. . . . None will regret making the acquaintance of this distinguished eccentric. [15]

Finally consider the long review-essay by Maximilian Harden, soon to become Germany's foremost critic, and himself a stylist of erratic brilliance.

The wide commercial success of a serious, estheticizing book in the country of poets and thinkers is in itself a not negligible miracle, which the exemplary cheapness of the price can only partly explain. In the best and in the worst sense, the book is ingenious and that is some explanation; the personality which speaks here in the style of an eccentric, is important, unique, and original, and that explains all. After so many people of uniform pattern, there appears a human being; after so many routine efforts, a literary individuality. . . . His strong and self-assured personality has all the virtues and all the weaknesses of passionate subjectivity, and the book will please only someone who does not expect objective truth and rigorously disciplined logic, but who seeks the acquaintance of a noble and eccentric spirit that is fully conscious of its eccentricity.

According to Harden, individualism was the guiding principle of the Rembrandt book, an individualism that recalls both Nietzsche's aristocratic radicalism and Lagarde's thought and style: "In the end, the author of the *Deutsche Schriften* may be the nameless German [of the Rembrandt book]." But Harden saw that Langbehn's individualism really meant a cult of genius, and that his "hatred against the age and against science, the power which most advanced democracy" derived from the fact that the age was inhospitable to the growth of genius. But it was a dangerous mistake to let one's hatred of an age turn into the desire to *"corriger le monde,"* and Harden warned against the author's fanatical faith in his *Weltanschauung,* which to him was like a religion. The book should carry the admonition: "Use with caution." The prophet—and Harden was not the only one to consider Langbehn a prophet —was the more effective because "in the first place [the author] is a master stylist, the like of which we have not had since Schopenhauer, with the possible exception of Nietzsche. His wide reading is astounding, but the brilliance of his imagery and the inexhaustible plenitude of his ingenious, if occasionally contrived, paradoxical, metaphors command still greater admiration." [16] These few strictures notwithstanding, the tone of Harden's review was immensely, indeed shockingly, admiring.

Other journals and less well-known critics were more critical, if sometimes for spurious reasons. *Die Gartenlaube,* that comfortable family journal, hailed *Rembrandt als Erzieher* because its individualism was antisocialist, hence good. On the other hand, its glorification of a single tribe of Germans, the *Niederdeutschen,* would divide Germans still further, and that was bad. From its untroubled vantage point, *Die Gartenlaube* found Langbehn's antimodernity, his attack on contemporary culture, much too radical, and hence repugnant.[17] An unpersuasive defense of modernity was written by the historian Otto Seeck, who in 1891, in the *Deutsche Rundschau,* devoted forty-two pages, in three installments, to what he meant to be a definitive demolition of the Rembrandt book. Seeck justified the extraordinary length and vigor of his attack by pointing to the acclaim with which this strange preacher had been received. The book came straight from the heart "and therein lies its significance: for so many people felt that it came straight from their hearts. . . . That his book could have created such a tremendous sensation is the most conclusive proof of the prevalence of the errors which he preached." Seeck proceeded to knock down these errors of antimodernity and antiscientism, all from the point of view that "the old, yet often unheeded saying that all that is, is good, remains valid." He sought as well to knock down the author. Seeck was the first, as far as I was able to discover, to reveal Langbehn's name. "What is more reckless or more frivolous than his abuse of great German scholars of whose works he knows at best a few brochures or popular lectures! That our German—but why talk of our German! As long as one argues about ideas, anonymity may be proper, but if one attacks individuals, then one should back one's attacks with one's own person—that Dr. J. Langbehn, by profession an archaeologist," has read the works of Mommsen, Ranke, or Du Bois-Reymond, even he would not claim. Alternating *ad hominem* attacks with an uncritical faith in science and in the "continuous progress of humanity," Seeck lashed out at the trivialities and pretensions of the Rembrandt book. This long review with its condescending and insulting tone, with its own triviality of argument, had that flavor of clever superficiality which the Germanic critics—and many other Germans besides—so resented in modern criticism and journalism.[18]

An attack similar to Seeck's came from the prolific literary critic, Leo Berg, who warned "against this foolish and dangerous book. It is dangerous because its foolishness and the general folly of the age are closely related." Berg, a Jew and a progressive, singled out Langbehn's "repulsive chauvinism: If the success of this book can be considered as a thermometer for the chauvinism of present-day Germany, then it is time indeed to think of some cooling, pain-relieving drug against the national fever." The book has no artistic or literary merits, and the author is an ignoramus. Berg concluded: "It is not modern to have intellect or to be liberal. Our Rembrandt philosopher has no intellect and he does not care about modern freedom. In short he is the perfect German man, provided he is not a woman." [19]

With one spirited exception, the Catholic reviewers liked the Rembrandt book; after having been for many years isolated and alienated because of the *Kulturkampf*, they welcomed this tract as a potentially sympathetic voice from a patently patriotic non-Catholic. Therefore the Catholics hailed the book, despite its many near-blasphemous remarks about Jesus and Christianity. The two leading Catholic historians, Johannes Janssen and Ludwig von Pastor, warmly endorsed the book, and the aged and distinguished editor of the *Historisch-politische Blätter für das katholische Deutschland,* Dr. Jörg, became a friend and correspondent of Langbehn's.[20] Jörg's journal carried two long and important reviews and one postscript by P. W. von Keppler, later Bishop of Rottenburg. These reviews, as pointed out in chapter 7, played a decisive role in preparing Langbehn for his eventual conversion.

From the first, Keppler's reviews struck a peculiarly indulgent, solicitous tone. Keppler found it strange that a man *not yet* of the faith, a man in fact ignorant of the faith, should have so many valuable insights and ideas. The book's success should not deflect Catholics, even though commercial success usually attested wickedness. On the contrary, this book had not yet attained all the success it deserved. Its critical, as against its constructive, side commanded Keppler's unbounded admiration; he relished Langbehn's attack on the predominance of reason, on "the contemporary barbarism with gas light," and his defense of the heart, of sentiment, of art, and of morality.

One can hardly read a single page of the book without running into ideas which one joyfully accepts and appropriates, without running into sentences in which one finds the resolving or redeeming word for things long sought or sensed, for unclear and enigmatic sides of the present. Not a page, but one admires anew the eminent richness of the author's intellect, the sovereign view of all fields of culture, the sharpness of his mind, as well as the depth of his soul, the brilliance of his eagle eye, and the pure and ideal purpose and the high ethical seriousness.

Such praise for a man who had explicitly repudiated the divinity, even the moral uniqueness of Jesus! How strongly antiliberal Keppler and his wing of the Church must have felt, to champion this unorthodox work! To be sure, there was regret tempered by anticipation that this promising author should deny the primacy of Christianity over other religions and over art. He would learn, Keppler thought: "His credo is certainly indistinct, vague, and colorless." Even in his present state, however, he was superior to modern atheists and naturalists, and with a little education in the faith, the author would come to understand that Rembrandt could never be the Saviour.[21]

A year later, in a review of the expanded thirty-seventh edition, Keppler reported considerable improvement. Many pro-Protestant statements had been dropped, many pro-Catholic sentiments added. Modernity had been still more vigorously attacked, and "Jewry was hit with powerful clubs." All that was to the good, and on the right path. Langbehn remained antimaterialist and antinaturalist, and his regard for the simple and the childlike justified the hope that he would yet find the true faith. "In the future the artist in him will have to die . . . so that the Christian can arise, the German will have to die in him, so that the man can arise." [22]

In a third review, dealing primarily with Langbehn's second anonymous book, *Der Rembrandtdeutsche,* Keppler noticed with alarm that his potential ally and convert had lost a good deal of ground. Keppler was appalled by the ferocity of Langbehn's attacks on his critics, and he chastised him for his ruthless outburst against the Jews, though Keppler himself called them bacilli. "To be sure, the Judaization [*Verjudung*] of the press, of literature, of the 'leading circles' is a terrible plague of the present age," but Langbehn's attack, nevertheless was a tactical error. Keppler urged him to be moderate, modest, even charitable. Keppler was afraid that Langbehn had lost the path to salvation, and on that note of troubled admonition ended this public wooing of a man's soul.[23]

How different from these reviews, so instrumental in converting Langbehn's mysticism to Catholicism, was the previously mentioned attack on the book by the Jesuit literary critic Alexander Baumgartner. What Keppler lauded—Langbehn's antimodernity—his Jesuit colleague condemned. To Baumgartner, Langbehn's "mighty intellect" seemed puny and his moral idealism appeared as sheer verbosity: "Here we stand before the crassest naturalism." He listed four fantasies of the book, and attacked them all, but most painstakingly the nonsensical assumption that the modern world should, or could, be undone. The worst fantasy he dismissed quickly: "The assumption that one could turn religion into art, that one can treat it as if it were a matter of taste. All approaches to Christian ideas are submerged as soon as they appear, in a staggering waterfall of words, in which paganism and Christianity, general nonsense about humanitarianism and German Protestantism, sentimental mysticism and the latest freemasonry are crazily mixed." Langbehn's lament was only "the anxious cry of resentful one-sidedness, of unsatisfied Germanism, and of ignorant *Kunstschwärmerei*." The book's success was in itself alarming; twenty-five printings in ten months was a "most serious and regrettable sign of the times. If thousands upon thousands can remain untroubled in the face of such massive blows to common sense, then this healthy sense must already have lost much of its virility and vitality, then the elementary principles of religion must have disappeared." [24] Like so many other hostile critics, Baumgartner thought Langbehn a dangerous and wrong-headed prophet, and his distress at the likely consequences of the Rembrandt book seemed fully justified by its immense impact on the culture of the 1890's.

In turning from the immediate reception of the Rembrandt book to a discussion of its more lasting effects on German life, one is forced back on speculative generalities. This would be true of any such attempt—to assess the influence of a book or a man is a notoriously hazardous task. This is doubly true when one deals with a book of prophecies; yesterday's popular prophet survives or not, but in neither case can one easily establish whether his prophecy helped to bring about or merely anticipated the actual developments. At the appropriate moment, and in an effective style, Langbehn had given expression to the thoughts and sentiments which later came to characterize a new cultural epoch. His success paved the way for many of the cultural movements of the Wilhelmine period, and these movements in turn kept alive his ideas and his memory. Many of the important innovators of the later period read and admired the "Rembrandtdeutsche." Langbehn appealed most strongly, however, to the nonintellectuals, to the young and the nonarticulate. Though his influence on them, no matter how great and far-reaching, is difficult to trace, it is possible to say with assurance that "his ideas appeared in hundreds of places." [25]

The year 1890 marked a turning point in the cultural life of Germany. The decade that followed witnessed a quickening of thought and hope, a new concern for the inner freedom of man, an anxious brooding on how this freedom could be realized in modern Germany.* Symptoms of this search could be seen everywhere: the sudden flowering of Nietzsche's fame, the concern for education and the critique of excessively intellectualized schools, the call for art and beauty, the vogue of sports for both sexes, the change in fashion, away from funereal attire—all these were new departures that Langbehn had in some way anticipated. The political situation had changed as well. The withering of the Bismarckian order led to a diffusion of authority which in turn favored the organization of the disaffected and the growth of countless pressure groups. In the 1890's everybody organized in Germany, but the greater the national divisiveness and the fumbling uncertainty of the Kaiser, the stronger the clamor for national unity and moral regeneration.

---

* When nearly eighty years old, Friedrich Meinecke, the great historian and sensitive recorder of his *Lebensweg,* recalled how some fifty years earlier he had witnessed a profound change: "In all of Germany something new can be detected around 1890, politically and intellectually as well. . . . Politically things went down, intellectually they went up again. . . . However one assesses the positive worth of what was accomplished then, first in the fine arts and poetry, later on in the humanistic disciplines, one thing is certain, there stirred a new and deeper longing for what was genuine and true, but also a new sense for the fragmentary and the problematic [*zerrissene Problematik*] in modern life, a sense which sought to penetrate from life's civilized surface to its now terrifying, now tempting depths. . . . Put in banal terms, the period after 1890 can at least boast of better taste than what on the average had prevailed in the two decades after 1870." Friedrich Meinecke, *Erlebtes 1862–1901,* Leipzig 1941, pp. 167–168.

I have said that Langbehn anticipated many of these movements and aspirations. More importantly, his peculiar conjunction of ideas—his esthetic concern with politics and his cultural defense of imperialism, his link between morality and the imaginary character of the old Germans, became the common line of the emerging new right-wing groups, which for sound tactical and psychological reasons emphasized its esthetic rather than political opposition to modernity. Simplicity, nature, energy, *Volkstum,* a Germanic art and a new Germanic community—these were some of the key words and ideas which Langbehn introduced or popularized, which separately had their appealing and idealistic side, but when taken ·together came to describe a new and pernicious force in German life.

Even Langbehn's crankiest notions—his ideas on health, for example—found a resounding echo in a decade in which "the belief in spirits flowered. The faith healers enjoyed a prosperous time." [26] Nowhere was his influence more direct, nowhere did all the strands of his being and all the strands of the period coincide more closely than in that spontaneous, activist revolt against modernity, the Youth Movement. The comradeship of youth with nature, the rebellion against bookish learning, the simple, hardy life—these were the living thoughts of the Rembrandt book. Between Langbehn and the style of the decade—its search for values and morality, its melancholy and its hope, its individualism and its craving to organize, its fear and its grandiosity—a close affinity prevailed.

With Langbehn, as with Lagarde, it was the gentle side that received the first and most enthusiastic acclaim. The prophet, the *praeceptor Germaniae,* the moralist—this is how Langbehn was remembered and how his fame was first exploited by the rising political movements of the right.* They

---

* The gentle Langbehn, the moral teacher, was still remembered in the very recent past: "He [Langbehn] carried the vocation of the writer to the highest level. Although the events of our time have confirmed his teachings, they have also superseded them. For the decline was irreversible. But his teachings will always be dug up again and will find imitators who will orient themselves by these teachings and, even more, by the personality of the author. Langbehn will join the ranks of the great conservative reformers of life and culture who will always be in demand as the leading opponents of the rise of the mass society." Rudolf K. Goldschmit-Jentner, *Vollender und Verwandler,* pp. 195 f.

gratefully invoked his plea that Germans should cherish their native traditions and spurn the false lure of intellectualism and cosmopolitanism. This resolve, so traditional among a people which for centuries had submitted to the cultural preëminence of others, became the rallying cry of "the invigorating Germanic Movement [that] swept through the land in the 1890's," and widely propagated Langbehn's nativist primitivism.[27]

This Germanic Movement was essentially the organized expression of a state of mind, of a feeling of discontent that had no clear source or goal. Small groups of men came together and formed patriotic societies, pledged themselves to keep alive and pure the old Germanic culture and to annihilate its enemies. At a time of shifting loyalties, when the Kaiser consorted with Jews and his government dared encroach on agrarian privileges, these groups embraced a new type of nationalism: "The nationalist does not fight for the German fatherland, but for the German people." * And whatever the specific aims of these organizations, they all sought, with characteristic illogicality, to purify and strengthen German culture, now embattled and declining, but destined nevertheless to establish its supremacy in the world. This type of imperialism, identified with the people, not the state, became closely intertwined with anti-Semitism and the desire for Caesarism. It was in the 1890's that cultural pessimism and antimodernity became the twin resentments of the disaffected, conservative elements of imperial Germany and hence could be manipulated by various interest groups as well. Modernity and the "progressive," official Germany suddenly became *undeutsch,* un-German.

To promote pure Germanism at home and abroad was the purpose of the *Deutschbund,* for example, which Friedrich Lange organized in 1894 "as a community, a *Burschenschaft*

---

* See M. R. Gerstenhauer's autobiographical guide to the Germanic Movement, *Der völkische Gedanke in Vergangenheit und Zukunft. Aus der Geschichte der völkischen Bewegung,* Leipzig 1933, p. 14. As a student in the *Gymnasium,* Gerstenhauer had read Langbehn "with great joy," and as a young man, in the early 1890's, he joined and rose to the top of all the Germanic organizations in sight. A devout disciple of Lagarde, he also showed his kinship to Langbehn in his several pamphlets for the Pan-German League, praising the *niederdeutsche* Boers and pleading for the annexation of all *niederdeutsche* countries.

of adults," open to all except Jews.[28] Its learned leaders and middle-class members carried on their anti-Semitic campaign to the end of the Weimar Republic. Another anti-Semite, Theodor Fritsch, who in a series of letters to Langbehn had converted him to a tougher brand of anti-Semitism, began to publish yet another journal, *Der Hammer,* in which the virtues of the soil and of racial purity were extolled as the potential conquerors of the Jews. To these and similar groups Langbehn was a kind of patron saint, and it was due to his success and personal intervention that the *Deutsche Schriften* of the other, even more prominent patron saint, Lagarde, were published in a second printing in 1891.*

In addition to these unpolitical groups, with their interlocking directorates and overlapping memberships, the Germanic ideology of antimodernity was exploited by some larger political organizations as well. Various groups that were socially or economically aggrieved—the agrarians and some other elements of the Conservative party—sought to recruit mass support by adopting this nationalist, populist, anti-Semitic ideology, as witness the Tivoli Program of the Conservatives adopted, in 1892, and the League of German Farmers, organized in 1893. In a rapidly changing Germany, the old pieties—Lutheranism, the monarchy, and Prussian patriotism—were no longer attracting enough votes. In an attempt to regain their strength, the conservative parties reached out for a new ideology and shifted their emphasis from what was to be conserved, to what should be recovered, the Germanic past, and to what was to be destroyed, modernity. To defend Germany's character and ancient culture against the grasping, corroding hands of the Jewish intelligentsia—this seemed a more viable program than the overt

---

* So Lagarde's widow asserted. See Anna de Lagarde, *Paul de Lagarde,* Göttingen 1894, p. 108. One of the most prominent and repugnant figures of the Germanic Movement, Adolf Bartels, a professor of literature, recalled that "in the last years of the nineteenth century, the German people and those writers who were consciously serving it, became thoroughly fed up with the style of 'the Berlin Modern,' especially as it now dealt in *fin de siècle* as well, and they developed a strong counterforce, which succeeded in establishing a place for itself even though the press and the theater were in Jewish hands. The stimulus often came from Langbehn's *Rembrandt als Erzieher.*" See *Einführung in das deutsche Schrifttum füur deutsche Menschen, In 52 Briefen,* 2d ed., Leipzig, Kohler und Amelang, 1933, p. 507.

defense of grain tariffs or the protection of class prerogatives. Such a program won support and votes from people whose immediate interests were not affected, but who were gratified by an ideology that flattered their resentments. In this enterprise, Langbehn's gospel seemed relevant indeed, and his success paved the way for the new dispensation. One contemporary observer, F. Greiffenrath, attributed the election of 1893, in which the Berlin radicals and intelligentsia were routed, and the anti-Semites won an unprecedented victory, to Langbehn's influence "the translation [of the Rembrandt book] into the will of the people, expressed in parliamentary language." [29]

The best-known political organization of the period, the Pan-German League, had its beginnings in 1890, was formally organized under a different name a year later, and again reorganized as the Pan-German League in 1894. In its manifesto of 1891 it called on all Germans, at home and abroad, to take part in its work:

We believe that in working for the preservation and expansion of the German spirit in the world our people most effectively promotes the construction of world morality. For our German *Kultur* represents the ideal core of human intellect [*Denkarbeit*], and every step which is taken for Germanism belongs therefore to humanity as such and to the future of our species [*Geschlecht*].[30]

The league, which had more academics as members than representatives of any other single group, never abandoned its double goal: the preservation of Germanism at home, which implied a reactionary, anti-Semitic policy, and the extension of German influence abroad. Its constitution stated: "The league strives to quicken the Germanic-national [*deutsch-nationale*] sentiment of all Germans and in particular to awaken and foster the sense of racial and cultural kinship of all sections of the German people. . . . [It seeks] the settlement of all cultural and educational . . . problems in ways that conform to the tradition of the German people [*Volkstum*]." [31] Material interests may at times have exploited and directed the Pan-German League for their own ends, but the strongest sentiment of the league sprang from the same kind of troubled utopianism as Langbehn's imperialism had. In that sense Charles Andler was right in placing Langbehn among the most important representatives of Pan-Germanism.*

Although the several Germanic groups could quite properly claim Langbehn as their own, they certainly had no monopoly of him. In the long run the importance of Langbehn to the nationalists was precisely this ubiquity of his influence; he was one of the bridges between the rabble-rousing nationalists and anti-Semites and the highly respectable, culturally discontented, politically disinterested groups in German life. It is in fact among the latter that Langbehn's greatest influence could be felt.

It was common for all critics to hail Langbehn's book as a defense of individualism, and nothing could have been timelier than his attack on the spiritual starvation of the individual.† Everywhere in the 1890's arose the cry for a new type of individualism, one that lay beyond the counting houses of Manchester or the electoral systems of the democrats. The new individualism was a plea for the natural man, for the psychological and biological self that was to be delivered from the shackles of society and conventions. This exaltation of the individual had analogues in the higher and more formal realms of thought, where the attack on positivism in the sciences and on naturalism in the arts attested a vital concern for the subjective and the volitional. In philosophy, there was the revival of Max Stirner's works,‡ in the arts,

---

* In our own time, the eminent Marxist critic, Georg Lukács, still arraigned Langbehn as an imperialist and incidentally placed him in some strange and distinguished company: In contrast to Nietzsche, he wrote, "the ordinary pamphleteers of reaction, from the *Rembrandt-deutsche* to Koestler and Burnham in our own days, never get beyond the point of satisfying, with more or less skillful demagogy, the immediate, tactical needs of the imperialist bourgeoisie." *Die Zerstörung der Vernunft*, Berlin 1954, p. 251.

† A few months after the appearance of *Rembrandt*, Leo Berg, a persistent critic of Langbehn's, commented: "The clamor for individuality is universal today. It arises whenever men of new and great ideas demand light and freedom; but it also appears when some feeble, sickly person, destined to decline and feeling his existence endangered, rallies for a last-ditch defense." *Zwischen zwei Jahrhunderten. Gesammelte Essays*, Frankfurt 1896, p. 293.

‡ John Henry Mackay, a native Englishman who had become a German, sponsored the Stirner revival. For the individualism of that period see Georg Steinhausen's somewhat tendentious *Deutsche Geistes- und Kulturgeschichte, von 1870 bis zur Gegenwart*, Halle 1931, pp. 302–365.

the cult of Stefan George. George's life and work resembled the *heimliche Kaiser* whom Langbehn had prophesied, though George's revolt against his age was not rooted in a primitive past, but looked toward the charismatic rule of the esoteric. The dramas of Ibsen and Strindberg, then at the height of their popularity, and the works of their German disciples, these too described the struggle of modern men against various forms of tyranny and propounded the duty of radical self-assertion. Above all it was the sudden, tragically belated, and at times wrong-headed recognition of Nietzsche as a great thinker and individualist that coincided with the popularity of Langbehn's ideas.

Nietzsche, who during the creative period of his life had been ignored or reviled by the German public and who then was succumbing to an incurable disease, was first hailed in 1890 as the preëminent German thinker. "The Germans of the 1870's and 1880's knew next to nothing of Nietzsche." [32] During the first decade of his new fame, he was celebrated primarily for his "aristocratic radicalism," for his soaring individualism.* This one-sided interpretation allowed for the pairing of Nietzsche and Langbehn on equal terms, a frequent error in German books before the First World War.† Many critics, indeed, assumed that the Rembrandt book had

---

* The phrase, of course, was Brandes's, who used it as the title of his essay of 1889—the first serious study ever written of Nietzsche. Two years earlier, Nietzsche had commented to Brandes that "Aristocratic Radicalism" was "the cleverest thing I have yet read about myself." Georg Brandes, *Friedrich Nietzsche,* London, Heinemann, 1914, p. 64.

† In 1904 another Scandinavian, August Strindberg, linked the two men: "At that time, in 1889 [*sic*], two new thinkers and prophets appeared, Langbehn, the author of *Rembrandt als Erzieher,* and Nietzsche, best known as the author of *Beyond Good and Evil.* However great the differences between these two were, however much the differences may have appeared as diametrical opposites, they nevertheless shared one common tendency: the reaction against the microscopic view [*Mikroskopie*]. Langbehn was above all a macroscopic viewer. . . . Langbehn, with whom the century was to close, was really a kind of resurrected Kant, with whom the century opened, and both sought salvation in postulates and imperatives because the faculty of judgment [*Urteilskraft*] and pure reason are not capable of solving the riddle of the world [an allusion to Haeckel's *Welträtsel*] and to give the individual the hold he needs to steer a safe course in the open sea." August Strindberg, *Die gotischen Zimmer. Familienschicksale vom Jahrhundertende,* transl. by Emil Schering, München and Leipzig, 1908, p. 113.

paved the way for the enthusiastic reception of Nietzsche. The young, however, preferred Langbehn, and it is probably correct that "until recently [1897] the philosophical textbook of the German youth was not the Zarathustra book, but the Rembrandt book." [33]

In that decade, while their elders talked reform, the young reached out for a life of their own making. For several decades there had been agitation for a reform of education in Germany, and Langbehn distilled much of this agitation into his diatribe against overintellectualized culture. For years the *Gymnasium* had been attacked for its excessive, deadening concentration on classical learning, for its remoteness from things German and patriotic, for its intolerable neglect of the natural sciences. William II, whose years at the Kassel *Gymnasium* had been something of an uninstructive ordeal, entered the struggle over education with his usual gusto. In December, 1890, on his initiative, a Reich Education Conference convened, at which he expounded his own educational theories. He registered many of the old complaints and urged many of the old reforms, but his additions, and even more the mood of his speech, suggested a striking, if accidental, affinity to Langbehn's beliefs. William II stressed the need for more exercise and greater strength and agility among students, demanded a more conscious devotion to the Germanic tradition, and an education adapted to modern needs.[34] The conference fulfilled only a few of his hopes; it reduced the students' total study load and increased their work in German studies at the expense of Latin. For years the agitation continued, and so strong were the conflicting interests that no thoroughgoing reform of the *Gymnasium,* that magnificent and dreaded barracks of the mind, was ever achieved. Langbehn's demand for a rigorous athletic program found limited realization in the establishment in 1891 of a Central Committee for the Promotion of National Youth Games in Germany, which "was intimately associated with nationalist thought." [35]

By the end of the decade, Langbehn's exaltation of childhood was no longer an uncommon sentiment. In 1902 appeared the popular German translation of the Swedish feminist Ellen Key's *The Century of the Child* which, with its prophetic title, epitomized the growing concern for the understanding and protection of the child.* The rigid discipline of school and home should no longer curb the creative talents of the child, and these demands found practical embodiment in several school experiments, especially Hermann Lietz's boarding school at Ilsenburg and Gustav Wyneken's more liberal experiment in student autonomy [*Freie Schulgemeinde*] at Wickersdorf. Many of these new educational ideals struck a note similar to Langbehn's hopes and like them were often cast in a populistic mold.

Toward the end of the century, the exaltation of art as salvation gripped a large number of students and beginning *bohémiens*. For that generation, the credo of art for art's sake, the impudent pleasure of *épater le bourgeois*, were no longer enough; now it was art for the sake of the nation, for the sake of one's higher moral self, art as the only meaningful way of life. For many of them, Langbehn's Rembrandt was a beguiling pedagogue, with his appealing mixture of art and morality.†

Even the ideal of art was organized in the 1890's, as witness the *Kunsterziehungsbewegung*, on which Langbehn had the most direct and most easily identifiable influence.[36] In that decade and beyond, under the leadership of artists and men of affairs, an attempt was made to translate this esthetic concern into workaday life and practice. Some men were primarily interested in promoting—through practical means like inexpensive reproductions, better art instruction in schools, and the like—the cultivation of artistic sensibility and imagi-

---

* The feminist movement, to which Langbehn as an antimodern and part-time misogynist was undoubtedly antagonistic, also appealed to his principles of individualism and self-development. In that organization-laden decade, women organized as well, and in 1894 the League of German Women's Clubs was founded.

† The biographies and autobiographies of the period abound in examples of this attitude. As one example, consider the reminiscences of Wilhelm von Scholz, noted poet and essayist; about his student life in Lausanne in 1893, he remembered the endless talking bouts with his fellow-students and their belief "that the monumental deed that has been vouchsafed us, is to usher in, after the centuries of faith with their inherent errors, the century of knowledge, and for the confused, emotional needs of mankind, the century of absolute' art." This was the common faith of all his friends, not just of the one fanatic who "was set afire by the ebullient confusions and the oracular commonplaces of the *Rembrandtdeutsche*." Wilhelm von Scholz, *Eine Jahrhundertwende. Lebenserinnerungen*, Leipzig, List, 1936, pp. 52, 54.

nation in order to enrich the individual's life. Others had a vision of a new harmony between the arts and the machine age; they were groping even then for a beauty to be found in modern, functional construction, in architecture, interior decoration, and industrial design. These were men deeply troubled about the future of their suddenly industrialized fatherland, about the alienation of the worker from his work, about the monumental ugliness of urban life that belied the esthetic promise of modern technology and planning. In the *Kunsterziehungsbewegung* there were instances of extravaganzas and flights into imaginary pasts, but for the most part it was a serious effort of devoted and disinterested men, who placed their hopes and lavished their efforts on these esthetic reforms which they hoped would solve Germany's intractable political problems as well.

This Arts and Crafts Movement sought through various means to improve the public taste. After 1901, biennial conferences—*Kunsterziehungstage*—were held, and Alfred Lichtwark, in his concluding address to the first such meeting spoke in a manner that underlined the close spiritual link between Langbehn's work and theirs:

The demand for an artistic education does not appear in isolation; from its first hour it was inextricably connected with the contemporaneous, more clearly formulated call of the mid-eighties for a moral renovation of our life. The two fields are inseparable. . . . For too long we have lived essentially for intellect. It is high time now for the moral-religious and artistic forces to reach their full development.[37]

In 1902, Ferdinand Avenarius organized the *Dürerbund*, a rapidly growing society that sought to advise the government, the public, and business on esthetic problems, in a general effort to combine utility with beauty. It became an effective lobby for cultural excellence. In 1907, Friedrich Naumann, together with the architect Hermann Muthesius, the publisher Eugen Diederichs, Ferdinand Avenarius, and Alfred Lichtwark, established the *Werkbund*, a long-lived society that sought to bring together artists and industrialists, designers and technicians, in order to raise the esthetic standards of modern life.* The *Werkbund*, a conscious adaptation

---

* Theodor Heuss, who had long been active in the *Werkbund*, rightly lamented that "the history of the *Werkbund*—one of the most im-

of the English Arts and Crafts Society, hoped to restore a measure of joy in life and work, to promote "the hallowing of labor by art." * In the diverse ambitions of the entire movement, many of which were realized only in the Weimar period, in the tacit linkage of art, morality, and nationalism, we see that Langbehn's influence on German culture truly endured.

It was an influence that did not go unchallenged. A decade after the furor over the Rembrandt book had subsided, the great philologist Hermann Diels, in an oration to the Prussian Academy of Sciences, denounced the modern apotheosis of art with its denigration of science. He traced the history of this onslaught on science, pointing out that since Rousseau there had been many men in different periods that had exalted art over science. At present, he said, there raged once again a struggle between the young and the old, and "The battle cry [of the young] is art, art at any price. . . . From our point of view two pioneer fighters stand out in the ranks of this bellicose youth; they were the first to intone the favorite battle slogan 'Forward to Art' in the field of science." The two pioneers were Langbehn and Nietzsche.

One of these youths, who had just learned the elements of science, appeared before the German people with a great reform plan. Cleverly he appealed to the patriotic mood, which had waxed after the great war and the political unification, and he recommended that patriotic art should be cultivated instead of a science that was alienated from the state and lost in mean minutiae. As a master and an example to art, he proposed the great painter of the

---

portant and most moving chapters of German *Geistesgeschichte* of the period—has not yet been written." Note also the explicit acknowledgment that Naumann had read Lagarde and Langbehn and that both had "exerted their influence on him." Theodor Heuss, *Friedrich Naumann. Der Mann, das Werk, die Zeit*, 2d ed., Stuttgart and Tübingen 1949, pp. 224 and 103. For the *Werkbund* see also the marvelously egotistical recollections of Ernst Jäckh, who for some years was executive director of the *Werkbund; Der Goldene Pflug, Lebensernte eines Weltbürgers*, Stuttgart 1954, pp. 195–208.

* The phrase was William Morris's, who was the dominant figure of the Arts and Crafts Society. There was one significant difference between the English society and the *Werkbund:* Morris was a socialist of sorts, and his German counterparts were staunchly antisocialistic, were hoping in fact to weaken Marxism through the *Werkbund.* Cf. Holbrook Jackson, *The Eighteen Nineties*, new ed., London 1927, pp. 246–247.

chiaroscuro, who would surely be a little surprised if he heard that he had been proclaimed the German national hero.

Langbehn's book had been successful partly because "of the heavy attacks on the ornaments of our academy; it apparently pleases certain circles to listen to the confessions of renegades, who as initiates instill special confidence in those more remote from the field. Despite the tremendous ephemeral success, the enthusiasm for this confused and immature book soon evaporated. Today it is already forgotten." [38] Even as the venerable Diels was burying the book, the memory of Langbehn was kept alive in the decade's fiercest rebellion against modern life, against the very elders whom Diels had pronounced victorious.

The German Youth Movement erupted like a great phenomenon of nature. Out of unsuspected depths leapt forth defiance, hate, yearning, love, all the hopes and fears that for decades had been repressed, denied, forcibly sublimated. The movement was spontaneous, translating sentiment directly into action, with thought as a kind of intermittent and subordinate guide. Even the briefest description of the Youth Movement will demonstrate its close affinity, historical and psychological, to Langbehn.[39] What he had confusedly articulated, the youths exuberantly acted out; they heeded his message, as they willingly acknowledged, and the few indispensable adults who helped and protected them, had also been followers of the Rembrandtdeutsche.

The Youth Movement had its simple beginnings in 1897, in Steglitz, a comfortable, bourgeois suburb of Berlin. Students from the local humanistic *Gymnasium*, enthralled by the charismatic leadership of an older comrade, Karl Fischer, bound themselves together and organized weekly hikes. Soon they wore their own distinct garb, and always tramped in rough, remote terrain, where physical toughness was rewarded by a new, longed-for proximity to nature. On their *Fahrten* and in their crude camps they sought once more the blue flower, sang their quaint student songs, and reveled in the *Bunderlebnis*, in the experience of belonging.* But in a

---

* Mario Domandi rightly calls attention to the significance of the mystical language of the Youth Movement; see "The German Youth Movement," Columbia University doctoral dissertation, 1960, chapter 8. According to Herbert Mau, "the vital center of the Youth Movement is an *Erlebnis*. As an irrational occurrence which has its most

country that was still strictly authoritarian, the very act of organizing brought the young to the brink of revolt, because student organizations in school or out were forbidden by law. By establishing a "front" organization of parents and friends, Fischer, the *Führer* whom his followers greeted with *Heil*, had won recognition of his group from the *Gymnasium's* director. In 1901, this innocent escape from city life, from the dull drill of the school and the uncomprehending authoritarianism of the home, turned into the *Wandervogel*, still under Fischer's leadership, and the organization spread at once to all parts of Germany, enrolling in its ranks *Gymnasium* students of middle-class origin.

The *Wandervogel* grew—and splintered—rapidly. Secession groups, dissidents, left- and right-wing deviationists, sprang up; some groups wanted to keep the movement pure and primitive, others wanted to make the *Fahrten* a little more comfortable and the movement a bit more respectable. After a few years, Fischer's leadership was repudiated, and fights over program and organization ensued. All of this attested the pathetic fact that the larger and more ambitious the *Wandervogel* became, the more certain was their failure. The movement had all the intensity of love in it, but of a love that had no future. The more enthralling the *Bunderlebnis,* the *Fahrten,* the greater the agony of its end, and of the gradual reëntry into the real world, into their father's culture. They had to "get-on," as it was called, get-on in a drab, grubby world, and neither the wisdom of the *Gymnasium* nor the wild exuberance of the *Fahrten* prepared a boy quietly to accept his ticket, to do his job, to scramble, and to die. The Youth Movement was a complicated failure, but it called attention to the deeply rooted resentments and unsatisfiable aspirations of German youth. The mood persisted, and eventually the pent-up energies were to prompt sports less innocent than *Fahrten ins Blaue.**

---

important effects in psychic developments, it eludes the possibility of definition. . . . The quest allows German bourgeois youth to experience male society and in that manner to overcome the perplexities of late-bourgeois conditions of life." "Die deutsche Jugendbewegung. Rückblick und Ausblick," *Zeitschrift für Religions- und Geistesgeschichte,* I (1948), 135 f.

* Consider the testimony of Hermann Rauschning, an astute observer: "The Youth Movement which we all know, the movement to which we all belonged in our time as senior schoolboys, was the first start of

Spontaneous and nonintellectual in the beginning, as the movement grew and began to demand sacrifices and decisions, it could not avoid acquiring self-consciousness and ideological justification. The young had to understand, and make others understand, what it was that their passions had driven them to do. At that moment in their history the *Rembrandt-deutsche* seemed to beckon as a short-cut to the articulation of their own feelings. By rebelling against the culture of their fathers and their teachers, against the whole stifling system of pedantry and overintellectualism, abstraction and artificiality, they were acting out Langbehn's rebellion. Hans Blüher, passionate historian of the Youth Movement and one-time participant, was right in calling it the *Romantik der Empörung*.

Its pleasures and activities, its delight in nature and the disciplined body, its revival of populist art, its revulsion from intellectuality—all betrayed a close affinity to Langbehn.* Beyond this general affinity there were the countless instances

---

the revolutionary dynamism which today is culminating in the doc-trineless revolution and turning into its own opposite. One is tempted to regard the years in which this movement started as marking a deep and radical cleavage in the general mental outlook. The generations which personally took part in the Youth Movement are able to understand and sympathize with many impulses with which the older generations, which had no personal experience of that first escape from the trammels of conventional existence, have no sympathy. Even the oldest ex-members of the Youth Movement, now in their fifties, are capable of a fellow-feeling for the youngest of the postwar generations. It is their common antiliberalism, their more or less radical rejection of the capitalist outlook on life, that unites all who have passed through adolescence since the turn of the century. The youthful restlessness of the original movement may have turned into a revolutionary restlessness of a very brutal sort, but there is no doubt that beneath the 'hiking' for its own sake, or the urge to get on the move in order to still the inner revolutionary unrest, and today's random revolutionary dynamism with its rage for marching, there are deep common elements." Hermann Rauschning, *The Revolution of Nihilism. Warning to the West*, New York 1939, pp. 64–65.

* Even in their attitudes toward sex there was some similarity. Both Langbehn and parts of the Youth Movement were characterized by a strong demand for purity, even prudery, mixed with a craving for male companionship, which in the *Wandervogel* went through every gradation to overt homosexuality. In his later works, Hans Blüher elaborated this erotic component of male societies, especially of the *Wandervogel*, much to the distress and disgust of some members.

of Langbehn's acknowledged influence. Three examples will suffice. The founder and greatest leader of the *Wandervogel,* Karl Fischer, was clearly a disciple of Langbehn, and Blüher was right in calling Fischer that "Germanically thinking *Rembrandt-Deutsche.*" * Frequently on the *Fahrten* he would read from the Rembrandt book, and he and others in the movement felt a greater affinity for Langbehn and Lagarde than for Nietzsche.[40] Again, the indispensable protector of the Steglitz group was the pedagogue and reformer Ludwig Gurlitt, who because of his radical proposals was dismissed from the Steglitz *Gymnasium;* he was a champion of Langbehn, whom in his father's house he had known well. Nor was it accidental that the historian of the movement, Hans Blüher, whose history was itself an historic step in the movement's search after an identity, inscribed as the motto of his book a passage from Langbehn, and quoted him admiringly throughout. Without Langbehn it would have been much harder for the Youth Movement to define its position and to make its way in what was always an adult world.†

Beyond the demonstrable historical link between Langbehn and the Youth Movement rests a deeper relationship, which helps to clarify his relationship to the other movements of his time as well. Langbehn was the prototype of the *Wandervogel* and of those Germanic movements which hoped to destroy the supremacy of reason and establish a vital, populistic, primitivistic society. At the beginning of a decisive cultural epoch in modern Germany, he had expressed his own alienation from society, his hatred of modernity and his search for salvation, finding it first in art and then in religion,

---

* We might note as well that Fischer's view of the Jews was similar to Langbehn's; he was not unfriendly, provided they would be content to cultivate a separate Semitic culture alongside the prevailing German culture. Jews came to be excluded from most of the branches of the later *Wandervogel.*

† Langbehn had a considerable influence on the later organization of Catholic youth as well. "Langbehn's fight against the ideal of intellectualized education coincided entirely with the aspirations of the Catholic youth movement and therefore received an enthusiastic response." Robert Scherer, "150 Jahre Geschichte des theologischen Denkens im Verlag Herder," in *Der Katholizismus in Deutschland und der Verlag Herder 1801–1951,* Freiburg im Breisgau, Herder, 1951, p. 44.

but always in the community of a regenerated *Volkstum*. His discontent and his utopian search were symptomatic for the next generation, which only in the First World War found a release from its discontent and thus, for a time, from itself.

III: Moeller van den Bruck

and the Third Reich

11: The Critic as Exile

*In no society so much as in Germany did the
eminent, the original, the truly individualistic
men become outsiders or were isolated against
their wills.*   MOELLER VAN DEN BRUCK

Arthur Moeller-Bruck came of age in the 1890's, in the decade
of Langbehn's success. An esthete and an outsider, Moeller
felt repelled by the culture of Wilhelmine Germany and early
joined the "inner opposition" to imperial Germany. A critic
of the Reich, and for a decade an expatriate as well, he constructed his own vision of an ideal Germany to which he
remained loyal all his life. The First World War and the
November revolution changed the course of his life, but not
of his thought. Whether *litterateur* or *Landsturmmann,* poet
or publicist, he longed for a new faith, a new community, a
new Reich. After 1918, he became the leading figure of the
conservative revolution; in 1922, he wrote *Das Dritte Reich,*
generally regarded as the prophecy of Hitler's regime, actually
the final political projection of his prewar cultural criticism.
He was the last and in some ways the most admirable of the
Germanic critics, and in him we can understand that the
conservative revolution was not a spontaneous or reactionary
opposition to Versailles or to the Weimar Republic, but was
the reformulation under more favorable historical conditions
of a nineteenth-century ideology.

Moeller was born on April 26, 1876, in Solingen, in the
Prussian Rhineland. On the paternal side he was descended
from a long line of Prussian officers, bureaucrats, and
Lutheran pastors; his father was an architect in the Prussian
civil service. His mother's family, van den Bruck, was of
Dutch and Spanish origin, and in his thirties, Moeller added

183

"van den" to his name. He felt and talked like a Rhinelander, and coming from that most Western of German lands, found it easier to acclimate himself to foreign cultures.

Moeller's biography has been sketched several times, but some events of his life are still obscure, and this has allowed some writers, notably his widow, to go on "mystifying forever," to touch up these obscurities with a tinge of Teutonic legendry.* From his early years on, Moeller was an outsider. As an adolescent, he was expelled from the *Gymnasium* and repudiated by his family; as a young man he left his native country in order to escape military service. He chose to remain outside any religious community as well, and the modest fortune he inherited, supplemented by his free-lance writing, freed him from the obligations of steady employment. For forty years he remained on the periphery of German society, an outsider who made a Nietzschean virtue of having drifted into isolation. How many youths of his time dignified their retreat from life by invoking Zarathustra, as if that superb self-conqueror had preached resignation and passivity in the face of an uncongenial culture! The abstract and fanciful quality of Moeller's thought was undoubtedly conditioned by his prolonged loneliness, as was his passionate desire to lead his people to a new community.

By the time he was of school age, Moeller's family had moved to Düsseldorf, and he entered the humanistic *Gym-*

---

* For an example of this "mystifying forever," see the only interview which Moeller's widow published concerning her husband's life, and which began with the remarkable sentence: "In trying to account for the question who was Moeller van den Bruck, you are really addressing a question to Germany's destiny." Lucy Moeller van den Bruck, "Erbe und Auftrag," *Der Nahe Osten*, V:20 (October 15, 1932), 430. In the bibliography are listed the several biographies of Moeller, all of which were published during the Hitler regime. There is a Moeller van den Bruck Archive in Berlin, jealously guarded by his widow. On my repeated visits to it in the summer of 1954, she was generous with her time and reminiscences, and allowed me to see some bits of correspondence, but remained impenetrably vague about the contents of the Archive, which, she claimed, was still being put in order. For the help she gave me, I wish to thank her. A large part of the Archive seems to have been captured and removed by the Russians; my impression is that the remains are thin. Various aspects of Moeller's life and thought I have discussed, in conversation or by correspondence, with Dr. Heinrich Brüning, Hedda Eulenberg, Max Fischer, Heinrich von Gleichen, Professor Heinrich Herrfahrdt, Ernst Jäckh, and Rudolf Pechel. I gratefully acknowledge their help.

nasium there. Three years before graduation, Moeller left or was expelled from the *Gymnasium,* and thus was barred forever from entering a German university. There have been countless contradictory conjectures about the circumstances of his departure; it is not clear whether he withdrew or was expelled, whether he courted expulsion or was victimized by uncomprehending pedagogues. All we know is that somehow he had run afoul of the *Gymnasium's* discipline.* It is probable that all the elaborate explanations reflected Moeller's own chronic uneasiness about this initial failure, however much he may have disguised it as an act of courageous defiance.

The end of his formal academic training precipitated a break with his parents as well, who had hoped that he would enter one of the traditional family professions, either the army or the ministry. He demurred and chose instead the independent life of the writer and artist. It is an important biographical fact that for the rest of his life Moeller was attuned to the familiar German theme, the *Generationsproblem,* the struggle of the young against the old, an idea that in different guises dominated his thought in all phases of his work.†

After his failure at school, Moeller began his *Wanderjahre,*

---

* This episode of Moeller's life has remained shrouded in mystery. Moeller's first wife wrote me that he withdrew voluntarily, after he had twice failed to be promoted. (Letter from Hedda Eulenberg, September 12, 1959.) His widow, along with other biographers, alluded to the school's vengeful acts against a gifted, sensitive lad who had precociously—and apparently illicitly—written newspaper articles about an exhibit of Edward Munch's paintings: "Of course, the real reasons for his departure from the Düsseldorf *Gymnasium* stemmed from his creative conception of life. What could he care for dead knowledge when through the artist Munch he could experience the living! He was repelled by the routine teaching of universities and thought he knew all that already—though this does not deny that occasionally something creative takes place at the universities. . . . He preferred to acquire knowledge from traveling, not books. He used to say that he only *saw* things [*er wäre ein Augenmensch*]." Letter from Lucy Moeller van den Bruck to me, August 8, 1951.

† His hero at the time was the German naturalist, Hermann Conradi, who in 1890 died at the age of twenty-eight. Of him and his time Moeller wrote a few years later: "The nation needed a change of blood, an insurrection of the sons against the fathers, a substitution of the old by the young." *Die Deutschen,* Minden 1904, Vol. I: *Verirrte Deutsche,* p. 142.

which, with a few short breaks, lasted for nearly twenty years. He went to Leipzig first, where he listened to a few lectures at the university, including Wilhelm Wundt's celebrated course in psychology and Karl Lamprecht's lectures on history.[1] There he met Hans Merian, Conradi's successor as the editor of *Die Gesellschaft,* and Moeller composed his first literary essays for that radically modern periodical. In those days, Moeller belonged to the *avant-garde* opposition to the empire; he was a partisan of the young writers, the moderns, who railed against the emptiness of the *Epigonenzeitalter.*

From Leipzig, Moeller went to Berlin, and there, at the age of twenty-one, married Hedda Maase, a friend of his childhood. The only intimate picture we have of Moeller as a youth comes from her; she remembered him as unbendingly serious, so much so that his friends were amazed when they saw him laugh for the first time.[2] From boyhood on he suffered from sporadic nervous complaints, even from *Angstvorstellungen* about school and military training. He became a prolific writer nevertheless, and his style reflected his relentless seriousness; pathos, not wit or ease, characterized his writing.

Moeller hated Berlin—by all accounts a hideous mixture of garrison town and parvenu capital. Some twenty years later he could still call it "the essentially ugliest city there is."[3] But it was astir with young artistic talent, and Moeller's life became more bearable after he had made his way into the literary world. He frequented the café *Das Schwarze Ferkel,* the *Stammlokal* of Richard Dehmel, August Strindberg, and several Scandinavians.[4] Conrad Ansorge, the pianist and composer, and Franz Evers, writer and theosophist, became his close friends. In 1901 he met, admired, and introduced to his wife Herbert Eulenberg, a young German dramatist whose bold plays on sexual themes were then being performed in Berlin.* For his part, Moeller was busy writing literary criticism, and by way of profitable distraction he translated, together with his wife, Defoe's *Moll Flanders,* some short stories by Maupassant, and the collected works of Edgar Allan

---

* Soon afterward, as we shall see, Moeller's wife attached herself to, and eventually married, Herbert Eulenberg. She wrote an engaging autobiographical account of her life with Eulenberg, in which she was tactfully reticent about her earlier marriage with Moeller. Hedda Eulenberg, *Im Doppelglück von Kunst und Leben,* Düsseldorf, n.d. (*ca.* 1950).

Poe. A short time later his wife translated Ruskin's lectures on art for a German reprint house.

Moeller's energies were soon absorbed in the first of his ambitious plans, few of which were ever completed. He set out to write a trilogy on modern German art, but finished only the first volume. For four years he published installments of that first volume, and in 1902 appeared his *Die Moderne Literatur,* an 800-page critique of contemporary prose and poetry. For a man so young—he began the book when he was 22—this critical survey of German literature after Nietzsche was an impressive achievement. He dealt competently with the various schools of literature; he was critical of the German naturalists, especially of Arno Holz, but praised Gerhart Hauptmann, celebrated Dehmel, and established the reputation of several young poets, among them Alfred Mombert and Stanislaw Przybyszewski.* His judgments of style and taste were generally sure and cogent; his prose, though already prolix, was vigorous, with only occasional flights into those mystical and prophetic realms that were increasingly to tempt him in later years.

Actually, Moeller intended to be more than a critic of literature; he sought to discover the spirit of his age in its esthetic creations. Accordingly he wrote a kind of didactic, subjectivist history—a willfully self-created past as a guide to an imaginary, ideal future. His acknowledged masters were Langbehn and Houston Stewart Chamberlain, whose *Foundations of the Nineteenth Century* had made a deep impression on Moeller, though he rejected its rigid racialist determinism.† Moeller's book was a simple version of German

---

* Dehmel, however, disagreed with some of Moeller's formulations, and wrote him a condescendingly amiable letter of rebuke. He was particularly indignant about Moeller's charge of "patriotic indifference." "It is true, of course, that I consider chauvinistic pathos the cheapest kind of bragging, but my honest German sentiment, my quiet *furor teutonicus* (which, by the way, has nothing to do with hypothetical drivel about race [*Rassengeschwafel*]), could be attested by dozens of passages." Nor did he accept Moeller's charge that in some of his leading poems he was exclusively concerned with sex. Letter of December 11, 1905, Richard Dehmel, *Ausgewählte Briefe aus den Jahren 1902 bis 1920,* Berlin 1923, pp. 85–86.

† A few years later Moeller wrote: "Already Langbehn's book, which in a thousand places opened new perspectives for a thousand fields, mentioned the revolution in historiography which was about to occur, as soon as historical writing would resolve to trace the influence

Geistesgeschichte: the *Zeitgeist* reveals itself in art, and art can best be understood through its representative men. In this fashion, meanings and symbols could be discovered that simplified and illuminated the complicated workings of history. In modern Germany there were a great many Spenglers before the master-metahistorian had his day. Moeller's method —so characteristic of German nonprofessional historiography —recalls Goethe's warning that "the spirit of the times" is at bottom the historian's "own spirit in which the times are reflected." [5]

Die Moderne Literatur elaborated Moeller's belief that over the past decades a great cultural upheaval had taken place, that Nietzsche had been the first to perceive it, and that now a new generation of artists would have to grasp and explain the meaning of this upheaval. "Liliencron and Nietzsche . . . stand at the sharp turn, at which our culture left the dull route of past centuries with its moral outlook on life and its moral activity in life, in order to make a pilgrimage to a new land, a land in which life was resurrected in all its might and greatness, and in its beauty and greatness." [6] This new land had to be charted by pioneering artists, and his great quarrel with the naturalists was their contention that art was only the imperfect imitation of nature. For Moeller, as for so many of his generation, art was "the signpost to the path that leads to the ultimate truth." Art soars higher still: "We already possess an art . . . which renders religion superfluous and which imbues every truly modern man with the same confidence in the universe [*Sicherheit zum Weltall*] which at other times only faith in God could provide." [7] A painting by Böcklin or a poem by Dehmel could give men this kind of religious experience.

Moeller's book was the first intimation of his *Lebensphilosophie* and of his incipient cultural thought. By combining a crude if popular version of Nietzsche's superman with an equally crude rendition of Darwin's struggle for survival, Moeller found intellectual grounds for his strong and probably torturing prejudice: "Fighting is magnificent and more worthy of man than self-indulgence in smug comfort. Battle gives us, especially when it is of spirits and passions, our

---

of blood on the development of peoples, tribes, and men." Moeller van den Bruck, *Die Zeitgenossen. Die Geister—Die Menschen*, Minden 1906, p. 105.

greatest kings and best heroes. . . . Eternal peace would be insupportable—it would be boredom, a yawning that would give us merely the philistine." [8] Given such sentiments it is no wonder that he turned against the drab, uncreative materialism of imperial Germany. If suffering was the prerequisite of creativity, then the prosperity of the new Reich was a disaster for culture. Nor is it surprising that Moeller came to believe that the virtues of struggle could ennoble a whole people and that war itself could have the same liberating and invigorating effects as spiritual self-conquest.

He also wrote two short books, *Das Variété* and *Das Théâtre Française*. The former was an appraisal of this new art form, especially of Wedekind's *Überbrettlei*, which proved so successful and popular a form of satire. By tracing its development, he sought to demonstrate that scenic art always sprang from a populist semi-art that stands half-way between life and fully embodied art.* The other book depicted the history of what Moeller regarded as the decline of the French theater.

Shortly after the publication of his first works Moeller fled from Germany, in dread of his still unfulfilled, and by now inescapable military service. His wife recalled the *Angstvorstellungen* which prompted his flight. Moeller's biographers disagree on the reasons for his sudden departure: technically and for a short time at least, he seems to have been branded as a deserter. In 1908, he tried without success to regularize his status; by 1914, he was formally cleared.

Moeller had left his pregnant wife in Berlin, and in December 1902 she gave birth to their only son, Wolfgang.† For the next four years he lived in Paris, again surrounded by friends in the artistic world. Together with Franz Evers and Max Dauthendey, and the painter Edward Munch, he frequented the café *La Closerie des Lilas,* and in his intermittent

---

* With this work Dehmel was in substantial agreement, and he wrote to the young author: "After happily surviving the first part, which is again written in this violent tapeworm style [*wühlenden Drehwurmweis*] which I cannot stomach, your Variété delighted me as much as possible; my most applauding thanks." Letter of March 23, 1902, Richard Dehmel, *Ausgewählte Briefe aus den Jahren 1883 bis 1902,* Berlin 1923, p. 408.

† The boy died twenty-one years later of pneumonia, a few months before his father committed suicide. Eulenberg, *Im Doppelglück,* pp. 18 and 362.

penury he lived off black coffee and little else.* He became a protégé of the Russian mystic, Dmitri Merezkowski—just as the Nazi ideologist Afred Rosenberg was to do a few years later.[9]

In Paris, Moeller met the Russian-born Lucy Kaerrick, who a few years later became his second wife. Moeller's first wife, whom he had virtually abandoned, was already living happily with Herbert Eulenberg, whose child she bore in 1904, and whom she married when it became legally possible to do so.† While under Merezkowski's influence, Moeller read Dostoevski and convinced Reinhard Piper, the Munich publisher, that a German edition of Dostoevski's works should at last be undertaken.[10] The publisher agreed, and appointed Moeller as the editor, who in turn commissioned E. J. Rashin—Lucy Kaerrick's sister—to translate more than twenty volumes, and secured the editorial coöperation of Merezkowski as well.

In the long run, Paris did not suit him either. He had lived in that politically alive city during the tumultuous days of the Russian revolution of 1905 and of the Moroccan crisis, and his interest in politics had been awakened. From Paris he went to Italy, where for two or three years he traveled extensively. There he turned to art again, and moved still closer to some of the leading figures of German expressionism. In Florence he met Ernst Barlach who left a delightful description of Moeller's successful midwifery in delivering Theodor Däubler's epic poem, *Nordlicht*, to the publisher. After negotiating for the contract, Moeller read the proofs of the poem as well, and Barlach recalled how Däubler would slip Moeller ever new "indispensable additions" to a work already scheduled to appear in three volumes.[11] The *Nordlicht* done, Moeller himself headed north, crossing Germany in the futile hope that he could make his peace with the Prussian military authorities. After a few months in the Baltic

---

* An intimate of his later years claimed that Moeller "ran through his fortune together with some satiated society people [*Gesellschaftsüberdrüssigen*] in order to show them that he did not care for society." Hans Schwarz, "Über Moeller van den Bruck," *Deutsches Volkstum*, XIV:14 (September, 1932), 690; his widow asserted that he was planning to emigrate to America when he lost his money. "Erbe und Auftrag," *Der Nahe Osten*, V:20 (October 15, 1932), 431.

† See her cheerful account of her romance with Eulenberg, which began, appropriately enough, in Triebschen. Eulenberg, *Im Doppelglück*, pp. 18–40.

provinces of Russia and a visit to England, he went to Scandinavia, where he remained until the outbreak of the war.

During his years abroad, he discovered his passionate love for Germany. Far removed from the source of discontent and annoyance, he constructed and succumbed to an idealized picture of Germany and of its past.* His foreign travels also clinched his view that each people had its own definable national character, and that the peoples of the world were divided into young peoples and old peoples—roughly, those that still had a future and those that did not. This remained the key idea of all of Moeller's later thought. Like so many of his ideas, this one was very much in the air, and among apprehensive Europeans at the end of the past century it was often used as an expressive metaphor.† To Moeller it was no metaphor, but a metaphysical truth describing a real phenomenon of nature and politics. This was a typical illustration of how Moeller mystified and obscured essentially clear biological ideas until they appeared as a kind of poetry of politics.

While abroad, Moeller published and planned books that embodied his new-found allegiances and insights. His nationalism was first expressed in an eight-volume history of the Germans, *Die Deutschen,* published between 1904 and 1910.[12] He also wrote a study of contemporary culture and its leaders, *Die Zeitgenossen,* which further elaborated the distinction between young and old peoples.[13] Finally he persuaded Reinhard Piper to accept a series of six volumes, to be entitled

---

* Germans have often discovered Germany from abroad. Theodor Mommsen recalled the experience of Ludwig Bamberger during his long exile after 1848: "Removed from his native soil and from the daily feeling of actual, annoying limitations, he saw the fatherland in its unsullied beauty and purity." Theodor Mommsen, *Reden und Aufsätze,* Berlin 1905, pp. 470–471.

† At a time of race-thinking and eugenics, this division of peoples into young and old, living and dying, proved a very appealing notion and cropped up everywhere. The Méline Commission, for example, charged in 1891 with the task of drawing up a new tariff for France, warned against the threat of competition from "the young countries," especially America and Russia. Eugene Golob, *The Méline Tariff,* New York, Columbia University Press, 1944, p. 182. In 1898, Lord Salisbury solemnly warned against the inevitable conflict between "living" and "dying" nations. Elie Halévy, *A History of the English People of the Nineteenth Century,* Vol. V: *Imperialism and the Rise of Labour,* New York, Peter Smith, 1951, p. 50.

"The Values of Peoples." Three volumes were to study the old peoples, three the young. The projected titles were revealing enough: French Skepticism [*Zweifel*], English Common Sense, and Italian Beauty; for the second series: German *Weltanschauung*, American Will, and Russian Soul.

The titles suggested that the style of each people could be epitomized in one characteristic; for the old peoples the titles revealed the main cause of national enfeeblement. The French had become too skeptical and irresolute, the English too shallow and utilitarian, the Italians too exclusively esthetic. As luck would have it, the old peoples became Germany's main enemies in the First World War, simplifying Moeller's later task of explanation. Piper agreed to publish the series, and Moeller submitted the first chapter of his book on Italy. This was at once printed on luxurious paper, but Moeller kept sending longer and longer sections of manuscript to the alarmed publisher. The finished work, dedicated to Theodor Däubler, was a magnificently produced and illustrated 760-page survey of Italian art and history from the Etruscans to the present, prematurely advertised as a tourist handbook.[14] Actually, it was an anti-Burckhardt history that fixed on the Middle Ages as "the classical age of the Italian nation," and that celebrated Piero della Francesca as the greatest, though neglected, painter.* It was the only work of this series to be completed and published.

Die Deutschen was the first work to bear Moeller's newly enriched name: he now signed himself Moeller van den Bruck, no longer Moeller-Bruck. Although the Dutch "van," unlike the German "von," connotes geographical origin and not aristocratic birth, it is likely that he appropriated it because of its seemingly distinguishing quality. There is a neat parallel between this decoration of the self and *Die Deutschen,* in which he sought to glorify and ennoble the history of his people.

Die Deutschen was an unconventional expression of a very conventional view of history. That the spirit and the history of a people finds clearest expression in the history of its great men was a common belief, and there was nothing extraor-

---

* Moeller van den Bruck, *Die italienische Schönheit*, München 1913, pp. 295 and 455–493. In its anti-Burckhardt slant as well as in its occasional excursions into racism, Moeller's book recalled Ludwig Woltmann's influential work, *Die Germanen und die Renaissance in Italien*, Leipzig 1905.

dinary in Moeller's attempt to recreate the history of Germany through biographical essays of its leading statesmen, thinkers, and artists. But to arrange these essays, not in chronological order but according to psychological categories, was unusual, and bore the stamp of Lamprecht's influence on Moeller. He established seven characteristic types of Germans, and each volume of *Die Deutschen* save one, was devoted to the lives of one particular *type* of German. Thus the first volume, "Drifting Germans," contained biographical sketches of eight Drifting Germans, from the early eighteenth-century poet Johann Christian Günther to the contemporary poet, Peter Hille. The Drifting Germans were followed by Leading, Dreaming, Decisive, Constructive, Frustrated, and Joyful Germans. One entire volume dealt with Goethe, in whom *all* German traits had found harmonious embodiment.* From beginning to end the mood of the series was hero-worship, and recalled Carlyle's *On Heroes, Hero-Worship and the Heroes in History* and Emerson's "On Representative Men," both of which were well known in Germany.

Each essay was brief, and none ranged beyond commonplaces known to all educated Germans. Moeller sought to evoke the man and his times and to moralize about both, and for this he did not require the detailed exactitude of scholarship. There were about fifty historical portraits, and on each was tagged Moeller's moralistic caption. All in all, it was a grand historical drama, and into it he poured all his passionate likes and dislikes.†

---

* The German titles were: *Verirrte Deutsche, Führende Deutsche, Verschwärmte Deutsche, Entscheidende Deutsche, Gestaltende Deutsche, Goethe, Scheiternde Deutsche, Lachende Deutsche.* It could not have been accidental that Moeller's first and most successful volume dealt with Germans adrift; he felt, I am sure, a particular affinity for these problematical Germans: "The strength and greatness that their age lacked became a personal disaster for them. Unable to find a unity outside themselves, they were unable to grow into a unity within, and thus they decayed in uncertainty and multiplicity." *Verirrte Deutsche,* p. 13.

† Moeller's good friend Ernst Barlach, the German Expressionist artist, wrote to him on August 24, 1913: "After reading all of your gigantic work I can, to be quite honest, say no more than what I wrote the other day on a postcard: It reads like a drama, and at best I might add that it is a drama in which divine and secular powers contend with one another. . . . I discover more religion than philosophy in it." Ernst Barlach, *Leben und Werk in seinen Briefen,* ed. by Friedrich Dross, München, Piper 1952, p. 69.

Moeller wrote his *Kulturgeschichte* with a definite purpose in mind. If he could do for the German spirit what Dostoevski had done for the Russian soul, that is, if he could bring it closer to self-consciousness, then he could help fashion its response to the radically new conditions of the modern age. In some of the biographical sketches, and slightly more systematically in the essays of *Die Zeitgenossen,* Moeller sought to depict the novelty of the modern age, the immense technological upheaval, the shrinking of the world, and the promise and threat of American civilization. The material progress of the new age had not yet found the appropriate "iron-and-steel style," as he called it. In a familiar vein, Moeller lamented the absence of great spiritual and artistic interpreters of modernity, barring magnificent exceptions like Walt Whitman, "the Homer of the modern world." As a consequence, modern man was adrift without spiritual moorings, and this, Moeller felt, was especially true of German youth. To them he formally dedicated *Die Deutschen,* in the hope that they would find in it the *Weltanschauung* which would give them the necessary hold on life.

His *Weltanschauung* was conservative in its premises, but hostile to the present. He came close to expressing the dilemma of a modern man with conservative instincts; liberalism, he knew, was the philosophic expression of the modern age, but it outraged Moeller's esthetic belief in the heroic and aristocratic nature of man and society. A retreat to old values, on the other hand, was impossible: Christianity had become obsolete; it had suffered too much at the hands of higher critics and scientists. Nor were the old political mores and institutions capable of being saved. Hence the desperate search for a new faith and the anguished resentment against liberalism which, its philosophic inadequacy notwithstanding, was so immensely strong. The new faith would have to be a Germanic *Weltanschauung* which would supplant religion and inspire a new state that would retain in a modern industrial society the political and cultural virtues of an idealized past. Once this state was built, Germany would become the dominant nation of Europe, perhaps of the world.

Moeller's thought was rooted in his interpretation of the character and destiny of man and history. It was also rooted in his unproved assumption, common to all neo-conservatives, that liberals believed man to be a good and rational being.

To this view Moeller opposed an essentially pessimistic view of man, and from this antithesis of his own making he deduced his undying enmity to liberalism. "Happiness and welfare enthusiasts who are still dreaming of a blessed age in which the Cain in man and the Abel in man will be reconciled and will become a single ideal man, should remember that in their utopia we would have to cease being fighters"— and fighting alone makes a man.[15] While everything has changed in the past few centuries, perhaps even improved, only "the naked human remains: our instincts have been differentiated, not modified; hunger and love, yearning and satisfaction, creative will and world eagerness still move us." [16] This traditionalism, rooted in his faith in the immutability of human nature, became one of the mainstays of Moeller's later revolutionary conservatism.

Moeller affirmed the inequality of men, their inherent limitations and irrationality, and recognized suffering and self-conquest as the only condition of human greatness. Men like Günther or Conradi, battling with themselves, or fiercely combating the customs of their times, or rebelling against the prejudices of the bourgeoisie—these were the real heroes of Moeller's work. Goethe's serenity or Kant's aloofness bored and distressed him. He liked fighters; and those fighters who failed or died young, or whose struggles were premature, received singularly solicitous attention. But there was nothing heroic about imperial Germany, and implicitly his vision of the heroic life was a denunciation of bourgeois life and an affirmation of an authoritarian or Caesarist society. Only heroes should govern, and such born leaders "incarnate the spirit, the great urge, and the yearning of their people. . . . Their people follows them and moves toward the unity which alone it could never have achieved." [17]

Each volume carried at least one essay about a contemporary figure and afforded Moeller a chance to express his disappointment at the decline of German culture after unification.* The first generation after the Franco-Prussian

---

* His attacks on imperial Germany, as I have said, were frank and frequent, yet one of the best formulations of his disdain occurred in thinly disguised form in *Die italienische Schönheit*, p. 36: "The culture which the Romans created at that time was in its pretensions and poverty the truly miserable *Unkultur* of founding years [*Gründungsjahre*], which in Rome, however, lasted not just a generation but for a third of its history. We must remember that this after all

war had been a dismal failure; it had been "an epoch of bureaucracy, of trembling before socialism, of empty and loud Hurrah-feelings, of flag-waving sentimentality and family-album stupidity." [18] He saw Bismarck's state endangered because of the growing gulf between the uncreative, "official" element of German society, that is, the army and bureaucracy, and the creative, popular element. Unless this estrangement were overcome by the creation of a national culture, the empire would eventually fall apart. [19]

Moeller frequently phrased this concern differently: Germany had too much civilization and too little culture. "Culture is of the spirit, and civilization of the stomach," the one permanent, the other transitory.* According to Moeller,

---

was the culture of emperors who themselves had come as bastards to the Roman Empire, the culture of rich merchants, grain traders, careerist officers, and armchair generals, and of that whole rabble that poured into the capital from all the provinces of the empire."
* *Die Zeitgenossen*, p. 8. This antithesis between civilization and culture was a favorite subterfuge of German "idealists"; it expressed in an unexceptionably cultured manner their resentment against modernity, democracy, and the West. During both world wars, German intellectuals pictured the Allied Powers as the protagonists of civilization and as the enemies of culture, represented chiefly by Germany. The most regrettable example of this specious antithesis appeared in Thomas Mann's *Betrachtungen eines Unpolitischen*. For a brief but suggestive summary of this distinction, see Norbert Elias, *Über den Prozess der Zivilisation*, Basel, Haus zum Falken, 1939, I, 1–64. Elias holds that Kant was the first to posit the distinction in the way here described; others have contended that Wilhelm von Humboldt fathered it. Whatever the paternity, it is beyond doubt that the idea of establishing a sharp dichotomy between civilization and culture was born at the time of German idealism, and has played an important and pernicious role in German thought ever since. Its centrality in Spengler's thought is well known. It is therefore disheartening to find the same vacuous antithesis prominently used in a recent American study, Amaury de Riencourt's *The Coming Caesars*, New York, Coward-McCann, 1957. "Culture predominates in young societies awakening to life, grows like a young organism endowed with exuberant vitality, and represents a new world outlook. It implies original creation of new values, of new religious symbols and artistic styles, of new intellectual and spiritual structures, new sciences, new legislations, new moral codes. . . . Civilization aims at the gradual standardization of increasingly large masses of men within a rigidly mechanical framework—masses of 'common men' who think alike, feel alike, thrive on conformism, are willing to bow to vast bureaucratic structures, and in whom the social instinct predominates over that of the creative individual" (pp. 10–11).

America was all civilization, Russia all culture; in ideal societies, as in the Germany of the future, the two would be perfectly balanced.[20]

Moeller's theme of cultural failure—common enough in Germany at the time—knew many variations, always playing up the artistic emptiness of the age, the rule of the satiated and joyless bourgeoisie, the decay of individualism and the triumph of mediocrity. His disgust was most readily evoked by the bourgeois' "impaired vitality," by his inability to contend with life.[21] In his attacks on the bourgeoisie—as well as in his sneaking admiration for their material achievements —Moeller was close to some of the characteristic attitudes of the Expressionists, penetratingly analyzed in Walter Sokel's *The Writer in Extremis*. But the bourgeoisie had become materialistic, and Moeller dismissed as cant their Darwinist justification of the economic struggle—as if his brand of Darwinism were any more persuasive or legitimate.

Moeller feared that the remaining unresolved antagonisms of German society, particularism, the religious conflict, and the social question, might yet undo Bismarck's creation and destroy the Reich. The gravest threat, however, to German society lay in the personal discontent, in the sense of spiritual malaise, which Moeller himself experienced, and which he expected would ultimately grip everyone: "We shall come to know a cultural discontent which is now felt by only a few, but which should seize everybody with furious indignation because it concerns the temporary as well as the eternal life of the entire nation." [22]

For Moeller, as for Lagarde, whom he had closely studied, the archenemy was liberalism: there was no evil for which liberalism was not responsible, and no danger which it would not bring to realization. What liberalism is, we are not told. It was synonymous with all that was thwarted and stunted, weak and spineless, helpless and tolerant, materialistic, democratic, and corrupt. Actually, Moeller—and many of his contemporaries—were not attacking a political or social philosophy but a style of life and a state of mind. They opposed the humaneness and rationality of liberalism, they resented what they thought was the insufferable arrogance of liberalism, the *Enrichissez-vous* of Guizot, which in Germany applied to education as well as to wealth, and which appeared more like a challenge to hardship than an invitation to equal opportunity. On the other hand, this type of attack on liberalism stopped short of a critique of the social structure which liberalism defended and which preserved the rights of private property.[23]

Moeller opposed his notion of aristocratic freedom to the liberal's defense of freedom: "Liberalism has not the slightest trait in common with freedom. . . . its freedom is only the freedom of the individual to become average humanity." [24] He attacked the liberals for preserving this "average humanity" by their humane aspirations, their indiscriminate charity and pity. His loathing for liberalism extended to the modern institutions, which embodied it: political parties and parliamentarianism. But what was the alternative to liberalism? This was the question with which Moeller wrestled all his life, for he knew from his innermost self that men needed a faith. Modern science, especially Darwinian biology, had destroyed the basis of religious belief, and—good evolutionist that he was—he thought that much of Christianity deserved to be destroyed: "Its history was the history of its corruption." [25] To be alive, a faith had to be creative, and Moeller thought that since the Reformation the Catholic Church had been spiritually bankrupt. His hostile attitude toward Protestantism, the faith of his forebears, was strongly influenced by Lagarde's criticism.* Still, his fundamentally ambiguous position was epitomized by his exclamation: "God himself nevertheless continues to exist, even though we know that he does not exist." [26]

The positive aspect of his attack on liberalism and his renunciation of Christianity was his search for a Germanic *Weltanschauung* which "would give us mortals a hold in the world." [27] It "would be only a new expression of religion," but for a long time to come its essence would have to be artistic, not philosophical, because philosophy had bogged down in epistemology, in questions of the limits, not the contents, of knowledge. In his uncritical critique of philosophy, as in his veneration for Dostoevski, Moeller anticipated the mood of modern existentialism.

In the distant future, even Christianity could perhaps be refurbished, provided it would also be "German, naturalistic . . . cultural and esthetic. . . . Perhaps now will come that

---

* This, at least, was the opinion of Moeller's widow, with whom I discussed the subject.

other Christianity of anger and will, which would be the true Christianity of our humanity." [28] Modern times demanded a heroic, muscular Christianity, and, part-Nietzschean that he was, he felt contempt for the comforting qualities of Christianity: "For whom does Christ exist? For the weak or the strong people, for the weak or the strong hours of humanity? The answer to this question of conscience can only be: for the very weakest hours and peoples, and our pride alone should prevent us from calling on Christ again and again." [29] In all his works Moeller strove for a final answer or formulation of the religious question, but never attained it; his dilemma exemplified the agony of the other critics who longed for a kind of secular mysticism which neither traditional religion nor philosophy could sanction but which, nevertheless, remained an overwhelming spiritual necessity for them.

The same difficulties dogged Moeller's thought on a new ethics. He rejected Christian ethics, especially the tradition originating in the Sermon on the Mount, as fiercely as he did the liberal and secular utilitarianism. But despite his tirades against modern skepticism and relativism, Moeller had himself abandoned all absolute ethical values. Morality must change as the evolutionary process unfolds. In a key sentence, Moeller argued that for modern man an ethical formula could be obtained only from sociological understanding; he anticipated a formula

which would be derived from a great evolutionary sense of justice, which would assume that every occurrence in the world has its inducement, every consequence its reason, every effect its cause, a formula for which the true, the good, and the beautiful—to talk in terms that have lately been overcome—is all which serves evolution, and evil, false, and ugly all which harms it, which delays the formation of a culture, and perhaps also everything that favors a too one-sided formation of civilization.[30]

To hitch morality to evolution was not to provide a very satisfactory answer. Moeller had rejected every value, save one: the struggle for existence. Struggle alone would not be overcome or abolished; it was inherent in man and history, and determined all evolutionary progress. This "moral Darwinism," so closely interwoven with Moeller's conception of the heroic life, had universal applicability. Because of his misconception of Darwin's theory, Moeller believed it legitimate to regard men and nations as commensurable units, with the ethics of the former necessarily applying to the latter as well.

The traditional antithesis in political thought between liberalism and conservatism reappeared in Moeller's thought. Characteristically, he stayed above partisan politics, but attacked every contemporary political force. He charged German conservatism with dodging the challenges of modern society and with merely defending existing privileges. He attacked the socialists, who promised a radical solution of modern problems, for clinging to two errors: that all men are equal, and that human affairs were reducible to economic problems. Still, "as a nation we can be proud of *this* social democracy," a sentiment that many conservative Germans harbored as well, for they knew that there was something Prussian and immensely patriotic about this allegedly internationalist movement.[31] In a country with growing prosperity, socialism would disappear; in America, Moeller pointed out, no worker would call himself a socialist because he was too proud of being an American. The time would come, after some necessary but unspecified reforms of capitalism, when the German worker would cease being a socialist and would be reabsorbed into the nation, which is the true historical unit.

Moeller was indefinite about the political form of the future Germany, but hoped for a closely knit community which would replace the so-called atomistic society of the liberal state. An elite, representing the will of the united people more truly than existing parliamentary machinery, would govern, while economic problems would be resolved by some form of corporatist organization.

Moeller had not yet arrived at a precise political program for Germany. His politics were never the result of an analysis of existing historical conditions or of actual need, but always a projection of an esthetic judgment and a criticism of culture. This was best shown in his celebrated distinction among old, young, and embryonic peoples and in his prophecy of their destinies. The yardstick for a people's youth was comparable to Moeller's qualitative distinction among individuals. And just as great men could claim preëminent privileges, so the young peoples—with their futures still ahead of them—must be accorded imperial power and responsibility. Germany was the only genuinely young people, bold, energetic, and capable of expansion and conquest; England, on the other hand, though seemingly young, was really a satiated young people, ready to graduate from the nursery to dotage. France was finished—its future already was mortgaged—because it had become sluggish and skeptical. Spain and Italy were done for too, though Italy with its impressive birth rate and the new nationalism of Corradini might yet touch off another Roman revival. A rising birth rate, a variation of the standard imperialist justification of a surplus population, was in fact the only material criterion which Moeller's imperialism would at times invoke. Beyond the young peoples were the embryonic: the Russians and the Americans. They stood at the beginning of their national development, their day was still very much in the future. Again, what was true of men was true of peoples: they lived by war alone. A few years before William James' cautioning *The Moral Equivalent of War* and Freud's regretful *Reflections on War and Death,* Moeller announced with untroubled brutality: "Does one want to make a pestilent heap out of humanity? . . . War has always been the national expression of the struggle for survival." [32]

At times Moeller expressed his nationalism in the language of a racialist and attributed to race a causal role in history. In other passages of his work he abjured the concept of race and pronounced it inapplicable to the history of modern nations. He was never at ease with the racialist doctrine and often sought to soften its deterministic character. "Race is almost a metaphysical concept, but on a physiological basis. . . . Race is a power. Whoever feels that power in him, possesses it, and exercises it. The racial view rests on the faith in that power, on the faith in man, on the belief that he is not the servant of his circumstances, but the master of his energies." * His distinction between a race of the spirit [*Rasse des Geistes*], a phrase he bandied about throughout his life, and a race of the blood, which he believed in intermittently

---

* Moeller's views on race were expressed in an attack on Dehmel published in 1908 and reprinted in *Das Recht der jungen Völker,* ed. by Hans Schwarz, Berlin 1932, "Rassenanschauung," pp. 193–196. Dehmel answered in turn, and criticized the follies of racism generally and of Moeller's intellectual backing and filling in particular: "Even as Moeller van den Bruck asserts, with some verbosity: 'the racial view rests on the *faith* in the power of race.' Well then, I believe in better-bred [*zuchtvollere*], that is, more loving, powers." Letter to the *Anthropologische Revue,* September 4, 1908, Richard Dehmel, *Ausgewählte Briefe aus den Jahren 1902 bis 1920,* p. 160.

and half-heartedly was quite idiosyncratic.* Both the English and the German peoples—the one castigated for its "utilitarian materialism," the other glorified for its idealistic spirit —belonged to the Germanic race, and Moeller concluded that the historical conditions of development were such powerful agents of change as to render the original identity of race insignificant. Nor did his racism apply to the Jews; in fact, in his prewar writings he never touched on the Jewish question—an attitude that was then characteristic of the Expressionists and the literary *avant-garde* in general, but did not sit well with the National Socialists at a later date.

For Germany, Moeller prophesied a great imperial future. Its destiny, after the annexation of Austria, was "to represent Europe in the racial and world-continental conflicts of the future, to become synonymous with Europe." [33] The world must not obstruct Germany; the very laws of nature decreed that Germany, because of its ever-growing population, must achieve the "domination of Europe." In particular, he enjoined the peoples of German nationality or those related to it, namely, the Dutch and the Central European peoples, to preserve their Germanic qualities and await their eventual inclusion into a *"Gesamtdeutschland."* [34]

Moeller's imperialist hope, briefly sketched here, was yet another instance of that new type of imperialism which was based neither on an appraisal of the objective political situation nor on the desire to further any material interests in society. It was as remote from the Prussian tradition of militarism as from the aims of the Pan-German League. Rather it was the vision of an esthete who analyzed nations and their foreign policies in the same impressionistic manner and with the same heroic ideals and prejudices as he did individuals. Hence Moeller's ruthless insistence on the unfettered power of great individuals found here its frightful counterpart. The intent of his imperialism closely corresponded to his general aim: it would induce a cultural rejuvenation of Germany. The characteristic conjunction of cultural discontent and the Darwinist creed which we have so frequently encountered as the root of Moeller's thought furnished here the inspiration for his imperialism. That this type of imperialism cannot be dismissed

---

* The term *Rasse des Geistes* had no compromising connotations even after the Hitler regime, and Moeller's widow, in letters and conversations, still used the phrase with awed delight.

as an individual aberration is made compellingly clear by the fact that in the 1920's the National Socialists—particularly Hitler and Alfred Rosenberg—arrived at their imperialist programs from essentially similar motives. Even their decision to unleash the Second World War can be better understood if this phenomenon of unrealistic, utopian imperialism is fully taken into account.

We have seen the persistent visions of Moeller's *Weltanschauung*. His work reflected the fact that he stood outside the ordinary categories of professional life, indeed outside his own country. But he remained always close to his own spiritual predicament. I believe that it was this transmutation of personal discontent into suggestions for political and cultural reform which distinguished the Germanic critics. Among these, Moeller was unquestionably the most introspective and self-critical. His work was intended to rescue others from a crisis which he himself knew all too well: "As a modern man, I too was used to drifting in doubt, just as our youth today drifts, and, because of all this relativism, cannot gain a firm grip on life." [35]

His prewar writing made little impression on his contemporaries—or on his later biographers. The latter overlooked the fact that here was the source of his later thought. As late as 1908, *Die Deutschen* had received but one review, and that in a children's section of a newspaper; Moeller attributed this silence to the fact that the book signified "a new fight to the finish against all that one may sum up as liberalism." *

Moeller continued fighting the official Germany, not only its liberal elements. In 1913, amidst the self-congratulatory chorus occasioned by the twenty-fifth anniversary of William II's accession to the throne, he publicly dissented. In an article on the Kaiser and architecture, he denounced his empty grandiosity and depreciated his taste.[36] For Moeller art and especially architecture were so overwhelmingly important that the Kaiser's dismal failure in this field was warning of still greater inadequacy to come. Moeller was not alone in this apprehension; many years later, a perceptive critic recalled: "However our fathers stood politically and whichever way

---

* See his letter to Ludwig Schemann, of January 22, 1908, as reprinted in *Deutschlands Erneuerung*, XVIII:6 (June, 1934), 323. His letters to Schemann, "the only German who had understood his books," were full of self-pitying humility and boundless arrogance.

they decided in 1918: in artistic matters the opposition was already almost general at the turn of the century. Is a political edifice which is no longer alive in the imagination not already endangered in reality as well?" *

In *Die Zeitgenossen* Moeller had warned that "the [contemporary] ideologists also belong to those to whom our age was clear, but they veiled it again for themselves in sociological-utopian or esthetic-utopian theories; for all their dreams of "Third Reichs" they began to stumble about in the modern world." [37] Irony would have it that Moeller fulfilled his own judgment to the letter. For it was he who in the years after Germany's defeat, when the illusions of the imperial Reich had vanished, wrote the most popular sketch of a Third Reich, and so veiled for himself and others the realities of their unhappy age.

---

* Otto Westphal, *Feinde Bismarcks. Geistige Grundlagen der deutschen Opposition, 1848–1914,* München and Berlin 1930, p. 186.—Or as the standard work on German art put it: "Modern German art has still one other foe, the German Kaiser." Cornelius Gurlitt, *Die deutsche Kunst des neunzehnten Jahrhunderts,* 3d ed., Berlin 1907, p. 661.

12: The Esthete's Turn to Politics

Frederick II recognized that one's literary works are less important for one's life than what stands behind literature: the state, the nation, the people, for whom one lives.

MOELLER VAN DEN BRUCK

The war and the subsequent collapse of imperial Germany were the decisive historical events for Moeller and his generation. From the exultation with which they greeted the war, the Germans were to plunge into the resentful passivity with which they endured defeat and revolution. The imperial regime that had seemed so glittering and stable collapsed, and the new, improvised republic seemed shabby and unstable. Both impressions were in fact wrong: the old order had sought to hide the terrible antagonisms that existed in German society, and the Weimar Republic, by the very nature of its political system, flouted and exaggerated them. But to a man like Moeller, who had been alienated from the old order, who fleetingly had found a home in wartime Germany, the new order inspired despair that turned into contempt.

Moeller had fully shared in the exultation that followed the outbreak of the war. In those first days of the war, the Germans not only rallied to the nation's defense—all peoples did that, and they all expected a short war and a decisive victory. But the intensity of their spiritual response, the exhilaration with which they welcomed the war, and the readiness with which they offered and demanded sacrifices, all this sprang from something deeper than patriotism.* For many

---

* Thirty years later, and after two crushing defeats, Friedrich Meinecke still remembered this period with a kind of glow: "The exaltation of the August days of 1914, despite its ephemeral character, is for all who lived through them one of the most precious and unforgettable

Germans, and certainly for Moeller, the war signified a release from an intolerable past, a final escape from the emptiness of bourgeois life. For them the exultation of August, 1914, was as well the implicit repudiation of the years before, a half-conscious indictment of the entire Wilhelmine Age. Few Germans were fully aware of this, and none could have put it as forcefully as Thomas Mann did in 1915:

> Let us remember the beginning—those never-to-be-forgotten first days, when what we no longer thought possible, happened. We had not believed in the war, our political insight had not sufficed to recognize the necessity of the European catastrophe. But as moral beings—yes, as such we had seen the trial [*Heimsuchung*] coming—and still more, in some way we longed for it, felt in the depth of our hearts that the world, our world, could not go on like this any more. We knew that world of peace, that *can-can* culture [*cancanisierender Gesittung*]. . . . Horrible world, which now no longer is, or no longer will be, after the great storm passed by. Did it not crawl with spiritual vermin as with worms? Did it not ferment and stink of the decaying matter of civilization? [1]

And can we properly understand the First World War without taking into account this disgust, this boredom, this "moral" longing for war?

Whatever the different emotions that informed the August spirit, its appearance epitomized the sense of unity and collective purpose that the Germans felt—for the first time in their modern history. The *Burgfrieden*, the suspension of all partisan struggles, was another, and to unpolitical Germans very attractive, manifestation of this unity. In the summer of 1914, then, Moeller may well have felt that his prewar glorification of war had been fully validated and that the sacrifices of the

---

memories of the highest sort . . . one perceived in all camps that the mere unity of a functional partnership would not suffice, but that a spiritual renovation of our state and culture was necessary." *Die Deutsche Katastrophe. Betrachtungen und Erinnerungen*, Wiesbaden 1946, p. 43. Meinecke was recalling an experience that had gripped nearly all Germans, from the poets Rilke and Ernst Toller to the Pan-Germans and to Hitler, who a few years after the war wrote: "The fight of the year 1914 was certainly not forced upon the masses, good God! but desired by the entire people itself. . . . To me personally those hours appeared like the redemption from the annoying moods of my youth. Therefore I am not ashamed today to say that, overwhelmed by impassionate enthusiasm, I had fallen on my knees and thanked Heaven out of my overflowing heart that it had granted me the good fortune of being allowed to live in these times." Adolf Hitler, *Mein Kampf*, New York 1940, p. 210.

war had indeed engendered a nobler spirit which in time would lead to a new society.*

This spontaneous experience of unity found intellectual embodiment in "the Ideas of 1914," in the wartime literature in which some of the best German minds sought to prove Germany's cultural apartness from, and superiority to, the West. Those were the years in which Ernst Troeltsch and Thomas Mann, among many others, grappled with the antithesis of German *Kultur* and Western *Zivilisation,* and in which lesser minds simply polemicized against the West.† In such a climate and amidst such endeavors, Moeller was thoroughly at home.

Because of the war, Moeller turned from his esthetic concerns to politics, and by the end of the war he had become a widely respected political writer. The war had fostered a similar change in all sections of German society; to remain unpolitical or *wirklichkeitsfremd* when every aspect of one's life was affected by the political and economic problems of the war proved impossible, and even the unpolitical had to mediate on politics.‡ Unfortunately, the Germans' turn to

---

* The memory of August 1914 and the myth of the *Fronterlebnis* were long cherished by Germans. In 1920 for example, the *Jungdeutsche Orden* was founded, dedicated to the preservation in peacetime of "the moral virtues [of the comradeship of the front] which must not remain the exclusive privilege of the military order." Klaus Hornung, *Der Jungdeutsche Orden,* Düsseldorf 1958, p. 15 and *passim.*

† Thomas Mann's *Betrachtungen eines Unpolitischen* was the classic example of this effort to define the essence of Germanism. It was a very personal document—the occasion, after all, was the break with his brother Heinrich, whom in the book he attacked as the *Zivilisationsliterat* and accused of siding with Germany's enemies. For the Ideas of 1914, see also Klemens von Klemperer's very suggestive *Germany's New Conservatism. Its History and Dilemma in the Twentieth Century,* Princeton 1957, pp. 47–69, and my essay, "The Political Consequences of the Unpolitical German," *History. A Meridian Periodical,* III (September, 1960), 104–134. For the gradual destruction of the August spirit, and the reappearance of old antagonisms over the question of war aims, see Hans W. Gatzke's excellent *Germany's Drive to the West (Drang nach Westen). A Study of Germany's Western War Aims During the First World War,* Baltimore 1950.

‡ Educated Germans before 1914 rarely dwelled on politics; a comparison of prewar and postwar biographies or collected letters reveals this suddenly aroused political interest. That prewar Germans lacked a sense of reality, that they were *wirklichkeitsfremd,* was Otto Baumgarten's felicitous phrase and contention in *Geistige und Sittliche Wirkungen des Krieges in Deutschland,* Stuttgart and Berlin 1927, pp. 5–14.

politics coincided with a steady decline of responsible political life in Germany; a stringent censorship of the press and the impotence of the Reichstag prevented any effective form of political debate or activity. Moeller's fame as a political publicist in the Weimar period depended in part on the fact that many Germans had become politically conscious without experiencing political responsibility, and hence found his peculiar esthetic and idealistic interpretation of politics relevant and profound.

Moeller's response to the war was unequivocal. Immediately after its outbreak, he ended his long stay in Scandinavia and returned to Berlin, where he remained until his death eleven years later.[2] Like so many other critics of Wilhelmine Germany, he now became an enthusiastic partisan of the German cause. In 1916, at the age of 40, he volunteered for the army and became a *Landsturmmann* on the eastern front. This gesture made, Moeller after a few months received a discharge on the grounds of excessive nervousness.* For the duration of the war, he was given a post at Army Headquarters in Berlin as a member of the Press and Propaganda Department for the eastern countries, which Ludendorff had organized. During that time, and by virtue of his official position, Moeller made new and important contacts. Gone were the days of the literary café with Expressionist writers; now he took weekly walks with Ernst Jäckh, with whom he worked in the *Werkbund* as well. He also wrote occasional pieces for various important newspapers, including *Die Kreuzzeitung* and the *Berliner Börsenblatt,* and articles on history and politics for such eminent periodicals as the *Deutsche Rundschau* and the *Preussische Jahrbücher.* Thus, just before the collapse of the old Reich, Moeller had won a foothold in its institutions and had established for himself a solid reputation as a critic of culture and politics.

---

* Or did he seek his discharge? His biographers of course assert that he was surprised and distressed by his discharge; the ubiquitous Ernst Jäckh, however, claimed that he obtained Moeller's release, as witness the following letter to Moeller: "We have done it at last! You can exchange your sword for your pen! In the end I had to trouble His Excellency von Falkenhayn, the Commander of the Field Army, personally, despite our disagreements concerning the conduct of the war in the Orient." *Der Goldene Pflug. Lebensernte eines Weltbürgers,* Stuttgart 1954, p. 342.

In 1914, Moeller appeared before the German public with what proved to be his most successful enterprise: the completion in twenty-three volumes of the first German edition of Dostoevski's collected works. Earlier and less adequate translations of individual works had been out of print for years. This new edition had been Moeller's idea, and he had supervised the entire venture. Finally he contributed a lengthy introduction to almost every volume—and Dostoevski was sent out into the German world with Moeller's mark clearly upon him.

The first volume of the new edition had already appeared in 1906—and by some timely irony it was *The Possessed,* which was immediately hailed as a profound commentary on the recent Russian revolution. More importantly, *The Possessed* allowed Moeller from the start to affix to Dostoevski a predominantly mystical and political interpretation which corresponded to nothing so much as to Moeller's own ideological inclinations. In Moeller's introductions, Dostoevski emerged as the great impenetrable mystic of the East, who had evolved "a conservative thinking which was based on a knowledge of human nature and was derived from his knowledge of the people." His political thought "was directed toward union [*Bindung*], not dissolution." Finally, as if to seal his kinship with Dostoevski, Moeller quoted Dostoevski as saying: "We are revolutionaries out of conservatism." [3]

Moeller's subsequent introductions were equally cloudy evocations of Dostoevski as the incarnation and the interpreter of the Russian soul, the prophet of Russia's destiny, and the archfoe of Western liberalism. Together with Dostoevski, Moeller made deep forays into the Russian soul, into Russian life, into the whole *Mysterium* of the Slav world which has alternately fascinated and repelled the Germans. Moeller's conception of Russia's geopolitical orientation—essential for his later sympathetic leanings toward national bolshevism and the Soviet Union—derived largely from his interpretation of Dostoevski. According to Dostoevski's vision, Russia's future lay in the East: "In Europe we are slaves. To Asia we come as masters. In Europe we were Tartars. To Asia we come as Europeans." [4] And from this, Moeller was to conclude that Russia would find itself in Asia and that consequently Germany would never again have to fear Russian power.

All of Moeller's introductions touched on Dostoevski's hatred of Western society and on his concern lest Russia become Westernized as well. "[Dostoevski] knew Europe and the West, and recognized liberalism . . . as the bearer of selfishness and individualism, as the spreader of the all-too Russian nihilism, and the bringer of the totally un-Russian industrialism, capitalism, and materialism." [5] Moeller had indeed converted Dostoevski into an ally.*

No other modern writer save Nietzsche had as great an impact on German thought as Dostoevski, and the character of that impact was largely shaped by Moeller.[6] In no other country was Dostoevski's legacy pressed into partisan strife, and only in Germany did he become the hero of the right, of the antiliberals and irrationalists. He was the conservatives' answer to Zola, the erstwhile hero of the progressives. His analysis of human depths, rather than of the surface of society, his pessimism drifting into mysticism—this appealed to Moeller and his friends. Appreciated in his own right, Dostoevski also offered an escape from the West, and it is significant that his triumph in Germany clinched a literary-political development that had freed the Germans from "the tyranny of the West," and had led them, via the theology of Kierkegaard and the pessimistic art of Ibsen, Strindberg, and Edward Munch, to the new prophet from the East.

For the conservative revolutionaries generally, Dostoevski was of central importance. Hermann Rauschning, one of the foremost politicians of the conservative revolution, often testified to his "positive reverence for Dostoevski," whom he had first read as a wounded soldier in a field hospital during the great war.[7] In Thomas Mann's early excursions into politics, Dostoevski was invoked time and again as the witness for the irrationality of man.†

Moeller's edition was a great commercial success as well; after a slow start, the sales rose sharply, strikingly so during

---

* He remained an ally even after the Bolshevik revolution. Dostoevski then was pictured as the great antithesis to Marx, as the writer who had foreseen, and already seen beyond, the materialistic intellectualism of social reformers. Defeated for a while, "Dostoevski belonged to those who rise from the dead." "Dostojewski der Politiker," *Gewissen*, II:30 (August 4, 1920).

† For quite different reasons, Nietzsche had warned against a German translation of Dostoevski: "I count any Russian book, especially Dostoevski (translated into French, for Heaven's sake not into German!!) as one of my greatest reliefs." Letter to Georg Brandes, October 20, 1888. *Friedrich Nietzsches Gesammelte Briefe*, 2d ed., Leipzig 1905, III, 318–319.

the terrible year 1916. After the German collapse, sales continued to soar, and various titles had to be reprinted several times. In 1920, 135,000 volumes were sold; in 1922, 179,000.[8] Since 1950 the same translations have appeared in new editions, but without Moeller's introductions.

Midway between the works of the *litterateur* and those of the political publicist stood *Der Preussische Stil,* Moeller's first wartime publication. Dedicated to Moeller's uncle, a Prussian lieutenant-colonel, "as a confession of faith in Hegel and Clausewitz," the book was the literary expression of his conversion and of his passionate support for Germany; the esthete had turned Prussian and political. Before creating the vision he called the Third Reich, Moeller turned back for the last time to German history and discovered in the Prussian tradition the noblest and most precious feature of German life. That tradition justified the defense of imperial Germany and vouchsafed its regeneration. Moeller's passionate commitment to Prussia—albeit a Prussia very much of his own myth-making —and his "confession of faith" in the Prussian state and army marked a break from his previous belief in the supremacy of art. In the Sandbox of the North, as Brandenburg was often called, there were some castles and churches, but little that could delight an esthete. For decades, in fact, many of the *Reichsdeutsche* regarded Prussia as an arrogantly poor and austere people that sought to put its boorish stamp on all of Germany. A new phase of the glorification of Prussia began only with the First World War.*

Der Preussische Stil has generally been hailed as Moeller's greatest work, and it certainly proved his most spirited and successful attempt to define the style or spirit of a people from a study of its geography and history, its art and politics.[9] For the occasion, his writing achieved a kind of austere simplicity,

---

* So strong in fact was the political and ideological opposition to Prussia in the years before the war, that in 1912 a *Preussenbund* for the defense of Prussianism was organized. Much of this antagonism was directed at Prussia's preëminence in the Reich. For the *Preussenbund* and the great concern over the preservation of Prussia, see Graf Westarp, *Konservative Politik im letzten Jahrzehnt des Kaiserreiches,* Vol. I: *Von 1908 bis 1914, Berlin, Deutsche Verlagsgesellschaft,* 1935, I, 210–211 and 358–366. It is interesting to note that Thomas Mann's prelude to politics also appeared in the guise of a Prussian tale, *Friedrich und die Grosse Koalition,* Berlin 1915.

except for those inevitable oracular-mythical pronouncements that explained or linked metahistorical essences. By means of impressionistic sketches of each historic period, Moeller traced the evolution of the Prussian spirit from its beginnings at the time of the Teutonic Knights to its decline in the decades after unification. For he contended that Prussia, which was "without *Mythos*," had been the only German tribe with sufficient realism to build a state, but once its political destiny had been fulfilled, with Germany's unification, its spirit was in jeopardy.[10]

The essence of the Prussian spirit was its simple matter-of-factness [*Sachlichkeit*], and—not surprisingly, given Moeller's method—he found this essence in all the characteristic forms of Prussian life. Prussian architecture and sculpture, especially the works of the younger Gilly and Schinkel, epitomized the Prussian spirit, as did its greatest ruler, Frederick William I. But that spirit was expressed as well by the Prussian's unbending devotion to duty, his ready obedience to authority, and his tough conquest of self. The Prussians were unyielding and practical, distinguished by their industry and talent, and living by a masculine strength harnessed to the purposes of the community. All of these characteristics were first personified in Frederick William I, *"Der Nurpreusse, der Urpreusse."* [11] Under such leaders and by such qualities, Prussians accomplished their great historical tasks; Frederick the Great and Bismarck brought about the final triumphs. The greatest achievement of the Prussians, the unification of Germany, ended with the near-annihilation of the Prussian style: "Prussia became the victim of Germany. . . . The collapse began by self-alienation; by completely misunderstanding its inherited values . . . Prussia denied its past . . . and its deprussianization began." [12]

The German spirit was antithetical to the Prussian spirit and was characterized by the persistence of the medieval romantic dream of a universal empire, by its poetic exuberance, its impracticability, and its feminine weakness. The idealistic bent of the German spirit promised great art, but the lack of a national state had historically obstructed the creation of a national style and thus German genius had wasted away. The Prussian tradition too, great as it was, suffered from the defects of its virtues: its austerity could never inspire fully articulated beauty.

Moeller delineated German and Prussian traits in such a

manner as to establish the usual thesis-antithesis relation between them. As always, when he posited a set of opposites, his synthesis was close at hand; and here the synthesis reconciled, not only his continued criticism of German culture with the promise of a great national future, but also with his support of Germany's war. As long as German and Prussian qualities remained unreconciled and alien to each other, cultural chaos and political disintegration threatened. During the war, however, the Prussian spirit would reassert itself in Germany, and a final synthesis would reconcile Prussia and Germany, and the great cultural epoch of Germany would begin. Moeller put it succinctly in his oft-quoted motto: "Prussia is the great colonizing deed of the German spirit [*Deutschtum*], just as Germany *will be* the great political deed of the Prussian spirit." (My italics.)

There was, of course, a clear connection between the war and Moeller's glorification of the Prussian tradition. The virtues he called Prussian were the prerequisites of Germany's victory: self-discipline, austerity, and obedience. They were also the virtues which the Ideas of 1914 praised as characteristically German; and when Moeller recognized the Prussian willingness to serve ". . . as our highest German and human freedom," he joined those writers in wartime Germany who redefined freedom in a defiantly anti-Western manner.[13]

Moeller certainly had shifted his ideal of human greatness. His former predilection for the struggling artist pitted against society had vanished; now his admiration went to the soldier's subordination of himself to the good of society. When at a later time Moeller developed the position of the conservative revolutionary, it was primarily this Prussian tradition which he sought to recover by a new revolution. His "Germanic" socialism, which he developed more fully in *Das Dritte Reich*, leaned strongly on the Prussian tradition of subordinating the individual's interests to the general good of the community.*

---

* Four years later, Oswald Spengler propounded much the same relationship in his *Preussentum und Sozialismus*, München 1920, p. 29: "Prussianism is a vital feeling, an instinct, an inability to act differently." Spengler delineated Prussian and German qualities in exactly the same manner as Moeller had. The philosophical premises of this national socialism are discussed in Karl Pribram, "Deutscher Nationalismus und deutscher Sozialismus," *Archiv für Sozialwissenschaft und Sozialpolitik*, XLIX:2 (Tübingen 1922), 298–376.

Der Preussische Stil was Moeller's last esthetic-historical work. As the war dragged on, he became more and more concerned with the political problems of the day, which he began to analyze *sub specie aeternatatis*. He was no armchair strategist, but a kind of metaphysician of crisis, a searcher after the deeper causes and prospects of the great trial. Like so many German thinkers, he sought to divine the basic spiritual meaning of a struggle which, after the initial enthusiasm had evaporated, threatened to become endless and senseless. If a world-historical meaning could be discovered, then a program for action and a prophecy of aggrandizement could be deduced as well. This Moeller proceeded to do. The meaning was buried in distant realms and could be approximated only by categories like race, space, and people's values, but the political consequences were tangible enough.

In one of his most important wartime essays, published in November, 1916, Moeller elaborated the proposition that Fate, not clever statesmanship, would decide the outcome of the war—and considering the egregious blunders of Germany's wartime leaders, this should have been a comfort to some of his more sophisticated readers.[14] Fate, like fortune, favored the young and the bold, and hence Germany's enemies—the old peoples—were doomed to defeat, and no degree of diplomatic finesse could rescue them. The war was at bottom a contest between young and old peoples. It also marked a phase in the historic march of power to the east. Fortunately this eastward trek of power would stop with Germany; Russia, he predicted, would shrink to its national boundaries and would lose its prewar hold on the Baltic. As Moeller once put it, in his characteristic poetic-prophetic manner: "The sea does not want the Russian." [*"Das Meer will den Russen nicht."*] [15]

These and similar laws of historical development guaranteed Germany's victory and foreshadowed the kind of peace she would establish. Moeller attacked the "merely pragmatic" claims of the Pan-Germans as well as of those superpatriots who sought the restoration of all land which had once belonged to the empire: "Restorations [*Rückgriffe*] such as the great-Latin, the neo-Celtic, the Pan-German aims demand, are a playing with history, not a command of history." [16] Only those peoples who had a community of interests or of ideas with Germany should be annexed. That Germany would expand after the war corresponded to yet another general development of history: in the nineteenth century peoples sought their national independence, in the twentieth century they sought their interdependence under Germany. This was particularly true of the *Baltikum,* where Esthonians and Letts had strong cultural and racial affinity with the Germans. To a lesser extent it was true of the Belgians as well; Flemish art and Baltic architecture were of German inspiration, and hence the rescue of these poples from other imperial powers or from their own ineffectual self-government was Germany's historic mission. "It is not so much a matter of the country, as it is of the people: it is a matter of the political preservation and intensification of the spiritual and economic belongingness which has always existed." [17]

Moeller's wartime imperialism, moderate by Pan-German standards, was a highly idiosyncratic compound of personal experience, literary imagination, and political observation, couched in terms of highest idealism. Consider, for example, his central idea of Germany's Eastern destiny, to which he clung to the end of the war. In early 1918, he wrote: "For a long time it·was almost a European certainty that Germany would win the war toward [*nach*] the East, even if it should lose in the West." [18] He knew all this because he had lived in the *Baltikum,* and had married into a Baltic family; he was drawn to the East by his image of a Dostoevskian Russia, and saw before his eyes the enforced, wartime community of Eastern nationalities with the far stronger German nation.* From these diverse strands he fabricated his particular imperialist pattern, with its strong Eastern tone. It was Moeller's good fortune that his visions and fantasies touched on reality and coincided with plans of more orthodox origins. Many of his arguments, for example, seemed to echo Friedrich Naumann's pioneering *Mitteleuropa,* published in October, 1915,

---

* This wartime *Schicksalsgemeinschaft* with other peoples was regarded by many Germans as the prelude to a peacetime commonwealth; few of them recognized the self-defeating quality of this wartime experiment, as Ernst Troeltsch did when he noted in 1919: "And one must not forget that our moral strength, at home and abroad, declined [during the war] so that the experience of the occupied areas aroused a hatred of Germany everywhere in the East and West. Our ruling class did not have the least talent for the government and management of the occupied areas." Ernst Troeltsch, *Spektator-Briefe. Aufsätze über die deutsche Revolution und die Weltpolitik 1918/22,* ed. by H. Baron, Tübingen 1924, pp. 319–320.

but they lacked the detailed evidence with which Naumann had bolstered his case.[19] Moeller's primary concern, moreover, was with the *Baltikum,* not with the Balkans or southeastern Europe as was the case with Naumann. The important point, however, was that Moeller's esthetic and metahistorical theorizing ran parallel to the political programs urged by men championing very real economic or political interests, and this coincidence of plans proved to be the precondition for his ever-growing influence.

In November, 1918, he published an essay in the *Deutsche Rundschau* on "The Right of Young Peoples," a passionate defense of Germany's right to victory, and a pathetic defiance of the military realities of the moment. Again he demonstrated that the war had divided the world into young and old peoples, and that Germany was on the side of the young. He recognized the obvious incongruities, that is, Japan and the United States fighting with the Allies while Turkey was supporting Germany; America had betrayed its character when it went to succor the old peoples, but it could still awaken and redeem itself, and gain its place as the leader of the young peoples. Moeller conceded the possibility of a short-term defeat, but proclaimed that ultimately the young peoples must emerge from the war—or the peace—as victors. It was a law of nature, a fate which men were powerless to alter. In the very month of publication, the Allied Armies defied this law of nature and forced Germany to sue for an armistice.

The German people were stunned by the sudden collapse; wartime censorship had concealed from them their rapidly deteriorating position, and even the leader of the Conservatives, von Heydebrand, cried out: "We have been lied to and duped." [20] The ill-timed appearance of Moeller's article was a striking illustration of this ignorance; the month of November, 1918, or indeed any time after August of that year, was a singularly inappropriate time to proclaim the inevitability of a German victory. But Moeller could revamp his theory in the midst of defeat, and in the interval between the armistice and the convening of the peace conference he expanded his earlier article into a book, *Das Recht der jungen Völker.* In it he addressed himself directly to President Wilson and demanded of him that Germany should not be inhibited in its natural growth. He flattered the president even as he threatened him; Wilson was challenged to deserve Moeller's respect by writing a peace which coincided with Moeller's demands.*

Moeller's appeal to President Wilson, whom he should have despised as an archliberal, is a striking example of the occasional practicality of his idealism. At times Moeller penetrated the mists of his own metahistory, and perceived the essence of political reality more clearly than most of his contemporaries, as he did in his early recognition of the central importance of Wilson and America. He believed in his theory of young peoples, and from this premise he deduced the expediency of his appeal, which coincided entirely with the opportunistic decisions of German politicians. Ironically, it had been Ludendorff, Moeller's nominal chief at Army Headquarters, who had first thought of elevating Wilson above his allies, of appealing to him in the hope of gaining an early armistice and a favorable peace. Moeller's line of reasoning was different, but the conclusion was identical. He was sure that his vision of America's destiny as the savior of young peoples corresponded to the true traditions of the country. As he put it later, in much the same context, "We have knowledge of America that America itself does not have." [21] For a while there was some possibility of having Moeller's book translated into English, and he was delighted because the book was written "for those circles that are not content to lead a purely materialistic life, but who want to keep alive the great idealistic tradition of the country and of the Emerson-and-Whitman period." [22] What Dostoevski had done for his *Ostpolitik,* Emerson and Whitman did for Moeller's short-lived *Amerikapolitik.* In this fashion, Moeller became a realist despite himself.

Moeller's book sought to serve two purposes: on the one hand it was in all seriousness meant to instruct President Wilson for his forthcoming task as peacemaker. On the other hand, it was meant to explain Germany's defeat, to exonerate it from the accusations levelled at home and from the vindictive charges of its enemies, to render comprehensible all the events which had left men stunned, to sketch the outlines of a

---

* Moeller's widow wrote to me that "toward the end of the war Moeller demanded that peace negotiations should be begun only under the condition that American troops should occupy the Rhine. If Moeller's suggestion had been accepted, Wilson would not have had to leave Paris with all of his ideas crushed." Letter of August 8, 1951.

new Germany. His several purposes were accomplished by his old notion that the war had been a contest of the young and the old peoples. Despite the unhappy end of the fighting, Germany remained a young people, because youth was a matter of will and Germany willed to be young. Or, as he put it often, the young lived off problems, and the old lived off "ideas"—and surely Germany had a superabundance of problems. Its youth, moreover, was attested by its capacity for work, its rising birth rate, and its ability to solve the social problems of the future.*

To write a fair peace, the true cause of the war had to be understood. The West's envy of German vitality had forced the war on Germany, and when the Allies were nearly vanquished they had turned for help to a gullible people, the Americans. To win American support the Allies had dusted off the old ideals of 1789, of liberalism and democracy, and Moeller considered the effectiveness of these false ideals to have been the major cause of Germany's defeat. Moeller, like Hitler, but unlike most other Germans, was greatly impressed by the enormous potential power of propaganda, as exemplified by the successful campaign of the Allies.[23] For the Germans, Moeller argued, were conquered not on the battlefield, but behind it. The Allied propagandists had not only succeeded in recruiting American help but with their liberal ideals had corrupted a part of the German people. This propaganda had put an end to the war: after four years of magnificent resistance, the German armies, unconquered in the field, broke off the fighting because the young peoples trusted President Wilson to give them a just peace.[24]

No single idea played so powerful and so pernicious a role in postwar Germany as the notion that an undefeated army had voluntarily laid down its arms in the hope of a just peace. Because of it, Germans were able to feel that the Allies had tricked, not defeated, them—hence, that a moral wrong had been committed. From it evolved the invidious belief that the great army had been betrayed by civilian elements at home, by socialists, liberals, and Jews, and that the republic had

---

* Germany's birth rate had fallen steadily since the 1880's, but despite this fact nationalistic publicists always justified their demands by Germany's rising birth rate. D. V. Glass, *Population Policies and Movements in Europe,* Oxford, Clarendon Press, 1940, p. 270.

been fathered by traitors.* Moeller's book appeared in January, 1919, and hence it is safe to say that he was one of the first Germans to spread this poisonous belief, though it would be futile to speculate on the exact share which he had in its propagation. As we shall see, Moeller's postwar politics, while arising from his own prewar commitments, expressed the aspirations of an ever-growing number of disgruntled German nationalists.

Moeller pleaded with Wilson for a peace that would release Germany's power. The right of the young peoples must not be ignored; they had "Darwin and Nietzsche on their side." [25] In other words, what Germany had failed to conquer on the battlefield, it should gain at the peace table: "Every war is decided only after the war." [26] Some sacrifices Moeller envisioned, but he urged, for example, that the fate of Alsace be decided by a plebiscite. France with its colored troops had become an African nation, and "Strasbourg in French hands would be for German feelings like a white girl in colored hands." As for Polish territory, Wilson was reminded that Poznan and Bromberg were German towns, even if the surrounding countryside was Polish: "Here quality comes before quantity." [27] It required considerable agility to dictate peace terms to the victor.

Moeller sounded his appeals to the Allies in a variety of discordant tones. He alternated between supplication and defiance, while avoiding an open break with the West. If Germany were allowed to retain its strength, it would become the West's ally. Only a powerful Germany could protect the

---

* In fairness to Moeller it must be remembered that the belief in an unconquered German army was at first shared by Germans of *all* parties. Thus, in December 1919, Friedrich Ebert welcomed the returning soldiers: "As you return unconquered from the field of battle, I salute you." Quoted in Robert G. L. Waite, *Vanguard of Nazism. The Free Corps Movement in Postwar Germany 1918–1923*, Cambridge 1952, p. 7. Moeller, however, kept harping on this theme, even when it had become the exclusive property of reactionaries. As early as December 1919, Ernst Troeltsch noted: "The great historical legend on which all the reactionary forces based themselves, namely that a victorious German army had been treacherously stabbed in the back by the uprooted [*vaterlandslose*] fellows from home . . . became the dogma and the flag of the discontented." *Spektator-Briefe*, p. 92. See also Lindley Fraser, *Germany between Two Wars. A Study of Propaganda and War-Guilt*, London 1944, esp. chapters 1–2, for a short history of the stab-in-the-back legend.

Allies from the Bolshevik revolution—a contention that Colonel House had already used in coercing Anglo-French approval of a German armistice, and that was destined to become a powerful political cliché for twenty years.* The promise of German support was accompanied by thinly veiled blackmail: if the Allies pressed their advantage and imposed crippling terms on Germany, then it would join with Russia against the West. Moeller exclaimed that in the open spaces of the East lay Germany's territorial destiny, and in the communal, antiliberal culture of Russia lay its ideological future. His policy was transparent: he was selling Germany to the highest bidder, still hoping, however, that the West would win.

The book was alive with one fervent hope: that Germany could solve the problems of modernity. There was a subterranean exaltation in Moeller's prose; the old culture had finally been destroyed, the young German people, freed from their past and sobered by the war, could reconstitute a new society. Germany alone could provide a solution to the two major questions of modern society: "What to do with our masses . . . and how to save human nature from the machine." [28] A German socialism could reconcile the antagonisms of industrial society and humanize its life, and it would do so by creating a synthesis between the individualistic Western society and the collectivistic society of the Soviet Union. Germany alone had the necessary moral energy and Germany alone had the tradition of *Innerlichkeit*, of idealism. It would devise some form of social harmony that would go far beyond the laissez-faire liberalism of the bourgeoisie and yet would stop short of the dictatorship of the proletariat.

Marxian socialism, he maintained, must fail in its promise

---

* In the spring of 1919, Winston Churchill, operating from very different premises, suggested a plan close to Moeller's: "I do not think that we can afford to carry on this quarrel with all its apparatus of hatred, indefinitely. I do not think the structure of the civilized world is strong enough to stand the strain. With Russia on our hands in a state of utter ruin, with a greater part of Europe on the brink of famine, with bankruptcy, anarchy, and revolution threatening the victorious as well as the vanquished, we cannot afford to drive over to the Bolshevik camp the orderly and stable forces which now exist in the German democracy. . . . A way of atonement is open to Germany. By combating Bolshevism, by being the bulwark against it, Germany may take the first step towards ultimate reunion with the civilized world." Quoted in *The New Europe*, April 17, 1919. I am grateful to Arno Mayer for calling this statement to my attention.

of social betterment. The workers could thrive only if Germany could obtain justice from other peoples. "The war should lead to a realization of the kind of justice that starts with peoples, and ends with men, not vice versa." [29] Here was the basic theme of Moeller's national—or social—imperialism, a socialism which would begin by expansion and lead to national unity and prosperity by means of imperialism.

Such was Moeller's case for Germany. Never again was he to attain the power and the passion of this book that was written under the sudden impact of defeat and dedicated to an immediate purpose. Here he had plucked the Ideas of 1914 from the ruins of defeat, and salvaged them for a new German order. As a defense of German interests, the book availed nothing. As a prophecy of slumbering hopes and aspirations, it was of terrifying accuracy.

13: The Conscience of the Right

We believe that everything in Germany has come too late; it would be better if decisions were made that came too early. CREDO OF THE JUNI-KLUB

The great danger of idealism lies in the fact that it turns men into fools. It can turn them into honest fools. It can turn them into sanctimonious fools. That is only a difference of degree. The decisive point is that because of all this idealism, and through the extravagant, everyday invocation of the highest ideals, reality may perish.
MOELLER VAN DEN BRUCK

On the ninth of November, the day of the German revolution, Moeller and some friends were walking down the streets of central Berlin, and as some trucks with revolutionaries rumbled by, Moeller said: "A revolution with no enthusiasm." [1] The comment was apt—for Moeller and for the revolution. This was his way of judging politics, and this was his expectation of the revolution. If the November revolution could have recovered some of the collective enthusiasm of August, 1914, then Moeller would have rallied to it as well. For a few weeks Moeller thought this might still happen, but enthusiasm and a great surge of hope and passion was the last thing the revolution could achieve. After the revolution became frozen in the Weimar Republic, and the Versailles treaty wrecked all hopes for a victory in defeat, Moeller rejected the republic and returned, consistent with his past, to his political vision of a much earlier time. He had longed for a new spiritual community amidst the political glitter of the Wilhelmine period; how much more would he seek an escape from the spiritual pluralism and the political disunity of Weimar.

The short interval between the revolution and the peace treaty Ernst Troeltsch once characterized as "the dreamland of the armistice period, when everyone could paint his own future—fantastically, pessimistically, or heroically, without [knowing] the conditions or practical consequences of the peace that was in the making." [2] In such a land, Moeller was very much at home. His appeal to President Wilson—sent to the latter with the approval of the German Foreign Office, but never answered—epitomized the strange mood of hope and despair that pervaded this dreamland period. Anything seemed possible—the crust of the old order had been broken through, and the outline of the new was still dim. Some foreign power, some greater destiny, might yet reverse the verdict of the war and rescue Germany from her defeat. Moeller was only exaggerating the hope that many Germans clung to in that period; even the pessimists believed that Germany would suffer nothing worse than the loss of some of her colonies and of a part of Lorraine. [3] The Germans were totally unprepared for the treaty which was eventually presented to them, and of which even Wilson had said that it was meant to be harsh. For six months the Germans deluded themselves; when the treaty shattered these delusions—and no treaty written under the conditions of 1919 could have preserved them—the Germans felt doubly betrayed and resentful. In four years of fighting, they had defined their apartness from, and their superiority to, the West. Now, in June, 1919, the West demonstrated its vengeful duplicity, and men like Moeller, who for decades had battled against the West and against liberalism, came into their own. Their message was heeded at last.

For Moeller this dreamland period marked the beginning of the most active and successful phase of his career. For years he had lived in his private political-esthetic dreamworld. That world had consisted of literary abstractions and political visions, tenuously linked to reality. Now, in the months between war and peace, between the destruction of the old order and the establishment of the new, others found themselves equally estranged from reality, and Moeller's vision, which he had learned to express in short oracular phrases and slogans, and which ultimately found full elaboration in his *Das Dritte Reich,* won grateful acclaim from the many men who were adrift and homeless among the parties of

Weimar. Under these conditions, and at a time when the democratization of Germany gave the political propagandist a considerable importance and prestige, Moeller decided to abandon his literary work altogether and to become a spiritual leader of his people. Time and again he extolled the war-tested power of propaganda; he was resolved to wage a propagandistic war on behalf of a new Germany. He would become the guide and conscience of a new group of young conservatives.

In this aim, he was immediately successful. Within weeks after the revolution, Moeller became the *spiritus rector* of a group of writers and publicists who, like himself, had no class to serve, no material interests to protect, no political ambition to satisfy, but who were impelled to action by the terrible fate that had befallen their defeated country. As the political parties reappeared—essentially in the old forms and with the old commitments—these men at once registered their "anti-party" stand, their fierce rejection of Marxism, liberalism, clericalism, and reaction, of the whole emerging pattern of party government. They were strongly anti-Bolshevik as well: "This group recognized as its most urgent German task in its highest political sense the salvaging, amidst the general dissolution, of the last authoritative ties, and thus as an immediate active step the repulse of all forces threatening the state." [4] In spirit they were closest to the nationalists, without the nationalists' nostalgia for Wilhelmine Germany. In some ways, they were close to the socialists, because they recognized the need for integrating or nationalizing the worker—but they loathed the Marxist ideology and its liberal-rational humanitarianism which clashed with their heroic-conservative values.

The basic difference between this group and every political party was the fact that they remained esthetes even when they talked and wrote politics. They carried a vague anti-liberal *Weltanschauung* into politics, as well as emotional grievances that could find no proper satisfaction in politics. Middle-aged though they were, they made a fetish of the fact that they were young: alternately they called themselves the *young* conservatives, the voice of the young, the front of the young, even as Moeller had fastened on the rights of the young peoples. They affirmed their youth and aim even in a Latin motto: *"Juvenum unio novum imperium."* [5] This cult of the young had many roots, some of which we already observed in

Langbehn's time and thought, and we know that many of these "young conservatives" had been close to the Youth Movement and had shared in the exaltation of August, 1914. In their postwar search, one characteristic stood out: they were no longer youth in revolt, but youth in search of an acceptable authority. No one in authority spoke to them with authority. Weimar had no voice and no symbol that commanded respect, and Moeller's friends hoped as much for moral certitude and social cohesion as for any definite political program. A few years later, under Moeller's inspiration, many of these groups called themselves conservative revolutionaries. So far as they were revolutionaries at all, they were so because they found Weimar's weakness and disunity unendurable, and this rebellion of the young *for* authority, not *against* authority, became one of the most important aspects of German politics.

To reach this audience Moeller did not have to recast his prewar ideas. Merely by relating them to topical problems, he captured the loyalty of hundreds of fellow writers and the attention of tens of thousands of readers. *He* did not change; the times did. After 1918 he lived and wrote in an historical setting which made his kind of thought popular. Discontent and a sense of alienation had seized many Germans after the defeat and the revolution, especially among the urban middle classes and the frequently unemployed former officers.[6] Moeller had found his audience, the malcontents; they in turn were attracted to his vague but proudly idealistic program. He impressed men by his passion, not by his partisanship; by his idealism, which to many was more appealing than the ideas of the left or the obviously resentful hatreds of the parties on the right. People responded to the abstractness of his thought, which they interpreted as a deeper kind of reality, and they were impressed by his apodictic prose, which bespoke a certainty that belied his own inner doubts. His style of writing came to possess the same quality of energetic sincerity that won him the admiration of the many men of affairs with whom he now worked. Long after his death, and across decades of disaster, friends still praised the luminous integrity of his character, and associates recalled his charisma.[7]

During this dreamland period, several of Moeller's friends set up their own organizations, designed to promote various patriotic ends. In the autumn of 1918, for example, Heinrich

225

von Gleichen-Russwurm, a descendant of Schiller, who during the war had been head of the Association of German Scholars and Artists, founded a league for national-social solidarity. Eduard Stadtler, a one-time prisoner of the Russians, was one of the first intellectuals to realize the immense importance of communism; he organized the Anti-Bolshevik League, with the munificent help of the chief patron of all these struggling groups, Hugo Stinnes. Moeller was close to all these organizations; in the spring of 1919 he joined Gleichen and Stadtler in an informal discussion group sometimes called the Front of the Young. To an interest in social solidarity and anti-bolshevism were added—in the person, for example, of Max Hildebert Boehm—a passionate concern for the fate of Germans abroad, born of Boehm's personal experience in border areas where Germans had become underprivileged minorities. The main ideas of these men were some form of corporatism, a national socialism, and a strong revulsion from the West, which grew much stronger after the signing of the Versailles treaty in June, 1919. That date provided the occasion and the name for the key organization of these young conservatives, the *Juni-Klub*. Here a distinguished and influential group of men met to discuss the national and social future of the Reich. "To this circle belonged young people, who came from all parties and who turned their back on all parties." [8]

The spiritual directorate of the Juni-Klub was in the hands of Moeller, Stadtler and the club's formal leader, Gleichen-Russwurm. The thirty-three principles which Moeller drafted for the club and which were to govern its admission policy, bore the clear traces of his style and moral fastidiousness. "The purpose is the merger [*Sammlung*]; the merger refers to people and to ideas. . . . Membership is a question of trust. . . . Nobody can be admitted for whom even one member harbors wellgrounded mistrust." In this way, the "fearful ones, the compromisers and the intellectual racketeers" would be kept out. The club was designed particularly for men whose war experience had led them to a new perspective, which made all partisan opinions obsolete. "Those who come from the right and those who come from the left shall meet in the fellowship of a third point of view, which we consider to be that of the future." [9]

Our knowledge of this group is still lamentably scant; a

complete membership list or the records of its weekly meetings have yet to come to light. In the first years of its existence, the Juni-Klub undoubtedly maintained its nonpartisan character, though men with conservative affiliations predominated. It was an impressive gathering; in addition to Moeller, Gleichen, and Stadtler, there were Max Hildebert Boehm, an expert on nationality problems who in 1920 became editor of the *Grenzboten;* Paul Fechter, *litterateur* and later managing editor of the Stinnes paper, *Deutsche Allgemeine Zeitung;* Hans Grimm, a close friend of Moeller's and author of the sensational *Volk ohne Raum;* Professor Heinrich Herrfahrdt, a student of constitutional law; Rudolf Pechel, editor of the *Deutsche Rundschau;* Walter Schotte, who in 1920 became editor of the *Preussische Jahrbücher* and in the mid-twenties was a frequent correspondent of Stresemann's; and Martin Spahn, leading Catholic theorist of corporatism. Albert Dietrich became one of the club's most articulate fighters against Marxism. Occasionally Heinrich Brüning, the later chancellor, and Otto Strasser, who went from national socialism to the founding of his own Black Front, attended these meetings. Hans Blüher, the celebrated historian of the *Wandervogel,* used to go to the Juni-Klub as well, and was deeply impressed by Moeller. Through him the writer Gustav Steinbömer was drawn to Moeller and the club. Still others, including Ernst Troeltsch and Otto Hoetzsch, dropped in occasionally. The list of members and friends was long, and in the recent spate of memoirs the Juni-Klub is often mentioned.[10] Although Gleichen presided over the club, Moeller in fact guided its activities. His new role was a high tribute to him, as well as a kind of personal trial: though a facile writer, he seems to have been a most reticent talker. But to be the respected leader of a group of men of great public influence and intellectual eminence redounded to Moeller's honor.

In those early years after the war, the club was an active force in German intellectual politics. Through its members and far-flung connections, it wielded considerable influence on young German intellectuals. Its headquarters at Motzstrasse 22, a solid, middle-class house in central Berlin, harbored several other nationalist groups as well. Intermittently the club was able to tap fairly sizable funds; industrialists, including Hugenberg, contributed funds for a while, without apparently infringing on the club's nonpartisan outlook.[11] In its efforts to reach ever wider circles among Germany's youth and intelligentsia, the club sponsored a series of subsidiary organizations. Moeller had thought of the Juni-Klub "as an example to all those organizations which shall evolve from this group" and until its demise in the mid-twenties the club was indeed a kind of spiritual holding company, often called *Der Ring,* which loosely linked all the other organizations with a similar nonpartisan conservative orientation.

The most important voice of the club was its weekly journal, the *Gewissen, Unabhängige Zeitung für Volksbildung,* which first appeared on April 9, 1919. Although it listed Werner Wirths as editor, and after 1920 Eduard Stadtler as publisher, for the first five years the dominant spirit was Moeller, who was also one of the most prolific contributors. The name of the journal was apt: it was intended to be the voice of conscience, the disinterested, detached voice of faith and tradition that would speak to all Germans, regardless of party and class. It would constrain and criticize the selfish promptings of politicians and party leaders. In its programmatic note, the *Gewissen* pledged itself to an unceasing struggle against "the lack of conscience *which is the most conspicuous feature of our age;* this lack of conscience dominates us; it dominates Europe; it dominates the world. Everywhere conscience has fallen silent." [12] Conscience and partisanship were antithetical, according to the *Gewissen,* and the journal continued to boast about its nonpartisan character even as it inclined more and more to the right.

The *Gewissen* was a kind of "national review," a journal of Germanic faith and conservative comment. In its weekly columns dealing with current developments it lamented the decline of Germany, caused by the vindictiveness of the Allies and hastened by their German agents. Its tone was unassailably idealistic. Although its goals were often couched in deliberately obscure abstractions, its enemies, both at home or abroad, were concrete enough. Its defense of culture, another of its primary concerns, had a pleasingly antidemocratic ring; Moeller's comment in a controversy over teachers' education—"half-education is the pestilence of our time"—epitomized the *Gewissen's* position on that subject.[13] Reflecting as it did the interests of so many conservatives, the *Gewissen* was particularly solicitous about the cultural well-being of the millions of Germans abroad. On the surface it was a perfectly

respectable paper, thoroughly *salonfähig,* as would befit the
organ of the Juni-Klub. It avoided the scurrility that marred
so much of Weimar's political pamphleteering. Occasional
slips—a reference, for example, to the "Jewish-metropolitan
press" or an excessively vitriolic *ad personam* attack on Erzberger—indicated how strong was the self-restraint the writers
of the *Gewissen* usually exercised.

Under the banner headline, "At the Eleventh Hour [*In
letzter Stunde*]," the first issue of the *Gewissen* proclaimed its
political credo. At this eleventh hour, when civil war threatened to destroy the Reich completely, "we appeal to the conscience of every German." The sole hope for avoiding national
disaster was social harmony, "the antithesis of bourgeois and
proletarian must vanish." In the other column on the front
page, entitled "More Enlightenment," the *Gewissen* explained
its attitude toward the republic in a way which recalled
Thiers's remark that the Third Republic was a *pis aller.* The
November revolution, it argued, had been legitimized by the
recent elections to the National Assembly, and the republic
had to be protected from its left-wing friends who threatened
to radicalize it. The Bolshevik danger was great, and the only
weapon against it was the type of propaganda which Lord
Northcliffe had used with such devastating success during the
war. The *Gewissen* promised to wage a propagandistic battle
for German unity.[14]

During the next year, as the republic acquired a kind of
shaky stability and the Bolshevik danger receded, the *Gewissen*
reversed its course; it attacked the republic, and first muted,
then transformed its antibolshevism. The history of the journal records this retreat of the intellectual right from the
republic, a retreat which separated the right sharply from
men like Thomas Mann who rallied to the republic, and
right-wing politicians, especially among the German Nationalists (*Deutschnationale*), who grudgingly collaborated with it.
The shift in the *Gewissen*'s policy became evident after the
Kapp putsch in March, 1920, which demonstrated the bankruptcy of the monarchical-reactionary opposition and the inability of the socialists to do more than passively defend the
republic. From this date on, the *Gewissen* moved to a systematic attack against the parties, all of which had been thoroughly discredited. At the same time, it made the first discreet
mention of a possible alternative source of power: the cap-

tains of industry. In an eight-point program, it demanded the virtual end of the parliamentary system and its replacement by an Economic Council and a "provisional representative body of the German people," formed by "elastic appointments and elections." The executive power of the state should at once be entrusted to a "directory of a few men, to an experienced industrialist [*Wirtschaftler*], a proved statesman, and to a man who possesses the confidence of the workers. . . . Parties may perish, but the people must live." [15] After this initial manifesto, every new crisis in Weimar, every new and largely inevitable surrender of republican governments to Allied demands, evoked the same demand for an end to parliamentarianism. The refrain was that the parliamentary regime at home was responsible for every German defeat abroad, and some of the republican leaders—the much maligned Erzberger, for example, or Walter Rathenau, an erstwhile friend of the *Gewissen*—were charged with actively selling out to the Allies.* Anticipating a common device and slogan of the National Socialists, the *Gewissen* demanded that the Wirth government should be tried for high treason because of its renunciation of Upper Silesia. Three months later, it declared: "In effect, the government is nothing but the executor of the will of our enemies." [16]

Gleichen and Stadtler took turns at attacking the party system in this fashion.† In phrases that were not uncommon in the early years of Weimar and that were to become the

* The *Gewissen*, particularly through its publisher, Eduard Stadtler, was one of the most embittered traducers of Erzberger. A few weeks before Erzberger's assassination, Stadtler inveighed against his new and eminently practical ideas on Christian solidarism: "Erzberger's teachings are the latest defraudings of the people by a defrauded fraud [*neuster Volksbetrug eines betrogenen Betrügers*]." *Gewissen*, III:26 (June 27, 1921); Stadtler may have felt cheated by this serious revival of his idea of solidarity, particularly at a time when he was moving away from advocating a genuine accommodation of the lower classes. He returned to the attack in a further polemic, "Erzberger und kein Ende," *Die Grenzboten,* July 27, 1921, pp. 90–100.

† In October 1921 Stadtler, still the publisher of the *Gewissen,* was briefly arrested on charges of high treason, charges which were quickly dropped by the government. At the time, it was revealed that he had shortly before become a member of the German People's party, which had been a partner of a Weimar cabinet. Despite his conversion, Stadtler maintained his antiparty stance, a stance not uncharacteristic of the party itself. See "In eigner Sache," *Gewissen,* III:43 (October 24, 1921).

stock-in-trade of the National Socialists, Gleichen and Stadtler denounced the stupidity of all parliamentarians, led as they were by stupid and selfish bosses. If one knew "that in a certain way the party struggles [were] artificially developed," then one wondered, Gleichen argued, why these parties could not be replaced by *one* German party that would rest on the principles of nationalism, Christianity, corporatism, and leadership.[17] It is not accidental that corporatism replaced socialism as the goal of the *Gewissen;* as early as December, 1920, the *Gewissen* had criticized all concessions to socialism and, in particular, it had attacked Wichard von Moellendorff, the most brilliant searcher after a non-Marxian planned economy. The Communists were also antiparty, and their only error was denying the need for aristocratic leadership. But the other parties, including "the rotten middle [*faule Mitte*]," were mired in the morass of party government. As a result, "under the guidance of the government, the parliament and the bureaucracy, the German people have been robbed in the last months of all satisfaction in self-government [*Lust am staatlichen Eigenleben*]," and this insidious theme of the superfluity of self-government constituted another link between the *Gewissen* and the National Socialists. The only alternative, and one from which the *Gewissen* did not shrink, was to establish a dictatorship that could reverse the disastrous course of Germany's foreign policy. Once Germany ceased surrendering to every Allied whim, it would be able to solve its internal problems as well.[18]

The *Gewissen* became more and more insistent in its antiparty position. Moeller championed this argument and enveloped it in his usual metahistorical mystique. In this instance, the difference between his tone and that of his colleagues may have corresponded to a real difference in motivation. Gleichen and Stadtler were closely attuned to the material interests in German society that sought to supplant the Weimar regime with an economic dictatorship of sorts; whereas Moeller, outraged by the undeniable pettiness of partisan squabbles, was much more representative of the kind of person who simply could not endure the continual turmoil and insecurity of the Weimar parliamentary regime. Even the fear that the public order might disintegrate can be a crushing burden to a certain type of man, just as the weakness of a system or of a man may

incite contempt in some people and desperate terror and resentment in others.

The direction of the *Gewissen,* though relatively subtle, was
unmistakable. In a democratic society, it is hard to launch a
frontal attack on democracy, yet the agitation against parties
was a veiled form of antidemocratic sentiment and one, incidentally, that had been popular in Germany since 1849. It
reflected the young conservatives' despair with the German
electorate, their tacit abdication of the hope of ever persuad-
ing a majority of the people to their own policy. As was common in Weimar, the *Gewissen* exaggerated the vices of democracy, and it had neither the wit nor the honesty to see the
likely pitfalls of its own vague schemes of leadership and elite
government. Could true conservatives honestly believe in the
stability and self-perpetuating quality of disinterested leadership? The writers of the *Gewissen* may have been seduced by
the grandeur of their own antidemocratic rhetoric; they would
not have understood the common-sensical view epitomized in
Winston Churchill's remark that democracy was the worst
form of government except for all the others that had been
tried before.

There was of course another ideological element in the
Gewissen's crusade against democracy. In Weimar Germany,
democracy was identified with the West, with the same group
of countries that had inflicted a crippling peace on Germany. After Versailles, the enemy stood in the West, and the
Gewissen's slogan became: No enemy to the East. Although it
did not adopt Moeller's scheme for an active *Ostpolitik,* the
Gewissen turned violently against a Western orientation in
foreign policy and against all those politicians in Weimar
who sought to conciliate Western politicians and emulate
Western political forms. The *Gewissen* believed—and who,
after the experience of Mussolini, could doubt it?—that a
dictatorship and an energetic foreign policy would go hand
in hand; the men of conscience succumbed to the lure of undefined, aimless power, believing as so many Germans had
before them that power was the best remedy, and its own
reward.

Particularly in its first few years, the *Gewissen* enjoyed considerable prestige among the educated conservative classes.
The journal, as we have seen, was long on faith, short on a
concrete program. In the intensely politicized atmosphere of

Weimar it retained some of the putative virtues of the political idealist, and it is therefore credible that the greatest representative of unpolitical Germany, Thomas Mann, wrote a warm endorsement of the journal. In 1920, in a letter to Gleichen, Mann wrote: "I have just renewed my subscription for the *Gewissen*, a paper which I always want to see and which I describe to everybody with whom I talk about politics as incomparably the best German newspaper." * A high recommendation for the *Gewissen*, if not for Mann's political sense of that time. Less than two years later, Mann, in his celebrated speech *"Von deutscher Republik,"* formally and brilliantly rallied to the republic and continued to defend it until 1933. In the intervening decade, he spoke often and contemptuously of the so-called conservative revolutionaries and sought to impress upon them the reasons for his own belated discovery of the virtues of the republic and of political reason. But the young conservatives, including the writers of the *Gewissen* who had once seen in the author of the *Unpolitical Meditations* their principal champion, thought the republican Mann a renegade, and he became a frequent target for their abuse.

Ernst Troeltsch, one of the most perspicacious observers of the early years of Weimar, took a very different view of the role of the *Gewissen*. He regarded it as a central link in what he thought was a sinister alliance of industrialists and writers —an alliance of which neither side was fully conscious, but by which both groups worked toward the substitution of an economic dictatorship for democratic rule. The function of the literati, he thought, was to disguise these aims—of which they

---

* Letter of July 7, 1920, in the possession of Heinrich von Gleichen, and quoted in Hans-Joachim Schwierskott, "Das Gewissen," in *Lebendiger Geist. Hans-Joachim Schoeps zum 50. Geburtstag von Schülern dargebracht*, ed. by Hellmut Diwald, Leiden 1959, p. 175; see also Gustav Hillard (pseudonym for Steinbömer), *Herren und Narren der Welt*, München, List, 1954, p. 293. Credible, but far from certain. It is odd that Gleichen, on January 26, 1951, answered my inquiry about material concerning the Juni-Klub and the *Gewissen* with the assurance that "all my material of the past has been burned or otherwise destroyed." The whole episode involving Mann seems a little doubtful considering the extremism of the *Gewissen* after the Kapp putsch and Mann's total repudiation of the conservative revolution in 1922. And given the *Gewissen*'s etiquette, is it likely that it would not have published this letter in the many attacks which were launched on Mann after his desertion to the republic?

were hardly aware—and, by propounding a German corporatism to undermine the existing barriers to the full exercise of economic power. Troeltsch was certain that Hugo
Stinnes was a leading agent in this campaign, and hence he
noted with concern that in 1920 "the writers of the *Gewissen*
[are] already moving into the newly acquired Stinnes papers." [19] At the time Troeltsch feared, somewhat prematurely
as it turned out, that the German industrialists and capitalists were engaged in a vast Americanization process of Germany, whereby they would gain control over the state as well
as society. Right-wing journalists, including the writers of the
Gewissen, were camouflaging this ultramodern drive as a
Germanic retreat from modernity: "For the captains of industry the literati have indeed wrapped the new Americanization in romantic, corporative, and medieval ideologies, in
Fichtean and Nietzschean ideas of leadership, and in truly
Germanic principles, and are thereby seeking a link to this
new conception of the state and of society." This tacit collaboration between the supermodern industrialists and the
irrational enthusiasts for the old Germanic character was
ironic indeed, and Troeltsch feared this Americanization of
Germany because it would lack the humane elements of the
real America, "the combination of Enlightenment, Christianity, and material progress which . . . constitutes the cultural
achievement of the modern Anglo-Saxons." [20]

The propaganda of the Juni-Klub and the *Gewissen* reached
a remarkably wide audience. The *Gewissen* was determined
to break out of the group of ephemeral and parochial journals, and its circulation figures attested its success. In January,
1922, it claimed to have 30,000 readers, many of them in the
lands of Germania Irredenta, especially in Poland and Czecho-
slovakia, as well as among Germans overseas.[21] A year later,
at the height of the inflation, it reported a weekly circulation
of 10,000, and even that figure was much above the average
of the little political magazines of Weimar.[22] In the early
years, when the journal struggled against financial odds as
well, it solicited and often received voluntary contributions.
From the beginning it had a small but select list of advertisers, ranging in a characteristic issue from a large recruiting
advertisement for the Lützow Free Corps and "its wild and
daring chase" against Germany's enemies, to a small, conventional box in which "two cultured gentlemen" expressed their

desire to meet two ladies of wealth, under twenty-four years of age, for purposes of matrimony.

Der Ring set up, through the *Gewissen*, a kind of patriotic book club which sold, or gave away as prizes to anyone who recruited new subscribers, a series of cheap reprints of Germanic works, including at the head of the list the works of Lagarde and Langbehn. In 1921, Max Hildebert Boehm arranged for the distribution of syndicated articles by men of the Ring Association to some thirty provincial newspapers.[23] Through its immediate readers and through its far-flung connections with other newspapers and journals, the *Gewissen* became, in the years after the war, the articulate conscience of those groups who, rejecting the reality of the Weimar Republic, strove for a new state, nationalistic and aggressive, dictatorial and corporatist.

The Juni-Klub resorted to still other means in its campaign to rally the eternally young among the German people. Its most ambitious offspring was the Political Seminar, directed by the Catholic historian and corporatist Martin Spahn. Conceived in the summer of 1919, it was designed to "deepen the political will through intensive schooling," in seminars of very short duration. The emphasis on brevity underlined the sponsors' contempt for the sustained, disinterested study of politics. This was to be a seminar for action.* The seminar

---

* Heinrich von Gleichen, "Das Politische Kolleg," *Deutsche Rundschau,* CLXXXVII (April, 1921), 106. With some acerbity Gleichen hinted that his idea for a political seminar hastened, if it did not inspire, the establishment in 1920 of Naumann's and Jäckh's *Hochschule für Politik,* which, he added, was more academic than activist. In point of fact, Gleichen was wrong; Friedrich Naumann had been concerned with the need for more "education to politics" as early as 1916, and in 1917 had already obtained the necessary funds from the liberal industrialist Robert Bosch. As so often in his life, Naumann's concern for this type of education was symptomatic of German thought and needs of the time. During the war, Jäckh organized discussion groups for men from all parties, which he thought of immense importance. The *Hochschule* and the Political Seminar were rivals for a short time, especially after the former had turned down Hugenberg's offer for generous financial support, provided economic interests would have a controlling vote on the board and Martin Spahn be appointed director. The *Hochschule,* Jäckh recalled in 1952, long outlived the "competitive bid of Spahn's and Gleichen's Political Seminar." See Theodor Heuss, *Friedrich Naumann,* pp. 410–413; Ernst Jäckh, *Goldene Pflug,* pp. 184–195; and Ernst Jäckh and Otto Suhr, "Geschichte der deutschen Hochschule für Politik," *Schriftenreihe der deutschen Hochschule für Politik,* Berlin 1952, p. 15.

sponsored lectures by leading Juni-Klub members to students from all parties, regions and walks of life, including some trade unionists. Max Hildebert Boehm, for example, spoke about the nationality problem, Martin Spahn about foreign policy, Moeller about the ideas of the World War and the question of war guilt, Stadtler (the most active lecturer and traveler) about the consequences of Versailles. These lectures were designed to mold political action on specific issues, and it was Gleichen's hope that the seminar would most especially reach teachers who in turn would indoctrinate future generations of students.

The club tried another means of persuasion as well; in 1922, it published its collective credo, *Die Neue Front,* to which thirty-eight members of the club contributed, and which was edited by Moeller, Gleichen, and Boehm. It covered a wide range of topics, from Moeller's long essay, "Liberalism is the death of nations [*An Liberalismus gehen die Völker zugrunde*]," which later became a part of the *Dritte Reich,* to articles on overpopulation and the colonial problem by Hans Grimm, and a treatise "Monism and Dualism as Fundamental Metapolitical Concepts." A brief exhortation by Rudolf Pechel, "The Word Gets Around," set the tone for the volume. Despite his attack on "today's wretched sham of slogans," Pechel's essay was a succession of mystical religious slogans designed to evoke feelings, not thoughts. "Loyalty to the populist tradition [*Volkstum*] becomes a religious demand. The path that leads to this religion and which is itself already religion, can be trod only by individuals." The Germans of course have a particular duty and destiny: "The West rests silent in spiritual paralysis. . . . Satan rules under the mask of God. All the great ideas of humanity are distorted and defiled." And the solution? "We want the *Führer* as Lagarde once described him, in whom shall be alive the noblest essence of the German nature, who in every fiber of his being possesses the feeling for our true nature, the hatred against everything unnatural, and who breathes the aspiration for a German future." [24] This was the characteristic message of the Juni-Klub, and it is striking that this reckless idealism and remoteness from reality should have appealed to a very successful publisher of a highly respectable bourgeois magazine.

Throughout the early 1920's, the Juni-Klub continued its separate existence, still proud of its suprapartisan attitude.

But the club and the *Gewissen* allowed their detachment from parties to harden into an uncompromising hostility for parties—a common attitude among the political moralists in Weimar Germany.* Determined to reach beyond all parties, the leaders of the club even talked with men of the extreme left, and in particular with Karl Radek, a leading member of the Comintern. Radek's decisive role in the later eruption of national bolshevism, that strange interlude in Weimar which was so intimately connected with Moeller and the Juni-Klub, will be discussed below.

In 1922, Moeller assented to Rudolf Pechel's suggestion that Adolf Hitler, a relatively unknown upstart from Munich, be given the opportunity to address the club. Hitler's appearance was a complete failure: "Whereas generally 120 to 130 people crowded the small rooms on our discussion nights, on that memorable night only thirty at the very most appeared—a very inauspicious beginning. Hitler spoke as if he were addressing a great mass meeting in a Munich beer hall. . . . After this catastrophic failure, Moeller was full of reproaches [for Pechel]." He nevertheless consented to have a private conversation with Hitler at which only Pechel and Dr. Lejune-Jung were present. "Afterward, Hitler, who had been very much impressed by Moeller, said: 'You have everything I lack. You create the spiritual framework for Germany's reconstruction. I am but a drummer and an assembler. Let us work together.'" Moeller gave an evasive reply, and after Hitler's departure remarked to Pechel: "That fellow will never grasp it." [25] Brüning contends that at the end of the meeting Moeller said: "I would rather commit suicide than see such a man in office." [26] A year later, after Hitler's abortive Putsch in Munich, it looked as if Hitler had committed po-

---

* Friedrich Naumann, for example, who in late 1918 had been close to Stadtler's anti-Bolshevik League, broke with him and his associates over the question of the place of parties in the new Germany. Essentially Naumann retained his prewar belief that "the party is a necessary form of life in the modern state," and he attacked Stadtler's and Gleichen's suprapartisan *Führergedanke*. Naumann proved to be far more responsible and realistic than his critics in the Juni-Klub, and his argument that the necessary machinery of politics should not be dismissed, in traditional German fashion, as "mechanistic," was timely. To Stadtler he wrote in March 1919: "The chaotic condition of having no parties precludes any political action." Heuss, *Friedrich Naumann*, pp. 500–501, and Klemens von Klemperer, *Germany's New Conservatism*, pp. 112–113.

litical suicide, and Moeller wrote a somewhat premature political obituary: "There are many things that can be said against Hitler. But one thing one will always be able to say: he was a fanatic for Germany. . . . Hitler was wrecked by his proletarian primitivism. He did not understand how to give his national socialism any intellectual basis. He was passion incarnate, but entirely without measure or sense of proportion." [27]

Moeller, as we have seen, was the central figure of the Juni-Klub. Active in its deliberations and intrigues, indefatigable in the pursuit of its propagandistic aims, and at the height of his literary power, Moeller had no equal in the camp of the conservative revolutionaries. So powerful and compelling had his voice become, that the young enthusiasts of the movement came to regard him as the leading political guide of the Weimar period.[28]

In those early years after the war, Moeller had learned to write with the speed of a journalist and the style of a prophet. His productivity was impressive; his signed articles alone numbered in the hundreds, and many others appeared anonymously in the *Gewissen*, which at times was but a disguised Moeller journal. Although his writing now focused on political problems, he occasionally returned to pure esthetics, as in his long article on Däubler's epic *Nordlicht*. The major excursion into another realm was his critique of Spengler, first set in print and then continued in the meeting rooms of the Juni-Klub. The historian of the whole Spengler-controversy considered Moeller's work as "a very important essay . . . which subtly penetrates the depths and contradictions of Spengler . . . and interprets them farther in his own way." [29]

He had begun the debate with Spengler in 1920, in the columns of the *Deutsche Rundschau*. The similarities in thought and motive between Spengler's *Decline of the West* and Moeller's far less systematic philosophy of history were unmistakable, and the tremendous popularity of the one helps to explain the appeal of the other. Both men were essentially metahistorians, who sought, in Nietzschean fashion, to define the styles of historical periods; both developed a philosophy of culture which posited the antithesis between *Kultur* and *Zivilisation,* between a decadent West and a still vital Prussia. Both derived their political judgments from this philosophy of culture, and both cherished vague ideas of Caesarism as a defense against cultural decay. Moeller, however, opposed Spengler's prophecy of doom and sought to refute the central vision of Spengler's work. Beneath the ornate rhetoric of Moeller's attack was a very simple and shrewd idea: Spengler, Moeller said, had rightly predicted the decline of the West when he assumed Germany would win the war; in that case even Germany might have succumbed to civilization. Defeat, on the other hand, "may have restored to us other possibilities—those final possibilities that are always the first: of simplicity, of a more natural life. . . . Did not the outcome of the war overthrow the premises on which Spengler had predicted the decline of the West? Was this not particularly true of the fate of the defeated? Did it not move our fate ahead [*hinausgerückt*]?" Nor was there a "homogeneous Occident. For that reason alone there can be no homogeneous decline." [30] Moeller pitted his belief in the vigor of the young peoples, especially of Germany and Russia, against Spengler's rigid pessimism concerning the inevitable decline of the entire West. He accepted the morphology of the *Decline,* but he contended that the defeat of Russia and Germany had cheated destiny of its prey. For these two peoples, the outcome of the war had restored the promise of life and growth, had separated them with finality from the decaying West. The debate between these two oracles of a new Germany may have seemed obscure to some, but both were deeply concerned about the practical consequences of their seemingly abstract speculations.* Moeller certainly was not the anti-Spengler; he was merely snatching free will from yet another deterministic system so that he could still bank on the ultimate resurgence of a New Germany, of a Third Reich.

His postwar articles on politics can be classified under three headings: they were either critiques of the democratic republic in the form of commentaries on contemporary events, or they

---

* Among others, Otto Strasser remembered them as oracles and wrote: "The author will never forget that fruitful discussion in Heinrich von Gleichen's 'June Club' when the Pessimist and the Optimist of the West expounded their versions of the coming decades. The two conceptions were opposed to each other and yet attuned to each other and complementary to each other, so that all of us, moved by this moment, solemnly swore to devote our lives to the realization ot these visions." Otto Strasser, *History in My Time* (transl. by Douglas Reed), London, Cape, 1941, p. 200.

were explorations of the historical origin of the German malaise, or they were prescriptions for the future, for what Germany should do. His discourses on the future always combined wish and prophecy—as a metaphysician he predicted what as a patriot he longed for. The three types overlapped, for Moeller could not write anything without touching on an imaginary past, a distorted present, or a visionary future. The future, after all, would resolve the struggle between the inadequacy of the present and the promise of a much earlier past. The unifying aspect of his writing was his exclusively spiritual interpretation of the world, combined with an almost total disregard for fact and reality, which allowed him sometimes to soar above the commonplaces of the day and to predict developments with amazing clairvoyance, but which at other times made him sound trivial and irrelevant.

For a short time after the revolution, Moeller unwillingly suspended his disbelief about the future of a democratic republic. He had been no partisan of the imperial regime, and he often admitted that the revolution had swept away a rotten system that deserved its fate. But how genuine was this brief gesture of judiciousness? Did not everything that he had believed in and yearned for dictate his rejection of a political system that was patterned after the West and was in close and humiliating communion with the West? The red thread that ran through all his thought and wishes was his loathing for what he had come to identify as the decadent West, with its philosophy of right and reason, its liberalism, its dull and unheroic life. For decades this abstraction of the West had been a fantastic exaggeration that corresponded only in a vague way to any verifiable reality. After 1918, the West became very real to Moeller and his compatriots; and the hatred that had such deep roots now fastened on a very tangible reality. Only a revolution that would have leapt across the Western phase of political development, that would have unified Germany in enthusiasm, would have satisfied him. But the revolution turned prematurely bourgeois, and Moeller became its enemy: "The socialist revolution forged the capitalistic republic." [31]

Although granting some merits to the postrevolutionary regime—especially the establishment of a closer link between the state and the people—Moeller decried as its worst failing its lack of leadership. He was certain, moreover, that this system would always block the emergence of a strong elite. For the weakness of Weimar politicians he had unbounded contempt, and he was convinced that their surrender to Allied demands derived from their moral cowardice. Moeller indicted not the flaws of a political system, but the integrity and character of public life in general—an unwarranted charge which by its very generality allowed neither rebuttal nor remedy.

In the months before the Kapp putsch, he clung to the hope that a union of youth, from the left and the right, would be achieved at last and that it in turn would create a national dictatorship. In Moeller's writings the idealistic justification of the dictatorial idea emerged clearly: the parliamentary regime produced irresponsibility and dictatorship required responsibility, or—and this neither Moeller nor his political friends ever envisioned—it would degenerate into tyranny. The myth of the German *Führer,* the myth of the inherent virtue of power, was so deeply imbedded in the minds and desires of these antiparliamentarians that the likely abuse of dictatorial power never troubled them. The Kapp putsch, which once more separated the right from the left, and which was followed by a series of Communist insurrections in central Germany, interrupted this drive toward a national dictatorship. After the insurrections of 1920 and 1921, Moeller, in an article entitled "Are Communists Germans?" concluded that of course they were German—their stupid and irresponsible political activism had proved it.[32] A few years later, Moeller wrote appreciatively of the National Socialist idea and of the small movement which bore that name.

Consistent with his past, Moeller railed against the cultural atmosphere of Weimar; in a bitter and prophetic article, entitled "The German Face," published a week before the Ruhr invasion, he exclaimed: "It is all true what they say of Germany today." Apathy, indifference, sloth, and petty selfishness—all these were true failings, and ringingly he denounced them. With solemn passion he lashed out against the materialistic, hedonistic attitude of the German people, and asked many times what it would take to save the Germans from themselves: "All men must be compelled, only Germans more so. Some people are brought to their senses by a danger. For Germans, apparently, nothing less than extinction [*Untergang*] will do." [33]

As so many conservative Germans did—often for good tactical reasons in order to preach the *Führeridee*—Moeller professed despair and contempt for the political ineptitude of the Germans. Since Bismarck, everything had failed. The generation of 1872 had taken the Reich for granted, unable even to comprehend the fury of a Lagarde or a Nietzsche; the generation of 1888 had been stupid and selfish and had nervously plunged the nation into all sorts of adventures; it had lost the First World War, and even now its epigoni sought to smile their way through disaster, content to pursue their profit and pleasure. This postwar generation did not even comprehend that it had been beaten, violated, and disgraced. The Germans, he asserted, have ever been a divided, self-annihilating people, intermittently capable of demonic, uncontrollable energy but only in the face of a dire threat. In an article, "Italia docet," written immediately after Mussolini's march on Rome, Moeller extolled the historic roots of fascism, and complained that the Germans did not even possess the requisite sense of a collective historical past that would allow them to establish a German variety of fascism. "The Italian people . . . lives in the conception of its freedom, its independence, its cohesion. The German people does not possess this tradition." [34]

So blind and unpolitical were the Germans, especially the governing classes of Weimar, that they did not even know that the heart of politics was foreign policy. In Moeller's thought, the *Primat der Aussenpolitik*—a principle which German historicism and political thought shared—reached an absurd height. Internal conflicts, which engaged and divided the people so deeply, should be suppressed, and all national energies should be thrown against the Western foes. For twenty years before Versailles, he had thundered against Western liberalism; the peace treaty merely confirmed his hatred, charged it with greater passion, and gave its expression a timeliness it never before had.

Germans should cease their internecine war and should learn to overcome or resolve their internal antagonisms. The only people who had learned this lesson and had acquired a political sense were the "Outsiders," the millions of Germans outside the national boundaries, in Europe and overseas. [35]

One of Moeller's most important contributions to the ideology of the conservative revolution was his espousal of a "socialist foreign policy," by which he meant a policy which would rectify the social grievances at home by punishing the exploiters abroad. "Socialism today must transform itself from a class socialism to a peoples' socialism." [36] The German proletariat must be torn from the false doctrines of Marxism and must be taught that social inequality could be abolished only if Germany's overpopulation could find an adequate outlet in enlarged territory. In subtler, and far less conscious form, this kind of argument—often called social imperialism—had appeared long before the First World War; in Weimar it gained plausibility because of the tangible deprivations imposed by the Western powers at Versailles.[37]

It was ironic that Moeller's socialist foreign policy depended on a prior change in the structure of domestic politics. Only a strong government—which came to mean a dictatorship—could pursue an aggressive policy abroad, and therefore Moeller too was faced by the inseparability of the domestic and external elements in the life of a state. "We are confident . . . that at some time the greater life force of the German people will assert itself over the French, and that the strength of seventy million people will prevail over that of forty million people. And our aim is to hasten that time, to fuse the seventy millions in a common direction, with the ready support of the masses as of the individuals." [38]

The direction of this socialist foreign policy was clearly outlined. Moeller was certain that the period of Western hegemony in the world had drawn to a close; the World War had given the final impetus to the rebellion against Europe: "The Orient, China, India, and Egypt seek to be free of European rule." Australia will become Australian, or American, but will cease to be British, just as South Africa had already become "Boerish." [39] The Germans abroad will not suffer from this process, because German imperialism is already dead and should not be revived. The whole colonial venture was a romantic mistake, and the time had come for a return to the *grossdeutsche Politik:* "This refers not only to the *Anschluss* with Austria. . . . Germany and Austria together . . . will be able to launch the boundary-struggle which runs from the Memel territory down to the Polish-German plebiscite area and across to Bohemia, Carinthia, and Tyrol until it reaches the threatened, nay the smashed-in and carved-up western boundary." [40]

But beyond these specific aims, which could and, according to Moeller, should be achieved largely by peaceful means, lay the dormant strength of German rage and fury. In one of his last articles before his death, entitled "The Mysterious Germany," Moeller predicted the eruption once again of this Teutonic furor. "Our annihilation harbors possibilities which our enemies never thought of. It carries with it the mysteriousness of a life in which there are men who have nothing more to lose, in which there is a people made up of such men." As a consequence, the world is afraid even of a disarmed Germany. "This fear is our only weapon," but the Germans were too decent to exploit this fear.

Germans who are unfamiliar with our German nature, and who are incapable of seeing historical processes in an intellectual unity, conclude from our political fate that we have no political mission at all. . . . But our mission is: not to let the world come to peace. Our calling is to be an irritation of the spirit to the people of comfort. And our miracle will be: when we, to whom it had been intimated that we should annihilate ourselves, will achieve out of our revolutionary suicide, our political rebirth.[41]

These were terrible threats, which originated in Moeller's perception of the violence that was smouldering beneath the surface of German society and in his wish that this violence should finally erupt. It was a violence so great that the enfeebled West would not be able to contain it. To this dark, destructive force, this nihilism that threatened to devour civilization, Moeller was drawn by a powerful fascination.

In his hatred of the West Moeller was willing to embrace this brutal and nihilistic force. He called for an alliance with bolshevism and sought to rally all the nationalistic discontents to his vision of the Third Reich. In his plea for national bolshevism and the Third Reich he came close to the main currents of German political life.

14: Toward the Third Reich

The idea of the Third Reich is an ideological idea which reaches beyond reality. . . . The German people is only too prone to succumb to self-delusion. The idea of the Third Reich could become the greatest of all the self-delusions that it ever held. It would be very German if it relied on it and if it found peace in it. It could perish by it.

MOELLER VAN DEN BRUCK

Reality is our only certain and inalienable possession. "Truth," however, suffered the same fate as "freedom" and "justice." The concept of truth became so abused that only the swindler defrauds with it and the fool is trapped by it. Truth, which once was a Christian certainty, according to which a man did or did not act, became a moral demand of the Enlightenment, which humanized, and thereby destroyed, the divine. For Western man, what is useful to him is true. The German is still occupied with a dangerous inclination for a truth "in itself." The new man will again divine the truth "in himself," but he will search and find it in reality.

FROM MOELLER'S ANSWER TO RADEK, 1923.

In the last years of his life, Moeller sought to be a political realist, a leader who would find a way out of the national degradation of Weimar and Versailles. He was surprisingly successful, and his success in becoming the dominant voice of the young conservatives attested the degree to which political reason was declining in the republic. Moeller's prominence as a political thinker was in some part due to his now eminently effective rhetoric of passion and patriotic wrath; to a larger degree it was due to the unreason that had swept over postwar Germany. Moeller's bridge to political reality was the intrusion into German politics of various manifestations of this unreason. When he poignantly depicted the mood of disillusioned Germans, he was in reality depicting his own mood, and when he prophesied the course of history, he was guided by his intuition of the mood of these people, an intuition quickened by desire.

Throughout this last phase of his work, Moeller preserved an exasperating indifference to fact or historical complexity. He clung to certain old ideas that had long been familiar to him, and he derived from these generalities—about the West, for example, or about liberal man—specious justifications for his political or cultural prejudices. The categories were old, as were the resentments, but the crisis of Germany, which Moeller had suffered from for decades, had become a burden for all.

After Versailles, after the vindictive measures of the victors and the submission of the vanquished, Moeller's long-standing hatred of the West as the repository of all that was old and putrid acquired specious justification. The bourgeois life and the liberal ideals had been equally loathsome to him, and his fight against both now engaged his heart and mind, and won for him a large political audience. In his espousal of a pro-Russian foreign policy and in his vision of the Third Reich he was devising new means to implement an old hope: to tear Germany from its Western course.

How closely his politics and his esthetic conceptions were still interwoven was demonstrated by his consistent championing of an Eastern orientation for German foreign policy and by his intermittent flirtation with national bolshevism. This complex of ideas, contemptuously called *Ostideologie* by the National Socialists, originated in a series of disparate reasons.[1] Initially Moeller had been drawn to the East by his esthetic imagination, and by his veneration of Dostoevski. For Moeller, Dostoevski *was* Russia, and because he mistook his abstract ideal of Russia for the live concrete society, Moeller could see in his Russia Germany's principal victim or ally; a bond of fate, a *Schicksalsgemeinschaft,* united Germany to that other young people, in a way it could never be united to the West. If the original premise is granted—that Dostoevski was Russia

and that art can grasp the totality of a nation's character—
then Moeller's conclusions follow as well, with that maddening
internal logic of fantasy.* Dostoevski had proved that Russia's
culture was non-Western and its destiny Asiatic. This allowed
Moeller to propagate a kind of spiritual geopolitics and to
continue his wartime prophecies concerning Germany's eastward expansion. Even Lenin could be fitted into this Dostoevskian scheme of things: he embodied another stage in
Russia's rejection of the capitalistic West, and Lenin's collectivistic society was preferable to the atomistic society of the
West. For all these reasons and in the light of Germany's
precarious condition, Moeller consistently urged a strong Eastern policy. To woo Russia as Germany's ally was Moeller's
hope—not as an instrument of *Realpolitik* but as an invitation from one young people to another to join in common
defiance of the decadent West.

Moeller's *Ostideologie* had two aspects. On the one hand,
he argued that Russia and Germany had a community of
interests and hence ought to form an alliance of sorts. But
beyond this tangible idea was the foggy notion that the political collaboration between the two states against the West
should be paralleled in the domestic politics of Germany as
well. There the West was represented by the republicans in
power, and the extreme opponents of the West, the Communists and the nationalists, should bury their differences in
order to fight the common enemy. Moeller was confident in
pressing for external collaboration, and despite the vagaries
of German communism, he never abandoned hope that the
two radical groups would unite to supplant the republic.

In the Weimar period, Moeller's fantasies often coincided
with the tough-minded plans of German leaders who were
working for the rapid recovery of German power and political
freedom. Certainly his pro-Russian and anti-Western policy,
with its leanings toward national bolshevism, had a large and
respectable body of adherents. As early as June, 1919, Count
Brockdorff-Rantzau, Germany's foreign minister, had written

---

* Moeller's views on German-Russian relations were collected by his
literary executor, Hans Schwarz, himself an enthusiastic Easterner.
A quantitative token of the importance of Dostoevski to Moeller's
reasoning was the fact that over half of these collected essays dealt
with Dostoevski. Moeller van den Bruck, *Rechenschaft über Russland*,
ed. by Hans Schwarz, Berlin 1933.

to Ebert in his letter of resignation: "The clear, unambiguous espousal of a policy of democratic self-determination and of social justice will in the future be the raison d'être [*Daseinsberechtigung*] of the German people; this raison d'être and *the declaration of uncompromising war against capitalism and imperialism, whose handiwork is the proposed peace of our enemies,* vouchsafe it a great future." * Some months later, in a very different spirit, General von Seeckt, sought close and illicit ties between the Red Army and the Reichswehr as the only feasible escape from the Versailles straitjacket.[2] At the other end of the political spectrum was Karl Radek, an old-guard Jewish Bolshevik, who in 1919, in his famous prison cell in Moabit, his "political salon," negotiated with German nationalists as well as with German Communists. Seeckt and Radek—a rather odd pair who shared nothing save mutual hatred—were at least realists, men of power who sought to exploit the needs of their prospective partners for their own purposes. In their shadows were the dissident ideologists of the left and right, who in their groping for a popular program concocted what was called national bolshevism.

It has usually been said that national bolshevism appeared at three distinct times in Germany, in 1919, in 1923, and in 1930.[3] But such chronological exactitude ill fits the character of the movement. Among the nationalists of the right, national bolshevism had a latent attraction throughout the Weimar period as a state of mind, and even more, as a willingness of the resentful heart. It had no definite program; it was impervious to changing conditions and incapable of action. Hence it is easy to understand why Moeller should have been the leading apostle of national bolshevism; his unwillingness to act at the decisive moment exemplified the spirit of the entire movement.

Moeller's chief concern, as we have seen, was the resurrection of German power abroad and of unity at home. He argued persuasively that Germany's chief enemy stood in the West and her only potential ally in the East. From time to time he contemplated a great Eastern crusade against the

---

* Graf Brockdorff-Rantzau, *Dokumente und Gedanken um Versailles,* 3d ed., Verlag für Kulturpolitik, Berlin 1925, p. 119. According to Ernst Jäckh, Moeller was in contact with Brockdorff-Rantzau at that time and later, and intended to dedicate *Das Dritte Reich* to him. *The War for Men's Souls,* New York 1943, p. 81.

West, a joining of the two young and oppressed peoples. He railed against the Weimar statesmen because they had rejected "the idea of seeking an alliance with Russia and of playing the revolutionary East against the capitalistic West. . . . The possibility of immediately altering the [Versailles] peace by the pressure of a great, threatening East-bloc—even if it were merely a bluff—succumbed to the anxiety of our statesmen that we might lose the good will of our enemies." [4] Power abroad required unity at home, and this could be attained only through a reconciliation of the political extremes; there is no doubt, moreover, that Moeller felt a closer affinity for the spirited revolutionaries of the left than the timid *Bürgers* or nostalgic reactionaries. And so the promptings of both heart and policy seemed to point to the *idea* of national bolshevism, so long as one did not reckon with the actual power of the Allies, the ruthlessness of the Kremlin's policy, or the material, not the spiritual, antagonisms that separated the proletariat from the representatives of German nationalism. Moeller's vague hopes heightened the intermittent hopes of a large number of German rightists who in the political frustration and disgust with Weimar looked to the East for support against the West.

In one of his early pronouncements on national bolshevism, in June, 1921, Moeller defined "the axis" between the Communists and the radicals of the right as consisting of the joint struggle against

the liberalism which spreads from the middle to all the parties and pollutes and corrupts them. In this liberalism, the revolutionaries and the conservatives see the expression of an individualistic *Lebensanschauung,* and what in the all-too-human consequence amounts to the same, an egoistical *Lebensanschauung.* That is why they both reject parliamentarianism in which they recognize a protective form which liberalism created for itself.

Hence they agreed on the need for a dictatorship, though one sought the dictatorship of the proletariat, and the other of the elite. Still, he insisted, they shared a common corporatist basis, and the only remaining obstacle was that the Communists would have to learn to think in national terms. The parliamentarians of the right did not see their relation to the Communists this way, but the nationalists outside parliament did:

"On the ephemeral surface of today's life, nationalists and Communists still face each other, weapon in hand. Despite this position of enmity, students, officers, and nationalist soldiers extend a certain sympathy to the workers and unemployed who stand as enemies before them." The educated classes also were unemployed because their specially trained talents were no longer required by the new German state. But this sympathy between right and left, Moeller continued, was founded on more than this—somewhat speciously argued —social solidarity: "This sympathy still goes back to the war. Time and again during those four years, the so-called educated groups had a unique experience when meeting the so-called uneducated. The discovery of the common man occurred." But when the common man became a proletarian, became a mass man, and put his faith in doctrines emanating from abroad, the bonds among classes snapped. The interests of the Communists and the nationalists were to some extent identical, but the question of actual collaboration depended entirely on the Communists. If they would rally to the fatherland as the only remaining possession, then the right and the left could jointly overthrow the tyranny of capitalism at home and imperialism abroad.[5]

In its domestic aspects Moeller's national bolshevism bogged down in the usual spiritual generalities. Actively he combatted the German opponents of his Eastern policy; in October, 1921, for example, he denounced Ludendorff's suggestion for an international crusade against the Soviet Union. Somewhat belatedly he recognized that the inability of his wartime chief "to grasp political reality was gradually becoming a danger for Germany. . . . He has always fashioned policies that ran against the spirit of the people. . . . No German worker will fight against Russia or even allow such a war to take place." [6]

Moeller welcomed the Rapallo treaty and prematurely proclaimed it "the [final] no to the West." [7] In May, 1922, he recalled Lloyd George's earlier warning that "there is a possibility that a hungry Russia might be armed by an angry Germany," and Moeller urged that this possibility be converted into reality.[8]

Some time later, the possibilities of national bolshevism were for the first time seriously contemplated in the Soviet

Union.* The Soviets had been frightened by the Ruhr invasion, and by the possibility of a decisive French triumph,
coming on the heels of several unfriendly acts by the British
in the Near East. Under these circumstances Radek in his
speech before the Enlarged Executive Committee of the Comintern reached out to the German right in an open bid for
collaboration. Acknowledging the friendly articles in the
Gewissen, Radek delivered a eulogy to the memory of the
martyred hero of the German nationalists, Leo Schlageter, a
former Free Corps fighter against Russian Communists in the
Baltic and in 1920 against German Communists in the Ruhr.
In 1923, he had been executed by the French for attempted
sabotage in the Ruhr. Did the German nationalists want to
fight the Russian people or the Entente capitalists? Should
they not make common cause "with the Russian workers and
peasants in order to throw off the yoke of Entente capital for
the enslavement of the German and Russian peoples?" Without such an alliance, Schlageter's death would have been a
meaningless sacrifice, and he would have been "a wanderer
into the void," a phrase taken from the title of a nationalist
novel. Recalling the emancipation of the peasantry under
Gneisenau and Scharnhorst before the war of liberation—
and these men are still the historic heroes of the latter-day
national bolsheviks of East Germany—Radek predicted that
only the emancipation of the proletariat could bring about
the emancipation of the German people. "If Germany wants
to be in a position to fight, it must create a united front of
workers, and the brain workers must unite with the hand
workers and form a solid phalanx. The condition of the brain
workers cries out for this union. Only old prejudices stand in
the way." The German Communists must find the path to the
"nationalist-minded masses." The Communists must do all in
their power "to make men like Schlageter, who are prepared
to go to their deaths for a common cause, not wanderers into
the void, but wanderers into a better future for the whole of
mankind; that they should not spill their hot, unselfish blood

* Cf. Edward Hallett Carr, *A History of Soviet Russia,* Vol. IV: *The
Interregnum 1923–1924,* New York 1954, chapter 7, "Communism and
German Nationalism," for the fullest account of the Soviet side; his
description of the *Gewissen* as a "national-socialist journal" and of
Moeller as "the intellectual of the Nazi movement," is significantly
wrong (pp. 177, 181).

for the profit of the coal-and-iron barons, but in the cause of the great toiling German people." The emancipation of the German people, "of all who toil and suffer," is the task of the Communists. "Schlageter himself cannot now hear this declaration, but we are convinced that there are hundreds of Schlageters who will hear it and understand it." [9] For a brief moment, in the streets, in meeting halls and in the columns of party newspapers, German nationalists and fascists collaborated with the Communists. Right and left extremists had met, but in the period of Leninism in Russia and of powerless ideologues in Germany, the collaboration was doomed. Under different circumstances and in a different form, it would be revived by Stalin and Hitler.

Radek explicitly solicited replies to his proposals from Ernst von Reventlow, the National Socialist writer, and from Moeller, whose articles he had originally singled out for commendation.* In the *Gewissen,* which Radek had called "the only thinking journal of German nationalistic circles," Moeller wrote three long articles in July, 1923, trying to explain why Radek's invitation should not be taken at face value. He appeared anxious to extricate himself from the threatened embrace; and he retreated from the sudden offer of Communist collaboration as rapidly as he could. His dreamland must remain inviolable, and he quickly disappeared behind a smoke screen of generalities.

Moeller's chief objection, though irrelevant to the immediate purpose, was in some ways prophetic. Capitalism, he told Radek, had changed its character since the war; it was now "a socially cohesive entrepreneurial capitalism in which 'capital' and 'labor' were synonymous. . . . From this capitalism, socialism had to fear the greatest reverses." [10] Shades of our American people's capitalism! Not quite, because Moeller readily agreed with Radek that an economic dictatorship of

---

* On the basis of an obscure reference in Troeltsch's *Spektator-Briefe,* pp. 269 f., Klemperer believes that Radek and Moeller had held a series of conferences. Klemperer, *Germany's New Conservatism,* p. 146. I have found no conclusive evidence for this. Ascher and Lewy lump Moeller's and Reventlow's replies together, creating the impression that Moeller shared Reventlow's anti-Semitism. Abraham Ascher and Guenter Lewy, "National Bolshevism in Germany. Alliance of Political Extremes against Democracy," *Social Research,* XXIII (Winter, 1956), 465–466.

sorts would be necessary, but not a proletarian dictatorship, not even a dictatorship of the proletariat and the brain workers together, but of the entrepreneurs alone. "For us the German entrepreneur belongs among the brain workers. In economic matters he belongs for us in the front row." [11] In foreign policy too, Moeller was no longer so certain about the viability of an Eastern orientation; perhaps the Soviet Union was not even strong enough for such a venture. In his alarm Moeller suddenly foresaw yet another later development, the Franco-Soviet alliance of 1935: "Germany must always be prepared for the restoration of certain political relations between France and Russia, which are suggested by their position towards England. . . . The French republic will no more shy away from a tie to the Soviet state than it shied away from contact with tsarism." [12] In his flight from Radek's offer, Moeller learned to think realistically. But the danger was soon over, the Communists abandoned the Schlageter line as suddenly as they had adopted it, and Moeller could, in due course, resume his pleadings for an Eastern policy, pleadings for which he was to be devoutly honored by the "Easterners" of the late twenties and early thirties.*

Moeller's most important and best-known political work, *Das Dritte Reich,* written in 1922 and published a year later, accidentally provided the National Socialist movement with one of its slogans and the National Socialist state with its historic name. The title came to Moeller as a happy afterthought; originally he had planned to entitle the work "The Third Party" or "The Third Point of View." [13] The intent was the same, but by appropriating an old German myth as the title for his work, he quite properly placed it in an old German tradition. The dream of the Third Reich went back to medieval mysticism, to Joachim of Floris, and recalled as well the memory of medieval imperial glory.[14] It had survived into the nineteenth century, and was powerfully revived after

---

* The later National Bolshevists, especially the groups around Ernst Niekisch and Karl Otto Paetel, were genuinely revolutionary, and their concern was with the radical reordering of German society. Unlike Moeller, they believed in the primacy of internal affairs, and it was not accidental that these groups, unlike the direct heirs of Moeller, did not make their peace with Hitler, not even with a triumphant Hitler.

the destruction of the second, the Bismarckian, Reich.*
Spengler called the Third Reich *"the Germanic ideal,* an
eternal tomorrow, to which all great men from Joachim of
Floris to Nietzsche and Ibsen tied their lives—arrows of yearning for the other side of the river, as Zarathustra says." [15] For
Moeller the emphasis was more on the magic "third" than
on the mythical Reich, for it incorporated his hope that the
great antitheses of German life—the antitheses of confessions,
classes, regions—could be subsumed under some higher and
harmonious synthesis. This thinking in thirds was singularly
appropriate to Moeller's argument: it allowed him to create
logical unities where none existed in reality. In form this
appeal to the "third position" was a vulgar imitation of
Hegelian dialectics; in intent it was but an incantation to
magically effect unity. The concept of the third position runs
through much of modern German thought and always be-
speaks a striving to get beyond the given in order to penetrate
regions beyond reality.†

Das Dritte Reich marked the culmination of Moeller's
thought, and it marked as well the culmination of the Germanic ideology. Moeller acknowledged his ineffectual forebears and hoped that his work would redeem their aspirations:
"The conservative thinkers [after Stein] were not statesmen
anymore, but outsiders, whose fate condemned them to walk
past the nation unrecognized, unheeded or soon forgotten,
beginning with the early conservatives around Adam Müller
to Paul de Lagarde and Langbehn." [16] It was Moeller who

* Moeller had long been familiar with this myth: see his remark about
it on p. 204. In *Die Moderne Literatur,* he had criticized Johannes
Schlaf's novel of the same title. He encountered it again in a manner
close to his own meaning in the wartime work of his later friend and
associate Ernst Krieck, *Die Deutsche Staatsidee. Ihre Geburt aus dem
Erziehungs-und Entwickelungsgedanken,* Jena 1917, p. 25.

† In Moeller's rhetoric, "third" and *Mitte* were often used synonymously,
and it is a significant coincidence that at the very time when *Das
Dritte Reich* attacked the Weimar Republic, Thomas Mann, in his
carefully wrought defense of the republic celebrated it as the best
juridical form of that German humanity which describes the *Mitte*
between "esthetic loneliness and disgraceful dissolution of the individual in the totality, between mysticism and ethics," between egoism
and statism. Moeller thought that the same opposites could only be
reconciled in the Third Reich, while Mann ended his address with
a salute to the republic: "Es lebe die Republik." Thomas Mann, "Von
Deutscher Republik," in *Bemühungen,* Berlin 1925, pp. 189–190.

brought this particular form of Germanic idealism to the threshold of the historic Third Reich.

Das Dritte Reich saw Moeller at the height of his literary power: the pace of the book was swift, the tone passionate and oracular, the argument speciously simple. His old enemies were vilified once again, but now with accusations of specific crimes. By having gained power in 1918, they had become palpable targets, and by having wielded their power meekly, they had become contemptible targets. *Das Dritte Reich* was the apotheosis of Moeller's prewar cultural prejudices and political aspirations.

Moeller's attacks on the revolution and the republic, on liberalism and social democracy, on the moral bankruptcy of every live political force in Germany had enough verisimilitude to be devastatingly effective. The only possible refutation would have been a pedantic recital of the historic limitations of political action, just as the only refutation of his mystical flight to a Third Reich would have been an insistence on the intractability of "stubborn and irreducible facts." But nothing is more impervious to fact or rational criticism than a political fantasy: like love, such a fantasy embodies the innermost aspirations and desires of the victim who, supreme delusion, thinks himself the master of his fate.

Moeller dedicated the book to Heinrich von Gleichen, in memory of their joint labors and in the belief "that all the wretchedness of German politics originates in the parties. . . . It is necessary to destroy the parties from the ideological side [*von der Seite der Weltanschauung*]." [17] This he proceeded to do by systematically reviewing every contemporary political position except the clerical position, that is, the Center, and the omission is significant in a work that has often been called an exercise in political religion. He examined the political culture of Weimar until, in the last chapter, he presented his vision of the Third Reich.*

In his analysis of Weimar, Moeller resorted to a method he had first used in *Die Deutschen*. He worked with ideal types, with the liberal man, the socialist man, and so on. By thus personifying liberalism, he could condemn it without coming to grips with its philosophy or political program. If a liberal was incapable of thinking or acting disinterestedly, then nei-

---

* The chapter titles were: Revolutionary, Socialistic, Liberal, Democratic, Proletarian, Reactionary, Conservative, The Third Reich.

ther his thought nor deed needed to be analyzed. This type of annihilation by label was not unique; the Marxists use the term "bourgeois" for the same purpose and often for the same groups that Moeller attacked as liberal. The label was a short-cut in the search for the villain as well. Once Moeller defined the liberal as the great dissolver and divider, as the coward and the opportunist, as the selfish traitor and forger, and alleged that the republic was ruled by such men, then it followed, in this infuriating mirror game, that the November revolution, indeed the whole Weimar Republic, was liberal and detestable.

The power and appeal of the book lay in its angry evocation of the mood of a betrayed and disillusioned people. Moeller's caricature of the ruling classes of Weimar was as brutal as anything Brecht wrote and Grosz drew.* He caught the smoldering anger of the right, the resentment of the masses, and the sense of corruption and disappointment that both left and right shared. His account of the force of this sentiment was incomparably better than his account of the more tangible forces in Weimar politics. And in the end, alas, that force conquered all others.

Enough has been said about Moeller's political ideas to render a full discussion of *Das Dritte Reich* unnecessary.[18] The book opened with an invocation to the need for a *successful* revolution: "A war can be lost. . . . The worst peace is never final. But a revolution must be won." [19] The November revolution had been a failure, executed by men who had stabbed the victorious army in the back and who had succumbed to the debased ideas of Germany's Western enemies. The revolution had destroyed the Wilhelmine age with its "self-satisfied and yet somehow insecure men, overeducated or totally uneducated, petty and pompous at once . . . satiated men of a mechanized, regulated, and at the same time boasting life, which was poor in all its wealth and ugly in all its ornamentation." [20] The Wilhelmine age was gone, but the Wilhelmine men were still dominant, and the revolution will

---

* Moeller was in fact much concerned over the predominance of literary talent on the left. In a letter to Ernst Krieck in 1923 he complained about the dearth of conservative writers: "The readers would of course be there. But the writers are missing. The political left, although without ideas—they have been fully exposed since 1918—still has all the talents on its side." Andreas Hohlfeld, *Unsere geschichtliche Verantwortung,* Leipzig 1933, p. 21.

succeed only if it achieves "a turning away from everything
that in the last generation was specifically German and what
today is still German." [21] When Moeller proclaimed himself
a revolutionary and called for another revolution, he envisioned a revolution in German culture and not in the
material conditions of German life.

His critique of socialism consisted essentially of a pedantic
elaboration of his opening sentence: "Every error of socialism
can be derived from Karl Marx's saying, 'hence men set themselves only those tasks which they can solve.' " [22] Socialism was
reduced to Marxism, Marxism to Marx, and Marx—to
Judaism. As a Jew he misunderstood the spiritual essence of
man, "as a Jew he was a stranger in Europe and nevertheless
mingled in the affairs of the European peoples. . . . As a Jew
he had no fatherland," and this homeless, uprooted intellectual sought to persuade the proletariat that it had no
fatherland either. "The effect [of his mission] was Jewish,
because it was corrosive." [23] How formidable the Marxist
threat must have appeared to Moeller can be inferred from
the fact that it was only when trying to destroy Marxism that
he resorted to anti-Semitism. Moeller and many of his friends
hesitated at adopting an anti-Semitism which in Weimar was
becoming ever more vulgar and opportunistic.

Moeller charged that Marx and his liberal epigoni had misconstrued the true nature of man and had totally ignored the
impact of foreign affairs on the social order. Moeller's socialism
remedied these deficiencies, and by combining the spirituality
of man with the rapacity of nations, he was able to devise a
scheme for the reconciliation of the German proletariat and
the German nation, without essentially altering the internal
structure of Germany. The heart of Moeller's purpose was
revealed in his remark that "our preoccupation with domestic
politics is still our national vice." [24] National unity—not in
any superficial sense, but in an active, willing, religious sense
—was still his overriding political passion.

The first step toward national unity was the destruction of
the proletariat, an end which could be accomplished by
spiritual means alone: "A proletarian is he who wants to be
a proletarian. Not the machine, not the mechanization of
labor, not the economic dependence on the capitalist mode of
production, makes a man a proletarian, but proletarian consciousness does." [25] In a curious way, this recalls Lenin's distinc-

tion between trade-union consciousness and proletarian consciousness, but Moeller of course drew different conclusions from the distinction. Let the proletarian return to the values of the folk, and he will abjure the whole materialistic claptrap of the Marxist. Let him learn that the whole Marxist analysis had been rendered obsolete by the war which divided nations, not classes, into capitalist and proletarian entities. Once the proletariat has become deproletarized it will understand that the German proletariat was nothing else but the twenty million Germans that Clemenceau had said were in excess in the world. These "surplus" Germans could regain their proper social status only through a "socialist foreign policy," that would heighten Germany's power and prosperity. Nebulous as all this was, in Moeller's rhetoric it appeared with oracular certainty. His scheme for the transformation of the proletariat and the transposition of the class struggle was another instance of the leap in German thought from excessive sentimentality to unrestrained aggressiveness.

Moeller wooed the German proletarians with his national socialism, but also sought to discredit their leaders and their achievements. Bitingly he exposed the nonrevolutionary character of the majority socialist leaders, and he exhorted the workers to leave "these proletarian Philistines" and the independent socialists who were but hirelings of France and Russia.[26] European socialism and Russian bolshevism had abandoned Marxism, without admitting it. Moeller counseled the German socialists to abjure formally what in fact they had long ago given up. A generation later, the German socialists did just that.

As promised in his oft-repeated slogan, "Every people has its own socialism," the new Germany would have a socialist basis. This Germanic socialism would embody a synthesis of the ideas of Fichte, List, and Stein, and of the medieval institutions of the guilds and the estates. It would be organic and corporatist, and in the new hierarchical society the differences among classes would unite, not divide, the people. But beyond these verbal gestures toward an ordered economy, toward a society that would willingly accept the inequalities of modern capitalism, there was nothing, and there could be nothing, in a mind that contemptuously dismissed material matters as "subaltern facts." Moeller's idealism was an example of the kind of noble indifference to economic realities that prompted Bertold Brecht to write the intentionally wounding lines:

> Erst kommt das Fressen,
> dann kommt die Moral.

The main force of Moeller's hatred was of course directed against liberalism and the liberal mind. In his attack on liberalism, his detestation of Weimar politics and of modern culture coincided, because in liberalism he saw the carrier of all modern evil and in Weimar the epitome of the liberal fraud. It was here too that Moeller most clearly posited the equation of liberalism with the Enlightenment, and he showed his disdain for both forms of post-Christian life. The roots of liberalism, he thought, went back to the dissolution of the traditional religious community: "Liberalism is the expression of a society that is no longer a community. . . . Every man who no longer feels a part of the community is somehow a liberal man." [27] Deftly he turned the liberal ideal of freedom against itself and insisted that the liberal had destroyed the true freedom of the Middle Ages and had substituted in parliamentarianism a sham form of freedom. The pre-1914 Germans, for example, were "the freest in the world," until the liberal revolution of 1918 had enslaved them. Moeller was in earnest when he proclaimed that liberalism was the death of nations, that liberalism was a deadly fraud which disguised its attack on traditional human bonds by sham slogans about freedom. "Liberalism has undermined cultures. It has annihilated religions. It has destroyed nations. It is the self-dissolution of humanity." [28]

Moeller considered liberalism synonymous with reason [*Vernunft*], which was inferior to the conservative faculty of understanding [*Verstand*]. The attack against reason, an attack against which Thomas Mann inveighed time and again after 1922, was certainly an integral part of Moeller's hostility to Weimar. The liberal, according to Moeller, was doctrinaire, unfeeling, and unrealistic, though he always knew how to translate abstract reason into concrete profit. In fact what seems to have driven Moeller frantic was his sense of an all-triumphant liberalism that was so contemptible, so intellectually threadbare. Hence he was certain that deceit must be the condition of its success, and to his conspiratorial theory of liberalism he added an attack on Freemasonry as the secret arm of rational liberalism.

The condition of Germany was the most revolting instance of liberal deceit. "A suspicion stalks the land that a fraud against the nation has been perpetrated." [29] The liberal fraud worked from within and without; the Allies had deluded the Germans during the war and betrayed them afterward, while the liberals at home persuaded their countrymen to lay down their arms and trust the benevolence of their liberal friends abroad. No wonder that Moeller felt an affinity for the Bolsheviks who like him were convinced that liberalism was a sham. He knew as well that the Bolsheviks were his only rivals in the struggle against liberalism, for he was convinced that there was a tremendous subterranean movement against liberalism that would some day erupt in revolution. The Communist revolution might break out first, but Moeller hoped that his conservative revolution, the articulate version of a great popular *Ruck nach Rechts* which he sensed everywhere, would forestall it.

But this conservative revolution could not rely on the traditional elements of German conservatism. Moeller was an able and severe critic of German conservatism, which since the days of Metternich and Frederick William III had been intellectually and morally bankrupt and exclusively dedicated to the preservation of material interests and privileges. In a much-discussed polemic, Moeller insisted that reactionaries and conservatives were entirely distinct, and that the reactionaries of 1922 were simply the heirs of the earlier and debased conservatism.* The touchstone of the difference between conservative and reactionary was the attitude toward the Wilhelmine past: "Anyone is reactionary who still thinks the life we led before 1914 was great, and beautiful, even superbly magnificent. Anyone will be conservative who yields to no flattering self-deception and honestly confesses that it was revolting." [30] The contemporary reactionary, moreover, was the

* This distinction has recently been revived in a brilliant article by the young Austrian historian, Friedrich Heer, "Der Konservative und die Reaktion," *Die Neue Rundschau*, LXIX:3 (1958), 490–527. Heer's typology, which is primarily psychological, would place Moeller and his friends among the reactionaries, which is in fact what Heer calls Spengler. Heer says, for example: "The conservative is cheerful and he can be recognized by this sign. The reactionary is crabbed, sad, dead serious, without cheerfulness or humor. He cannot be cheerful because he is not his own master. . . . For the reactionary . . . the most important thing is suspicion. Enemies are everywhere" (pp. 503, 505).

most powerful obstacle to the union of right and left extremes, a union that Moeller still occasionally favored.

The conservative, on the other hand, was a realist, both in his principles and in his understanding of the limitations of a given situation. He recognized the immutability of human nature: "The great facts of human life are still love, hate, and hunger, necessity which fosters invention, challenge that incites, enterprise, discovery, the self-assertion of the ego among men and peoples, commerce and competition, will, ambition, and the drive to power itself." [31] The conservative disdains the optimism of the liberals and their idea of human perfectibility.

For the present, the conservative, unlike the reactionary, must accept the November revolution and the German republic. But he must complete the former and alter the latter so that Germans would at last have a political organization that would be consistent with their ancient traditions and with the eternal laws of human nature. Beyond this, beyond the glimpse of a national socialism and a social imperialist program, there was nothing more definite than the myth of the Third Reich, which somewhat like Marx's Communist society would herald the end of all domestic strife and reconcile all classes. The only definite aspect of this Third Reich was that old German ideal, the *Führergedanke,* which itself represented an escape from politics and social reality. The *Führer* would embody the aspirations of all social groups, and in his person would be transcended the contradictions of the German people. Here was the old rationalization of monarchical absolutism, rendered more modern by its nationalist appeal, and more appealing by its mystical overtones.

The Third Reich was otherwise left vague, as befits a myth. It was depicted as the fulfillment of the "final empire" that would mark the culmination of all German history. But a myth it remained. The Third Reich "is always promised. It is never fulfilled. It is perfection that can only be attained in the imperfect." [32]

In the Third Reich the Germans would have the strength to live with their historic antagonisms. Some of these have already diminished: the fratricidal tendencies of the German tribes have disappeared, and in the modern period the German tribes subsume their tribal pride under the more comprehensive consciousness of being German. Likewise the confessional antith-

eses have been pushed to a higher plane, where the consciousness of Christian unity reconciles Protestants and Catholics.
In like manner, the three remaining antitheses will be resolved.
Moeller promised a synthesis between Reich and *Länder*, and
between capitalists and proletariat through the introduction of
a "socialism of entrepreneurship." His last concern was with
"German pacifism," that is with the dispute between the paci-
fists and the militarists. "The idea of eternal peace is of course
the idea of the Third Reich," but it would have to be a peace
secured by German arms.[33] The final Reich would be *gross-
deutsch*, and in the Western world that was actually declining
despite its temporary triumph, Germany alone would stand
strong and inviolable. All danger and conflict had been
banned; truly the Third Reich was the dream of dreams, and
in its promise were fused all the hopes of the German right.

The ideas of the *Dritte Reich* were not new; they were the
stock-in-trade of the antidemocratic right wing.[34] But Moeller
infused them with life, and by associating them with the myth
of redemption, with the Third Reich, charged them with hope
as well. His work has been called "truly a political religion"; it
was a work of faith and wrath and prophecy.[35] The Third
Reich—that never-attainable realm of unity and strength—was
a religious idea. The fervor and urgency of Moeller's voice, of
a very personal voice, was that of a preacher, seeking a response
in passion.

The response to Moeller was not immediate. The book appeared in 1923, when the republic was for the first time on the
verge of collapse. But it survived, purged by the ordeal, and in
1924 began its period of deceptive stability. Even the German
Nationalists joined the government, radical opposition to the
republic seemed futile, and many of the Juni-Klub members
began to look for more profitable alliances with the parties of
the right. The dissolution of the Juni-Klub and its transformation into the wealthier and more worldly *Herrenklub* took
place at this time.[36] Moeller refused to join this exodus and became estranged from most of his former associates, including
Heinrich von Gleichen, whose capacity for political accommodation was very much greater than Moeller's. After years of
being the central figure of a group in quest of a new program,
Moeller seemed once again to be left an outsider, alone, except
for a few undistinguished disciples. The burden proved too

great; Moeller's mind and nerves gave way, and in 1924 he suffered a nervous breakdown. A few months later, he committed suicide.

Even in the darkest days of republican stability—and it is a mistake to think that the period from 1924 to 1929 reconciled more than a few people to the republic—Moeller's work was kept before the public. In 1928, his literary executor Hans Schwarz, together with A. von Trotha, the former chief of the German high-sea fleet, started a new bimonthly journal called *Der Nahe Osten,* which they published at the old headquarters in the Motzstrasse. The programmatic note announced: *"Der Nahe Osten* demands the recovery of the lost provinces and a settling of accounts [*Auseinandersetzung*] with Poland. . . . It continues the legacy of Moeller van den Bruck and prepares for a European reordering which spiritually and politically will correspond to the rural character of the entire east." [37] In its first year, *Der Nahe Osten* published mostly jottings from Moeller; the remaining pages featured bellicose articles by others, including many by Moeller's widow, who pretended that Moeller had believed in her own brand of racism and extreme aggression. By 1930, there were spirited debates about the "real" Moeller, and many critics rightly felt that his legacy was being distorted by his former intimates.[38]

Moeller did not live to see the ultimate fulfillment of his prophecies. But he had been right in his intuitive sense of the great subterranean anger against the republic. After the parliamentary crisis of 1928, after the death of Stresemann and the collapse of the brief Weimar boom, the clamor against the republic broke out afresh. It preceded, accompanied, and idealized the actual, cynical destruction of the Weimar Republic by the amateur politicians of the right. Moeller's myth of the Third Reich was at once revived, and by 1929 this myth, still more closely attached to Moeller's name than Hitler's, "dominated the conceptual world of *all* nationalist groups." [39] Hermann Rauschning remembered Moeller's book as the main inspiration of "the renewal of Conservatism," and even the socialist enemies of Moeller noted that the influence of "this apostle of the Third Reich, especially on the leading intellectual circles of the right, can ever be detected afresh and can hardly be overestimated." [40] Between 1929 and 1933, Moeller's main works were reprinted several times, excerpts from them appeared in countless cheap pamphlets, and his political miscellany were collected in four volumes by Schwarz.

In the final retreat from the republic and from parliamentarianism, Moeller's ideas were invoked time and again. In the conservative-revolutionary camp—to use a phrase of Moeller's that had at last gained great popularity—he was used by both conservative and revolutionary groups, for in the face of political reality the false synthesis quickly disintegrated into its original, antagonistic components. The conservative ideologists, as we shall see, became the apologists for the right-wing gravediggers of the republic; the revolutionary elements, scattered in a hundred little bands, ill-organized and always obscure, were genuinely committed to a revolution and to the hope that the anticapitalistic radicals of the right and left could be united. However ineffectual the latter groups may have been, they added a distinctive and appealing element to the intellectual fervor of that macabre period.

The *Gewissen* had died in 1927, but within a year or two several more prominent journals took its place. In 1929, Hans Zehrer became the editor of *Die Tat,* and converted it into an intellectually respectable and highly popular journal of the nonpartisan young conservatives. At once he proclaimed the advent of the final crisis and called for a revolution and a dictatorship, for a union of right and left extremes, for a national socialism of the Moeller type. Moeller's name was repeatedly invoked and his Third Reich prophesied.* Zehrer even hailed the later Brüning government as a "third front," as an admirable and irreversible step toward "a nonliberal, authoritarian government." [41] The same themes appeared in *Der Ring,* which was the direct successor to the *Gewissen,* and was sponsored, by the aristocratic Herrenklub, the heir to the Juni-Klub. *Der Ring,* with its frequent contributions by Gleichen, who was also the head of the Herrenklub, found in Moeller's work a complete justification for the successive undermining of the parliamentary democracy, first by Brüning, then by Papen and Schleicher. The journal was closest to Papen, him-

---

* In style, too, *Die Tat* was close to Moeller; it has recently been described as "an impenetrable mishmash of clarity and mysticism, fatalism and ruthless activism, resentment and good will, presumption and insight." Kurt Sontheimer, "Der Tatkreis," *Vierteljahrshefte für Zeitgeschichte,* VII:3 (July, 1959), 259.

self a member and patron of the Herrenklub. Papen's presidential cabinet, which in its nonparliamentary character was an extreme reactionary version of the old imperial regime, was hailed by *Der Ring* as the final embodiment of the conservative revolution, and Papen was proud to dignify his maneuverings and frivolous opportunism by the same name.[42] The ideology of this "new state" was derived directly from Moeller.[43] After Papen's fall, *Der Ring* continued to announce that the hour for Moeller's Third Reich had struck, and when, contrary to its expectations, Hitler's Third Reich came instead, *Der Ring* readily succumbed to the temptation to justify the latter by identifying it with the former. Its disgracefully swift surrender to the Nazis culminated in an article in June, 1933, defending the government's prohibition of some nationalist groups and appropriately entitled, "Die Logik der Totalität." [44]

The truly revolutionary enemies of capitalism and of Hitler's national socialism preserved Moeller's legacy in a very different manner. Ernst Niekisch, for example, that brave uncompromising National Bolshevist, started his *Widerstand* movement in 1926, dedicated "to a socialist and national-revolutionary policy." He too identified Versailles with capitalism, Prussia with socialism, and alleged that Communist Russia was more Prussian than Weimar Germany was.[45] Years later, after Hitler's defeat and his own re-conversion to historical materialism, Niekisch recalled Moeller's type of socialism "as a mood which gripped us." [46]

Moeller was also the hero of the Black Front, which the "socialist" Otto Strasser organized after his break with Hitler in 1930. Strasser had been a friend of Moeller's in the early days of the Juni-Klub, and his Black Front became "a front against everything *Zivilisatorisch-Intellektuelles.* . . . The banner of all its members is the black banner of Moeller, who is its great teacher and whose book, *Das Dritte Reich,* is *the* basic book of the Black Front." [47] Strasser, it was claimed, had first carried the idea of the Third Reich into the camp of the National Socialists.

The National Socialists, whose relations with Moeller will be discussed below, said little about Moeller—or about any of the conservative revolutionaries. We know from Goebbels's unpublished diary that in 1925 he had been deeply moved by Moeller's Third Reich: "So calm and clear, yet gripped by passion, he writes everything that we, the young people, have long known in our hearts and instincts." [48]

Such was Moeller's influence in the final years of the republic. He was the hero of most right-wing intellectuals; he had given the antirepublicans a goal, the Third Reich, and in their final onslaught against Weimar, in their desperate leap into political uncertainty, they believed that they were fulfilling Moeller's program and prophecy. The manysidedness of the Moeller cult confirms what a German nationalist wrote shortly after 1933: "There came something entirely irrational, that is according to the then prevailing opinions: the idea of the Third Reich. This idea gripped the Germans; it gripped the political adventurers and the politically homeless; it gripped the deeply rooted and the totally uprooted; it gripped the beings with whom one could neither talk nor argue." [49]

Moeller died before this sudden boom of his myth and before its putative realization in 1933 by Adolf Hitler. In his last months, he had suffered new disappointments. He was dismayed by the meager response to *Das Dritte Reich* as well as by the acceptance of the Dawes Plan and the subsequent Stresemann policy of aggressive reasonableness. He was disappointed in the political opportunism of his former associates. He maintained an intermittent interest in politics to the end, and his last political message, in April, 1925, concerned the Hindenburg election: "Tell my wife that I have been immensely pleased by the Hindenburg election and that I must ask the people to forgive my pessimism. It was a victory of sentiment over utility and there is no purer victory." [50] A few days later, in despair over his ever-worsening condition, he took his life.

It was fitting that friend and foe alike "mystified" his death, and elaborately accounted for what they called his Germanic sacrifice. His widow and her friends exalted his suicide as a protest, a gesture of despair about Germany's future; others have suggested that he took his life because he feared that the Nazis had perverted his ideas, that he had become "one of the first victims of Hitler's Third Reich." [51] Martyrdom of course enhanced the appeal of his ideas. But there is not a shred of evidence for any of this mystification. It is true only in the much larger sense, as a hint that the personal despair and disintegration of one of the leading Germanic critics was deeply and lamentably intertwined with the future of German politics, and thus with the survival of the Western world.

Conclusion:

From Idealism to Nihilism

> *Weariness that wants to reach the ultimate with one leap, with one fatal leap, a poor ignorant weariness that does not want to want any more: this created all gods and other worlds.*
>
> NIETZSCHE

Lagarde, Langbehn, and Moeller belonged to different generations, but their style of thought and their aspirations were remarkably alike. The unity of their thought allows us to speak of the rise of the Germanic ideology; the similarities in their lives and the common psychological and intellectual roots of their struggle against modernity allow us to speak of them as a distinct cultural type, a new version of the alienated intellectual in the modern world. Once this type has been defined, it will be possible to assess the place of these writers in German culture, and to analyze their relation to earlier intellectual traditions and to later political movements.

These three critics witnessed the gradual destruction of the old Germany and the emergence of a new, urban, secular country. They hated the temper and the institutions of this new Germany and decried the conditions of modernity. Their protests, as we have seen, were not unique. Others were dismayed as well: conservatives saw their beliefs and privileges challenged, Christians saw their faith attacked, and a new class, the urban proletariat, attacked the exploitative and inegalitarian character of modern industrial society. These groups and their spokesmen had a stake in the past or a tangible goal for the future. But Lagarde, Langbehn, and Moeller had no commitment to the past nor were they defending existing social privileges. Even their nationalism was an idealistic abstraction, a recollection of an ideal Germanic type that was supposed to have flourished once, but had since been betrayed. They had reluctantly repudiated the faith and the philosophical traditions of their ancestors. Dispossessed in a double sense, Lagarde, Langbehn, and Moeller cast their discontent into political visions which were as divorced from reality as their creators were from their society.

Our critics were simultaneously proud and resentful of their alienation. They were proud of the perspicacity which their "untimeliness" had granted them, but their deepest longing was for a new Germanic community in which they and all their countrymen would at last find the peace of complete unity. Because of this longing they made the leap from cultural criticism to politics, assuming that cultural evil could be dissolved by the establishment of the right kind of faith and community. However prescient their cultural criticism was, their political thought revealed the willful ignorance of political reality that often characterizes the alienated and unexperienced critic. Their political imagination grasped lifeless abstractions and the petty details of their proposed reforms. The middle range of practicality was foreign to them.

They knew that they were radically different from all those who had a real stake in society. To emphasize their apartness they called themselves conservative revolutionaries. They were conservative out of nostalgia and revolutionary out of despair. They were not concerned with compromise; they sought to destroy the present in order to usher in a future Reich—one which would realize on this earth some of the bliss that had once been promised for the hereafter. They exemplified in the realm of thought what the National Socialists were later to demonstrate with such practical thoroughness: that the annihilation of a culture can only be willed by the uprooted, the dispossessed.

These men, as I have said, have to be understood as a cultural type, a type moreover that made its simultaneous appearance in all Western countries.* The distinctive quali-

---

* The type clearly emerged in the 1880's, and ranged from Charles Maurras, Maurice Barrès, and Knut Hamsun to the poet Miguel de Unamuno. It thus included men of diverse interests and unequal talents who were linked by a feeling of alienation in the modern

ties of these men are not to be found in their thought or their lives alone, but in the tension between their thought, their personalities and their culture, as well as in the form in which this tension was expressed. The conventional categories of social types have little relevance; for these three men were intellectuals *faute de mieux,* intellectuals whose work was emotional and seldom reflective; they were artists without talents of creative expression, prophets without a god. They exemplified and encouraged what they sought to combat and annihilate, the cultural disintegration and the collapse of order in modern Germany. They were the accusers, but also the unwitting proof of their charges. As a consequence, they were forever wrestling with themselves even as they were fighting others.

Their writings rang with the prophecy of impending doom, lightened only by an occasional note of hope that redemption might still be possible. It was as if their own Jeremiads on the real evils of the present so frightened them that they were forced to project a future or a regeneration beyond all historical possibility. Having abjured religious faith, they could not fall back on the promise of divine deliverance. Having abjured reason, they could not expect a natural human evolution toward the community they sought. The goal, consequently, was a mystique, and the means, though left obscure, suggested violence and coercion.

To speak of a cultural type requires us to show that these men had common personal and biographical characteristics, and that their lives and works described a similar and novel position in culture. This, I think, can be done, without violating the facts or reducing men to formulas; description will show these men to have been a complex instance of the search for salvation, by a type of mind that can neither endure nor overcome the conditions of modern life.

---

world and an attendant search for a new faith. The type was also depicted in a long line of fictional characters from *The Possessed* to D. H. Lawrence's James Sharpe in *Kangaroo* "who is half an artist, not more, and so can never get away from it or free himself from its dictates" (Penguin edition, London, p. 258). This type dominated the literature of the *fin de siècle* and of the German Expressionists. Philip Wylie's *Generation of Vipers* may be taken as a contemporary instance of the enduring quality of this genre. Note his bombast: "We have cancer—cancer of the soul. Religion has failed." This was already a commonplace among the Germanic critics. Philip Wylie, *Generation of Vipers*, New York, Farrar and Rinehart, 1942, p. 7.

These men were born, or early in their lives became, urbanites, cut off from nature and the simple rural life that in their dreams they idealized. They were brought up in modest surroundings and challenged by the parental expectation that they should find for themselves a place in society, so as to live in comfortable distinction. Born into families with professional pretensions, they sought to attain status, to achieve recognition which would set them apart from other men. Was it an accident that two of our writers adopted new and more ornamental names, and that Langbehn sought to win fame from his elaborate mask of anonymity? They turned their backs on the abundant economic opportunities of business and finance. To live as free intellectuals was their ambition, but Moeller and Langbehn both spurned, or accepted only with reluctance, the customary employment of intellectuals. With neither secure employment nor sufficient independent means, they groped for something better, more rewarding than mere survival, always believing that others, usually the wicked men of power, owed them admiring deference and substantial help.

Their intellectual ambition, first roused at home, was furthered by their education. All three attended the *Gymnasium,* though Moeller did not complete his studies. The German *Abiturient,* after his nine exacting years of Greek and Latin, acquired both an excellent education and the means for attaining greater prestige. He could, and often did, enter the university, or he could seek a managerial career in business. Lagarde and Langbehn proceeded to the university, earned their doctorates and thus won a certain kind of social distinction. But distinction often brings with it loneliness and, after their break with the academic world, they found it difficult to fit into any social group.

In the course of their formal education, notes of dissent and discord already began to appear. They experienced the inherent shortcomings of the nineteenth-century *Gymnasium,* its disdain for the natural sciences, and its carefully preserved isolation from the "real" world. Given its original impulse by Humboldt, the *Gymnasium* remained throughout a century of modernization the citadel of humanistic learning and of philosophical idealism. It was essentially a conservative force, controlled by anxious officials who feared that knowledge of social evils or of politics would breed corruption and radicalism. The role of the *Gymnasium* in German culture has yet to be assessed; its pedagogical excellence we are familiar with, but we have still to understand why so many young Germans felt such revulsion for it. The Youth Movement was only the most dramatic rebellion against what its members called the artificiality and pedantry of these schools. Much of the irrationalism and the hatred of "system" which characterized German youth sprang up in opposition to these schools. Even men who after graduation had themselves become teachers or academics remembered an ill-defined discontent with this prison-like ivory tower; it is a significant fact that most of the autobiographies of that age express simultaneous admiration and hatred of the *Gymnasium*.* Certainly Lagarde, Langbehn, and Moeller had loathed this kind of education. It had widened the gulf between them and society without giving them the training which would have enabled them to define logically or in historical perspective their opposition to modernity. Moreover, they spurned the positive values of the *Gymnasium;* they rejected the discipline of the mind which the less gifted student accepted as a matter of course, and they forsook the humanistic tradition which left its imprint on the better student. Lagarde's and Langbehn's writings bristled with scornful attacks on German schools and thus helped to unsettle the minds of countless other students.

Langbehn's and Moeller's years at school seem also to have reinforced their temperamental disinclination for rigorous thought and study. The customary pedantic instruction which completely starved the imagination confirmed them in their predilection for intuitive and nonsystematic knowledge. Langbehn's certainty, so proudly maintained in his mature years, that he had learned everything from his own travels found its counterpart in Moeller's cheerful courting of expulsion from the *Gymnasium*. He, too, ridiculed the inadequacy of mere "bookish" learning and proceeded to educate himself —from books.

Langbehn, it will be remembered, had once begun to study chemistry but had quickly shifted to fine arts, before depart-

* Friedrich Meinecke, for example, records with considerable puzzlement that even some sixty years after graduation, "The sudden sight of the red brick building of my old *Gymnasium* did not evoke any warm memories." *Erlebtes, 1862–1901,* Leipzig 1941, p. 63.

ing from the academic scene altogether. Lagarde and Moeller fared little better in their occasional studies of the sciences and were content with the conventional claptrap about the dangers of the age of science. In many ways, their lives, and Moeller's in particular, illustrate the shortcomings of the self-tutored man. Lagarde, it is true, had achieved great eminence in his field of scholarship, but he sought power and influence in areas that were removed from his training. In their political and social criticism they were all dilettantes who had not even mastered the art of acquiring knowledge. Moeller's perceptive understanding of contemporary literature was a measure of his ability, and yet in other fields, in his historical and political writings for example, he gained only a superficial breadth and uncritical knowledge. The political constructions of the Third Reich, like the antiscientific tirades of Langbehn, bore the stamp of an almost willful disregard of common knowledge. Their writings appealed not by their intellectual force but because they were suffused with passion, the passion of their indignation and their suffering.

Beyond their troubled education lay their individual unhappiness, already apparent in early childhood and perpetuated to the ends of their lives. Tragedy had touched each of them in his earliest years, depriving Lagarde of his mother and Langbehn of his father; of Moeller it is said that even as a child he had never been known to laugh. None of them had experienced a pleasant youth or even a moderately warm relationship with his parents. One further recalls Lagarde's numbness at his father's death, Langbehn's invariably disastrous attempts at friendship, or Moeller's long exile from Germany. Little is known of their marriages or their relationships with women, but Lagarde's and Moeller's silence about or indifference to their childless marriages and Langbehn's failure to convert his fitful attraction for women into abiding companionship deepens the impression of sadness, as do his obscure attempts at repressing what seem to have been strong sexual impulses. As a final element in their characters, one must remember that their achievements never measured up to their own extravagant images of themselves, largely because of the limitation of their talents but partly because of the stubborn opposition of society. Frustration forced them ever more inward, exaggerating Lagarde's crotchetiness and Langbehn's insane priggishness, and contributing to Moeller's breakdown, leading, perhaps, to his suicide. Their lives, one senses, lacked comforts or rewards; neither joy nor even self-acceptance made their journey easier. Only Langbehn found in the Catholic Church a release from himself.

Langbehn's conversion points to the fundamental unhappiness of their lives which was at once personal and cultural in origin; they had been born into an age of unbelief, an age when not only the overwhelming number of intellectuals but large parts of the public as well had withdrawn from organized religion into a personal, deistic religion, agnosticism, or atheism. The motives and conditions for this retreat were complex; they cannot be simply explained, as is often done, by referring to the rise of scientism or the pressures of the industrial society. Corresponding to the complexity of motives is the diversity of the manifestations of this break from Christianity, and neither can be dealt with here at any length. It suffices to say that in Germany the retreat was usually disguised, without the sharp struggle between believers and nonbelievers that characterized the same process in France. The educated German tended to glide into unbelief. For many Germans, Basil Willey's description of an English type applies: "The devout skeptic, the sage who rejects traditional religion not because he is shallow or immoral, but because he is too earnest to accept it—because he understands and tolerates all forms of religion too well to adopt any one of them." [1] And, one might add among the younger generation another type, the suffering son who inherited his father's doubt but not the will to endure it. So it was with Lagarde, Langbehn, and Moeller, who were moved by strong religious compulsions.* They had from childhood been troubled by

---

* To define a person's religious consciousness is difficult at best, but is rendered more difficult here by the reluctance of Lagarde, Langbehn (except in the last years of his life), and Moeller to probe into their religious feelings and by the abstrusity of their scattered comments. Rudolf Otto, *The Idea of the Holy*, 2d ed., London 1950, in particular chapter 4, "Mysterium Tremendum," is perhaps the most penetrating insight into a similar state of mind. A recent definition of the religious view would certainly fit this type: "According to the religious view of the world there is a purpose in the scheme of things, into which human life must presumably in some way fit, so that human life is itself meaningful as being a part of the cosmic plan. The world is

what they called the mystery of life and nature, and were never satisfied with the abstractions of "cold" science, longing for a more grandiose view of the world than that offered by atoms swirling endlessly and aimlessly in space. They felt and were awed by a mysterious power, inexplicable and yet immediately real to them, which they believed to rule the fate of man and the laws of nature. They avowed the existence of a supernatural order and of a deity and yearned to live in a community of dedicated believers.

But these sentiments did not lead them to the orthodoxy of the Christian faith; in fact, they broke with the Protestant faith into which they had been born, and heaped abuse upon its moral and political opportunism which sought to compromise with the modern world. Nor could Lagarde and Moeller accept the stricter Catholic religion, for their path was blocked by an inherited naturalism and agnosticism from which they could not escape. Like so many others, they were the victims of, not the participants in, the struggle over the validity of revealed religion; in the end, they hoped to invest their own beliefs with the passion of religion. They could neither banish the sense of awe and mystery nor could they submit to a faith whose dogmas had been riddled by generations of scientists and textual critics. Even the pantheistic love of Nature, which had inspired some of the great romantic writers, they rejected, largely because science and scientism had in the interval pronounced that faith "unreal" and puerile. Only Langbehn succeeded in placing his faith in the Catholic Church, while Moeller and Lagarde cast about unable to join either the Church or the secular opposition. Moeller had avowed that God must exist even if we know that he is dead, and he proceeded to resolve the obstinate contradictions of mind and temper, culture and individuality, by fusing into art and politics the mystical impulses of his consciousness.

The portrait of this type emerges now with some clearness; certainly isolation, alienation, and self-hatred are the out-

governed 'in the end' (whatever that phrase may mean) not by blind physical forces, but by spiritual forces which, in most actual religions, are conceived under the name God. Moreover, the world is a moral order in which, in spite of all appearances to the contrary, goodness must prevail and justice be done." W. T. Stace, *Religion and the Modern Mind*, Philadelphia, Lippincott, 1952, p. 179.

standing characteristics.* The Germanic critics had refused to accept society on any of its traditional terms; they had been hostile to its education and had accepted neither the formal beliefs of the majority nor the dogmas of the *avant-garde*. Equally, they brushed aside the possibilities of employment, even when this might have opened to them a career in harmonious relation with their professional peers. Langbehn and Moeller would have none of the humdrum of daily work; only Lagarde continued to wrestle with the authorities for his rightful place in the academic world. Yet when his ambition had at last been amply satisfied and he had gained his well-deserved place of distinction, he quickly trained his guns on his new colleagues and after a while angrily complained that he was being snubbed. In fact all three were slighted upon occasion, though less often than they imagined. After all, they offended others with the abandon of men indifferent to civility, yet they resented and suffered from the slightest hint of criticism. One need only recall, for instance, Lagarde's egotism, or Langbehn's pose as the secret emperor, to realize that they were anything but independent of external recognition. They desperately wanted it, though on their own impractical terms. Perhaps no trait of the Germanic critics was more representative of a new type of discontent than this agonized search for status and prestige while denouncing the source of the honor sought and continuing to cling to isolation and self-inflicted cultural martyrdom. Among the leaders and the early followers of the National Socialist movement this conflict was often the mainspring of political action.

---

* I note an interesting correspondence between my impression of these men and Eric Hoffer's description of the character of the true believer: "The most incurably frustrated—and, therefore, the most vehement—among the permanent misfits are those with an unfulfilled craving for creative work. . . . That hatred springs more from self-contempt than from a legitimate grievance is seen in the intimate connection between hatred and a guilty conscience." Eric Hoffer, *The True Believer. Thoughts on the Nature of Mass Movements,* New York 1951, pp. 46, 93. I should also mention the similarities between my views of these men and the authoritarian personality as defined by T. W. Adorno and his collaborators. I have purposely avoided the strictly psychological analysis which the authors of that book pressed. Cf. T. W. Adorno and others, *The Authoritarian Personality,* New York, Harper, 1950, esp. "Syndromes Found Among High Scorers," pp. 753–771.

It is a truism that men can suffer from the burden of their time as easily as from their own failure; or they may, as did Lagarde, Langbehn, and Moeller, suffer from the convergence of the two. They had rejected the contemporary bourgeois world, partly following the dictates of their nature, partly because that society had made acceptance difficult and unrewarding. But how bitter that withdrawal made them! How they hated being monks without monasteries! As secular mendicants they preached the evils of this world, hoping still that their weariness and the weariness of all their fellow sufferers would some day be dispelled in a new Reich.

ii

Lagarde, Langbehn, and Moeller thought of themselves as prophets, not as heirs. They were proud of their originality, proud of their intuitive sense of the crisis of their times. In fact, however, they had been much more influenced by past traditions than they realized, and without knowing it they served as cultural middlemen, transmitting old ideas in new combinations to later generations.

They acknowledged no intellectual masters and rarely mentioned earlier thinkers at all. Even in the realm of ideas, they felt lonely. But their silence attested also their distrust of the intellectual life, their unwillingness to wrestle with previous philosophers. They took seriously their own denigration of bookish learning, they were in truth "anti-intellectual intellectuals." [2] What they read, they usually read uncritically, and what was said of one of them—"Lagarde was not a systematic thinker, but a rhapsodist"—was true of all of them.[3] The irrationalism that they preached, they practiced as well.

Still, their thought contained many important themes from past traditions, and their influence was enhanced by the familiar ring of so much of their work. In dealing with their intellectual dependency, we must once more recall that they were essentially uninterested in abstract ideas, that they were more concerned with the moral tone or the idealistic commitment of an author. As a consequence, they were more attracted to men than to ideas, and especially to men whose fate resembled their own—to lonely, suffering, and unfulfilled geniuses. Langbehn, for example, felt an affinity for Novalis,

Moeller for Nietzsche. Equally illuminating are their anti-
pathies: they sneered at the "older," successful Goethe, they
loathed Heine, and they were indifferent to Kant. From men
they liked, they would appropriate certain "key ideas," or
tags, which popular memory had fastened to these thinkers.
These ideas reappeared in the works of the Germanic critics,
as unidentified components of their own ideology. Their indebtedness to past thought was at once vast and insignificant.
They were eclectics as well as *terribles simplificateurs*—those
whom Burckhardt feared*

They appropriated something from every intellectual tradition of modern Germany, except one. They consistently
warred against the ideas of the Enlightenment and of the
French Revolution—the so-called ideas of 1789—and hence
they were most powerfully influenced by the men who shared
this hostility, to wit, the romantics, the cultural nationalists
of the late eighteenth century, and the more aggressive
nationalists, like Jahn and Arndt, of the Napoleonic period.
They illustrated what Nietzsche called "the hostility of the
Germans to the Enlightenment," this "obscurantist, enthusiastic, and atavistic spirit" which Nietzsche thought had
been overcome, but which a half century later Thomas Mann
noted was stronger than ever.†

The Germanic critics, following the accepted judgment of
their time, condemned the romantics as ineffectual dreamers.
Yet theirs was an essentially romantic temper: they exalted
energy, will, passion, heroism—the demonic—and they de-

---

* In 1920, Moeller wrote about his political program: "At bottom it is
all *very, very, very* simple: only by using concepts do we make everything complicated. What we seek is the *Word*." Letter to Ernst Krieck,
quoted in Andreas Hohlfeld, *Unsere geschichtliche Verantwortung,*
Leipzig 1933, p. 18. Italics in original.

† Nietzsche's aphorism is of particular relevance to the Germanic critics:
"The whole tendency of the Germans ran counter to the Enlightenment, and to the revolution of society which, by a crude misunderstanding, was considered its result: piety toward everything still in
existence sought to transform itself into piety toward everything that
had ever existed, only to make heart and spirit full once again and to
leave no room for future goals and innovations. The cult of feeling
was erected in place of the cult of reason." *Morgenröte,* in *Friedrich
Nietzsche, Werke in Drei Bänden,* ed. by Karl Schlechta, München
1954, I, 1145. Thomas Mann's remarks were contained in one of his
attacks on the conservative revolution, "Die Stellung Freuds in der
modernen Geistesgeschichte," *Gesammelte Werke,* East Berlin 1955, XI,
197–200.

spised the rational, contemplative, and conventional life. Hence they were particularly drawn to the *Stürmer und Dränger,* to the romantic genius as rebel.* They further exaggerated the already distorted notion of the romantics concerning the grayness of all theory and the emptiness of all "mechanistic" thought. They also shared the romantics' rejection of what they alleged was the eighteenth-century view of man as an essentially good and rational creature. They thought of man as a volitional and spiritual being, in need of a faith and a community, and they extolled the romantic sense of the tragic and the inexplicable in human fate. In much of this, unknown to themselves, they were remote Rousseauans, and like so many German conservatives they acknowledged their debt only by vilifying Rousseau's democratic thought.

Far greater and more direct, especially on Lagarde and Langbehn, was the impact of Herder. Lagarde's view of language, for example, and Langbehn's emphasis on the primitive, populistic quality of true art seem to be clear adaptations of certain aspects of Herder's cultural nationalism. Herder had been one of the first to associate nationalism with German folk traditions, with the primitive and spontaneous expression of the *Volksseele.* In 1773 appeared the original manifesto of this new nationalism, *Von deutscher Art und Kunst,* to which Goethe and Möser contributed as well. A few years later, Herder exclaimed: "Great Reich, Reich of ten peoples, Germany! You have no Shakespeare, but have you no ancient songs of which you can be proud? . . . Were we poor Germans from the beginning destined only to translate, only to imitate?" [4] Herder's appeal to national self-consciousness was still subordinated to his cosmopolitan ideal of a common humanity, though he already believed that the German people had a unique calling for the realization of the goals of humanity. Under the impact of the revolutionary wars, later thinkers dissolved this association of nationalism and cosmopolitanism.

---

* In German usage, there is a sharp distinction between *Sturm und Drang* and *die Romantik,* the latter typically identified as "everything unreal and without substance, everything which is neither capable of life nor deserving of it." Rudolf Haym, *Die Romantische Schule,* 5th ed., Berlin 1928, p. 14. I am following the non-German usage of considering *Sturm und Drang* as the most vigorous expression of German romanticism.

The Germanic critics were obviously influenced by the early nationalists, by the patriots who at the time of the French Revolution sought to liberate Germany from the tyranny of foreign rule and fashion. They were particularly attracted to Fichte, who at the moment of Germany's humiliation sought to exalt the cultural destiny of the nation. Moeller, we know, appeared to his contemporaries—and perhaps to himself—as a latter-day Fichte, who, at a time of still greater disaster, sought to save the nation.*

Certainly the "main ideas" of Fichte's *Addresses to the German Nation* reappeared in the works of the Germanic critics. Fichte's famous dictum "to have character and to be German [*Charakter haben und deutsch sein*] undoubtedly mean the same," became a principal tenet of later Germanic nationalism. Likewise his emphasis on *inner* freedom as the sufficient condition of human self-realization, his reconciliation of individualism and authority by means of a *Kulturstaat,* his appeal to youth because its "age lies nearer to the years of childlike innocence and of nature," and his projection of a great future for Germany, his echo of Schiller's "each people has its day in history, but the day of the Germans is the harvest of all times"—all of these were themes of the later ideology as well. The Germanic critics were still moved by the same faith that Fichte expounded at the end of his *Addresses:* "You are of all modern peoples the one in whom the seed of human perfection most unmistakably lies, and to whom the lead in its development is committed. If you perish in this your essential nature, then there perishes together with you every hope of the whole human race for salvation from the depths of its miseries." [5]

Lagarde, Langbehn, and Moeller shared more with Fichte than the ideas they snatched from his much subtler and more complex philosophic thought. Fichte had inaugurated a new genre of political thinking; as Meinecke said, "among pure thinkers there is no more important example of the invasion of unpolitical ideas into Germany's political life than

---

* Max Hildebert Boehm, Moeller's friend and associate, wrote in his article on Moeller in the *Encyclopedia of the Social Sciences,* New York, Macmillan, 1948, X, 569: "His [Moeller's] thought was intuitive in character and his influence on the younger generation in post-war Germany might be compared to that of Fichte's *Reden an die Deutsche Nation* during the War of Liberation."

Fichte's." [6] This metaphysical, moralistic, and thoroughly unempirical manner of dealing with political questions characterized other German romantics as well. Consider, for example, Novalis's poetic approach to politics, his lyrical evocation of a Christian empire, his vision of a Germany reborn, whose faith and spirit would lead and reconcile the warring parties of Europe. Langbehn thought himself inspired by Novalis, as did so many of the neo-romantics of the early twentieth century—and yet how remote Langbehn and his followers were from the Novalis who in his *Christendom or Europe* glorified not only the sublimity of the past but also the promise of the new world, which he saw in the "delightful feeling of freedom, the unqualified expectation of vast domains, pleasure in what is new and young, informal contact with all fellow citizens, pride in man's universality and joy in personal rights and in the property of the whole, and strong civic sense"![7]

The Germanic critics quarried many ideas from the romantics—the organismic view of the state, the idealization of a corporatist and religious organization of society, and finally Schelling's belief in the resolution [*Aufhebung*] of opposites in "higher thirds." * More importantly, they emulated the German romantics' esthetic and spiritual interpretation of politics and history, and their disdain for the empirical and material fact. Because of these similarities, Lagarde, Langbehn, and Moeller have often been called romantics, but such a designation overlooks the fact that they were indiscriminate and partial borrowers, who appropriated from incompatible traditions only the elements they happened to know about and that corresponded to their own prejudices.†

---

* Note the similarity of style and intent between Schelling and our critics, as evidenced by this description of Schelling: "The opposition [*Gegensatz*] of the two sexes is resolved in *Gesamtmenschen*, the opposition of individuals in a higher organism, in the 'state' or the people, the division among states by the higher organization of the Church." Carl Schmitt, *Politische Romantik*, 2d ed., München and Leipzig, Duncker and Humblot, 1925, p. 127.

† Thus the Germanic critics overlooked the humanistic, cosmopolitan ideas of the romantics. This was also Thomas Mann's charge against the German right which used the romantics in order to malign the Weimar Republic. Mann saw a correspondence between the ideas of the romantics and the *Democratic Vistas* of Walt Whitman. See, for

Lagarde's and Langbehn's primitivist and anti-Semitic notions were foreshadowed by the works of Arndt and Jahn, by their glorification of the German folk, and by the xenophobic spirit of the *Burschenschaften*. Throughout the restoration period, this kind of folk ideology and *Germanomanie* was kept alive by journalists like W. Menzel, and by various artisan groups that blamed their decline on the Jewish exploitation of liberal free-trade principles.[8] We saw that Lagarde's father was close to these groups.

Lagarde's attack on Hegel coincided with the general spirit of anti-Hegelianism that pervaded the second half of the nineteenth century. Hegel's intellectual domination had disintegrated rapidly; his thought was discounted by philosophers and historians, and satirized by Schopenhauer and Nietzsche. Among the educated, some of Hegel's ideas survived in isolation—as slogans and popular generalities—and these we encounter in Langbehn and Moeller. Both of them adopted a vulgarized form of the dialectics, and the "higher thirds" that characterized their writings resembled Schelling's obscure model and Hegel's celebrated but dissimilar method. Even anti-Hegelians found that Hegel's dialectic offered a convenient rhetoric for reconciling or overcoming conflict, and the abolition of conflict was a central aim of Langbehn's and Moeller's. In Moeller's conception of history we find echoes of Hegel's philosophy as well; Moeller's panorama of the history of *The Germans* was filled with world-historical figures that embodied and realized the aim of the World Spirit.[9] His emphasis on these world-historical figures, on the importance of the personality in history, bolstered his antiliberal arguments for a Caesar. The differences between the Germanic critics and Hegel were of course immense; it is especially important to recall that Hegel considered the modern state as the final embodiment of a progressive historical process, while the Germanic critics, anticipating National Socialist usage, sneered at the "mechanistic" state and preferred a kind of folk community.[10]

Lagarde's first essay was written shortly before the rise of Schopenhauer's fame. Both men attacked Hegel's rationalism, but, more importantly, Schopenhauer taught the Germanic critics that the primacy of the human will brought about the

---

example, "Von deutscher Republik," in *Bemühungen*, Berlin 1925, esp. pp. 163–183.

CONCLUSION

irrationality of life and that this, in turn, must fill men with a cosmic pessimism. Beyond the pessimism of his formal philosophy lay Schopenhauer's despair concerning the decline of German culture, and his counsel that only a contemplative, ascetic life offered an escape from the basic evil force in the world, the will. Although accepting Schopenhauer's voluntarism and pessimism, Lagarde and Moeller could not endure his contemplation of the futility of action; rather, they sought an escape into a projected activism, a release through still greater will.*

The Germanic critics had reached out to the German romantics and to Fichte and Hegel across the dominant intellectual current of their own day—the empirical, positivist direction in the natural sciences. The growth of science and its institutionalization in the universities constituted one of the most important developments in nineteenth-century Germany, and one that the Germanic critics dreaded. The natural scientists generally avowed their separation from philosophy, but the popularizers of science went even further; Büchner and Haeckel, for example, propagated a mechanistic materialism which denied the possibility of autonomous consciousness. "The idolatry of science" had upset all previous beliefs. Mind was once more banned from a universe whose fundamental reality was conceived to be matter, and after 1850 the claims of eighteenth-century materialistic science were revived, grown more extravagant, by the tangible achievements of the physical sciences of the intervening years.

Darwin's evolutionary theory had an incomparable impact on European culture. After Darwin, the fact of evolution could no longer be denied, and the popular imagination, long prepared for such a theory, extended it to ever new

* A recent critic described the grandeur of Schopenhauer's position: "To look upon man, as Schopenhauer and Burckhardt did, as the fallen creature, on sin and evil as constituent and ineradicable factors in human history, on human affairs as pathological, without believing in the reality, existence, possibility and indeed the definite offer of spiritual health, must needs create a profound spiritual predicament. . . . The predicament persists; and it did, throughout their lives, persist for men like Schopenhauer and Burckhardt. They bore it nobly, and with a strength of spirit and character which is rare among human beings." Erich Heller, *The Disinherited Mind. Essays in Modern German Literature and Thought,* Cambridge (England) 1952, p. 62.

fields. The Germanic critics, despite their hostility to science and materialism, were influenced by the various strands of Darwinism. Moeller, as we saw, believed that the theory of evolution had destroyed all moral absolutes, all truths, all timeless religions. The truth of Darwin, Moeller felt, had swept aside the moral truths of earlier times and thus prepared the way for the triumph of relativism. His own prescription for a new ethics incorporated the evolutionary principle, and he tacitly accepted the belief of the social Darwinists that the laws of nature and of society were identical. Lagarde and Moeller also resorted to the rhetoric of social Darwinism and justified the role of struggle by appealing to the dubious principle of natural selection. The idea of the struggle for survival was transposed by them to the international realm and turned into an exhortation to war, because war would select and ennoble the superior people. Actually social Darwinism was a new and "scientific" guise for their romantic sense of the nobility of struggle and self-conquest, and in this curious mixture of romantic heroism and mechanistic materialism they were once again anticipating the later, and more dangerous, concoctions of the National Socialists.

Darwinism was the last common intellectual experience of the three generations of Germanic critics. Only Moeller felt the full force of Nietzsche's impact on German culture. For Moeller, as for so many of his contemporaries, Nietzsche proved to be of towering importance. The very magnitude of that impact also carried with it the likelihood of terrible misunderstandings. Under no circumstances is a great man's work easily appropriated, but when revolutionary ideas are cast in an irresistible style, as they were in Nietzsche's prose aphorisms, then seduction rather than comprehension is likely to follow. Nietzsche sensed the difficulty, even the obscurity of his thought, for "everything profound loves a mask."

Nietzsche had expected that he would be misunderstood and had demanded university courses of instruction in Zarathustra's philosophy—in vain. There was no academic exegesis of Nietzsche in prewar Germany; everybody had his own sense of "what Nietzsche really meant." Nietzsche's sister tried to create an official—and thoroughly distorted—interpretation. By clever editing and attempted suppression, she sought to convert him, posthumously, into the kind of narrowminded patriot that she herself was.*

The terrible dangers of this cultural free-for-all were well exemplified in Moeller's interpretation of Nietzsche. Here we shall see some of the distortions and simplifications that falsified Nietzsche's thought in Germany and that bear out Camus's contention—that few men have suffered so much from posterity: "In the history of the intelligence, with the exception of Marx, Nietzsche's adventure has no equivalent; we shall never finish making reparation for the injustice done to him." [11]

The charge has often been made that Nietzsche fathered Germanic nationalism and the irrational cult of violence. The National Socialists claimed him as one of their distant forerunners, and many of their Western opponents agreed, because they had for a long time regarded Nietzsche as the intellectual source of German nihilism. But the case of the Germanic critics is one instructive illustration of the nature of that "influence." We will see that Nietzsche's thought differed radically from that of the Germanic critics, that the latter were uneasily aware of these differences, and that in essence the Germanic ideology had been formulated before Nietzsche's work was even available. Lagarde, Langbehn, and Moeller were not disciples of Nietzsche—and it is doubtful if anyone ever was a legitimate disciple.

The differences between Nietzsche and these critics were immense. In the first place, Nietzsche was a philosopher, a great and self-critical writer, to whom the search for truth and reality was a measure of his own integrity. Half-truths and the comforts of unreason he loathed. His style was experimental without being precious; witty without being trivial; profound without being ponderous. The reverse held true for the Germanic critics—proof again that style is the man.† Nietzsche hoped to learn from his sufferings and weak-

---

* On Elizabeth Förster-Nietzsche, as well as on every other aspect of Nietzsche's life and thought, see the exemplary study of Walter A. Kaufmann, *Nietzsche: Philosopher, Psychologist, Antichrist,* Princeton 1950.

† Their contemporaries recognized the difference. Franz Overbeck, a friend of Nietzsche's and a sympathetic reader of Lagarde's, wrote: "I already find Nietzsche too 'rhetorical,' but how pure is his rhetoric and how much it is based on *genuine* feeling compared to Lagarde's. Both are great in self-appraisal, but how much stronger is the place of

nesses, in order to understand the condition of man; the Germanic critics succumbed to their weaknesses and sought to reform the world because of them. In their trivializing and mystifying, the Germanic critics manifested the intellectual qualities that Nietzsche most despised.

Beyond these differences in style and character were the many substantive issues on which their positions were antithetical. Nietzsche admired the Enlightenment, the Germanic critics dreaded it. Joyfully he acknowledged the influence of many earlier thinkers; the Germanic critics were loath to acknowledge anyone. He started and ended as the "good European" and tirelessly denounced German nationalism, anti-Semitism, and other proto-Nazi beliefs. He never abandoned the individualistic premise of his thought. The individual could achieve greatness and fulfillment, but only in opposition to society. Nietzsche loathed every collective tyranny, and he would have battled the Germanic community as fiercely as he did the existing state.* He never sought to overcome his cultural despair by facile solutions; there was

---

vanity in Lagarde's case. Nietzsche was incapable of such lack of taste as Lagarde showed when he depicted in his poem on the Last Judgment his own glorification at the Last Judgment. Nietzsche measured himself against what was real and living; only Lagarde got ecstatic over this matter and measured himself against the hereafter. Nietzsche never took himself so 'seriously' as this schoolmaster." Carl Albrecht Bernoulli, *Franz Overbeck und Friedrich Nietzsche. Eine Freundschaft,* Jena 1908, I, 133.

* He did, in fact: M. P. Nicolas quotes two letters that Nietzsche wrote to Theodor Fritsch, rebuking the entire anti-Semitic movement, including Lagarde. "If you only knew how I laughed last spring when I read the works of that vain, obstinate, and sentimental man who calls himself Paul de Lagarde—I obviously lack that 'viewpoint of the supreme ethics' of which he makes so much on each page" (Letter of March 23, 1887). And a week later: "Believe me, this hateful craze on the part of feeble amateurs to want to discuss at all cost the *value* of men and races; this submission to the 'authorities' who reject all reasonable spirit with cold contempt (for example, E. Dühring, Richard Wagner, Ebrard, Wahrmund, P. de Lagarde . . . one does not know which of these is least qualified, the most inept at judging moral and historical questions!); these constant and absurd falsifications, these vague expressions ('Germanic. . .'). All of this, in the long run, would seriously anger me and would dispel that ironic good will with which until now I have observed the good velleities and the Pharisaism of the Germans of our day." M. P. Nicolas, *De Nietzsche à Hitler,* Paris, Fasquelle, 1936, pp. 131–134. These two letters have not been included in the available collection of Nietzsche letters in German.

pride as well as truthfulness in his oft-repeated assertion that
he was the last "unpolitical German." Truly, Zarathustra's
prophet was worlds apart from the parochial revivers of
Wotan.

What appealed to Langbehn and to Moeller, and to their
followers, was Nietzsche's relentless denunciation of cultured
Philistinism, which could be read as an attack on all learning,
and used as an excuse for intellectual illiteracy. Because he
loved wisdom and integrity, Nietzsche—in this the friend
and ally of Burckhardt—attacked German pedantry and
Philistinism, and these attacks became the ammunition of
those who feared wisdom or learning of any kind. Nietzsche's
intermittent brutality, the violence of his phrases, his glorification of power and the elite—all of these were echoed as well.
Above all, Moeller—and countless other Germans—used
Nietzsche's biography, his loneliness, suffering, and final
breakdown, as the validation of their own attacks on German
culture; the severity of Nietzsche's sacrifice was taken as a
measure of Germany's decay. This indecent idolatry of
Nietzsche's illness and death was the epitome of the Nietzsche
myth.

In one of his essays, Moeller celebrated Nietzsche as Germany's greatest cultural critic and as the reviver of metaphysical thought after the aridity of positivism. He admired
Nietzsche's heroic morality and his individualism, and saw
in them the sources of his own attacks on liberal and
Christian humanitarianism. Somewhat condescendingly he
praised Nietzsche's psychological insights and the political
views which he had derived from them. Nietzsche, he admitted, had destroyed the foundations of a decadent culture
—and for this he deserved the gratitude of his compatriots,
but he had built nothing on the ruins of the old world. In
short, Nietzsche was "impractical," or, conversely, Moeller
was "too practical to be a Nietzschean"—which was precisely what his widow said of him.[12] Moeller was always ready
with a formula of reconciliation, with a myth that would
promise salvation. Contrast Moeller's insistence that "God
himself . . . continues to exist, even if we know that he does
not exist," with Nietzsche's comment: "How many people
still make the inference: 'one could not stand life if there
were no God!' (or as they say in the circles of the Idealists:
'one could not stand life if it lacked the ethical significance

of its ground!')—consequently there *must* be a God (or an ethical significance of existence)! . . . what presumption to decree that all that is necessary for my preservation must also really *be there!* As if my preservation were anything necessary!" [13]

The gulf between Nietzsche and Moeller seems widest in their respective interpretations of Darwin. Moeller sought to mediate between Darwin and Nietzsche, and argued that Nietzsche's conception of the superman provided the metaphysical meaning of evolution. Quite aside from Nietzsche's disdain for such mediation—"Anyone who wants to mediate between two resolute thinkers is characterized as mediocre; he does not have the eye for the unique"—we know that Nietzsche's superman was the negation, not the fulfillment, of Darwinian evolution.[14] By self-conquest, by a tremendous effort of the will, superman fashions himself, and thus the elements of purpose and will, which Darwin had banished, were reintroduced. Moeller failed to see that Nietzsche was Darwin's greatest antagonist; more than that, Nietzsche feared the consequences of Darwinism as acutely as Tocqueville had feared the consequences of Gobinism.*

Moeller's misreading of Nietzsche emerged clearly in his complaint that Nietzsche did not sufficiently extend the will to power: "It is perhaps obvious that Nietzsche himself should have undertaken the transfer of his principles . . . to the race and to its will to power." [15] Moeller, in short, accused Nietzsche of not being a social Darwinist, of not extending his individualistic morality to the *Volk*. Nietzsche had, of course, warned against this illicit transfer of the will to power from man to the state. Not so Moeller. He was "practical,"

---

* Tocqueville warned his friend Gobineau about the consequences of his racial and fatalistic theories: "The consequences of both theories is that of a vast limitation, if not a complete abolition, of human liberty. . . . I believe that [these theories] are probably quite false; I know that they are certainly very pernicious." Alexis de Tocqueville, *The European Revolution and Correspondence with Gobineau,* ed. by John Lukacs, Doubleday Anchor Books, New York 1959, p. 227. Nietzsche wrote: "If the doctrines of sovereign Becoming, of the liquidity of all . . . species, of the lack of any cardinal distinction between man and animal—doctrines which I consider true but deadly— are hurled into the people for another generation . . . then nobody should be surprised when . . . brotherhoods with the aim of robbery and exploitation of the non-brothers . . . will appear on the arena of the future." Quoted in Walter A. Kaufmann, *Nietzsche,* p. 141.

and did not hesitate to translate Nietzsche's thoughts to society, to preach a kind of social Nietzscheanism.

Moeller marked an important stage in the vulgarization of Nietzsche. Through him, the authority of a distorted Nietzsche was brought still closer to the antidemocratic movements of Weimar. After the war, as before, Nietzsche's influence was great, and on the surface at least, more evil than good.* But this was the work of history rather than of the man; just as Anabaptists followed in Luther's wake, or revolutionary terrorists in Rousseau's, so antidemocrats attached themselves to Nietzsche.†

The course and character of Nietzsche's influence were exemplified by his relation to Moeller and the Germanic critics. Though Moeller had appropriated some Nietzschean thoughts, the Germanic ideology as a whole had preceded Nietzsche's works. Lagarde, it will be remembered, had written his first two essays in 1853, and his third, complete with the important themes of his life's work, in 1873. Also in 1873, but unknown to Lagarde, Nietzsche had published his first explicit criticism of German culture, the incomparable polemic against David Friedrich Strauss. There is no evidence to suggest that Lagarde was influenced by Nietzsche after that date.

Nietzsche, then, had nothing to do with the birth of the Germanic ideology, though he did powerfully affect its historical development—not intellectually, for the contention that Nietzsche and his doctrine of the eternal recurrence "stands at the center" of the conservative revolution greatly overestimates the philosophical foundation of the entire movement.[16] Rather, an uneasy generation, further unsettled

---

* Nietzsche had anticipated this, too: "Posthumous men—I, for example —are understood worse than timely ones, but *heard* better. More precisely: we are never understood—*hence* our authority." *Götzendämmerung,* in *Friedrich Nietzsche. Werke in Drei Bänden,* ed. by Karl Schlechta, München 1955, II, 944.

† This was true of antidemocrats everywhere. Mussolini thought of himself as a Nietzschean, and the later Action Française was sympathetic to his work. See Reino Virtanen, "Nietzsche and the Action Française," *Journal of the History of Ideas,* XI:2 (April, 1950), 191–214. On National Socialist efforts to claim Nietzsche, see Crane Brinton, *Nietzsche,* Cambridge (Mass.) 1941, chapter 8, as well as Walter Kaufmann's comments, in his *Nietzsche,* pp. 255–256.

by Nietzsche's work, accepted the Germanic critics more readily for their apparent closeness to Nietzsche. Such "disciples" Nietzsche had always feared, and had prophesied: "You had not yet sought yourselves, when you found me." [17]

iii

We have seen how Lagarde, Langbehn, and Moeller appropriated and distorted some of the major intellectual traditions of Germany. Their thought in turn was distorted and usurped; it was distorted by the several generations of "unpolitical" Germans, who shared with our writers a sense of alarm at the direction of German life. Thomas Mann and Ernst Troeltsch, Friedrich Naumann and Christian Morgenstern were deeply affected by Lagarde, and men of equal eminence admired Langbehn and Moeller. These men responded, as I suggested earlier, to the "gentle" Lagarde— the Lagarde stripped of what these admirers commonly called his crotchetiness, his anti-Semitism, and imperialism. The National Socialists, on the other hand, usurped the thought of our writers by fastening exclusively on the "tough," nihilistic side; in this way they could claim all three as part of their legacy. In actual fact, Lagarde, Langbehn, and Moeller had a powerful impact on both groups, and thus forged a link between them. The Germanic ideology was one of the traditions that the German elite and the National Socialists shared.

For many years, the Germanic critics were the acknowledged apostles of cultural despair, and their memory was invoked whenever men dreamed of a new Germany, a Germany beyond Philistinism, materialism, and conventional patriotism. There was much genuine idealism in these rumblings of discontent, much danger and much nobility in those German writers who, before and after 1914, refused to see in imperial Germany the perfect society or "the good old days!"

The Youth Movement believed in Lagarde and Langbehn, as did many of the *Bürger* and nationalist reformers who found prewar Germany ugly and unsatisfying. The critics of the republic—who saw in Weimar an enfeebled version of the Wilhelmine Reich—were confirmed in their despair by Moeller and Lagarde. The stronger a certain kind of patriotic discontent, the greater was the popularity of the three writers. The height of their influence, as measured by the circulation of their works, the number of studies about them, and the public references to them, came at the time of the dissolution of Weimar, in the years of Hitler's rise to power. The Germanic critics had predicted the death of liberal society, and when its agony began, they were duly remembered.

The course of German history had a curious way of fulfilling our critics' predictions. From 1890 to 1933, German life was characterized by the successive explosions of discontent, always half-cultural and half-political in outlook and intent. Did not the rebellion of the Youth Movement, the exaltation of August 1914, the *Fronterlebnis,* and the idealistic brutality of the postwar years bear out our critics' sense of the inadequacy of liberal, rational society, of the boredom of the nation, of the yearning for a collective faith? They believed as well that liberal politics would not be able to contain the discontent that it bred—and they prefigured the resentful rejection of the Weimar Republic that had little to do with objective grievances and everything with a disdain that was compounded of loneliness and embittered expectations of the unattainable.

By heightening the dissatisfaction of many men, theirs had been a self-fulfilling prophecy. But their opponents helped as well; barring a few exceptions, political leadership in Wilhelmine and Weimar Germany was not of a caliber that would disprove the charges of the Germanic critics. The failure of German parliaments in years of crisis was all too real and tended to validate the earlier complaints of the Germanic critics.*

---

* The despair about German politics in general, and Weimar parliamentarianism in particular, was widespread; as the merest example, consider the comments of a moderate bourgeois journal, written in 1923, after Germany had barely weathered the storm of the Ruhr occupation and the inflation. Reference is made to Stresemann's decision to permit the German crown prince to return from exile as well as to Hitler's Beerhall putsch. The crown prince's "return at this time will remain a classic example that German politicians of the Wilhelmine period were concerned only with their internecine fights, and regardless whether in 1917 they were called Ebert and Erzberger or in 1923 Stresemann and Hitler, they had neither enough insight nor discipline to have the least regard for the exigencies of their people's foreign position." Of Hitler's putsch it said: "With us, fascism lacks the force for a breakthrough. It is not *volkstümlich.* But we could not do without this

The fact that Lagarde, Langbehn, and Moeller were right in so many of their predictions increased their influence, but does not necessarily validate their arguments. Their analysis of Germany's problems, as we saw, was intellectually threadbare; the analysis of many of their liberal and socialist opponents was infinitely subtler—and less accurate. Lagarde, Langbehn, and Moeller anticipated and to some degree created the mood of many Germans, and it was this mood of cultural despair that became a political force which rational thinkers had not reckoned with. Our critics, moreover, had foreshadowed the kind of response that would appeal to this mood: their own despair had prompted their political utopianism, their weariness had inspired their mystique.

After the experiences of war, defeat, and impotent republicanism, this mood of despair and political mysticism had seized both the German right and the National Socialists. Without that pervasive mood, the National Socialists would not have been able to succeed. A thousand teachers in republican Germany who in their youth had read and worshiped Lagarde or Langbehn were just as important to the triumph of National Socialism as all the putative millions of marks that Hitler collected from German tycoons.

The long history of the Germanic ideology throws light on what has been called "the real problem in German history . . . , why so few of the educated, civilized classes recognized Hitler as the embodiment of evil. University professors; army officers; business-men and bankers—these had a background of culture, and even of respect for law. Yet virtually none of them exclaimed: 'This is anti-Christ.' " * A partial answer to this problem is given in this book: long before Hitler, long before Versailles, there appeared in Germany deep national

---

stimulating poison in our blood. Also it has a natural magic for the freshest and most passionate of our youth." The article concludes that if parliamentarians continue to play politics while the nation is in crisis, then the army must act. It alone has "authority and it alone has a residue of the German political spirit of the Bismarck period." "Politische. Rundschau," *Deutsche Rundschau*, CXCVII (December, 1923), 333.

* This was A. J. P. Taylor's definition of the problem; his answer is unsatisfactory: The responsible classes in Germany were fighting communism and "Hitler's hostility to Communism was his strongest asset." A. J. P. Taylor, "The Seizure of Power," in *The Third Reich*, ed. by Edmond Vermeil *et al.*, London 1955, p. 525.

frustrations, galling cultural discontents, which inspired nationalist fantasies and utopias which found ready assent among this German elite. Even without Hitler and without political disasters, the presence of such a force would have had to be reckoned with in an analysis of the political culture of modern Germany.

The educated, civilized classes had been moved by the Germanic ideology when it was only a dream; is it strange that they continued to believe in it when it appeared as a live political reality? By 1930, this generation of Germans clung all the more desperately to the heroic and nationalistic values of men like Lagarde and Moeller; all that they had felt in the Youth Movement, endured in the war, and suffered under Versailles, prepared them to accept—or at least not to reject—Hitler. To them the appeal of the *Führer* was immense, even if the *Führer* adulterated the idealism of his prophets with the nihilism of his brutal followers. The propaganda of the National Socialists, in turn, emphasized the cultural rottenness and political irresponsibility of Weimar—the very themes that Moeller had been driving home as well. The promise of the Third Reich, of the unity of the racial *Volk*, of its aggrandizement, of the resolution of its internal conflicts, the invocation of heroism, of individual exertion and national will—all of these seemed timely echoes of an ideology first disseminated in the days of Bismarck. Finally the National Socialist movement had the élan, the dynamism, the religious tone that our critics, in their lives and thought, had longed for and that their admirers sought as well.*

---

* Thomas Mann was one of the first to point out the historic roots of national socialism. Immediately after the disastrous Reichstag elections of 1930, Mann, in his famous address to the Germans, warned against the "spiritual sources of support" that the Hitler movement could draw on. "It may seem bold to make a connection between the radical nationalism of today and the ideas of a romanticizing philosophy; nevertheless the connection exists and must be recognized by anyone who wants to understand the context of the present developments. . . . We find here a certain ideology of philologists, a romanticism of professional Germanists, a superstitious faith in the Nordic—all these emanate from the academic-professorial classes, and the Germans of 1930 are harangued . . . with phrases like racist, populistic, *bündisch*, heroic, and this contributed to the [Hitler] movement an ingredient of cultured barbarism, more dangerous and less

The cultural pessimism which they helped to propagate in German society has been recognized as an important factor in converting men to national socialism.* The various attempts to understand the triumph of national socialism have consistently underestimated the deeply rooted spiritual longings which inspired so many of Hitler's followers, and which also restrained members of the German elite from recognizing or resisting the approaching catastrophe. This aspect of the rise of Hitler has been overlooked by Marxist or psychoanalytical explanations of national socialism; it is misunderstood

---

realistic . . . than the estrangment from reality and the political romanticism that led us into the war." Mann also noted that the new nationalism hated the opposition at home far more than it hated Germany's enemies abroad. "Its chief goal . . . is the internal purification of Germany and the return to an earlier condition of Germany such as would correspond to the conception of the Germans that the radical nationalism cherishes. But even supposing such a return to be desirable, is it possible? Is this fantasy of a primitive, pure-blooded, simple-hearted and simple-minded, heel-clicking, blue-eyed, obedient, disciplined sobriety, this complete national simplicity, to be realized, even after ten thousand expulsions and purification raids . . . in an old, mature, deeply experienced and deeply demanding *Kulturvolk?*" Thomas Mann, *Deutsche Ansprache. Ein Appell an die Vernunft*, Berlin 1930, pp. 16–18. A more detailed description by a contemporary of the relations of the new nationalism to old traditions, including the thought of our three writers, can be found in Walter Gerhart, *Um des Reiches Zukunft. Nationale Wiedergeburt oder polititische Reaktion*, Freiburg im Breisgau 1932, pp. 60–62 and chapter 5.

* In the best study of actual *individual* conversions to national socialism, we find in first place an account of "four cultural pessimists" who early became active National Socialists. "In general, one can perhaps say that when national socialism appeared, cultural pessimism as a secular mood was already widely disseminated and appealed to the minds and tempers of people, so that it prepared some people for a sudden leap from a purely bemoaning attitude to the new activist outlook. . . . We now can summarize the result of our examples: the isolation of the 'intellectuals' that we have described manifested itself in their social position. . . . The persons we discussed were 'rootless,' that is, free of all compelling personal examples. They had the task to find themselves, to decide for themselves who they wanted to be. Neither religion nor political tradition, neither an occupational model nor any other indisputable model provided them with a pattern for their ego foundation. Therefore, they acted in the political realm, as if that were a vacuum into which one can safely and at the same time experimentally channel the destructive drives of one's neurosis." Wenda von Baeyer-Katte, *Das Zerstörende in der Politik. Eine Psychologie der politischen Grundeinstellung*, Heidelberg 1958, pp. 42, 45.

by the "intellectual" approach to national socialism, that is, by those men who blame the ideas of Hitler on every German thinker after Luther. It has found no place in the empirical studies of sociologists who seek to analyze the social base of National Socialist strength.*

To some extent, this idealistic element of national socialism was directly derived from Lagarde, Langbehn, and Moeller. We saw how difficult it was to define with precision the relationship of the Germanic critics to earlier movements of thought; similar difficulties obstruct a clear understanding of their relationship to the leaders of national socialism. The question is a particular instance of the larger problem of intellectual influence, of the diffusion and power of ideas. But it is especially delicate because one deals with the effect of confused ideas on irrational men and movements. We are in fact confronted by a mounting process of abstraction and usurpation: the ideas of the romantics, of the critics of democracy, and, above all, the ideas of Nietzsche, were distorted and then appropriated by the Germanic critics and were ultimately vulgarized by men who held thought itself in contempt and regarded ideas as mere weapons in the political fight for power. It is a process which descends from the level of detached contemplation to that of nihilistic activism, from nonpartisanship to fanatical factionalism. As thinkers, the Germanic critics were simultaneously related to European philosophy and to National Socialist ideology; as personalities

* See S. M. Lipset's excellent analysis of the sources of National Socialist support, which he found chiefly among those that had formerly voted for liberal or moderate parties. In a footnote, he remarks that "Catholic affiliation constantly overrides class or other allegiances as a major determinant of party support in practically all election data for Germany, in both the Weimar and Bonn republics." If belonging to a religious group can override all other considerations, then one wonders whether the political choice of non-Catholics may not have been decisively affected by similar ties or ideological considerations. It is important to know that the National Socialists scored heavily among the self-employed and other formerly liberal groups, but since these groups did not act as a unit, the question remains what spiritual or psychological factors may have predisposed some members of a given group to embrace national socialism and others to resist it. See Seymour Martin Lipset, *Political Man. The Social Bases of Politics*, New York, Doubleday, 1960, p. 147.

they stood midway between the detached philosopher and the uneducated rabble rouser.

The National Socialist ideology, in motive, form, and content, resembles the Germanic ideology. Their negative views were indistinguishable. For both, liberalism was the chief enemy, an alien and corrosive force that was devouring the true Germanic spirit and destroying the German Reich. Both demanded the unity and aggrandizement of a folkish Reich, and both insisted that only a *Führer* could establish and rule such a Reich. Both were embittered critics of the bourgeois way of life, of the spirit of capitalism, and Moeller anticipated the National Socialist belief in a Germanic socialism. Lagarde and Langbehn had emphasized the central place of anti-Semitism in such an ideology, and the Germanic critics as well as the National Socialists believed—with more or less literal-mindedness—in the racial determination of character and history. Lastly, their common thoughts sprang from a common hatred and alienation. We may conclude from this resemblance that the National Socialist leaders were not creating a false ideology with which to manipulate the political will of the masses. The example of the Germanic critics demonstrates that such an ideology has a great intrinsic appeal, and the success of national socialism convinces us that this particular translation of resentment and discontent into political myth offered hope to those who, caught in the throes of economic disaster and social disintegration, craved the certainty of a spiritual redemption.

The two movements then sprang from similar psychological conditions and professed similar ideologies. More, their lines of march often crossed. Abundant evidence attests the direct influence of Lagarde and Langbehn on the most important National Socialist ideologists. Alfred Rosenberg, the chief ideologist of the Hitler movement, considered himself Lagarde's disciple. Ernst Krieck, the National Socialist theorist of education, freely borrowed from and acknowledged the works of Lagarde and Langbehn.[18] The several founders of the Germanic religion based themselves on Lagarde's work.[19] The young idol of National Socialist historians, Christoph Steding, attempted a metahistorical critique of European civilization and placed Langbehn's thought at the center of his own work.[20] The National Socialists celebrated the older pair as their forebears and, although at one time or another repudiating every other influence, never wavered in their loyalty to these two.*

Still more clearly is the junction seen in the person and the work of Moeller. He was the dominant figure of the conservative revolution in the Weimar Republic, and his idea of the Third Reich constituted the most powerful myth of the antirepublican forces.† His direct influence on the National Socialists was not very great: when *Das Dritte Reich* appeared, Hitler was already concerned with disengaging himself from the National Socialist program, rather than elaborating it. Goebbels, on the other hand, had been immensely impressed by the book in 1925, and seven years later, on the occasion of a new edition of *Das Dritte Reich*, he enthusiastically endorsed it: "I welcome the dissemination of Moeller's work which is so very important for the history of National Socialist political ideas." [21]

The secondary influence, however, was considerable. Because Moeller's conservative revolution had no means of self-fulfillment, its followers had no path to political power. Despite some misgivings about Hitler's demagogy, many conservative revolutionaries saw in the *Führer* the sole possibility of achieving their goal.‡ In the sequel, Hitler's triumph

---

* The first issue of the *Nationalsozialistische Monatshefte*, the "intellectual" voice of the party, took stock of all forebears and singled out Lagarde, but mentioned Langbehn as well. See also Georg Schweinshaupt, "Nationalsozialismus und Lagarde," *Nationalsozialistische Monatshefte*, III:32 (November, 1932). Erich Unger, ed., *Das Schrifttum zum Aufbau des neuen Reiches 1919–1934*, Berlin 1934, lists among works of National Socialist prophets nine books by Lagarde and seven for Langbehn. He also lists four books on or about Moeller under "National Socialist *Weltanschauung*."

† It seems, nevertheless, far fetched to assert that "with all his paradoxes and lack of clear reasoning, van den Bruck gave Hitlerism its inspiration, and scores of political writers elaborated and extended his basic ideas about the Folkic State in which socialism found its best expression in dictatorship, and in which progress meant nationalism." Stephen H. Roberts, *The House that Hitler Built*, New York, Harper, 1938, p. 47. For Rohan d'O. Butler, Moeller's thought "was not only the culmination of advanced political thought in post-war Germany. In a very real sense it was the climax of 150 years of persistent theory." *The Roots of National Socialism, 1783–1933*, London 1941, p. 265.

‡ As can be seen in the postelection statement in 1932 of a leading conservative revolutionary among Catholics, Edgar Jung: "What was at issue in the past election? The liquidation of Weimar liberalism, together with its defeatism at home and abroad, which had brought us to the brink of the abyss. This dying liberalism was in a terrible

shattered the illusions of most of Moeller's followers, and the twelve years of the Third Reich witnessed the separation of conservative revolution and national socialism again.*

This disentanglement was a heartbreaking and heroic experience for the conservative revolutionaries. It is a tribute to the genuine spiritual quality of the conservative revolution that the reality of the Third Reich aroused many of them to opposition, sometimes silent, often open and costly. Some, like Rauschning and Treviranus, sought refuge abroad; others, like Edgar Jung, were killed in the purge of June 30, 1934. In the final plot against Hitler, in July, 1944, a few former conservative revolutionaries risked and lost their lives, martyrs to the genuine idealism of their earlier cause.†

For their part, the National Socialists repudiated Moeller and his circle as well. After a few months of adulation in 1933, the National Socialists disavowed Moeller, and Rosenberg formally denied that he had been a forerunner of na-

---

state. . . . We not only rejoice [at the growth of national socialism] but we have done our bit to bring it about. In untold work on a small scale, especially among the educated classes, we created the prerequisites for the day when the German people would give its vote to the National Socialist candidates.—I do not know where Moeller van den Bruck would stand today. Since he is dead, he has had the honor of being claimed by the National Socialists, but this has not materially advanced the understanding of his work." Edgar J. Jung, "Neubelebung von Weimar? Verkehrung der Fronten," *Deutsche Rundschau,* CCXXXI (June, 1932) 154, 159.

* Hermann Rauschning is the typical representative of this group. "Many Conservatives who had become spiritually homeless found their way into the ranks of National Socialism, from the very best of motives and in perfect good faith." *The Revolution of Nihilism. Warning to the West,* New York 1939, p. 112. In his next book, *The Conservative Revolution,* New York 1941, he attempts, not very convincingly, to explain at length how one could have strayed from one revolution to the other.

† See Rudolf Pechel, *Deutscher Widerstand,* Zürich 1947, pp. 71–114, for an analysis of the link between the German opposition to Hitler and the conservative revolution. Pechel was himself a participant in the conspiracy against Hitler. Other conservative revolutionaries survived: Joachim Tiburtius is now a senator in West Berlin, Hans Zehrer is at present the editor of *Die Welt,* and Moeller's close political associate, Max Hildebert Boehm, who wrote voluminously under the National Socialist regime, recently served the Bonn government as coeditor of a trilogy, *Die Vertriebenen in Westdeutschland. Ihre Eingliederung und ihr Einfluss auf Gesellschaft, Wirtschaft, Politik und Geistesleben,* ed. by Eugen Lemberg *et al.,* in 3 vols., Kiel, Hirt, 1959.

tional socialism. In 1939, the party sponsored an official study of Moeller's work with the avowed purpose of investigating the relation between Moeller's "unrealistic ideology which has nothing to do with the actual historical developments or with sober *Realpolitik*" and Hitler, "who was *not* Moeller's heir." [22] Moeller was praised for his attacks on the intellectual refuse of the nineteenth century, but the final verdict pronounced that he "never was, and also never wanted to be, the 'spiritual founder' of our National Socialist state." [23]

For us the National Socialist repudiation of Moeller and the opposition of some conservative revolutionaries to the Hitler regime is a partial exoneration of Moeller and of the Germanic critics as a group. Their ideological influence on national socialism was, after all, not decisive, nor did the National Socialists honor *all* aspects of their thought. Above all, Moeller—and the other Germanic critics—did not want *that* Third Reich, and would not have acknowledged the reality of Hitler's Reich as a realization of their dream.

But, we must ask, could there have been any other "Third Reich"? Was there a safe stopping place in this wild leap from political reality? Can one abjure reason, glorify force, prophesy the age of the imperial dictator, can one condemn all existing institutions, without preparing the triumph of irresponsibility? The Germanic critics did all that, thereby demonstrating the terrible dangers of the politics of cultural despair.

Notes

Introduction

(Pp. xi–xxx)

[1] Paul de Lagarde, *Symmicta*, Göttingen 1880, II, 106.

[2] Eduard Spranger, "Wesen und Wert politischer Ideologien," *Vierteljahrshefte für Zeitgeschichte*, II:2 (April, 1954), 122–123.

[3] Alfred Fouillée, *Morale des Idées-Forces*, Paris, Alcan, 1908, p. 353.

[4] Hugo von Hofmannsthal, *Das Schrifttum als geistiger Raum der Nation*, München 1927, pp. 27 and 31.

[5] Julien Benda, *The Betrayal of the Intellectuals (La Trahison des clercs)*, Boston 1955, pp. 135 and 21.

[6] There are two studies of the conservative revolution in Germany after 1918: Armin Mohler, *Die konservative Revolution in Deutschland 1918–1932. Grundriss ihrer Weltanschauungen*, Stuttgart 1950, and Klemens von Klemperer, *Germany's New Conservatism. Its History and Dilemma in the Twentieth Century*, Princeton 1957. Klemperer's study is a searching analysis of the intellectual currents of Germany's new right-wing groups.

[7] John Henry Cardinal Newman, *Apologia Pro Vita Sua*, Everyman's Library, London n.d., p. 233.

[8] Lionel Trilling, *The Liberal Imagination. Essays on Literature and Society*, New York, Viking, 1950, p. ix.

[9] See Michael Curtis, *Three Against the Third Republic. Sorel, Barrès, and Maurras*, Princeton 1959; see also the incisive commentary on Italian nationalism in Richard A. Webster's "The Cross and the Fasces. Christian Democracy and Fascism in Italy," Columbia University doctoral dissertation 1959, chapters 1 and 2. On "The Folklore of Populism," see Richard Hofstadter, *The Age of Reform. From Bryan to F.D.R.*, New York, Knopf, 1955, chapter 2.

[10] Cardinal Spellman, as quoted in the *New York Times*, June 14, 1955, and Dr. William S. Carlson, then president of the State University of New York, as quoted in the *New York Times*, October 22, 1956.

[11] The best study of German liberalism is Leonard Krieger's *The German Idea of Freedom. History of a Political Tradition*, Boston 1957.

[12] Ludwig Curtius, *Deutsche und Antike Welt. Lebenserinnerungen*, Stuttgart, Deutsche Verlagsanstalt, 1950, p. 455.

[13] The problems of the social and historical consequences of German idealism are immense, and central to an understanding of

301

German history; see the important essay by Hajo Holborn, "Der deutsche Idealismus in sozialgeschichtlicher Beleuchtung," *Historische Zeitschrift*, CLXXIV:2 (October, 1952), 359–384. See also my essay, "The Political Consequences of the Unpolitical German," *History. A Meridian Periodical*, III (September, 1960), 104–134.

[14] Friedrich Meinecke, *The German Catastrophe. Reflections and Recollections*, transl. by Sidney B. Fay, Cambridge (Mass.) 1950, p. 14.

[15] Theodor Mommsen, "Rede zur Vorfeier des Geburtstages des Kaisers," March 18, 1880, in *Reden und Aufsätze*, Berlin 1905, p. 91. For a discussion of the general sense of decline, see D. Wilhelm Lütgert, *Das Ende des Idealismus im Zeitalter Bismarcks*, Gütersloh 1930, pp. 224–298.

[16] Max Weber, *Gesammelte politische Schriften*, München 1921, pp. 24 ff.

Chapter 1

(Pp. 3–26)

[1] Ludwig Schemann, *Paul de Lagarde, Ein Lebens- und Erinnerungsbild*, 3d ed., Leipzig 1943, is the most complete biographical study. It first appeared in 1919, went through two editions in that year, and was reprinted in 1943. Lagarde himself scattered autobiographical details throughout his writings and I have used these to temper Schemann's adulation. See also Anna de Lagarde, *Paul de Lagarde. Erinnerungen aus seinem Leben für die Freunde zusammengestellt*, Göttingen 1894. The best introduction to Lagarde's scholarly work is the essay of his sometime pupil, Alfred Rahlfs, *Paul de Lagardes wissenschaftliches Lebenswerk im Rahmen einer Geschichte seines Lebens dargestellt*, Berlin 1928. I was able to supplement the published material by consulting the Lagarde Archive at Göttingen, which includes, *inter alia*, his entire correspondence.

[2] Rahlfs, *op. cit.*, p. 13.

[3] Paul de Lagarde, *Ausgewählte Schriften*, ed. by Paul Fischer, 2d ed., München 1934, p. 34. This anthology of Lagarde's writings will henceforth be cited as *A.S.*

[4] Anna de Lagarde, *op. cit.*, p. 5.

[5] Lagarde, "Erinnerungen an Friedrich Rückert," *A.S.*, p. 42.

[6] *Ibid.*, p. 43.

[7] For a summary of Hengstenberg's thought, see Emanuel Hirsch, *Geschichte der neueren evangelischen Theologie im Zusammenhang mit den allgemeinen Bewegungen des europäischen Denkens*, Gütersloh, Bertelsmann, 1954, V, 118–130.

NOTES

⁸ On Tholuck, see Karl Barth's fine account, *Die protestantische Theologie im 19. Jahrhundert. Ihre Vorgeschichte und ihre Geschichte,* 2d ed., Zürich 1952, pp. 459–468.

⁹ Lagarde, *Mittheilungen,* Göttingen 1887, II, 94.

¹⁰ See the liberal historian Alfred Stern in "Waldeck," *Allgemeine Deutsche Biographie,* Leipzig 1896, XL, 672.

¹¹ Anna de Lagarde, *op. cit.,* pp. 12–13.

¹² Lagarde, "Über einige Berliner Theologen und was von ihnen zu lernen ist," *A.S.,* p. 75.

¹³ On this damaging episode in Lagarde's career, see Rahlfs, *op. cit.,* pp. 38–39 and 95–97 and Helmuth M. Pölcher, ed., "Symphilologein. Briefe von Paul de Lagarde an Adolf Hilgenfeld aus den Jahren 1862–1887," in *Lebendiger Geist. Hans-Joachim Schoeps zum 50. Geburtstag von Schülern dargebracht,* ed. by Hellmut Diwald, Leiden-Köln 1959, pp. 24–26.

¹⁴ For Bunsen's exceptionally close ties to English intellectual life, see Dr. Wilma Höcker, *Der Gesandte Bunsen als Vermittler zwischen Deutschland und England,* Göttingen, Musterschmidt, 1951, esp. pp. 99–147.

¹⁵ Anna de Lagarde, *op. cit.,* p. 25.

¹⁶ *Ibid.,* pp. 42–43.

¹⁷ Lagarde, "Nachrichten über einige Familien des Namens Bötticher," *A.S.,* pp. 24–31.

¹⁸ Rahlfs, *op. cit.,* p. 16.

¹⁹ Pölcher, *op. cit.,* p. 31.

²⁰ As an example of this sense of conspiracy, see the introduction to Lagarde's *Symmicta,* Göttingen 1880, II, iii–viii.

²¹ Quoted in Schemann, *op. cit.,* p. 132.

²² *Ibid.,* p. 132.

²³ Paul de Lagarde, *Aus dem deutschen Gelehrtenleben,* Göttingen 1880, p. 6.

²⁴ George F. Moore, "Paul Anton de Lagarde," *University Quarterly,* XVI:4 (July, 1893), 19.

²⁵ Schemann, *op. cit.,* p. 50. Lagarde's one-time student, Alfred Rahlfs, also maintained that the general opinion of Lagarde as a querulous man could not have gained credence without his help.

²⁶ G. Nathanael Bonwetsch, "Aus vierzig Jahren deutscher Kirchengeschichte. Briefe an E. W. Hengstenberg," *Beiträge zur Förderung christlicher Theologie,* 2d series, XXIV:2 (Gütersloh 1919), 5–6.

²⁷ Rahlfs, *op. cit.,* p. 60.

²⁸ Lagarde, *Gelehrtenleben,* p. 80, and pp. 73–86 *passim.*

²⁹ Anna de Lagarde, *op. cit.,* pp. 76–78.

³⁰ Pölcher, *op. cit.,* p. 28.

³¹ Anna de Lagarde, *op. cit.,* p. 84.

³² Andrew L. Drummond, *German Protestantism since Luther,* London 1951, p. 134.

³³ Lagarde, "Bescheinigung über den richtigen Empfang eines von Herrn Otto Ritschl an mich gerichteten offenen Briefes," *A.S.,* pp. 267–301. On the conflict between Ritschl and Lagarde, see also Götz von Selle, *Die Georg-August-Universität zu Göttingen 1737–1937,* Göttingen, Vandenhoeck & Ruprecht, 1937, pp. 318–323.

³⁴ Copy of Lagarde letter to King William I, September 4, 1870, in Lagarde Archive.

³⁵ *L'Allemagne aux Tuileries de 1850 à 1870,* ed. by Henri Bordier, Paris 1872, pp. 36–37.

³⁶ Anna de Lagarde, *op. cit.,* pp. 96–103.

³⁷ Paul de Lagarde, "Drei Vorreden" (1878), *Deutsche Schriften,* 3d ed., München 1937, pp. 93–94. Cited hereafter as *D.S.* The first time a particular essay is cited, its date of composition will be given.

³⁸ His plan will be discussed below. In the recent *Festschrift zur Feier des zweihundertjährigen Bestehens der Akademie der Wissenschaften in Göttingen,* Berlin, Springer, 1951, II, xiii, Rudolf Smend praised Lagarde's "opinions on the reform of the Society . . . which despite the mixture of the significant and the trivial, the utopian and the exact, diagnosed the feebleness of the patient."

³⁹ Schemann, *op. cit.,* pp. 81–82.

⁴⁰ Rahlfs, *op. cit.,* p. 70.

⁴¹ *Ibid.,* pp. 78–79.

⁴² *A.S.,* pp. 187–188.

⁴³ *Ibid.,* p. 190.

⁴⁴ Paul de Lagarde, *Die königliche Gesellschaft der Wissenschaften in Göttingen betreffend. Ein zweites und letztes Gutachten,* Göttingen 1889, p. 4.

⁴⁵ Schemann, *op. cit.,* p. 369.

⁴⁶ Richard J. H. Gottheil, "Bibliography of the Works of Paul de Lagarde," *Proceedings of the American Oriental Society,* XV (April, 1892), ccxi–ccxxix.

⁴⁷ S. R. Driver, "Recent Literature Relating to the Old Testament," in *The Contemporary Review,* LV (March, 1889), 393–394. He listed fourteen recent publications by Lagarde and reviewed all but one: a polemic on "Jewish Pedantry."

⁴⁸ Ulrich von Wilamowitz-Moellendorf, *Reden und Vorträge,* Berlin, Weidmann, 1901, pp. 90–96.

⁴⁹ *Mommsen und Wilamowitz Briefwechsel, 1872–1903,* ed. by F. and D. Hiller von Gaertringen, Berlin, Weidmann, 1935, pp. 452–453. Letters of December 28, 1891, and of January 5, 1892. The correspondence between the two scholars, the younger of whom was an ardent nationalist, offers valuable insights into the German academic scene. See also Ulrich von Wilamowitz-Moellendorff, *My*

Recollections, 1848–1914, transl. by G. C. Richards, London, Chatto and Windus, 1930, pp. 277–283.

[50] William James, *The Principles of Psychology,* New York, Holt, 1893, I, 310–311.

[51] Anna de Lagarde, *op. cit.,* p. 125.

[52] Lagarde, *Gedichte,* Göttingen 1885, and *Gedichte von Paul de Lagarde. Gesamtausgabe besorgt von Anna de Lagarde,* 2d enlarged ed., Göttingen 1911.

[53] Karl Ernst Knodt, "Paul de Lagarde, der Dichter. Eine literarische Studie," *Monatsblätter für Deutsche Literatur,* IV:1 (October 1899), 132.

Chapter 2

(Pp. 27–34)

[1] Lagarde, "Über das Verhältnis des deutschen Staates zu Theologie, Kirche und Religion. Ein Versuch, nicht Theologen zu orientieren" (1873), *DS,* p. 82, and "Zum Unterrichtsgesetze" (1878), *DS,* p. 221.

[2] Anna de Lagarde, *Erinnerungen,* p. 38.

[3] Lagarde, "Konservativ?" (1853), *DS,* p. 10, and "Die Reorganization des Adels" (1881), *DS,* p. 333.

[4] Lagarde, "Noch einmal zum Unterrichtsgesetze" (1881), *DS,* p. 325.

[5] Lagarde, "Zum Unterrichtsgesetze" *DS,* p. 201.

[6] Lagarde, "Die Reorganisation des Adels" *DS,* p. 333.

[7] Lagarde, "Über die gegenwärtigen Aufgaben der deutschen Politik" (1853), *DS,* p. 29.

[8] Quoted in Anna de Lagarde, *op. cit.,* p. 163.

[9] *Ibid.,* p. 164.

[10] See Georg Steinhausen, *Deutsche Geistes- und Kulturgeschichte von 1870 bis zur Gegenwart,* Halle 1931, pp. 17–61 and pp. 305–399 for a documentation of this general type of criticism in pre-1914 German thought.

[11] Lagarde, "Die Reorganisation des Adels," *DS,* p. 334.

[12] Lagarde, "Über die Klage, dass der deutschen Jugend der Idealismus fehle" (1885), *DS,* p. 439.

[13] Lagarde, "Über die gegenwärtige Lage des deutschen Reichs" (1875), *DS,* p. 184.

Chapter 3

(Pp. 35–52)

1 Lagarde, *Mittheilungen*, Göttingen 1887, II, 256.
2 Lagarde, *A.S.* p. 41.
3 *Ibid.*, p. 28.
4 Lagarde, *Mittheilungen*, II, 75.
5 Lagarde, "Die Religion der Zukunft" (1878), *D.S.*, p. 267.
6 Lagarde, "Über das Verhältnis des deutschen Staates zu Theologie, Kirche und Religion. Ein Versuch, nicht Theologen zu orientieren," *D.S.*, p. 69.
7 *Ibid.*, p. 67.
8 Lagarde, "Über die gegenwärtigen Aufgaben der deutschen Politik," *D.S.*, p. 30.
9 Lagarde, *A.S.* p. 93.
10 Lagarde, "Über das Verhältnis des deutschen Staates," *D.S.*, p. 54.
11 Lagarde, *A.S.*, p. 293.
12 *Ibid.*, p. 292.
13 Lagarde, "Über das Verhältnis des deutschen Staates," *D.S.*, p. 57.
14 Lagarde, *A.S.*, p. 98.
15 Lagarde, "Konservativ," *D.S.*, p. 18.
16 Lagarde, *A.S.*, pp. 97–98.
17 Lagarde, *Die königliche Gesellschaft*, p. 4.
18 Lagarde, "Über das Verhältnis des deutschen Staates," *D.S.*, p. 57.
19 *Ibid.*
20 *Ibid.*, p. 62.
21 Lagarde, *A.S.*, p. 192.
22 Lagarde, "Die Stellung der Religionsgesellschaften im Staate" (1881), *D.S.*, p. 300.
23 Lagarde, "Über die gegenwärtige Lage des deutschen Reichs," *D.S.*, p. 158.
24 Lagarde, "Die Religion der Zukunft," *D.S.*, pp. 251–286.
25 *Ibid.*, p. 270.
26 *Ibid.*, p. 273.
27 *Ibid.*, p. 278.
28 *Ibid.*, p. 276.
29 *Ibid.*, p. 274.
30 *Ibid.*, p. 286.
31 *Jakob Burckhardts Briefe an seinen Freund Friedrich von*

Preen, 1864–1893, ed. by Emil Strauss, Stuttgart and Berlin, Deutsche Verlagsanstalt, 1922, letter of July 3, 1870, p. 18.

[32] G. B. Shaw, *Androcles and the Lion,* New York 1919, p. cxxv.

[33] Lagarde, "Über das Verhältnis des deutschen Staates," *D.S.,* p. 79.

[34] Lagarde, "Die Religion der Zukunft," *D.S.,* p. 286.

Chapter 4

(Pp. 53–70)

[1] As quoted in Erich Brandenburg, *Die Reichsgründung,* 2d ed., Leipzig, Quelle und Meyer, n.d. (1922?), I, 362.

[2] See the comprehensive survey of the thought of "The Reactionary Fifties," in William O. Shanahan's *German Protestants Face the Social Question,* Vol. I: *The Conservative Phase 1815–1871,* Notre Dame, Indiana, 1954, chapter 6, and the illuminating comments in Theodore S. Hamerow, *Restoration Revolution Reaction. Economics and Politics in Germany 1815–1871,* Princeton 1958, chapter 11.

[3] Lagarde, "Über die gegenwärtigen Aufgaben der deutschen Politik," *D.S.,* p. 33.

[4] Quoted in Schemann, *Paul de Lagarde,* p. 79.

[5] Lagarde, "Die nächsten Pflichten deutscher Politik" (1886), *D.S.,* pp. 473–475.

[6] Lagarde, "Über die gegenwärtige Lage des deutschen Reichs," *D.S.,* pp. 136–140.

[7] Lagarde, "Programm für die konservative Partei Preussens," *D.S.,* pp. 418–419.

[8] *Ibid.,* p. 375.

[9] Lagarde, "Konservativ?" *D.S.,* pp. 9–21. The idea of a new gentry is fully developed in "Die Reorganisation des Adels," *D.S.,* pp. 326–333.

[10] See Eugene N. Anderson, *The Social and Political Conflict in Prussia 1858–1864,* Lincoln 1954, chapter 2, esp. pp. 20–22.

[11] Lagarde, "Die Reorganisation des Adels," *D.S.,* pp. 326–327.

[12] "Programm für die konservative Partei Preussens," *D.S.,* pp. 421–422.

[13] "Über die gegenwärtigen Aufgaben der deutschen Politik," *D.S.,* p. 41.

[14] *A.S.,* p. 223.

[15] "Über die gegenwärtigen Aufgaben der deutschen Politik," *D.S.,* p. 30.

[16] "Die Stellung der Religionsgesellschaften im Staate," *D.S.,* p. 295.

[17] *A.S.,* p. 248.

[18] *Ibid.,* p. 239.

19 On this subject, see the useful monograph by S. Adler-Rudel, *Ostjuden in Deutschland 1880–1940. Zugleich eine Geschichte der Organisationen, die sie betreuten,* Tübingen, Mohr, 1959.

20 See, for example, the pertinent statistics in Bernard D. Weinryb, "The Economic and Social Background of Modern Antisemitism" in *Essays on Antisemitism,* ed. by Koppel S. Pinson, New York, Conference on Jewish Relations, 1946, pp. 17–34.

21 Lagarde, "Die graue Internationale" (1881), *D.S.,* p. 370.

22 *Ibid.,* p. 358.

23 Lagarde, "Konservativ?" and "Die Religion der Zukunft," *D.S.,* pp. 20 and 283.

24 Lagarde, "Noch einmal zum Unterrichtsgesetze," *D.S.,* p. 318.

25 Schemann, *op. cit.,* p. 216.

26 Henry Cord Meyer, in his excellent study, *Mitteleuropa in German Thought and Action 1815–1945,* The Hague 1955, pp. 30–33, considers Lagarde as the most important *Mitteleuropa* proponent at a time when this sentiment was rapidly waning.

27 Lagarde, "Über die gegenwärtigen Aufgaben der deutschen Politik," *D.S.,* pp. 33–34.

28 *Ibid.,* pp. 30–35.

29 *Ibid.,* p. 37.

30 *A.S.,* p. 245.

31 "Über die gegenwärtige Lage des deutschen Reichs," *D.S.,* p. 129.

32 "Die nächsten Pflichten deutscher Politik," *D.S.,* pp. 449–450.

33 "Über die gegenwärtige Lage des deutschen Reichs," *D.S.,* p. 116.

34 "Die nächsten Pflichten deutscher Politik," *D.S.,* pp. 442–481.

35 Lagarde, "Die Finanzpolitik Deutschlands" (1881), *D.S.,* p. 355.

Chapter 5

(Pp. 71–81)

1 Lagarde, "Noch einmal zum Unterrichtsgesetze," *D.S.,* p. 312.

2 *A.S.,* p. 141.

3 *Ibid.,* p. 181.

4 For a summary of "The Criticisms and Satire of Academic Culture," see Frederic Lilge, *The Abuse of Learning. The Failure of the German Universities,* New York 1948, chapter 4. See also Karl Löwith, *Von Hegel zu Nietzsche. Der revolutionäre Bruch im Denken des Neunzehnten Jahrhunderts. Marx und Kierkegaard,* Stuttgart 1950, 2d printing, pp. 312–326.

5 It should be noted that while Nietzsche and Lagarde offered a sweeping indictment of German education, a host of teachers and

publicists demanded minor reforms within the existing system. These are discussed in Friedrich Paulsen, *Geschichte des gelehrten Unterrichts,* 3d ed., Berlin and Leipzig 1921, II, 362–389.

6 Anna de Lagarde, *Erinnerungen,* p. 110.

7 Lagarde, "Diagnose," *D.S.,* p. 109.

8 "Zum Unterrichtsgesetze," *D.S.,* p. 198.

9 "Über die gegenwärtige Lage des deutschen Reichs," *D.S.,* pp. 148–149.

10 On the Prussian *Gymnasium,* see the short summary in Franz Schnabel's *Deutsche Geschichte im Neunzehnten Jahrhundert,* Vol. II: *Monarchie und Volkssouveränität,* 2d ed., Freiburg im Breisgau 1949, pp. 342–354.

11 Quoted in Edward H. Reisner, *Nationalism and Education since 1789. A Social and Political History of Modern Education,* New York 1923, p. 145.

12 Lagarde, "Über das Verhältnis des deutschen Staates," *D.S.,* p. 84.

13 "Die graue Internationale," *D.S.,* p. 365.

14 "Zum Unterrichtsgesetze," *D.S.,* p. 198.

15 *A.S.,* p. 125.

16 "Die Religion der Zukunft," *D.S.,* p. 284.

17 *A.S.,* p. 103.

18 "Über die gegenwärtige Lage des deutschen Reichs," *D.S.,* p. 181.

19 "Zum Unterrichtsgesetze," *D.S.,* p. 237.

20 "Noch einmal zum Unterrichtsgesetze," *D.S.,* p. 322.

21 "Zum Unterrichtsgesetze," *D.S.,* p. 233.

22 Lagarde, *Die königliche Gesellschaft der Wissenschaften in Göttingen betreffend. Ein zweites und letztes Gutachten,* Göttingen 1889, p. 6.

Chapter 6

(Pp. 82–94)

1 Thomas Carlyle to Lagarde, May 20, 1875, Lagarde Archive, Göttingen.

2 Ludwig Curtius, for example, writes that he devoured Lagarde's *Deutsche Schriften* one night in Rome, just before the end of the century, and "from then on I remained faithful to it." *Deutsche und Antike Welt. Lebenserinnerungen,* Stuttgart, Deutsche Verlagsanstalt, 1950, pp. 175–176. See also Richard Dehmel, *Lebensblätter. Gedichte und Anderes,* Berlin, Genossenschaft Pan, 1895, pp. 19 and 27.

[3] Thomas Mann, *Betrachtungen eines Unpolitischen*, Berlin 1919, p. 262.

[4] *Ibid.*, pp. 260–263. The phrase that democracy was "present only in the press" was taken from Richard Wagner's "Was ist Deutsch?" *Gesammelte Schriften und Dichtungen von Richard Wagner*, 3d ed., Leipzig, Fritzsch, 1898, X, 50.

[5] Ernst Troeltsch, *Gesammelte Schriften*, Vol. II: *Zur religiösen Lage, Religionsphilosophie und Ethik*, Tübingen 1913, pp. 20–21.

[6] Ludwig Schemann, "Paul de Lagarde. Ein Nachruf," *Bayreuther Blätter*, XV: 6 (June, 1892), 185–210. See also Adolph Wahrmund, "Paul de Lagarde," in *ibid.*, pp. 210–222.

[7] Houston Stewart Chamberlain, *Die Grundlagen des neunzehnten Jahrhunderts*, 5th ed., München 1904, p. lxii.

[8] See, in particular, Friedrich Lange, *Reines Deutschtum. Grundzüge einer nationalen Weltanschauung*, Berlin 1894, and Theodor Fritsch, *Antisemiten-Katechismus*, 17th ed., Leipzig 1892.

[9] Lagarde's correspondence with these and other professional anti-Semites can be found in the Lagarde Archive, Göttingen.

[10] Adolf Bartels, *Der völkische Gedanke. Ein Wegweiser*, Weimar 1923, p. 23.

[11] See below, pp. 176–180, on the German Youth Movement; on Lagarde's influence on the Youth Movement, see Else Frobenius, *Mit uns zieht die neue Zeit. Eine Geschichte der deutschen Jugendbewegung*, Berlin 1927, pp. 32 and 415, and Mario Domandi, "The German Youth Movement," Columbia University doctoral dissertation, Department of History, 1960, *passim*.

[12] Adolf Rapp, *Der deutsche Gedanke: Seine Entwicklung im politischen und geistigen Leben seit dem 18. Jahrhundert*, Bonn 1920, p. 328.

[13] See Hans Buchheim, *Glaubenskrise im Dritten Reich. Drei Kapitel nationalsozialistischer Religionspolitik*, Stuttgart 1953, pp. 45 ff.

[14] Lagarde certainly played a significant role in the development of the Pan-German ideology; therefore Charles Andler rightly included him in his collection, *Les Origines du Pangermanisme (1800 à 1888)*, ed. by Charles Andler, Paris 1915, pp. 231–263.

[15] On this subject, see the excellent article by Felix Gilbert, "Mitteleuropa—The Final Stage," *Journal of Central European Affairs*, VII:1 (April, 1947), 58–67, and also Henry Cord Meyer's *Mitteleuropa*, *passim*.

[16] Wilhelm Hartmann, *Paul de Lagarde, ein Prophet deutschen Christentums. Seine theologische Stellung, Religionsanschauung und Frömmigkeit*, Halle 1933, p. 10.

[17] Alfred Rosenberg, *Der Mythus des 20. Jahrhunderts. Eine Wertung der seelisch-geistigen Gestaltenkämpfe unserer Zeit*, 25th-26th printing, München 1934, p. 457.

Chapter 7

(Pp. 97–115)

[1] The main biographical source is a panegyric by Langbehn's avowed friend and disciple, Benedikt Momme Nissen, *Der Rembrandtdeutsche Julius Langbehn,* Freiburg im Breisgau 1927. Shorter and less biased works are cited below. A German psychiatrist wrote a "pathopsychological" analysis of Langbehn's work and character as a contribution to clinical psychiatry. Hans Bürger-Prinz and Annemarie Segelke, *Julius Langbehn der Rembrandtdeutsche. Eine pathopsychologische Studie,* Leipzig 1940.

[2] See Lawrence D. Steefel, *The Schleswig-Holstein Question,* Cambridge (Mass.), Harvard University Press, 1932, chapter 1, for a guide to the political maze of these troubled provinces.

[3] Quoted in Nissen, *op. cit.,* p. 18.

[4] *Ibid.,* p. 22.

[5] *Ibid.,* p. 24.

[6] Julius Langbehn, *Flügelgestalten der ältesten griechischen Kunst,* München 1880.

[7] Hermann Brunn, "Julius Langbehn, Karl Haider, Heinrich von Brunn," *Deutsche Rundschau,* CCXVIII (January, 1929), 22.

[8] *Ibid.,* p. 32.

[9] Quoted in Nissen, *op. cit.,* p. 52.

[10] Cornelius Gurlitt, "Der Rembrandtdeutsche," *Die Zukunft,* LXIX (December 18, 1909), 371.

[11] Nissen, *op. cit.,* p. 50.

[12] *Ibid.,* p. 54.

[13] Cornelius Gurlitt, "Der Rembrandtdeutsche," *Die Zukunft,* LXII (February 1, 1908), 143.

[14] *Ibid.,* p. 142.

[15] Cornelius Gurlitt, "Der Rembrandtdeutsche," *Westermanns Monatshefte,* LV: 2 (July, 1911), 681–682.

[16] Letter of Langbehn to Lagarde, December 12, 1887, Lagarde Archive.

[17] Letter of Langbehn to Anna de Lagarde, April 9, 1889, Lagarde Archive.

[18] Hermann Brunn, *op. cit.,* p. 21.

[19] Hermann E. Busse, ed., *Hans Thoma. Sein Leben in Selbstzeugnissen Briefen und Berichten,* Berlin, Propyläen-Verlag, 1942, pp. 134–143.

[20] From a letter of 1883, quoted in Nissen, *op. cit.,* pp. 89–90.

[21] Frau Forster Nietzsche, *The Life of Nietzsche,* Vol. II: *The Lonely Nietzsche,* New York, Sturgis & Walton, 1915, p. 395. A more

thorough and far more critical study of Langbehn's intervention may be found in Erich F. Podach, *Gestalten um Nietzsche, mit unveröffentlichen Dokumenten zur Geschichte seines Lebens und seines Werks,* Weimar, Lichtenstein, 1932, pp. 177–199.

[22] Carl Albrecht Bernoulli, *Franz Overbeck und Friedrich Nietzsche. Eine Freundschaft,* Jena 1908, II, 318.

[23] Liselotte Ilschner, *Rembrandt als Erzieher und seine Bedeutung. Studie über die kulturelle Struktur der neunziger Jahre,* Danzig n.d. (1928?), p. 78. This monograph has also appeared under the name of Liselotte Voss.

[24] *40 Lieder. Von einem Deutschen.* Dresden, Glöss, 1891. A selected, expurgated edition of these poems appeared posthumously, *Langbehns Lieder,* ed. by Benedikt Momme Nissen, München n.d. (1931?). For a critical review of Nissen's benevolent censorship and of the poems themselves, see Josef Hofmiller, "Der Rembrandt-Deutsche als Dichter," *Süddeutsche Monatshefte,* XXVIII: 11 (August, 1931), 819–821. Two of the explicitly erotic poems are reproduced in Podach, *Gestalten um Nietzsche,* p. 177. Some of the poems are reprinted and analyzed in Hans Bürger-Prinz's "Über die künstlerischen Arbeiten Schizophrener," in Oswald Bumke, ed., *Handbuch der Geisteskrankheiten,* Vol. IX, part v, *Die Schizophrenie,* ed. by K. Wilmanns, Berlin 1932, pp. 685–690.

[25] Cornelius Gurlitt, "Langbehn, der Rembrandtdeutsche," *Protestantische Studien,* No. 9 (Berlin 1927), p. 87.

[26] Nissen, *op. cit.,* p. 177.

[27] *Ibid.,* p. 187.

[28] *Ibid.,* p. 207.

[29] *Ibid.,* pp. 296–298.

[30] *Langbehn-Briefe an Bischof Keppler,* ed. by Benedikt Momme Nissen, Freiburg im Breisgau 1937, letter of December 28, 1901, p. 39.

[31] Paul Wilhelm von Keppler, *Wahre und Falsche Reform,* 3d ed., Freiburg im Breisgau 1903; see p. i for Cardinal Rampolla's letter conveying Pope Leo XIII's approval.

[32] Bishop Keppler's introduction to Nissen, *op. cit.,* p. 7.

[33] *Langbehn-Briefe,* ed. by Nissen; letter of July 1901, p. 37.

[34] The initial controversy was conducted by the Catholic *Hochland* and Harden's *Zukunft.* In 1908, Cornelius Gurlitt began publishing some of his recollections of Langbehn in *Die Zukunft,* not knowing that he had died. Heinrich Vorwald, "Neues über den Rembrandt-Deutschen," *Hochland,* VI: 1 (October, 1908), 126–127, revealed how he had discovered, by chance, that Langbehn had been converted to Catholicism in Rotterdam. E. M. Roloff, "Julius Langbehn, der Rembrandt-Deutsche," *Hochland,* VII: 8 (May, 1910), 206–213, divulged that Langbehn had in fact died, and he described the improbable circumstances which had led him to

Langbehn's unmarked grave. Gurlitt, in turn, gratuitously questioned the authenticity of this report, and an acrimonious exchange, soon joined by others, ensued.

Chapter 8

(Pp. 116–136)

[1] *Rembrandt als Erzieher. Von einem Deutschen,* 33d ed. Leipzig 1891, p. 300. This edition is hereafter cited as *Rembrandt.*

[2] The pejorative use of *Weltanschauung* is largely due to National Socialist usage. Before its recent vulgarization, the term had philosophical respectability; cf. Wilhelm Dilthey, *Gesammelte Schriften,* Vol. VIII: *Weltanschauungslehre. Abhandlungen zur Philosophie der Philosophie,* Leipzig, Teubner, 1931, and as relevant to this study, a brief dialogue, "Der moderne Mensch und der Streit der Weltanschauungen," 1904, pp. 225–233. See also Karl Joël, *Wandlungen der Weltanschauung. Eine Philosophiegeschichte als Geschichtsphilosophie,* Tübingen, Mohr, 1934, II, 747–947, for a critique of the major *Weltanschauungen* since the mid-nineteenth century.

[3] *Rembrandt,* p. 1.

[4] *Ibid.,* p. 60.

[5] Franz Schnabel, *Deutsche Geschichte im neunzehnten Jahrhundert,* Vol. III: *Erfahrungswissenschaften und Technik,* 2d ed., Freiburg im Breisgau 1950, p. 199.

[6] Jacques Barzun, *Darwin, Marx, Wagner. Critique of a Heritage,* Boston 1941, pp. 110–137, and chapter 5, identifies this movement in its late nineteenth-century cultural setting. See also Richard von Mises, *Kleines Lehrbuch des Positivismus. Einführung in die empiristische Wissenschaftsauffassung,* The Hague, Stockum and Zoon, 1939, pp. 46–61 for a critical summary of the "anti-scientific" philosophy: *"The present age is dominated by ideas which we have defined as negativistic and which aim to assign a subordinate, even pernicious role to Reason and which expect salvation from fundamentally different qualities, such as instinct and sentiment"* (p. 61, italics in original). A more detailed treatment may be found in Professor Aliotta, *The Idealistic Reaction Against Science,* transl. by Agnes McCaskill, London 1914.

[7] *Rembrandt,* p. 187.

[8] *Ibid.,* p. 67.

[9] *Ibid.,* p. 70.

[10] *Ibid.,* p. 58.

[11] *Ibid.,* p. 184.

[12] *Ibid.,* p. 96.

[13] *Ibid.,* p. 290.

[14] *Ibid.*, p. 328.

[15] *Ibid.*, p. 302.

[16] *Rembrandt als Erzieher*, von einem Deutschen, 49th ed., Leipzig 1909, p. 312. This edition is hereafter cited as *Rembrandt*, 49th ed.

[17] *Rembrandt*, pp. 315–316.

[18] On Heroic Vitalism, see Eric Russell Bentley, *A Century of Hero-Worship*, Philadelphia 1944, esp. pp. 205–230 and Part V.

[19] *Rembrandt*, pp. 288 and 317.

[20] Julius Langbehn, *Der Geist des Ganzen*, ed. by Benedikt Momme Nissen, Freiburg im Breisgau 1930, p. 77. This is a collection of Langbehn's literary remains, ordered and embodied in a book by his old disciple.

[21] *Rembrandt*, p. 329.

[22] *Ibid.*, p. 308.

[23] *Ibid.*, p. 268.

[24] *Ibid.*, p. 269.

[25] *Ibid.*, pp. 323–327 and *passim*; for the important literary controversy in Germany concerning Zola, see the pedestrian account of Winthrop H. Root, *German Criticism of Zola 1875–1893*, New York, Columbia University Press, 1931, which discusses Langbehn's critique, pp. 88 ff.

[26] *Rembrandt*, p. 209.

[27] *Ibid.*, p. 201.

[28] *Ibid.*, p. 255.

[29] The impact of Langbehn's book will be discussed in Chapter 10; its influence on the art-education movement headed by Avenarius and Lichtwark is discussed in Konrad Lange, *Die künstlerische Erziehung der deutschen Jugend*, Darmstadt 1893, which takes Langbehn's book as a point of departure.

[30] *Rembrandt*, p. 216.

[31] *Ibid.*, p. 37.

Chapter 9

(Pp. 137–152)

[1] Ziegler speaks of the "estheticizing of the idea of power" in Friedrich Naumann's thought. See Theodor Ziegler, *Die geistigen und sozialen Strömungen Deutschlands im neunzehnten Jahrhundert*, Berlin 1911, p. 512.

[2] *Rembrandt*, p. 120.

[3] *Ibid.*, p. 119. Cf. Hans Naumann, *Die deutsche Dichtung der Gegenwart 1885–1923*, Stuttgart 1923, esp. pp. 8–11, for the naturalists' credo concerning the relation of milieu and character.

[4] *Rembrandt*, p. 182.

[5] *Ibid.*, p. 284.

[6] *Der Rembrandtdeutsche. Von einem Wahrheitsfreund,* Dresden 1892, p. 184.

[7] *Rembrandt,* 49th ed., p. 352.

[8] *Ibid.,* p. 317.

[9] The literature on German anti-Semitism before 1914 is already large and is still growing. Among the best studies are Paul W. Massing, *Rehearsal for Destruction. A Study of Political Anti-Semitism in Imperial Germany,* New York 1949; Eva G. Reichmann, *Hostages of Civilisation. The Social Sources of National Socialist Anti-Semitism,* Boston 1951. See also the relevant parts of Hannah Arendt's *The Origins of Totalitarianism,* New York 1951; and Adolf Leschnitzer, *The Magic Background of Modern Anti-Semitism. An Analysis of the German-Jewish Relationship,* New York, International Universities Press, 1956; the short essay by Waldemar Gurian, "Antisemitism in Modern Germany," in *Essays on Antisemitism,* ed. by Koppel Pinson, New York, Conference on Jewish Relations, 1946, and Kurt Wawrzinek, "Die Entstehung der deutschen Antisemitenparteien 1873–1890," *Historische Studien,* No. 168, Berlin 1927. None of these studies sufficiently emphasizes the role of cultural discontent and antimodernity as an important source of anti-Semitism.

[10] *Rembrandt,* p. 310.

[11] *Ibid.,* p. 312.

[12] *Ibid.,* p. 186.

[13] *Ibid.,* p. 175.

[14] *Rembrandt,* 49th ed., pp. 327–331.

[15] *Der Rembrandtdeutsche. Von einem Wahrheitsfreund,* Dresden 1892, p. 127.

[16] *Rembrandt,* p. 153.

[17] *Ibid.,* p. 152.

[18] Langbehn, *Geist des Ganzen,* p. 33.

[19] *Rembrandt,* p. 154.

[20] *Ibid.,* p. 227.

[21] *Ibid.,* p. 262.

[22] *Ibid.,* p. 158.

[23] *Ibid.,* p. 271.

[24] *Ibid.,* p. 274.

[25] *Ibid.,* pp. 230–233.

[26] Cf. Charles Andler, ed., *Le Pangermanisme philosophique (1800 à 1914),* Paris 1917, pp. 188 and 190–239 for selections from Langbehn's writings.

Chapter 10

(Pp. 153–180)

[1] The advertisers' slogan was quoted in Leo Berg, "Monsieur Chauvin als Philosoph," *Zwischen zwei Jahrhunderten. Gesammelte Essays*, Frankfurt am Main 1896, p. 434; Berg's article, a spirited attack on the Rembrandt book, first appeared in 1890.

[2] "Rembrandt als Erzieher," *Börsenblatt für den Deutschen Buchhandel* (May 25, 1926), pp. 661–662. *Rembrandt als Erzieher*, new revised ed. by Momme Nissen, 61st–84th printing, Hirschfeld, Leipzig 1925–1928; 85th–90th printing, W. Kohlhammer-Verlag, Stuttgart 1938; also *Illustrierte Volksausgabe*, ed. by H. Kellermann, 1st–31st printing, Duncker, Weimar 1922–1944; also *Rembrandt als Erzieher*, ed. by Gerhard Krüger—with a fierce polemic against Nissen's earlier and different edition—Fritsch, Berlin 1944. See C. G. Kayser's *Bücher-Lexicon*, vol. 26, Leipzig 1891, and subsequent volumes, as well as a letter to me dated April 8, 1959, from W. Kohlhammer, Stuttgart. This large circulation accounts for the fact that a second-hand copy of *Rembrandt als Erzieher* today costs less than the original book.

[3] Herbert Cysarz, *Von Schiller zu Nietzsche. Hauptfragen der Dichtungs- und Bildungsgeschichte des jüngsten Jahrhunderts*, Halle 1928, p. 361.

[4] H. Stuart Hughes, *Oswald Spengler. A Critical Estimate*, New York 1952, p. 89.

[5] Frederic Lilge, *The Abuse of Learning. The Failure of the German University*, New York 1948, p. 112.

[6] Quoted in Nissen, *Der Rembrandtdeutsche*, p. 126.

[7] For a detailed study of the book's critical reception, though a study biased in favor of Langbehn, see *Rembrandt als Erzieher und seine Bedeutung. Studie über die kulturelle Struktur der neunziger Jahre*, Danzig n.d. (1928?), esp. pp. 55–74.

[8] See, for example, such unsparing parodies as *Höllenbreughel als Erzieher. Auch von einem Deutschen*, 4th ed., Leipzig, Reissner, 1890; *Billige Weisheit*, Leipzig 1890; *Goethe als Hemmschuh*, Berlin 1892. Among the many admiring tracts were Heinrich Pudor, *Ein ernstes Wort über Rembrandt als Erzieher*, Göttingen 1890, and Max Bewer, *Bei Bismarck*, Dresden 1891.

[9] *Kladderadatsch*, XLIII:30 (July 13, 1890).

[10] Quoted in Ilschner, *op. cit.*, p. 63.

[11] "Vom Zeitalter deutscher Kunst," *Der Kunstwart*, III:12 (March 18, 1890), 177–179.

[12] *Die Kunst für Alle*, V:13 (April 1, 1890), 193–197.

13 "Kritik," *Die Gesellschaft,* No. 5 (May, 1890), p. 767.

14 W. Bode, "Rembrandt als Erzieher von einem Deutschen," *Preussische Jahrbücher,* LXV:3 (March, 1890), 301–314.

15 Georg Brandes, "Rembrandt als Erzieher," *Freie Bühne für Modernes Leben,* Berlin, I:14 (May 7, 1890), 390–392.

16 Maximilian Harden, "Rembrandt als Erzieher," *Das Magazin für die Litteratur des In- und Auslandes,* LIX:27 (July 5, 1890), 417–421.

17 Johannes Proelss, "Rembrandt als Erzieher. Ideen eines niederdeutschen Idealisten," *Die Gartenlaube,* No. 12 (1890), pp. 382–386.

18 Otto Seeck, "Zeitphrasen," *Deutsche Rundschau,* LXVII (June, 1891), 407–421; LXVIII (July, 1891), 86–104; LXIX (August, 1891), 230–240.

19 Leo Berg, *op. cit.,* p. 444.

20 Nissen, *op. cit.,* pp. 139, 147.

21 Anonymous, "Ein nationalpädagogischer Versuch," *Historisch-politische Blätter für das katholische Deutschland,* CVI (1890), 266–288.

22 Anonymous, " 'Rembrandt als Erzieher.' Zur 37. Auflage nocheinmal," *Historisch-politische Blätter für das katholische Deutschland,* CVIII (1891), 900–910.

23 Anonymous, "Der Rembrandtdeutsche," *Historisch-politische Blätter für das katholische Deutschland,* CXI (1893), 48–56.

24 A. Baumgartner, S. J., "Rembrandt als Erzieher," *Stimmen aus Maria-Laach: Katholische Blätter,* XL (1891), 86–104.

25 Adolf Rapp, *Der deutsche Gedanke. Seine Entwicklung im politischen und geistigen Leben seit dem 18. Jahrhundert,* Bonn 1920, p. 295.

26 Paul Weiglin, "Fin de siècle," *Deutsche Rundschau,* LXXVIII:11 (November, 1952), 1128.

27 Rapp, *op. cit.,* p. 295, and for a detailed history of the "Germanic Movement" in the 1890's, pp. 295–336; for the organizations of the "Germanic Movement," see also Philipp Stauff, *Das Deutsche Wehrbuch,* Wittenberg 1912, and Fr. Guntram Schultheiss, "Deutschnationales Vereinswesen. Ein Beitrag zur Geschichte des deutschen Nationalgefühls," in *Der Kampf um das Deutschtum,* München 1897.

28 See Friedrich Lange's best known work, *Reines Deutschtum,* 4th ed., Berlin 1904, pp. 351–353. See p. 40 for his appreciation of Langbehn.

29 F. Greiffenrath, "Bischof von Ketteler und die deutsche Sozialreform," *Frankfurter zeitgemässe Broschüren,* 1893, pp. 363 ff., as quoted in Nissen, *op. cit.,* p. 125.

30 Alfred Kruck, *Geschichte des Alldeutschen Verbandes 1890–1939,* Wiesbaden 1954, p. 10. Kruck attributes far more importance to the Pan-Germans than either Mildred S. Wertheimer, *The Pan-*

German League 1890–1914, New York 1924, or Lothar Werner, "Der Alldeutsche Verband 1890–1918," *Historische Studien*, No. 278, Berlin 1935. See also the excellent summary in Pauline Relyea Anderson, *The Background of Anti-English Feeling in Germany, 1890–1902*, Washington 1939, pp. 194–210.

[31] Kruck, *Geschichte*, pp. 10–11.

[32] Gisela Deesz, *Die Entwicklung des Nietzsche-Bildes in Deutschland*, Würzburg, Triltsch, 1933, p. 9.

[33] Leo Berg, *Der Übermensch in der modernen Literatur. Ein Kapitel zur Geistesgeschichte des 19. Jahrhunderts*, Leipzig 1897, p. 213.

[34] A summary of William's speech can be found in *Deutschland unter Kaiser Wilhelm II*, ed. by S. Körte and others, Berlin 1914, II, 1085.

[35] R. H. Samuel and R. Hinton Thomas, *Education and Society in Modern Germany*, London 1949, p. 156.

[36] This is fully discussed in Hans Strobel, *Der Begriff von Kunst und Erziehung bei Julius Langbehn. Ein Beitrag zur Geschichte der Kunsterziehungsbewegung*, Würzburg 1940.

[37] Alfred Lichtwark, "Der Deutsche der Zukunft" in *Eine Auswahl seiner Schriften*, ed. by Wolf Mannhardt, Berlin 1917, I, 3–4 and 17.

[38] Hermann Diels, "Festrede," January 23, 1902, *Sitzungsberichte der königlich Preussischen Akademie der Wissenschaften zu Berli··*, Berlin 1902, IV, 25–43.

[39] The history of the Youth Movement is, of course, beyond the scope of this book. The existing literature, especially in German, is overwhelming; particularly relevant for this study are Hans Blüher, *Wandervogel. Geschichte einer Jugendbewegung*, 2 vols., 4th ed., Berlin and Prien, 1919; Luise Fick, *Die deutsche Jugendbewegung*, Jena, Eugen Diederichs, 1939; Else Frobenius, *Mit uns zieht die neue Zeit. Eine Geschichte der deutschen Jugendbewegung*, Berlin 1927; and, most recently, Hermann Mau, "Die deutsche Jugendbewegung. Rückblick und Ausblick," *Zeitschrift für Religions- und Geistesgeschichte*, I (1948), 135–149. In English: Howard Becker, *German Youth: Bond or Free*, London 1946, and the thorough and imaginative doctoral dissertation by Mario Domandi, "The German Youth Movement," Columbia University, Department of History, 1960.

[40] Blüher, *op. cit.*, I, 133, and II, 126; Frobenius, *op. cit.*, pp. 33–34, and Domandi, *op. cit.*, pp. 60 ff. and *passim*.

Chapter 11

(Pp. 183–204)

[1] For Moeller's days in Leipzig, see Paul Ssymank's recollections of him, "Es gellt wie Trommelklang," *Velhagen und Klasings Monatshefte*, IL:9 (May, 1935), 262–265.

[2] Paul Fechter, *Moeller van den Bruck. Ein politisches Schicksal*, Berlin 1934, p. 19.

[3] Moeller van den Bruck, *Der Preussische Stil*, 3d ed., Breslau 1931, p. 193.

[4] Hedda Eulenberg's letter to me, September 12, 1959; and Harry Slochower, *Richard Dehmel: Der Mensch und der Denker*, Dresden, Reissner, 1928, p. 94.

[5] *Faust*, Part I, "Night."

[6] Arthur Moeller-Bruck, *Die Moderne Literatur*, Berlin and Leipzig 1902, p. 137.

[7] *Ibid.*, p. 440.

[8] *Ibid.*, p. 608.

[9] Professor Brüning told me of Moeller's association with Merezkowski (letter to me, March 26, 1947). It is well known that Merezkowski longed "for a Third Reich." See Bernhard Schultze, *Russische Denker. Ihre Stellung zu Christus, Kirche und Papsttum*, Wien, Thomas Morus-Presse, 1950, p. 245.

[10] See Reinhard Piper, *Vormittag. Erinnerungen eines Verlegers*, München, Piper, 1947, pp. 406–416, for a discussion of the Dostoevski edition, one of the most important achievements of the publishing house.

[11] Ernst Barlach, *Ein selbsterzähltes Leben*, Berlin, Paul Cassirer, 1928, pp. 68–69, and Theodor Däubler, *Dichtungen und Schriften*, ed. by Friedhelm Kemp, München, Kösel, 1956, pp. 868–869 for a discussion of Däubler's friendship with Moeller.

[12] Arthur Moeller van den Bruck, *Die Deutschen. Unsere Menschengeschichte*, in eight volumes, Minden 1904–1910.

[13] Moeller van den Bruck, *Die Zeitgenossen. Die Geister—die Menschen*, Minden 1906.

[14] Moeller van den Bruck, *Die italienische Schönheit*, München 1913, and Piper, *op. cit.*, p. 414. Piper ruefully comments on this commercial fiasco, but praises the book nevertheless.

[15] Moeller, *Die Zeitgenossen*, p. 26.

[16] *Ibid.*, p. 16.

[17] Moeller, *Führende Deutsche*, Vol. II of *Die Deutschen*, p. 5.

[18] Moeller, *Verirrte Deutsche*, Vol. I of *Die Deutschen*, p. 140.

[19] Moeller, *Die Zeitgenossen,* pp. 75–80.

[20] *Ibid.,* pp. 326–336.

[21] *Ibid.,* p. 37.

[22] Moeller, *Scheiternde Deutsche,* Vol. VII of *Die Deutschen,* p. 262.

[23] For a discussion of this problem, see Herbert Marcuse, "Der Kampf gegen den Liberalismus in der totalitären Staatsauffassung," in *Zeitschrift für Sozialforschung,* III:2 (1934), 161–194.

[24] Moeller, *Entscheidende Deutsche,* Vol. IV of *Die Deutschen,* p. 33.

[25] Moeller, *Verschwärmte Deutsche,* Vol. III of *Die Deutschen,* pp. 13–14.

[26] Moeller, *Die Zeitgenossen,* p. 22.

[27] *Ibid.,* p. 21.

[28] Moeller, *Entscheidende Deutsche,* pp. 234–235.

[29] Moeller, *Die Zeitgenossen,* pp. 118–119.

[30] *Ibid.,* p. 27.

[31] Moeller, *Scheiternde Deutsche,* p. 275.

[32] Moeller, *Entscheidende Deutsche,* pp. 260–261.

[33] *Ibid.,* p. 17.

[34] See Moeller, *Scheiternde Deutsche,* pp. 243–318, for a discussion of Germany's future.

[35] Moeller's letter to Ludwig Schemann, January 22, 1908, reprinted in *Deutschlands Erneuerung,* XVIII:6 (June, 1934), 323.

[36] Moeller, "Der Kaiser und die architektonische Tradition," *Die Tat,* V:6 (September, 1913), 595–601.

[37] Moeller, *Die Zeitgenossen,* p. 202.

Chapter 12

(Pp. 205–221)

[1] Thomas Mann, *Friedrich und die grosse Koalition,* Berlin 1915, pp. 12–13.

[2] Helmut Rödel, *Moeller van den Bruck,* Berlin 1939, p. 27.

[3] F. M. Dostojewsky, *Die Dämonen,* 2d ed., München 1921, Introduction by Moeller von den Bruck, I, xviii–xix.

[4] F. M. Dostojewsky, *Politische Schriften,* München 1920, Introduction by Moeller van den Bruck, p. xxi.

[5] *Ibid.,* pp. xii ff. Hans Kohn, *Prophets and Peoples. Studies in Nineteenth Century Nationalism,* New York 1946, wrote of Dostoevski: "Liberalism and rationalism appeared to him as the mortal danger. . . . Westernized liberals might not be criminals themselves . . . their liberalism by necessity corrupted and produced criminal nihilism" (p. 145).

[6] See Leo Löwenthal's remarkable essay, "Die Auffassung Dostojewskis im Vorkriegsdeutschland," in *Zeitschrift für Sozialforschung*, III:3 (1934), 343–382, for a study of that impact.

[7] Hermann Rauschning, *The Conservative Revolution*, New York 1941, p. 254; for Dostoevski's "lasting imprint on German Expressionism," see Walter H. Sokel's *The Writer in Extremis. Expressionism in Twentieth-Century German Literature*, Stanford 1959, p. 154 and *passim*.

[8] Piper, *Vormittag*, p. 411.

[9] Fechter and Rödel considered the book his greatest "Germanic" work. Fechter, *Moeller van den Bruck*, p. 59. Rödel, *op. cit.*, p. 30. S. D. Stirk labeled it also Moeller's "greatest work" and employed it at length to bolster his thesis that national socialism was but the culmination of Prussianism. S. D. Stirk, *The Prussian Spirit. A Survey of German Literature and Politics 1914–1940*, London, Gollancz, 1941, p. 45; and pp. 42–59 for a review of Moeller's works.

[10] Moeller, *Der preussische Stil*, 3d ed., Breslau 1931, p. 15.

[11] *Ibid.*, p. 77.

[12] *Ibid.*, pp. 189–190.

[13] *Ibid.*, p. 33.

[14] Moeller, "Schicksal ist stärker als Staatskunst," in *Deutsche Rundschau*, CLXIX (November, 1916), 161–167.

[15] Moeller, "Belgier und Balten," *Der Deutsche Krieg. Politische Flugschriften*, No. 59, ed. by Ernst Jäckh, Stuttgart 1915, p. 29.

[16] *Ibid.*, p. 36.

[17] *Ibid.*, p. 37.

[18] Moeller, "Politik nach Osten," in *Stimmen aus dem Osten*, (January 18, 1918), as reprinted in *Das Recht der jungen Völker*, ed. by Hans Schwarz, Berlin 1932, p. 188.

[19] For Friedrich Naumann, see Henry Cord Meyer's *Mitteleuropa in German Thought and Action 1815–1945*, The Hague 1955, esp. chapter 9.

[20] As quoted in Hermann Rauschning, *The Revolution of Nihilism. Warning to the West*, New York 1939, p. xiii.

[21] Moeller, "Stellung zu Amerika," *Gewissen*, V:17 (April 25, 1921).

[22] Letter to Theodor Däubler, November, 1919; by chance, this was the only letter which Frau Moeller van den Bruck could locate for me in the Moeller Archive.

[23] For Hitler this experience had been a decisive influence; see *Mein Kampf*, New York 1940, chapter 6.

[24] Moeller, *Das Recht der jungen Völker*, München 1919, p. 115. This volume is not identical with a previously cited book of the same title, containing a collection of his essays.

[25] *Ibid.*, p. 25.

[26] *Ibid.*, p. 42.

[27] *Ibid.*, p. 84
[28] *Ibid.*, pp. 60, 62.
[29] *Ibid.*, p. 95.

Chapter 13

(Pp. 222–244)

[1] Max Hildebert Boehm, "Moeller van den Bruck im Kreise seiner politischen Freunde," *Deutsches Volkstum,* XIV:14 (September, 1932), 693.

[2] Ernst Troeltsch, *Spektator-Briefe. Aufsätze über die deutsche Revolution und die Weltpolitik 1918–22,* ed. by H. Baron, Tübingen 1924, p. 69. For the atmosphere of the dreamland, see also Klemens von Klemperer's *Germany's New Conservatism. Its History and Dilemma in the Twentieth Century,* Princeton 1957, pp. 76–80.

[3] See Alma Luckau, *The German Delegation at the Paris Peace Conference. A Documentary Study of Germany's Acceptance of the Treaty of Versailles,* New York 1941, pp. 28–53, for an excellent summary of German expectations concerning the peace.

[4] Heinrich von Gleichen, "Das politische Kolleg," *Deutsche Rundschau,* CLXXXVII (April, 1921), 105.

[5] See, for example, Max Hildebert Boehm's account of Moeller's group: "Die Front der Jungen," *Süddeutsche Monatshefte,* XVIII:1 (October, 1920), 8–12; for the Latin motto, see "Das Erbe," *Gewissen,* III:4 (January 26, 1921).

[6] Robert G. L. Waite, *Vanguard of Nazism. The Free Corps Movement in Postwar Germany 1918–1923,* Cambridge (Mass.) 1952, chapter 2, gives a good description of this mood among the Free Corps men.

[7] Nearly thirty years later, Rudolf Pechel wrote: "One may disagree about Moeller as a political thinker, but as a personality he was very attractive, a thoroughly artistic being and a person of utter integrity and of great ethical will power" (letter to me, May 16, 1947). Professor Joachim Tiburtius, now Senator for Education in West Berlin, recalled his frequent contacts with Moeller, and the pleasure which he derived "from this tender and lively intellect" (letter to me, December 2, 1959).

[8] Boehm, "Die Front der Jungen," p. 8. I am primarily concerned with Moeller's thought, not with the organizations of the conservative revolution after 1918. For the latter, see Klemperer, *Germany's New Conservatism,* pp. 97–112. See also Armin Mohler, *Die Konservative Revolution in Deutschland 1918–1932. Grundriss ihrer Weltanschauungen,* Stuttgart 1950, pp. 50–70, and *Gewissen,* III:4 (January 26, 1921). Ralph F. Bischoff, *Nazi Conquest through Ger-*

man Culture, Cambridge (Mass.) 1942, pp. 63–72 presents an unreliable account of the Juni-Klub, based largely on his conversations with Max Hildebert Boehm.

[9] I wish to thank Professor Heinrich Herrfahrdt for sending me a copy of Moeller's "Thirty-three Principles of the Juni-Klub"; letter of March 8, 1951.

[10] Heinrich von Gleichen, "Das Politische Kolleg," *op. cit.,* pp. 105–106; letter to me from Heinrich Brüning, March 26, 1947, and interview with him, July 30, 1954; Otto Strasser, *History in My Time,* transl. by Douglas Reed, London, Cape, 1941, p. 200; Hans Blüher, *Werke und Tage. Geschichte eines Denkers,* München, List, 1953, pp. 328–329; Gustav Hillard (pseud. for Gustav Steinbömer), *Herren und Narren der Welt,* München, List, 1954, pp. 292–293.

[11] Klemperer, *Germany's New Conservatism,* pp. 108–109, and Hans-Joachim Schwierskott, "Das Gewissen," in *Lebendiger Geist: Hans-Joachim Schoeps zum 50. Geburtstag von Schülern dargebracht,* ed. by Hellmut Diwald, Leiden-Köln 1959, p. 165.

[12] *Gewissen,* I:11 (June 24, 1919). The italics were in the original. I am grateful to the Hoover Institution on War, Revolution, and Peace, Stanford (Calif.), for its permission to photostat its holdings of the *Gewissen.*

[13] *Gewissen,* II:29 (July 28, 1920).

[14] *Ibid.,* I:1 (April 9, 1919).

[15] Eduard Stadtler, "Chaos und Ziel," in *ibid.,* II:12 (March 31, 1920).

[16] *Ibid.,* III:43 (October 24, 1921); and IV:1 (January 2, 1922).

[17] *Ibid.,* III:9 (March 2, 1921).

[18] *Ibid.,* IV:1 (January 2, 1922).

[19] Troeltsch, *Spektator-Briefe,* article of July 1, 1920, p. 146.

[20] *Ibid.,* article of December 12, 1921, p. 247.

[21] See the note to subscribers, *Gewissen,* IV:1 (January 2, 1922).

[22] Helmut Hüttig, *Die politischen Zeitschriften der Nachkriegszeit in Deutschland,* Magdeburg 1928, pp. 33 and 90.

[23] Schwierskott, "Das Gewissen," p. 174.

[24] Rudolf Pechel, "Das Wort geht um," in *Die Neue Front,* ed. by Moeller van den Bruck, Heinrich von Gleichen, Max Hildebert Boehm, Berlin 1922, pp. 72–75.

[25] Rudolf Pechel, *Deutscher Widerstand,* Zürich 1947, pp. 277–280.

[26] Letter to me from Dr. Brüning, March 26, 1947.

[27] *Gewissen,* V:45, quoted in Schwierskott, "Das Gewissen," p. 167.

[28] He was remembered as "the only Realpolitiker of his generation." Wolfgang Herrmann, "Moeller van den Bruck," *Die Tat,* XXV:4 (July, 1933), 274.

[29] Manfred Schroeter, *Der Streit um Spengler. Kritik seiner Kritiker,* München, Becksche Verlagsbuchhandlung, 1922, p. 12.

30 Moeller, "Der Untergang des Abendlandes. Für und Wider Spengler," *Deutsche Rundschau*, CLXXXIV (July, 1920), 61, 63.

31 "Revolution, Persönlichkeit, Drittes Reich," *Gewissen* (May 30, 1920), reprinted in Moeller van den Bruck, *Der politische Mensch,* ed. by Hans Schwarz, Breslau 1933, p. 83.

32 "Sind Kommunisten Deutsche?" *Gewissen*, III:26 (June 27, 1921).

33 "Freiheit," in *ibid.*, IV:1 (January 2, 1922).

34 "Italia docet," *Gewissen* (November 3, 1922), reprinted in Moeller van den Bruck, *Das Recht der jungen Völker,* ed. by Hans Schwarz, Berlin 1932, p. 123.

35 See Moeller's articles, "Der Auslandsdeutsche," *Grenzboten* (April 28, 1920) and "Der Aussenseiter als Weg zum Führer," *Der Tag* (January 15, 1919) reprinted in Moeller, *Der politische Mensch,* pp. 44–75.

36 "Sozialistische Aussenpolitik," reprinted in Moeller van den Bruck, *Sozialismus und Aussenpolitik,* ed. by Hans Schwarz, Breslau 1933, p. 81.

37 See Abraham Ascher, *National Solidarity and Imperial Power; the sources and early development of social imperialist thought in Germany, 1871–1914,* University microfilm, Ann Arbor 1958, who argues that social imperialism was a dominant theme in the work of Schmoller, Naumann, Moeller, and others, and through them, in German society.

38 "Wirklichkeit," *Gewissen* (August 30, 1923), reprinted in Moeller, *Das Recht der jungen Völker,* ed. by Hans Schwarz, p. 98.

39 "Der Auslandsdeutsche," *Grenzboten* (April 28, 1920) reprinted in Moeller, *Der politische Mensch,* p. 63.

40 "Deutsche Grenzpolitik," *Grenzboten* (May 19, 1920) reprinted in Moeller, *Sozialismus und Aussenpolitik,* pp. 70–71.

41 "Das unheimliche Deutschland," *Gewissen* (January 7, 1924) reprinted in Moeller, *Das Recht der jungen Völker,* ed. by Hans Schwarz, pp. 103–108.

Chapter 14

(Pp. 245–266)

1 Woldemar Fink, *Ostideologie und Ostpolitik. Die Ostideologie ein Gefahrenmoment in der deutschen Aussenpolitik,* Berlin 1936, was an official Nazi repudiation of Moeller's plans for German collaboration with the Soviet Union. Three years later, at the time of the Hitler-Stalin pact, Fink was the fool and Moeller the prophet —such are the professional hazards of party ideologists.

2 See Hans W. Gatzke, "Russo-German Military Collaboration

during the Weimar Republic," *American Historical Review*, LXIII:3 (April, 1958), 565–597.

³ See, for example, Erich Müller, "Zur Geschichte des Nationalbolschevismus," *Deutsches Volkstum*, XIV:16 (October, 1932), 782–790; Klemperer, *Germany's New Conservatism*, pp. 143–150; Abraham Ascher and Guenter Lewy, "National Bolshevism in Weimar Germany. Alliance of Political Extremes Against Democracy," *Social Research*, XXIII (Winter, 1956), 451, 456, 471. On national bolshevism, see also Ruth Fischer's unreliable *Stalin and German Communism. A Study in the Origins of the State Party*, Cambridge (Mass.) 1948, pp. 189–287, and Edward Hallett Carr, *A History of Soviet Russia*, Vol. IV: *The Interregnum 1923–1924*. New York, Macmillan, 1954, chapter 7. The present book was already in press when Otto-Ernst Schüddekopf's *Linke Leute von Rechts. Die nationalrevolutionären Minderheiten und der Kommunismus in der Weimarer Republik*, Stuttgart, Kohlhammer, 1960, was published. I could therefore not take it into account.

⁴ "Deutsche Grenzpolitik," *Grenzboten* (May 19, 1920), reprinted in Moeller, *Sozialismus und Aussenpolitik*, pp. 65 f.

⁵ "Sind Kommunisten Deutsche?" *Gewissen*, III:26 (June 27, 1921).

⁶ "Kritik der Presse," *Gewissen*, III:41 (October 10, 1921).

⁷ "Politik wider Willen," *Gewissen* (April 24, 1922), as reprinted in Moeller van den Bruck, *Rechenschaft über Russland*, ed. by Hans Schwarz, Berlin 1933, p. 188.

⁸ "Die deutsch-russische Seite der Welt," *Gewissen* (May 15, 1922), as reprinted in Moeller, *Rechenschaft über Russland*, p. 196.

⁹ Karl Radek, "Leo Schlageter—The Wanderer into the Void," *The Labour Monthly*, V:3 (September, 1923), 152–157.

¹⁰ "Der Wanderer ins Nichts," *Gewissen* (July 2, 1923), reprinted in *Schlageter. Eine Auseinandersetzung*. Karl Radek, P. Frölich, Graf Ernst Reventlow, Moeller van den Bruck, Berlin, Vereinigung Internationaler Verlags-Anstalten, n.d. (1923?), pp. 9–10.

¹¹ "Wirklichkeit," *Gewissen* (July 30, 1923), reprinted in Moeller, *Das Recht der jungen Völker*, ed. by Hans Schwarz, p. 96.

¹² *Ibid.*, p. 95.

¹³ Max Hildebert Boehm, "Moeller van den Bruck im Kreise seiner Freunde," *Deutsches Volkstum*, XIV:14 (September, 1932), 695.

¹⁴ For Joachim of Floris's prophecy of the coming of the Third Reich, the Reich of the Holy Ghost, see Alois Dempf, *Sacrum Imperium. Geschichts- und Staatsphilosophie des Mittelalters und der politischen Renaissance*, München, Oldenbourg, 1929, pp. 269–284; for an incomplete and partisan history of the idea of the Third Reich, cf. Julius Petersen, *Die Sehnsucht nach dem Dritten Reich in deutscher Sage und Dichtung*, Stuttgart, Metzler, 1934. The best

summary of the importance of the political myth may be found in Jean Neurohr, *Der Mythos vom Dritten Reich. Zur Geistesgeschichte des Nationalsozialismus,* Stuttgart 1957, *passim.*

[15] Oswald Spengler, *Der Untergang des Abendlandes. Umrisse einer Morphologie der Weltgeschichte,* Vol. I: *Gestalt und Wirklichkeit,* 33d–47th rev. ed., München 1923, p. 467. Italics in the original.

[16] Moeller van den Bruck, *Das Dritte Reich,* 3d ed. by Hans Schwarz, Hamburg 1931, p. 116. An English version exists, but the translator simplified and condensed Moeller's rhetoric, to the great benefit of the book. As a consequence, Moeller appears as a thoroughly rational critic, without the mystical note that dominated the original. *Germany's Third Empire,* authorized (condensed) English ed. by E. O. Lorimer, London 1934.

[17] Moeller, *Das Dritte Reich,* p. vii.

[18] Most critics of Moeller's Third Reich slighted or omitted altogether his prewar cultural writings and thus missed the deeper, nonpolitical sources of his major work. For summaries of the book, see Gerhard Krebs, "Moeller van den Bruck: Inventor of the 'Third Reich,'" in *American Political Science Review,* XXXV:6 (December, 1941), 1085–1105, and Edmond Vermeil, *Doctrinaires de la Révolution Allemande, 1918–1938,* new ed., Paris, Sorlot, 1948, chapter 3. Albert R. Chandler, "The Political Typology of Moeller van den Bruck," in *Essays in Political Theory, presented to George H. Sabine,* ed. by Milton R. Konvitz and Arthur E. Murphy, Ithaca 1948, pp. 228–245, compares Moeller's typological method of political analysis to Plato's. Except for this unpersuasive thesis, his essay is a useful introduction to Moeller's work. See also Roy Pascal, "Revolutionary Conservatism: Moeller van den Bruck," in *The Third Reich,* ed. by Edmond Vermeil, *et al.,* London 1955, chapter 7.

[19] Moeller, *Das Dritte Reich,* p. 1.

[20] *Ibid.,* p. 6.

[21] *Ibid.,* p. 13.

[22] *Ibid.,* p. 29.

[23] *Ibid.,* pp. 34, 180.

[24] *Ibid.,* p. 144.

[25] *Ibid.,* p. 189.

[26] *Ibid.,* p. 164.

[27] *Ibid.,* pp. 97, 99.

[28] *Ibid.,* p. 100

[29] *Ibid.,* p. 79.

[30] *Ibid.,* p. 219.

[31] *Ibid.,* p. 234.

[32] *Ibid.,* p. 320.

[33] *Ibid.,* p. 317.

[34] See, for example, the excellent summary by Kurt Sontheimer, "Antidemokratisches Denken in der Weimarer Republik," *Vierteljahrshefte für Zeitgeschichte*, V:1 (January, 1957), 42–62.

[35] Professor Tazerout called it a political religion in "La Pensée politique de Moeller van den Bruck," *Revue Internationale de Sociologie*, XLIX:1–2 (January–February, 1936), 65.

[36] The actual demise of the Juni-Klub is still a matter of controversy. Klemperer, *Germany's New Conservatism*, p. 120, dates the dissolution from 1924 and attributes it to internal dissension and the withdrawal of funds. Others, including Moeller's widow, accused Gleichen and his friends of having sold out and having become "liberal and capitalistic." Wilhelm Wunderlich, "Die Spinne," *Die Tat*, XXIII:10, (January, 1932), 842, and Lucy Moeller van den Bruck, "Erbe und Auftrag," *Der Nahe Osten*, V:20 (October 15, 1932), 435.

[37] *Der Nahe Osten*, I (January 1, 1928), 1.

[38] Wolfgang Herrmann, for example, complained about the Moeller cult and its blind veneration of Moeller; see his "Moeller van den Bruck," *Die Tat*, XXV: 4 (July, 1933), 273.

[39] Ernst H. Posse, *Die politischen Kampfbünde Deutschlands*, Berlin, Junker und Dünnhaupt, 1930, pp. 73 f.

[40] Hermann Rauschning. *The Revolution of Nihilism. Warning to the West,* New York 1939, pp. 111–115, and Otto Friedlaender, "Die ideologische Front der Nationalen Opposition," *Sozialistische Monatshefte*, XXXV (March 18, 1929), 209.

[41] Quoted in Karl Dietrich Bracher, *Die Auflösung der Weimarer Republik*, 2d ed., Stuttgart and Düsseldorf 1957, p. 537. Bracher's work is the best study of the period.

[42] See Gert Buchheit, *Franz von Papen. Eine politische Biographie*, Breslau 1933, who entitled the chapter dealing with Papen's thought "Revolutionärer Konservatismus," and cites Papen's speeches denouncing liberalism and praising Lagarde and Langbehn, pp. 77–93.

[43] Bracher, *Die Auflösung der Weimarer Republik*, "Ideologie des 'Neuen Staates,' " pp. 536–545.

[44] *Der Ring*, VI:25 (June 23, 1933); the collapse of this branch of the conservative revolution in the face of the National Socialists can be traced in the pages of *Der Ring* from February 3 to June 30, 1933.

[45] Hans Buchheim, "Ernst Niekischs Ideologie des Widerstands," *Vierteljahrshefte für Zeitgeschichte*, V:4 (October, 1957), 334–361, *passim*.

[46] Ernst Niekisch, *Gewagtes Leben. Begegnungen und Begebnisse*, Köln, Kiepenheuer und Witsch, 1958, p. 136.

[47] Richard Schapke, *Die Schwarze Front*, Leipzig, Lindner, 1932, p. 77.

[48] Joseph Goebbels, *The Goebbels Diaries,* 1925, p. 58, December 18, 1925. At the Hoover Institution on War, Revolution, and Peace, Stanford, (Calif.).

[49] Andreas Hohlfeld, *Unsere geschichtliche Verantwortung,* Leipzig 1933, p. 5.

[50] Quoted in Schwierskott, "Das Gewissen," p. 173.

[51] So Ernst Jackh, *The War for Man's Soul,* New York 1943, p. 86. Otto Strasser wrote: "I think of my old comrade Moeller van den Bruck, the Rousseau of the German Revolution (he committed suicide on the day he realized that Hitler had betrayed his ideas)." *Hitler and I,* transl. by Gwenda David and Eric Mosbacher, Boston, Houghton Mifflin, 1940, p. 15.

Conclusion

(Pp. 267–298)

[1] Basil Willey, *Nineteenth Century Studies,* New York 1949, p. 221.

[2] On the problem of interpreting "the literature of the unliterary," or the "intellectual anti-intellectualism," see Armin Mohler, *Die Konservative Revolution,* pp. 27–29.

[3] Ludwig Schemann, "Paul de Lagarde. Ein Nachruf," *Bayreuther Blätter,* XV:6 (June, 1892), 202.

[4] J. G. von Herder, "Aehnlichkeit der mittlern englischen und deutschen Dichtkunst," *Sämmtliche Werke,* Carlsruhe 1821, VIII, 58, 55.

[5] Johann Gottlieb Fichte, *Addresses to the German Nation,* The Open Court Publishing Company, Chicago and London 1922, pp. 208, 256, 268.

[6] Friedrich Meinecke, *Weltbürgertum und Nationalstaat. Studien zur Genesis des deutschen Nationalstaates,* 5th ed., München and Berlin, Oldenbourg, 1919, p. 111.

[7] Novalis, "Die Christenheit oder Europa," *Sämtliche Werke,* ed. by Ernst Kamnitzer, München, Paetel, 1924, III, 25.

[8] On this *Germanomanie* and anti-Semitism, see Eleonore Sterling, *Er ist wie Du. Aus der Frühgeschichte des Antisemitismus in Deutschland (1815–1850),* München 1956, esp. pp. 128–143; on the artisans generally see Theodore S. Hamerow, *Restoration Revolution Reaction. Economics and Politics in Germany, 1815–1871,* Princeton 1958, *passim.*

[9] See Charles W. Cole, "The Heavy Hand of Hegel," in *Nationalism and Internationalism. Essays Inscribed to Carlton J. H. Hayes,* ed. by Edward Mead Earle, New York, Columbia University Press, 1950, pp. 64–78, for a discussion of the generally pernicious influence of Hegel's *Philosophy of History* on some modern German

interpreters of history. Franz Schnabel, *Deutsche Geschichte im Neunzehnten Jahrhundert*, Vol. III: *Erfahrungswissenschaften und Technik*, 2d. ed., Freiburg im Breisgau 1950, pp. 22–30, supports the view that Hegel's reputation waned quickly after his death. See also Walter Kaufmann's brilliant "The Hegel Myth and Its Method," which is at once a critique of Karl Popper's *Open Society* and a brief exposition of Hegel's central ideas. *From Shakespeare to Existentialism: Studies in Poetry, Religion and Philosophy*, Boston, Beacon Press, 1959, pp. 88–119.

[10] For "National Socialism versus Hegel," see Herbert Marcuse, *Reason and Revolution. Hegel and the Rise of Social Theory*, New York, Oxford University Press, 1941, pp. 409–419.

[11] Albert Camus, *The Rebel. An Essay on Man in Revolt*, rev. translation by Anthony Bower, New York, Knopf (Vintage Books), 1956, p. 75.

[12] Interview with Moeller's widow in Berlin, July, 1954.

[13] Moeller van den Bruck, *Die Zeitgenossen*, p. 22. Quoted in Walter A. Kaufmann, *Nietzsche*, p. 312.

[14] *Die fröhliche Wissenschaft*, in *Friedrich Nietzsche, Werke in Drei Bänden*, ed. by Karl Schlechta, München 1955, II, 152–153.

[15] Moeller van den Bruck, *Führende Deutsche*, Vol. II of *Die Deutschen*, pp. 248 ff.

[16] Armin Mohler, *Die Konservative Revolution*, p. 206.

[17] *Also Sprach Zarathustra*, in *Friedrich Nietzsche, Werke in Drei Bänden*, ed. by Karl Schlechta, München 1955, II, 340.

[18] See Ernst Krieck, *Nationalpolitische Erziehung*, 11th ed., Leipzig, Armanen-Verlag, 1933, *passim*, and George Frederick Kneller, *The Educational Philosophy of National Socialism*, New Haven, Yale University Press, 1941, chapters 4 and 8.

[19] Ernst Bergmann, *Die deutsche Nationalkirche*, Breslau, Hirt, 1933, *passim*.

[20] Christoph Steding, *Das Reich und die Krankheit der europäischen Kultur*, Hamburg 1938.

[21] Quoted in Joachim H. Knoll, "Der Autoritäre Staat. Konservative Ideologie und Staatstheorien am Ende der Weimarer Republik," in *Lebendiger Geist*, ed. by Hellmut Diwald, p. 205.

[22] Helmut Rödel, *Moeller van den Bruck*, pp. 3–5.

[23] *Ibid.*, p. 164. Even at the height of the war, the National Socialist party concerned itself with the ideological purity of Moeller. In 1942, a high Saxon functionary prefaced a report with a motto from Moeller; his superiors removed the motto and rebuked the author. The latter complained to party headquarters in Berlin, which handed the matter to Rosenberg's office; a few weeks later, the authoritative answer disavowed Moeller and concluded: "Above all, it must be remembered that three years before the appearance of Moeller's book, the *Führer* had already proclaimed the program

of the party and had built on this basis a fighting movement that did not have to derive its *Weltanschauung* from Moeller, because national socialism was not only the political, but the spiritual, work of Adolf Hitler." Letter of Dr. Kulp, Hauptamt Wissenschaft, July 11, 1942. Microcopy T-81, roll 198, records of the National Socialist German Labor party, National Archive, Washington, D.C.

Acknowledgments

Acknowledgments

This book was begun as a dissertation in the graduate seminar of Jacques Barzun and Lionel Trilling. It is a pleasure to record at last my deep gratitude to them. Their counsel and their inspiration have been of lasting benefit to me.

The dissertation was completed some years later, under Jacques Barzun's supervision and with the help of his incomparable combination of advice, encouragement, and relentless expectation. Before completing the thesis, I discussed it on several occasions with the late Franz Neumann, whose critical interest helped me in this and other efforts. I remain grateful to his memory.

After the dissertation was completed, I parted from the company of the Germanic critics. I returned to them some years later, encouraged by the advice of Peter Gay, Richard Hofstadter, and Paul Seabury. I began the revision of the manuscript, which turned out to be a more radical revision than I had originally planned, in the winter of 1957–58, at the Center for Advanced Study in the Behavioral Sciences, Stanford, California. There under the ideal conditions that Ralph W. Tyler, the director of the Center, has created, I had the particular advantage of long and leisurely talks with John Bowlby and Ralf Dahrendorf—conversations continued at a later time in New York. I discussed various aspects of my book with J. Christopher Herold, David S. Landes, Henry Cord Meyer, Philip Rieff, and Walter Sokel. I also wish to express my thanks to the Hoover Institution on War, Revolution and Peace, at Stanford, California, to the Niedersächsische Staats- und Universitätsbibliothek in Göttingen, and most especially to the unfailing courtesy of the Columbia University libraries and the Baker Library of Dartmouth College. The Social Science Research Council of Columbia University provided me with funds for clerical assistance, and Miss Susan Rubin typed the manuscript, with expert care and great forbearance.

When the revised manuscript was completed, I inflicted it once more on Jacques Barzun, who read it with the same magnificent attention to style and substance as he had read the earlier version. I am grateful to Richard Hofstadter who read parts of the manuscript, and to Beatrice K. Hofstadter who read all of it, and brilliantly and ruthlessly called my attention to many infelicities. Leonard Krieger and R. K. Webb read the revised manuscript as well, and their counsel and encouragement were of great help. Finally, I am grateful to my friend and neighbor, Henry L. Roberts, for the many conversations we have had, about this book and much else.

To all these friends and colleagues I am grateful. I am most grateful to my wife who shared the pleasures and eased the burdens of this work.

Rochester, Vermont   F. S.
August 9, 1960

Selected Bibliography

Selected Bibliography

NOTE: This bibliography does not list all the works cited in the notes and footnotes. I have included only those works that I have found particularly important for the study of these three men and their times. For books mentioned in the text but omitted from the bibliography, I supplied the necessary bibliographical information the first time I cited them. I hope that a somewhat shorter, selective bibliography will be of greater use than the indiscriminate listing of all works consulted and mentioned.

I. PRIMARY AND SECONDARY SOURCES FOR LAGARDE, LANGBEHN, AND MOELLER VAN DEN BRUCK

A. WORKS BY AND ON PAUL DE LAGARDE

1. *Unpublished material*
Lagarde *Nachlass,* containing his unpublished correspondence and some papers. Niedersächsische Staats- und Universitätsbibliothek, Göttingen.

2. *Published works by Lagarde*
Lagarde, Paul de, *Aus dem deutschen Gelehrtenleben. Aktenstücke und Glossen,* Göttingen, Dieterich, 1880.
————, *Ausgewählte Schriften,* ed. by Paul Fischer, 2d ed., München, Lehmanns, 1934.
————, *Bemerkungen zu einem von Herrn Professor Felix Klein über die Reorganisation der königlichen Gesellschaft der Wissenschaften zu Göttingen abgegebene Gutachten,* Göttingen, Dieterich, 1889.
————, *Deutsche Schriften,* 3d ed., München, Lehmanns, 1937. The first edition was published by Dieterich, Göttingen, 1878. Other editions and anthologies are listed in the notes.
————, *Gedichte,* Göttingen, Dieterich, 1885.
————, *Gedichte von Paul de Lagarde,* ed. by Anna de Lagarde, 2d enlarged ed., Göttingen, Dieterich, 1911.
————, *Gesammelte Abhandlungen,* Leipzig, Brockhaus, 1866.

————, *Die königliche Gesellschaft der Wissenschaften betreffend. Ein Gutachten,* Göttingen, Dieterich, 1887.

————, *Die königliche Gesellschaft der Wissenschaften betreffend. Ein zweites und letztes Gutachten,* Göttingen, Dieterich, 1889.

————, *Mittheilungen,* 4 vols., Göttingen, Dieterich, 1884, 1887, 1889, 1891.

————, *Symmicta,* 2 vols., Göttingen, Dieterich, 1877, 1880.

3. *Books and articles on Lagarde*

Albrecht, Karl, "Paul de Lagarde," *Burschenschaftliche Bücherei,* II: 2, Berlin, 1904.

Anstett, Jean-Jacques, "Paul de Lagarde," in *The Third Reich,* ed. by Edmond Vermeil *et al.,* London, Weidenfeld and Nicolson, 1955, pp. 148–202.

Berliner, Dr. Abraham, *Professor Paul de Lagarde nach seiner Natur gezeichnet,* Berlin, Benzian, 1887.

Breitling, Richard, "Die Einflüsse der Aufkärung und Romantik auf Lagarde," *Archiv für Kulturgeschichte,* XVIII: 1 (1927), 97–103.

————, *Paul de Lagarde und der grossdeutsche Gedanke,* Wien, Braumüller, 1927.

Christlieb, Max, "Paul de Lagarde," *Die Tat,* V:1 (April, 1913), 1–9.

Driver, S. R., "Recent Literature Relating to the Old Testament," *The Contemporary Review,* LV (March, 1889), 393–402.

Gottheil, Richard J. H., "Bibliography of the Works of Paul de Lagarde," *Proceedings of the American Oriental Society,* XV (April, 1892), ccxi–ccxxix.

Grabs, Rudolf, *Paul de Lagarde und H. St. Chamberlain,* Weimar, Verlag deutscher Christen, 1940.

Hahne, Fritz, "Lagarde als Politiker," in *Deutscher Aufstieg. Bilder aus der Vergangenheit und Gegenwart der rechtsstehenden Parteien,* ed. by Hans von Arnim and Georg von Below, Berlin, Schneider, 1925, pp. 287–295.

Hartmann, Wilhelm, *Paul de Lagarde: Ein Prophet deutschen Christentums. Seine theologische Stellung, Religionsanschauung und Frömmigkeit,* Halle, Akademischer Verlag, 1933.

Hippler, Fritz, *Staat und Gesellschaft bei Mill, Marx und Lagarde. Ein Beitrag zum soziologischen Denken der Gegenwart,* Berlin, Junker und Dünnhaupt, 1934.

Karpp, Heinrich, "Lagardes Kritik an Kirche und Theologie," *Zeitschrift für Theologie und Kirche*, IL (1952), 367–385.

Kaufmann, David, *Paul de Lagardes jüdische Gelehrsamkeit*, Leipzig, Schulze, 1887.

Knodt, Karl Ernst, "Paul de Lagarde, der Dichter. Eine literarische Studie," *Monatsblätter für Deutsche Literatur*, IV: 1 (October, 1899), 125–165.

Koselleck, Arno, "Die Entfaltung des völkischen Bewusstseins bei Paul de Lagarde," *Historische Vierteljahrschrift*, XXX: 2 (1935), 316–360.

Krammer, Mario, "Paul de Lagarde," *Die Grossen Deutschen*, ed. by Willy Andreas and Wilhelm von Scholz, Vol. IV, Berlin, Propyläen, 1936, pp. 24–38.

———, "Deutschtum als Prophetie," *Preussische Jahrbücher*, CCII:2 (November, 1925), 175–192.

Lagarde, Anna de, *Paul de Lagarde. Erinnerungen aus seinem Leben für die Freunde zusammengestellt*, Göttingen, Kaestner, 1894.

Lougee, Robert W., "Paul de Lagarde as Critic. A Romantic Protest in an Age of Realism," *Journal of Central European Affairs*, XIII (October, 1953), 232–245.

Mehring, Franz, "Man nennt das Volk," *Die Neue Zeit*, XIII:8, part 1 (November 15, 1894), 225–228.

Moore, George F., "Paul Anton de Lagarde," *University Quarterly*, XVI:4 (July, 1893), 166–179.

Overbeck, Franz, *Über die Christlichkeit unserer heutigen Theologie. Streit- und Friedensschrift*, Leipzig, Fritzsch, 1873.

Platz, Hermann, *Grossstadt und Menschentum*, chapter iv: "Paul de Lagarde," München, Kösel und Pustet, 1924.

Pölcher, Helmut M., "Symphilologein: Briefe von Paul de Lagarde an Adolf Hilgenfeld aus den Jahren 1862–1887," in *Lebendiger Geist. Hans-Joachim Schoeps zum 50. Geburtstag von Schülern dargebracht*, ed. by Hellmut Diwald, Leiden-Köln, Brill, 1959, pp. 19–47.

Rahlfs, Alfred, "Paul de Lagardes wissenschaftliches Lebenswerk im Rahmen einer Geschichte seines Lebens dargestellt," in *Mitteilungen des Septuaginta-Unternehmens der Gesellschaft der Wissenschaften zu Göttingen*, Berlin, Weidmann, IV:1 (1928), 1–98.

Saitschick, Robert, *Bismarck und das Schicksal des deutschen Volkes. Zur Psychologie und Geschichte der deutschen Frage,* chapter viii: Paul de Lagarde, Basel, Reinhardt, 1949.

Schemann, Ludwig, *Paul de Lagarde. Ein Lebens- und Erinnerungsbild,* 3d. ed., Leipzig, Matthes, 1943.

Schiffmann, Käte, *Lagardes Kulturanschauung,* Münster, Coppenrath, 1938.

Schmid, Lothar, *Paul de Lagardes Kritik an Kirche, Theologie und Christentum,* Stuttgart, Kohlhammer, 1935.

Schweinshaupt, Georg, "Nationalsozialismus und Lagarde," *Nationalsozialistische Monatshefte,* III:32 (November, 1932), 500–503.

Wilamowitz-Moellendorff, Ulrich von, *Rede gehalten im Auftrage der königlichen Georg-August-Universität am Sarge von Paul de Lagarde am 25. Dezember 1891,* Göttingen, Dieterich, 1892.

Wittig, Hans, *Die geistige Welt Paul de Lagardes,* Borna-Leipzig, Noske, 1937.

B. WORKS BY AND ON JULIUS LANGBEHN

1. *Published works by Langbehn*

Langbehn, Julius, *Flügelgestalten der ältesten griechischen Kunst,* München, Ackermann, 1881.

———, *Der Geist des Ganzen,* ed. by Momme Nissen, Freiburg im Breisgau, Herder, 1930.

———, *Langbehns Lieder,* ed. by B. M. Nissen, München, Kösel und Pustet, n.d. (1931?).

———, *Rembrandt als Erzieher. Von einem Deutschen,* 33d ed., Leipzig, Hirschfeld, 1891.

———, *Rembrandt als Erzieher,* ed. by Gerhard Krüger, Berlin, Fritsch, 1944.

———, *Der Rembrandtdeutsche. Von einem Wahrheitsfreund,* Dresden, Glöss, 1892.

———, *Langbehn-Briefe an Bischof Keppler,* ed. by Momme Nissen, Freiburg im Breisgau, Herder, 1937.

———, *40 Lieder von einem Deutschen,* Dresden, Glöss, 1891.

———, *Deutsches Denken. Gedrucktes und Ungedrucktes vom Rembrandtdeutschen. Ein Seherbuch.* Leipzig, Hirschfeld, 1933.

2. *Books and Articles on Langbehn*

Andersen, Friedrich, *Der wahre Rembrandtdeutsche. Eine notwendige Auseinandersetzung,* Stuttgart, Roth, 1927.

Bewer, Max, *Bei Bismarck,* Dresden, Glöss, 1891.

———, *Rembrandt und Bismarck,* 10th ed., Dresden, Glöss, 1891.

Brunn, Hermann, "Julius Langbehn, Karl Haider, Heinrich von Brunn," *Deutsche Rundschau*, CCXVIII (January, 1929), 20–34.

Bürger-Prinz, Hans, "Über die künstlerischen Arbeiten Schizophrener," in Oswald Bumke, ed., *Handbuch der Geisteskrankheiten*, Vol. IX, part v: *Die Schizophrenie*, ed. by Karl Wilmanns, Berlin, Springer, 1932.

Bürger-Prinz, Hans, and Segelke, Annemarie, *Julius Langbehn der Rembrandtdeutsche: Eine pathopsychologische Studie*, Leipzig, Barth, 1940.

Carr, C. T., "Julius Langbehn—a Forerunner of National Socialism," *German Life and Letters*, III:1 (1938), 45–54.

Diels, Hermann, "Festrede" January 23, 1902, *Sitzungsberichte der königlichen Preussischen Akademie der Wissenschaften*, Berlin 1902, IV, 25–43.

Gurlitt, Cornelius D., "Langbehn, der Rembrandtdeutsche," *Protestantische Studien*, No. 9, Berlin 1927. A brochure of 92 pp.

Hartwig, Hermann, *Langbehn als Vorkämpfer der deutschen Volkswerdung*, Mannheim, Gengenbach und Hahn, 1938.

Ilschner, Liselotte, *Rembrandt als Erzieher und seine Bedeutung: Studie über die kulturelle Struktur der neunziger Jahre*, Danzig, Kafemann, n.d. (1928?). This monograph has also appeared under the name of Liselotte Voss.

Keppler, Paul Wilhelm von, *Wahre und falsche Reform*, Freiburg im Breisgau, Herder, 1903.

Müller, Karl Alexander von, "Zwei Münchener Doktordiplome," in *Festgabe für seine königliche Hoheit Kronprinz Rupprecht von Bayern*, ed. by Walter Goetz, München-Pasing, Bayerische Heimatforschung, 1953, pp. 180–193.

Nissen, Momme Benedikt, *Der Rembrandtdeutsche Julius Langbehn*, Freiburg im Breisgau, Herder, 1927.

Pudor, Heinrich, *Ein ernstes Wort über Rembrandt als Erzieher*, Göttingen, Dieterich, 1890.

Roloff, E. M., "Julius Langbehn, der Rembrandt-Deutsche," *Hochland*, VII:8 (May, 1910), 206–213.

Seillière, Ernest, *Morales et religions nouvelles en Allemagne. Le Néoromantisme au delà du Rhin*, Paris, Payot, 1927. On Langbehn: pp. 69–125.

Strobel, Hans, *Der Begriff von Kunst und Erziehung bei Julius Langbehn. Ein Beitrag zur Geschichte der*

Kunsterziehungsbewegung, Würzburg, Triltsch, 1940.

Vorwald, Heinrich, "Neues über den Rembrandtdeutschen," *Hochland, VI*:1 (October, 1908), 126–127.

C. WORKS BY AND ON MOELLER VAN DEN BRUCK

1. *Published works by Moeller van den Bruck*

Moeller van den Bruck, Arthur, *Die Deutschen. Unsere Menschengeschichte,* 8 vols., Minden, Bruns, 1904–1910.

———, F. M. Dostojewski, *Sämtliche Werke,* ed. by Moeller van den Bruck, München, Piper, 1906–1914.

———, *Das Dritte Reich,* 3d ed. by Hans Schwarz, Hamburg, Hanseatische Verlagsanstalt, 1931.

———, *Germany's Third Empire,* authorized English ed., transl. and condensed by E. O. Lorimer, London, Allen and Unwin, 1934.

———, *Die italienische Schönheit,* München, Piper, 1913.

———, *Die Moderne Literatur in Gruppen- und Einzeldarstellungen,* Berlin and Leipzig, Schuster und Loeffler, 1902 (published under Moeller-Bruck).

Moeller van den Bruck, Heinrich von Gleichen, and Max Hildebert Boehm, *Die Neue Front,* Berlin, Paetel, 1922.

———, *Der politische Mensch,* ed., by Hans Schwarz, Breslau, Korn, 1933.

———, *Der preussische Stil,* 2d. ed., München, Piper, 1922.

———, *Rechenschaft über Russland,* ed. by Hans Schwarz, Berlin, Der Nahe Osten, 1933.

———, *Das Recht der jungen Völker,* München, Piper, 1919.

———, *Das Recht der jungen Völker. Sammlung politischer Aufsätze,* ed. by Hans Schwarz, Berlin, Der Nahe Osten, 1932.

———, *Sozialismus und Aussenpolitik,* ed. by Hans Schwarz, Breslau, Korn, 1933.

———, *Das Théâtre Français,* Berlin und Leipzig, Schuster und Loeffler, 1905.

———, *Die Zeitgenossen. Die Geister—die Menschen,* Minden, Bruns, 1906.

———, "Belgier und Balten," in *Der Deutsche Krieg,* ed. by Ernst Jäckh, No. 59, Berlin 1915.

———, "Der Kaiser und die architektonische Tradition," *Die Tat,* V:6 (September, 1913), 595–601.

———, "Schicksal ist stärker als Staatskunst," in *Deutsche Rundschau,* CLXIX (November, 1916), 161–167.

———, "Der Untergang des Abendlandes. Für und wider

Spengler," *Deutsche Rundschau,* CLXXXIV (July, 1920), 41–70.

———, "Briefe Moeller van den Brucks an Ludwig Schemann," *Deutschlands Erneuerung. Monatsschrift für das deutsche Volk,* XVIII:6 and XVIII:7 (June and July, 1934), 321–327 and 396–399.

2. *Books and Articles on Moeller van den Bruck*

Adam, Reinhard, "Moeller van den Bruck," *Schriften der königlichen Deutschen Gesellschaft zu Königsberg,* No. 9, Königsberg, 1933.

Boehm, Max Hildebert, "Moeller van den Bruck im Kreise seiner politischen Freunde," *Deutsches Volkstum,* XIV:14 (September, 1932), 693–697.

———, *Ruf der Jungen: Eine Stimme aus dem Kreise von Moeller van den Bruck,* 3d ed., Freiburg im Breisgau, Urban, 1933.

Chandler, Albert R., "The Political Typology of Moeller van den Bruck," in *Essays in Political Theory, Presented to George H. Sabine,* ed. by Milton R. Konvitz and Arthur E. Murphy, Ithaca, Cornell University Press, 1948, pp. 228–245.

Eulenberg, Hedda, *Im Doppelglück von Kunst und Leben,* Düsseldorf, Die Faehre, n.d. (1948?)

Fechter, Paul, *Moeller van den Bruck: Ein politisches Schicksal,* Berlin, Frundsberg, 1934.

Fink, Woldemar, *Ostideologie und Ostpolitik. Die Ostideologie als Gefahrenmoment in der deutschen Aussenpolitik,* Berlin, Götz und Bengisch, 1936.

Herrmann, Wolfgang, "Moeller van den Bruck," *Die Tat,* XXV:4 (July, 1933), 273–297.

Hohlfeld, Andreas, *Unsere geschichtliche Verantwortung: Eine zeitgeschichtliche Betrachtung zu einer politischen Aufgabe,* Leipzig, Armanen, 1933.

Krebs, Gerhard, "Moeller van den Bruck: Inventor of the Third Reich," *American Political Science Review,* XXXV:6 (December, 1941), 1085–1105.

Moeller van den Bruck, Lucy, "Erbe und Auftrag," *Der Nahe Osten,* V:20 (October 15, 1932), 429–436.

Pascal, Roy, "Revolutionary Conservatism: Moeller van den Bruck," in *The Third Reich,* ed. by Edmond Vermeil *et al.,* London, Weidenfeld and Nicolson, 1955, pp. 316–349.

Rödel, Helmut, *Moeller van den Bruck. Standort und Wertung,* Berlin, Stollberg, 1939.

Schwarz, Hans, "Über Moeller van den Bruck," *Deutsches Volkstum,* XIV:14 (September, 1932), 689–692.

343

Schwierskott, Hans-Joachim, " 'Das Gewissen.' Ergebnisse und Probleme aus den ersten Jahren der Weimarer Republik im Spiegel einer politischen Zeitschrift," in *Lebendiger Geist: Hans-Joachim Schoeps zum 50. Geburtstag von Schülern dargebracht,* ed. by Hellmut Diwald, Leiden-Köln, Brill, 1959, pp. 161–176.

Seddin, Wilhelm, "Nachwort zu Moeller van den Bruck," *Wille und Macht,* III:23 (December 18, 1935), 1–6.

Ssymank, Paul, "Es gellt wie Trommelklang," *Velhagen und Klasings Monatshefte,* IL:9 (May, 1935), 262–265.

Tazerout, Professor, "La pensée politique de Moeller van den Bruck," *Revue Internationale de Sociologie,* XLIV:1–2 (January–February, 1936), 65–100.

Wunderlich, Wilhelm, "Die Spinne," *Die Tat,* XXIII:10 (January, 1932), 833–844.

II. GENERAL WORKS

A. Selected Works Relating to German History

Anderson, Pauline Relyea, *The Background of anti-English Feeling in Germany, 1890–1902,* Washington, American University Press, 1939.

Anderson, Eugene N., *The Social and Political Conflict in Prussia 1858–1864,* Lincoln, University of Nebraska Press, 1954.

Andler, Charles, ed., *Les Origines du Pangermanisme,* Paris, Conard, 1915.

———, *Le Pangermanisme philosophique* (1800 à 1914), Paris, Conard, 1917.

Baumgarten, Otto, *et al., Geistige und sittliche Wirkungen des Krieges in Deutschland,* Stuttgart, Berlin, Deutsche Verlagsanstalt, 1927.

Becker, Howard, *German Youth: Bond or Free?* London, K. Paul, Trench, Trübner, 1946.

Bischoff, Ralph F., *Nazi Conquest through German Culture,* Cambridge, Harvard University Press, 1942.

Blüher, Hans, *Wandervogel. Geschichte einer Jugendbewegung.* Vol. I: *Heimat und Aufgang,* 4th ed., Charlottenburg, Blüher, 1919. Vol. II: *Blüte und Niedergang,* 4th ed., Prien (Oberbayern), Anthropos, 1919.

Bordier, Henri, ed., *L'Allemagne aux Tuileries de 1850 à 1870. Collection de documents tirés du Cabinet de l'Empereur,* Paris, Beauvais, 1872.

Bracher, Karl Dietrich, *Die Auflösung der Weimarer Republik. Eine Studie zum Problem des Machtverfalls in der Demokratie*, Stuttgart and Düsseldorf, Ring, 1957.

Bracher, Karl Dietrich and Wolfgang Sauer and Gerhard Schulz, *Die nationalsozialistische Machtergreifung. Studien zur Errichtung des totalitären Herrschafts-systems in Deutschland 1933–34*, Köln and Opladen, Westdeutscher Verlag, 1960.

Buchheim, Hans, *Glaubenskrise im Dritten Reich. Drei Kapitel nationalsozialistischer Religionspolitik*, Stuttgart, Deutsche Verlagsanstalt, 1953.

Butler, Rohan d'O., *The Roots of National Socialism, 1783–1933*, London, Faber and Faber, 1941.

Cysarz, Herbert, *Von Schiller zu Nietzsche. Hauptfragen der Dichtungs- und Bildungsgeschichte des jüngsten Jahrhunderts*, Halle, Niemeyer, 1928.

Deesz, Gisela, *Die Entwicklung des Nietzsche-Bildes in Deutschland*, Würzburg, Triltsch, 1933.

Dehio, Ludwig, *Deutschland und die Weltpolitik im 20. Jahrhundert*, München, Oldenbourg, 1955.

Dehmel, Richard, *Ausgewählte Briefe aus den Jahren 1883 bis 1902*, Berlin, Fischer, 1923.

———, *Ausgewählte Briefe aus den Jahren 1902 bis 1920*, Berlin, Fischer, 1923.

Drummond, Andrew Laudale, *German Protestantism since Luther*, London, Epworth Press, 1951.

Eschenburg, Theodor, *Das Kaiserreich am Scheideweg. Bassermann, Bülow und der Block*. Berlin, Verlag für Kulturpolitik, 1929.

Fischer, Fritz, "Der Deutsche Protestantismus und die Politik im 19. Jahrhundert," *Historische Zeitschrift*, CLXXI:3 (May, 1951), 473–518.

Fischer, Ruth, *Stalin and German Communism. A Study in the Origins of the State Party*, Cambridge (Mass.), Harvard University Press, 1948.

Fontane, Theodor, *Briefe an Georg Friedlaender*, ed. by Kurt Schreinert, Heidelberg, Quelle und Meyer, 1954.

Fraser, Lindley, *Germany between Two Wars. A Study of Propaganda and War Guilt*, London, Oxford University Press, 1944.

Gatzke, Hans, *Germany's Drive to the West (Drang nach Westen). A Study of Germany's Western War Aims during the First World War*, Baltimore, Johns Hopkins Press, 1950.

Glum, Friedrich, *Philosophen im Spiegel und Zerrspiegel.*

Deutschlands Weg in den Nationalismus und Nationalsozialismus. München, Isar, 1954.

Gurlitt, Cornelius, *Die deutsche Kunst des neunzehnten Jahrhunderts. Ihre Ziele und Taten,* 3d ed., Berlin, Bondi, 1907.

Hamerow, Theodore S., *Restoration Revolution Reaction. Economics and Politics in Germany 1815–1871,* Princeton, Princeton University Press, 1958.

Heiden, Konrad, *Der Fuehrer. Hitler's Rise to Power,* Boston, Houghton Mifflin, 1944.

Heller, Erich, *The Disinherited Mind. Essays in Modern German Literature and Thought,* Cambridge (England), Bowes and Bowes, 1952.

Heuss, Theodor, *Friedrich Naumann. Der Mann, Das Werk, Die Zeit,* 2d ed., Tübingen, Wunderlich, 1949.

———, *Hitlers Weg. Eine historisch-politische Studie über den Nationalsozialismus.* Stuttgart, Union deutsche Verlagsgesellschaft, 1932.

Hitler, Adolf, *Mein Kampf,* annotated American ed., New York, Reynal and Hitchcock, 1940.

———, *The Speeches of Adolf Hitler April 1922–August 1939,* ed. by Norman H. Baynes, 2 vols., London, New York, Oxford University Press, 1942.

Höfele, Karl Heinrich, "Selbstverständnis und Zeitkritik des deutschen Bürgertums vor dem ersten Weltkrieg," *Zeitschrift für Religions- und Geistesgeschichte,* VIII (1956), 40–56.

Holborn, Hajo, "Der deutsche Idealismus in sozialgeschichtlicher Beleuchtung," *Historische Zeitschrift,* CLXXIV:2 (October 1952), 359–384.

Hornung, Klaus, *Der Jungdeutsche Orden,* Düsseldorf, Droste, 1958.

Jäckh, Ernst, *Der Goldene Pflug. Lebensernte eines Weltbürgers,* Stuttgart, Deutsche Verlagsanstalt, 1954.

Jahn, Friedrich Ludwig, *Deutsches Volksthum,* Lübeck, Niemann, 1810.

Kahler, Erich, *Der deutsche Charakter in der Geschichte Europas,* Zürich, Europa, 1937.

Kehr, Eckart, "Schlachtflottenbau und Parteipolitik 1894–1901. Versuch eines Querschnitts durch die innenpolitischen, sozialen und ideologischen Voraussetzungen des deutschen Imperialismus," in *Historische Studien,* No. 197, Berlin, Ebering, 1930.

Klemperer, Klemens von, *Germany's New Conservatism. Its History and Dilemma in the Twentieth Century,* Princeton, Princeton University Press, 1957.

Krieger, Leonard, *The German Idea of Freedom. History of a Political Tradition*, Boston, Beacon, 1957.

Kruck, Alfred, *Geschichte des Alldeutschen Verbandes 1890–1939*, Wiesbaden, Steiner, 1954.

Künneth, Walther, *Der grosse Abfall. Eine geschichts-theologische Untersuchung der Begegnung zwischen Nationalsozialismus und Christentum*, Hamburg, Wittig, 1947.

Kupisch, Karl, *Zwischen Idealismus und Massendemokratie. Eine Geschichte der evangelischen Kirche in Deutschland von 1815–1945*. Berlin, Lettner, 1955.

Lilge, Frederic, *The Abuse of Learning. The Failure of the German University*, New York, Macmillan, 1948.

Lukács, Georg, *Die Zerstörung der Vernunft. Der Weg des Irrationalismus von Schelling zu Hitler*, East Berlin, Aufbau, 1948.

Lütgert, Wilhelm D., *Das Ende des Idealismus im Zeitalter Bismarcks*, Gütersloh, Bertelsmann, 1930.

Mann, Golo, *Deutsche Geschichte des neunzehnten und zwanzigsten Jahrhunderts*, Frankfurt am Main, Fischer, 1959.

Mann, Thomas, *Bemühungen. Neue Folge der gesammelten Abhandlungen und kleinen Aufsätze*, Berlin, Fischer, 1925.

——, *Betrachtungen eines Unpolitischen*, Berlin, Fischer, 1918.

——, *Deutsche Ansprache. Ein Appell an die Vernunft. Rede gehalten am 17. 10. 1930*, Berlin, Fischer, 1930.

——, *Friedrich und die grosse Koalition*, Berlin, Fischer, 1915.

——, *Gesammelte Werke*, Vols. X–XII, East Berlin, Aufbau, 1955.

Mayer, Carl, "On the Intellectual Origin of National Socialism," *Social Research*, IX:2 (May, 1942), 225–247.

Meinecke, Friedrich, *Erlebtes 1862–1901*, Leipzig, Koehler und Amelang, 1941.

——, *The German Catastrophe. Reflections and Recollections*, transl. by Sidney B. Fay, Cambridge (Mass.), Harvard University Press, 1950.

——, *Weltbürgertum und Nationalstaat. Studien zur Genesis des deutschen Nationalstaates*, 5th ed., München and Berlin, Oldenbourg, 1919.

Mendelssohn Bartholdy, Albrecht, *The War and German Society. The Testament of a Liberal*, New Haven, Yale University Press, 1938.

Meyer, Henry Cord, *Mitteleuropa in German Thought and Action 1815–1945,* The Hague, Nijhoff, 1955.

Michels, Robert, *Umschichtungen in den herrschenden Klassen nach dem Kriege,* Stuttgart-Berlin, Kohlhammer, 1934.

Mommsen, Theodor, *Reden und Aufsätze,* Berlin, Weidmann, 1905.

Naumann, Hans, *Die deutsche Dichtung der Gegenwart 1885–1923,* Stuttgart, Metzler, 1923.

Neumann, Franz, *Behemoth. The Structure and Practice of National Socialism,* Toronto, New York, Oxford University Press, 1942.

Neumann, Sigmund, "Die Stufen des preussischen Konservatismus. Ein Beitrag zum Staats- und Gesellschaftsbild Deutschlands im neunzehnten Jahrhundert," in *Historische Studien,* No. 190, Berlin, Ebering, 1930.

Neurohr, Jean F., *Der Mythos vom Dritten Reich. Zur Geistesgeschichte des Nationalsozialismus,* Stuttgart, Cotta, 1957.

Nietzsche, Friedrich, *Werke in Drei Bänden,* ed. by Karl Schlechta, München, Hanser, 1954–1956.

Paulsen, Friedrich, *Geschichte des gelehrten Unterrichts auf den deutschen Schulen und Universitäten vom Ausgang des Mittelalters bis zur Gegenwart,* 2 vols., Leipzig, Veit, 1919–1921.

Petersdorff, Herman von, *Die Vereine deutscher Studenten. Zwölf Jahre akademischer Kämpfe,* 3d. ed., Leipzig, Breitkopf und Härtel, 1890.

Plessner, Helmuth, *Die verspätete Nation. Über die politische Verführbarkeit bürgerlichen Geistes,* Stuttgart, Kohlhammer, 1959.

Rosenberg, Alfred, *Der Mythus der 20. Jahrhunderts. Eine Wertung der seelisch-geistigen Gestaltenkämpfe unserer Zeit,* 25th–26th printing, München, Hoheneichen, 1934.

Rosenberg, Arthur, *The Birth of the German Republic, 1871–1918,* transl. by Ian F. D. Morrow, London, Oxford Press, 1931.

Rousset, David, *The Other Kingdom,* transl. by Ramon Guthrie, New York, Reynal and Hitchcock, 1947.

Samuel, Richard H. and Thomas R. Hinton, *Education and Society in Modern Germany,* London, Routledge and K. Paul, 1949.

Scheler, Max, *Die Ursachen des Deutschenhasses. Eine nationalpädagogische Erörterung,* Leipzig, Wolff, 1917.

Schemann, Ludwig, *Gobineau und die deutsche Kultur,* 7th ed., Leipzig, Eckardt, 1910.

Schnabel, Franz, *Deutsche Geschichte im neunzehnten Jahrhundert,* 2d ed., 4 vols., Freiburg im Breisgau, Herder, 1937–1949.

Shanahan, William O., *German Protestants Face the Social Question,* vol. I, *The Conservative Phase 1815–1871,* Notre Dame (Ind.), University of Notre Dame Press, 1954.

Sokel, Walter H., *The Writer in Extremis. Expressionism in Twentieth-Century German Literature,* Stanford, Stanford University Press, 1959.

Stechert, Kurt, *Wie war das möglich?* Stockholm, Bermann-Fischer, 1945.

Steinhausen, Georg, *Deutsche Geistes- und Kulturgeschichte von 1870 bis zur Gegenwart,* Halle, Niemeyer, 1931.

Sterling, Eleonore, *Er ist wie Du. Aus der Frühgeschichte des Antisemitismus in Deutschland (1815–1850),* München, Kaiser, 1956.

Stern, Fritz, "The Political Consequences of the Unpolitical German," *History. A Meridian Periodical,* III (September, 1960), 104–134.

Troeltsch, Ernst, *Gesammelte Schriften.* Vol. II: *Zur religiösen Lage, Religionsphilosophie und Ethik,* Tübingen, Mohr, 1913; Vol. IV: *Aufsätze zur Geistesgeschichte und Religionssoziologie,* ed. by Hans Baron, Tübingen, Mohr, 1925.

———, *Spektator-Briefe. Aufsätze über die deutsche Revolution und die Weltpolitik 1918–1922,* ed. by Hans Baron, Tübingen, Mohr, 1924.

Veblen, Thorstein, *Imperial Germany and the Industrial Revolution,* 2d ed., New York, Viking, 1939.

Wahl, Adalbert, *Deutsche Geschichte, 1871–1914. Von der Reichsgründung bis zum Ausbruch des Weltkriegs,* 4 vols., Stuttgart, Kohlhammer, 1926–1936.

Waite, Robert G. L., *Vanguard of Nazism. The Free Corps Movement in Postwar Germany 1918–1923,* Cambridge (Mass.), Harvard University Press, 1952.

Weber, Max, *Gesammelte politische Schriften,* München, Drei Masken, 1921.

Westphal, Otto, *Feinde Bismarcks. Geistige Grundlagen der deutschen Opposition 1848–1918,* München and Berlin, Oldenbourg, 1930.

Windelband, Wilhelm, *Die Philosophie im deutschen Geistesleben des 19. Jahrhunderts,* Tübingen, Mohr, 1909.

Ziegler, Theobald, *Die geistigen und sozialen Strömungen Deutschlands im neunzehnten Jahrhundert,* Berlin, Bondi, 1911.

Ziekursch, Johannes, *Politische Geschichte des neuen deutschen Kaiserreiches,* 3 vols., Frankfurt am Main, Frankfurter Societäts-Druckerei, 1925–1930.

B. Works Relating to European Politics and Culture

Aliotta, Antonio, *The Idealistic Reaction against Science,* transl. by Agnes McCaskill, London, Macmillan, 1914.

Arendt, Hannah, *The Origins of Totalitarianism,* New York, Harcourt, Brace, 1951.

Bahr, Hermann, *Der Antisemitismus. Ein Internationales Interview,* Berlin, Fischer, 1894.

Barth, Karl, *Die protestantische Theologie im 19. Jahrhundert. Ihre Vorgeschichte und ihre Geschichte,* 2d ed., Zollikon/Zürich, Evangelischer Verlag, 1952.

Barzun, Jacques, *Darwin, Marx, Wagner. Critique of a Heritage,* Boston, Little Brown, 1941.

———, *Race. A Study in Modern Superstition.* New York, Harcourt, Brace, 1937.

Bäumer, Gertrud, *Die soziale Idee in den Weltanschauungen des 19. Jahrhunderts. Die Grundzüge der modernen Sozialphilosophie,* Heilbronn, Salzer, 1910.

Bentley, Eric Russell, *A Century of Hero-Worship. A Study of the Idea of Heroism in Carlyle and Nietzsche, with Notes on Wagner, Spengler, Stefan George, and D. H. Lawrence,* 2d ed., Boston, Beacon, 1957.

Berg, Leo, *Der Übermensch in der modernen Literatur. Ein Kapitel zur Geistesgeschichte des neunzehnten Jahrhunderts,* München, Leipzig, Paris, Langen, 1897.

Bernoulli, Carl Albrecht, *Franz Overbeck und Friedrich Nietzsche. Eine Freundschaft,* 2 vols., Jena, Eugen Diederichs, 1908.

Brinton, Crane, *Nietzsche,* Cambridge (Mass.), Harvard University Press, 1941.

Casserley, Julian Victor Langmead, *The Retreat from Christianity in the Modern World,* London, Longmans, Green, 1952.

Fouillée, Alfred, *Moral des Idées-Forces,* 2d ed., Paris, Alcan, 1908.

Friedell, Egon, *Kulturgeschichte der Neuzeit,* Vol. III: *Romantik und Liberalismus,* München, Beck, 1931.

Fromm, Erich, *Escape from Freedom,* New York and Toronto, Farrar and Rhinehart, 1941.

Gundolf, Friedrich, *Caesar im neunzehnten Jahrhundert,* Berlin, Bondi, 1926.

Hughes, H. Stuart, *Consciousness and Society. The Reorientation of European Social Thought,* New York, Knopf, 1958.

——, *Oswald Spengler. A Critical Estimate,* New York, Scribner, 1952.

Huizinga, Johan, *Mein Weg zur Geschichte. Letzte Reden und Skizzen,* transl. by Werner Kaegi. Basel, Schwabe, 1947.

Jackson, Holbrook, *The Eighteen Nineties. A Review of Art and Ideas at the Close of the Nineteenth Century,* new ed., London, Cape, 1927.

Kaufmann, Walter A., *Nietzsche: Philosopher, Psychologist, Anti-Christ,* Princeton, Princeton University Press, 1950.

Löwith, Karl, *Von Hegel zu Nietzsche. Der revolutionäre Bruch im Denken des neunzehnten Jahrhunderts. Marx und Kierkegaard,* 2d ed., Stuttgart, Kohlhammer, 1950.

Marck, Siegfried, *Der Neuhumanismus als politische Philosophie,* Zürich, Aufbruch, 1938.

Marcuse, Herbert, "Der Kampf gegen den Liberalismus in der totalitären Staatsauffassung," *Zeitschrift für Sozialforschung,* III:2 (1934), 161–194.

Merz, John Theodore, *A History of European Thought in the Nineteenth Century,* 4 vols., Edinburgh and London, Blackwood, 1896–1914.

Namier, Lewis Bernstein, *In the Margin of History,* London, Macmillan, 1939.

Otto, Rudolf, *The Idea of the Holy. An Inquiry into the Non-rational Factor in the Idea of the Divine and Its Relation to the Rational,* transl. by John W. Harvey, London, Oxford University Press, 1950.

Ranulf, Svend, *Moral Indignation and Middle-Class Psychology. A Sociological Study,* Copenhagen, Levin and Munksgaard, 1938.

Schemann, Ludwig, *Die Rasse in den Geisteswissenschaften. Studien zur Geschichte des Rassengedankens,* 3 vols. München, Lehmanns, 1928–1931.

Voegelin, Eric, *Die politischen Religionen,* Stockholm, Bermann-Fischer, 1939.

Willey, Basil, *Nineteenth Century Studies. Coleridge to Matthew Arnold,* New York, Columbia University Press, 1949.

Williams, Raymond, *Culture and Society, 1780–1950,* New York, Columbia University Press, 1958.

C. Works Relating to the Conservative Revolution in Germany and to Analogous Movements Elsewhere

Alter, Junius (pseudonym of Franz Sontag), *Nationalisten. Deutschlands nationales Führertum der Nachkriegszeit,* 2d ed., Leipzig, Koehler, 1932.

Bartels, Adolf, *Der völkische Gedanke. Ein Wegweiser,* Weimar, Fink, 1923.

Bayer-Katte, Wanda von, *Das Zerstörende in der Politik. Eine Psychologie der politischen Grundeinstellung,* Heidelberg, Quelle und Mayer, 1958.

Bell, Daniel, ed., *The New American Right,* New York, Criterion, 1955.

Benda, Julien, *The Betrayal of the Intellectuals (La trahison des clercs)* Boston, Beacon Paperback, 1955.

Böhm, Franz, *Anti-Cartesianismus. Deutsche Philosophie im Widerstand,* Leipzig, Meiner, 1938.

Bowen, Ralph, *German Theories of the Corporative State. With Special Reference to the Period 1870–1919,* New York, McGraw-Hill, 1947.

Chamberlain, Houston Stewart, *Die Grundlagen des neunzehnten Jahrhunderts,* 2 vols., 5th ed., München, Bruckmann, 1904.

Class, Heinrich, *Wider den Strom. Vom Werden und Wachsen der nationalen Opposition im alten Reich,* Leipzig, Koehler, 1932.

Curtis, Michael, *Three Against the Third Republic. Sorel, Barrès, and Maurras,* Princeton, Princeton University Press, 1959.

Domandi, Mario, "The German Youth Movement," doctoral dissertation, Columbia University, Department of History, 1960.

Ernst, Paul, *Der Zusammenbruch des deutschen Idealismus,* München, Müller, 1918.

Frank, Walter, *Hofprediger Adolf Stoecker und die christlichsoziale Bewegung,* 2d ed., Hamburg, Hanseatische Verlagsanstalt, 1935.

Frobenius, Else, *Mit uns zieht die neue Zeit. Eine Geschichte der deutschen Jugendbewegung,* Berlin, Deutsche Buchgemeinschaft, 1927.

Fünfzig Jahre J. F. Lehmanns Verlag. 1890–1940. Zur Erinnerung an das 50 jährige Bestehen, München, Lehmanns, 1940.

Gerhart, Walter (pseudonym for Woldemar Gurian), *Um des Reiches Zukunft. Nationale Wiedergeburt oder politische Reaktion?* Freiburg im Breisgau, Herder, 1932.

Gerlach, Hellmuth von, *Von Rechts nach Links,* Zürich, Europa, 1937.

Gerstenhauer, Max Robert, *Der völkische Gedanke in Vergangenheit und Zukunft. Aus der Geschichte der völkischen Bewegung,* Leipzig, Armanen, 1933.

Heer, Friedrich, "Der Konservative und die Reaktion," *Die Neue Rundschau,* LXIX:3 (1958), 490–527.

Hentschel, Cedric, *The Byronic Teuton. Aspects of German Pessimism 1800–1933,* London, Methuen, 1940.

Hesse, Hermann, *Zarathustras Wiederkehr,* Berlin, Fischer, 1924.

Hoffer, Eric, *The True Believer. Thoughts on the Nature of Mass Movements,* New York, Harper, 1951.

Hofmannsthal, Hugo von, *Das Schrifttum als geistiger Raum der Nation,* München, Bremer Presse, 1927.

Hotzel, Curt, *Deutscher Aufstand: Die Revolution des Nachkriegs,* Stuttgart, Kohlhammer, 1934.

Kolnai, Aurel, *The War against the West,* New York, Viking, 1938.

Krüger, Horst, "Vom Irrationalismus zum Nationalsozialismus," *Das Goldene Tor,* II:8–9 (1947), 108–111.

Massing, Paul W., *Rehearsal for Destruction. A Study of Political Anti-Semitism in Imperial Germany,* New York, Harper, 1949.

Mau, Hermann, "Die Deutsche Jugendbewegung. Rückblick und Ausblick," *Zeitschrift für Religions- und Geistesgeschichte,* I (1948), 135–149.

Metnitz, Gustav Adolf von, *Die deutsche Nationalbewegung 1871–1933,* Berlin, Junker und Dünnhaupt, 1939.

Michels, Robert, "Psychologie der antikapitalistischen Massenbewegungen," *Grundriss der Sozialökonomik,* Vol. IX, part i, Tübingen, Mohr, 1926.

Mohler, Armin, *Die konservative Revolution in Deutschland 1918–1932. Grundriss ihrer Weltanschauungen,* Stuttgart, Vorwerk, 1950.

Müffling, Wilhelm Freiherr von, *Wegbereiter und Vorkämpfer für das neue Deutschland,* München, Lehmanns, 1933.

Nicolas, M.-P., *De Nietzsche à Hitler,* Paris, Fasquelle, 1936.

Niekisch, Ernst, *Das Reich der niederen Dämonen,* Hamburg, Rowohlt, 1953.

Nohl, Herman, "Die Deutsche Bewegung und die idealistische Systeme," *Logos,* II (1912), 350–359.

Pechel, Rudolf, *Deutscher Widerstand,* Erlenbach-Zürich, Rentsch, 1947.

Quabbe, Georg, *Tar a Ri. Variationen über ein konservatives Thema,* Berlin, Verlag für Politik und Wirtschaft, 1927.

Radek, Karl, "Leo Schlageter—The Wanderer into the Void," *The Labour Monthly. A Magazine of International Labour,* V:3 (September, 1923), 152–157.

Rapp, Adolf, *Der deutsche Gedanke. Seine Entwicklung im politischen und geistigen Leben seit dem 18. Jahrhundert,* Bonn, Schroeder, 1920.

Rauschning, Hermann, *The Conservative Revolution,* New York, Putnam, 1941.

———, *The Revolution of Nihilism. Warning to the West.* Transl. by E. W. Dickes. New York, Alliance, 1939.

Reichmann, Eva G., *Hostages of Civilization. The Social Sources of National Socialist Anti-Semitism,* Boston, Beacon, 1951.

Rohrbach, Paul, *Der deutsche Gedanke in der Welt,* Düsseldorf and Leipzig, Langewiesche, 1912.

Rosteutscher, J. H. W., *Die Wiederkunft des Dionysos. Der naturmystische Irrationalismus in Deutschland,* Bern, Franke, 1947.

Rüsten, Rudolf, *Was tut Not? Ein Führer durch die gesamte Literatur der Deutschbewegung,* Leipzig, Hedeler, 1914.

Schmal, Eugen, *Der Aufstieg der nationalen Idee,* Stuttgart, Berlin, Union deutsche Verlagsgesellschaft, 1933.

Schultheiss, Fr. Guntram, *Deutschnationales Vereinswesen. Ein Beitrag zur Geschichte des deutschen Nationalgefühls.* A pamphlet in the series *Der Kampf um das Deutschtum,* München, Lehmanns, 1897.

Sontheimer, Kurt, "Antidemokratisches Denken in der Weimarer Republik," *Vierteljahrshefte für Zeitgeschichte,* V:1 (January, 1957), 42–62.

———, "Der Tatkreis," *Vierteljahrshefte für Zeitgeschichte,* VII:3 (July, 1959), 229–260.

———, "Thomas Mann als politischer Schriftsteller," *Vierteljahrshefte für Zeitgeschichte,* VI:1 (January, 1958), 1–44.

Spengler, Oswald, *Preussentum und Sozialismus,* München, Beck, 1920.

———, *Der Untergang des Abendlandes. Umrisse einer Morphologie der Weltgeschichte,* 2 vols., München, Beck, 1923.

Spranger, Eduard, "Wesen und Wert politischer Ideologien," *Vierteljahrshefte für Zeitgeschichte,* II:2 (April, 1954), 118–136.

Stauff, Philipp, *Das deutsche Wehrbuch,* Wittenberg, Ziemsen, 1912.

Steding, Christoph, *Das Reich und die Krankheit der europäischen Kultur,* Hamburg, Hanseatische Verlagsanstalt, 1938.

Stoffregen, Goetz Otto, *Aufstand. Querschnitt durch den revolutionären Nationalismus,* Berlin, Brunnen, 1931.

Ullmann, Hermann, *Das Neunzehnte Jahrhundert. Volk gegen Masse im Kampf um die Gestalt Europas,* Jena, Eugen Diederichs, 1936.

Unger, Erich, *Das Schrifttum des Nationalsozialismus von 1919 bis zum 1. Januar 1934,* Berlin, Junker und Dünnhaupt, 1934.

Vermeil, Edmond, *Doctrinaires de la Révolution Allemande 1918–1938,* Paris, Sorlot, 1938.

Viereck, Peter, *Metapolitics. From the Romantics to Hitler,* New York, Knopf, 1941.

Virtanen, Reine, "Nietzsche and the Action Française," *Journal of the History of Ideas,* XI:2, (April, 1950), 191–214.

Webster, Richard A., "The Cross and The Fasces. Christian Democracy and Fascism in Italy," doctoral dissertation, Columbia University, 1959.

Whiteside, Andrew G., "The Nature and Origins of National Socialism," *Journal of Central European Affairs,* XVII:1 (April, 1957), 48–73.

Index